Knowledge and passion:
Ilongot notions of self and social life

Cambridge Studies in Cultural Systems

Clifford Geertz, Editor

Knowledge and passion: Ilongot notions of self and social life

MICHELLE Z. ROSALDO

Associate Professor of Anthropology
Stanford University

CAMBRIDGE UNIVERSITY PRESS

Cambridge

London   New York   New Rochelle

Melbourne   Sydney

Published by the Press Syndicate of the University of Cambridge
The Pitt Building, Trumpington Street, Cambridge CB2 1RP
32 East 57th Street, New York, NY 10022, USA
10 Stamford Road, Oakleigh, Melbourne 3166, Australia

First published 1980
Reprinted 1986

Printed in the United States of America

Library of Congress Cataloging in Publication Data
Rosaldo, Michelle Zimbalist.

Knowledge and passion.

(Cambridge studies in cultural systems; 4)

Bibliography: p.

Includes index.

1. Ilongot (Philippine tribe) – Psychology.
2. Ilongot (Philippine tribe) – Social life and customs
I. Title.   II. Series.
DS666.I4R67   301.29′599   79-12632
ISBN 0 521 22582 5 hard covers
ISBN 0 521 29562 9 paperback

To my mother, Dorothy, and my son, Samuel

Contents

Preface

Shortly after we left the Philippines in November 1974, Manila news-
papers published stories of an assembly of The New Bugkalut Nation.
Led by "Chieftan Gomiad" (in my transcription, Rumyad), several
hundred of the people popularly known as Ilongot[1] met and appealed to
the Philippine National Government for support and education, an-
nouncing that their traditional practice of headhunting was now offi-
cially foresworn. The tone of the articles, which spoke of schooling,
land development, and irrigation, differed markedly from that of news-
paper reports Renato Rosaldo and I had read before and during our
fieldwork with the Ilongots, beginning in 1967. In the late 1950s and
early 1960s, we read headlines that spoke of "Ilongots on the Warpath," reports of picnickers beheaded, of a "mating season" that required "braves" to offer up a Christian head to future in-laws, and of
conclaves where proven warriors had sworn blood brotherhood with
lowland authorities. As late as June 1967 – three months before our
departure for the Philippines – the *Manila Daily Mirror* reported "Ilongots Embracing Civilization: Headhunting Ritual Abandoned," but on
May 14, 1968 when we were beginning to feel some confidence in our
grasp of the Ilongot language – the *Manila Chronicle* warned local
sportsmen, "To Hunters: Don't Lose Your Heads": "Fire trees are in
bloom and Ilongot headhunters are again on the warpath. The bloom of
fire trees is said to arouse the primitive instincts of the Nueva Vizcaya
Ilongots and goad them into leaving their forest homes to hunt for
'heads'." These reports recalled Spanish accounts, dating from the
eighteenth century, of a "miserable" people who would kill without a
thought for the humanity of their victims, of a people who swore that
they would "break like eggs" if they engaged in future violence, and
who yet persevered, when driven by the blossoms of a fire tree in
springtime, to slaughter innocent Christians in their bloodthirsty quest
for heads.[2]
  Although mistaken in detail, what these accounts accurately reflect
is the fact that headhunting was a central aspect of Ilongot social prac-

ix

tice until at least the early 1970s. However, reduced in numbers by the onslaughts of Japanese during the Second World War, constrained by settlers who have claimed their lands increasingly since 1960, converted to fundamentalist Christianity in the last two decades, and, finally, intimidated by the power of a military government that has ruled the Philippines since 1972, Ilongots appeared by 1975 to have abandoned a traditional stance not just of violence but of autonomy. Although fieldwork in the period from 1967–9 had shown a people only beginning to respond to mission efforts, there were no Ilongot settlements at the time of our return fieldwork in 1974 without a number of adults who demonstrated through their behavior that they considered themselves Christians, and probably none where people failed to speak of water buffaloes and irrigation, or to attend the possibilities of wage labor at sawmills and road construction projects in areas where, just years before, the customary occupation had been hunting. After centuries of raiding, trading, and occasional shows of deference toward colonial governments and Philippine lowland neighbors, the Ilongots declared themselves a "nation." Ironically, in asserting their integrity and independence, they accepted the hegemony of a modern state.

Radical change, as this most clearly was, is at the very least an embarrassment to a traditionally oriented ethnographer like myself. My interests in choosing the Ilongots as a subject for investigation and for examination in the text that follows has been in the meaning and organization of Ilongot practices such as headhunting – not as they have been for all time, but as they were experienced by the adults who served as our informants in the field. And yet, by 1974, these very individuals had come to view their customs of only years before as aspects of distant history. In certain ways, the values of their recent past were lively: People explained, for example, that they 'followed' one another in accepting Christianity in much the same terms that they used to convey how, in previous days, young men had 'followed' peers in taking heads. But at the same time, our friends would speak as though we had not known that the game consumed in 1968 was roughly twice what we could eat in the mid-1970s. A thirty-three-year-old woman, telling about 'ancients' who hung the jawbones of hunted boar over household fires to call 'companion' animals to their hearths, recalled in a tone suggesting bygone eras, 'Even I have seen this practice of our elders' – and then looked at us in mute surprise when we reminded her that the now-abandoned practice had been lively when her youngest child was born. And the men who declared themselves leaders of The New Bugkalut nation in early 1975 rejected as a slight the 'lowland' appellation 'Ilongot' (from the indigenous *'irungut,* 'from the forest')—a name that was in fact accepted as a self-appellation in certain dialects

– because, I believe, it suggested that being 'of the forest' made them more "wild" than they thought they were. Clearly, their image of their past and of themselves had as much to do with idioms in the Manila papers as it did with more traditional concerns that formed the focus of my interest – issues that seemed to me to underlie both prior deeds and present discourse, and, as such, provide the subject of this book.

Because of my own preference, in the field I sought out adults who had resisted mission influence, and their descriptions and accounts of their experience sustained my own feeling that I stood witness to a passing way of life that had, along with conflict, a certain beauty and a telling sense. The style of understanding developed in our discussions acquired something of the nostalgic cast one sees in histories that recount the fading of an era – a style I believe to be uniquely appropriate to an appreciation of the distinctive quality of a particular way of living, though problematic insofar as it leads to a denial of process, inconsistency, strain, and contradiction in an idealized past. The danger I confront here is, then, one of misconstruing their concerns and our relation, either ignoring present change and the conditions of my fieldwork, or – even worse – permitting the illusion that up until a period of two or five or ten years previous, the Ilongot world was integrated, fixed, coherent, in a way that it is not today. My analysis seeks to capture continuities in cultural form and characterize the underlying shape, or meaning, that actors find in changing social practice; but in so doing, I have found it difficult to portray as well the social forces that make meanings change. Thus, although I have attempted to convey the interaction between traditional features of Ilongot thought and the contingencies of historical situation, it is the former that predominate in my account.

What I hope this book will do is document the enduring and intelligible shapes of Ilongot social action – and, by exploring Ilongot views of their emotional life as it relates to conduct in their social world, to tell not of A Culture as a "seamless web," but rather of certain partially consistent themes in Ilongot activity and thought. Adapting a distinction used by Clifford Geertz, I seek to capture neither timeless essence nor a "point" in time, but some of the "lines" or patterns that, inferred from present adult discourse, lend an intelligible form to quickly changing social practice, thereby making accessible some of the terms in which Ilongots have understood their fellows' motives and made sense of themselves. The focus and style of my presentation reflects the difficulties that I found in discovering what is orderly in Ilongot experience of their social world and in appreciating its pattern. At the same time it reflects my view of "culture" as the intelligible form of peoples' lives, a view suggesting that the analyst can and should perceive in the diverse remarks of very different individuals the threads of mutual bearing and coherence necessary to support an integrative account. In introduction, I will, then, outline first the way the Ilongot society "looks" more or less to an outsider, and then discuss the analytical concerns that guided my investigations and interpretations of the things Ilongots said.

October 1979   *Michelle Z. Rosaldo*

Acknowledgments

The fieldwork on which this book is based includes my predoctoral researches and those of Renato Rosaldo from 1967–9, and our return field trip of about nine months in 1974. Neither of us planned our research with any more than a vague premonition of the direction of our present writings; as I recount in this book, the idea of using "emotional" idioms to interpret Ilongot headhunting and to situate it in relation to other aspects of Ilongot social experience did not occur to me until the summer of 1974. At the same time, a perusal of notes from our earlier encounters with Ilongots suggests to me that this book is a kind of crystallization of the concerns that first interested me in anthropology; and I feel that many of the strengths and limitations of the text that follows are consistent with a long-standing intellectual bent. Although as an undergraduate I majored in English literature and found myself particularly drawn to lyric poetry, a reading of Benedict's *Patterns of Culture* just before the beginning of my freshman year led me to take a seminar with Professor E. Z. Vogt on the Maya. The seminar led in turn to a field trip to southern Mexico and to the realization that in anthropology I could explore what, for me, was the first fascination of literature: the relation between "language" and "experience" or "culture" – or, to cast this relation in terms more appropriate to my present study, between "forms of discourse" and "forms of life." Professor Vogt did everything he could to support my developing interests, and his confidence in my abilities was, in a very real sense, much of what made me an anthropologist.

My problem, when I turned from literature to serious anthropological study in graduate school, was to learn how to "go beyond" language – or rather, to learn how to understand and describe the social and physical factors that both constrain and are organized by the meanings of things people say. The "translation" of language or culture is, I learned, only as rich as our understanding of the social and historical context in which meanings are made. While I was in graduate school, David Maybury-Lewis taught me to think about social structure; James

Fox made "translation" a "problem"; and friends who were feminists and antiwar activists demanded that I find ways of describing the organization of social experience that linked social process, conflict, and inequality to ideology, symbols, and speech. At much the same time, Professor Harold C. Conklin (who first suggested that Renato Rosaldo and I work with the Ilongots) taught me a good deal of what it is to be a responsible scholar, accountable to the details of Ilongot living and to their place in Philippine history and in the contemporary Philippine state.

Although my field diaries are replete with evidence of Malinowski's now scandalous ambivalence, and our first field trip, in particular, was by far the most emotionally and physically demanding experience of my life, I find it difficult to recall old feelings of pain and confusion. Instead, my memories of Ilongot living are touched with the romantic cast that was, of course, part of what led me to seek such "exotic" surroundings. Writing at this moment, I find myself overwhelmed with gratitude and nostalgia for a world that is typified by the warmth, consideration, and playfulness of people who tolerated and cared for us, and finally, became our dear friends. Their names (or rather, their words, because the names of these persons are changed to ensure their privacy and safety) provide a human thread that unites much of what I recount in this monograph. Rumors from the Philippines – of dams, counterinsurgency training, and established settlements of outsiders on lands I know they hoped to save – are probably a fair testimony to the difficulties of their present situation. And I am certain that this book embodies my desire to celebrate these Ilongots in the context of political and economic developments that seem more than likely to crush them – developments that I have not learned how to change.

Ilongots introduced me to their world, but they could not teach me to translate the categories of their experience into the descriptive and theoretical discourse of Western social science. The list of friends, students, and teachers who have read large portions of this text, pushed my thinking, and offered me everything from editorial assistance to deep conceptual guidance is a long one. Clifford Geertz, by inviting me to the Institute for Advanced Study in 1975, provided the time and intellectual environment necessary to get me started. That year's "symbolic anthropology" seminar at the Institute combined support and criticism in responding to early chapters. To four of its participants – Clifford Geertz, William Reddy, and Ellen and William Sewell – I give special thinks for their continued interest in and commentary on the developing text. Jane Collier, Sherry Ortner, and Bridget O'Laughlin have read and reread the text in its entirety and have forced me to probe conceptual issues in ways I could not have done alone.

xv *Acknowledgments*

Jane Atkinson, Amy Burce, Harold Conklin, Michael Dove, Shelly Errington, Charles Frake, Duncan and Helene Foley, Thomas Kuhn, Richard Maddox, Leslie Nadelson, Robert Paul, Forrest Robinson, Amelie Rorty, Terence Turner, and Sylvia Yanagisako all read and provided useful commentary on large portions of the manuscript. Finally, Renato Rosaldo has grown with me through periods of both support and conflict. It is not easy to share fieldwork and career so fully with one's husband, but I am lucky. Without Renato, I fear I would be both less happy and less honest.

My initial fieldwork was made possible by a National Institutes of Health Predoctoral Fellowship and a National Institutes of Health Research Grant (5 FI MH-33, 243-02 BEH-A). Research in 1974 was funded by National Science Foundation Research Grant No. GS-40788. Within the Philippines, I enjoyed the support of the staff at the National Museum and the cooperation of Dell and Sue Schultz, along with the other members of the New Tribes Mission, who facilitated our first contacts with the Ilongots, supported our researches, and let us use their airplane.

1. The Ilongots

There are probably some 3,500 Ilongots, inhabiting a forested area of about 1,536 square kilometers, primarily in the province of Nueva Vizcaya, Northern Luzon, Philippines (see Map 1). An initial survey of the Ilongot region, which included visits to and hikes in the vicinity of current and abandoned mission bases, revealed a world of over thirty-five dispersed settlements, each from twenty minutes to a several-hour hike from its nearest neighbors, and composed of two to nineteen households, with an average of seven inhabitants in each household.[1] Excepting the four instances where houses clustered around a mission home and airstrip, the most striking feature of these settlements was their apparent lack of physical organization. Houses, built near gardens under immediate cultivation, were as much as half an hour from each other, and between them there were no communal buildings, no recognized public grounds — only rivers, ill-marked forest trails, and an occasional field of ripening rice.

William Jones, an American anthropologist whose diary record of the "picturesque" and fertile country where he was killed in 1909 first interested us in the Ilongots, had also noted this lack of any local organization: "Village life as I know it in America is wholly absent. At this moment, I can only liken it to a country community, with the Ilongot community on a much abbreviated scale" (1908:6). And Jones remarked, as we soon did – when seeking in vain for words to denote "big man," "chief," or "leader" – on the perplexing absence of formal structure, the casual and informal quality of Ilongot social life: "Society is pretty simple, and government is largely according to custom" (Rideout 1912:105).

Though William Jones would find himself attracted by "the free life in these wild rugged hills and silent gloomy jungles" (1912:198), this lack of an articulated system of local controls ultimately proved fatal to him. His ethnological interests led him to develop an extensive collection of material culture during his year of research with the Ilongots, a laborious and disappointing process among people who, as he would

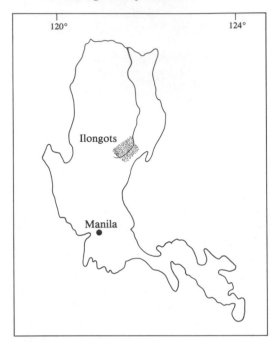

Map 1. The Ilongots on Luzon

write just weeks before recalcitrant helpers killed him, were "definitely exasperating from a practical point of view" (Rideout 1912:198). Much like his contemporaries in the colonial government, Jones struggled to make sense of men who did not share his view of obligation: "These . . . people sorely disappointed me. I expected better treatment. It is not a case of their having forgotten. They have their pay and do not intend to give a single thing. They have things but expect me to pay for them. Some things they have kept out of sight." He was particularly disturbed to find that government-appointed headmen lacked authority, an observation that may still hold true today: "The headman has no power whatever. Even if he spoke his people would not heed" (Diary, Book 9, 49).

To ship his goods, Jones required a small battalion of bamboo river rafts, but rumors of cholera in the lowlands as well as the sheer difficulty of mobilizing services from the necessary numbers of adults so frustrated him that he threatened to arrest the men he held responsible for his belongings. What we can glean from Jones's own account, reports of the constabulary who investigated his death,[2] and the memories of contemporary adults who themselves had seen the odd American known as 'Doctor' is that Jones's threats to his reluctant

Forest and garden newly planted in rice

hosts were themselves so disturbing that the local Ilongots arranged to take his life. Over fifty years later, Renato Rosaldo and I experienced similar difficulties in organizing Ilongot carriers and guides – so much so that, on Ilongot persuasion, we built an airstrip where a mission plane could land with our belongings. We thus avoided problems Ilongots never face: of making formal claims on people by purchasing their labor, when, ideally, cooperation should be governed by the reciprocity appropriate to kin.

The "customary" ordering of Ilongot social life as we encountered it is, as Jones remarked, quite "simple." As hunters and horticulturalists whose environment – to Jones in 1908 and even to us in the late 1960s – appeared both fertile and abundant, Ilongots recognize no differences in class or status. The only imbalances in their social field obtain between unmarried youths, who labor in the homes and gardens of adults, and their married seniors, and between women cultivators and men who choose their garden sites, clear their swiddens, gather wild foods, fish, and hunt. Society, much as Jones observed, ". . . is on a very simple plan. I cannot yet make out if anything like social caste exists. If it exists, it is very, very feeble. Where a good hunter is mated to an industrious wife there is a commodious dwelling and one or two grannaries (sic); in his home there is much to eat all the time" (1908:5). The Ilongot diet, consisting of dry rice, supplementary root crops, fish, deer, wild boar, and more periodic cultivated sugar cane, fruits and greens, wild ferns, palm hearts, frogs, and birds is as universally available as it is diverse. Although they exchange meat (and, in Jones's time, tobacco and rattan) for bullets, ornaments, knife blades, pots, and cloth, Ilongots are not dependent for subsistence goods on trade. Encroaching settlers since 1960 have led individuals in certain areas to lay claims to previously cleared territory, but Ilongots do not recognize among themselves exclusive rights to land. In fact, differential status identities have decreased since Jones's day, when shamans had not yet been killed by Japanese, or converted, as they have been since 1955, to fundamentalist Christianity:

: . . over here is a man who is reputed to have mysterious power; he can see into the future, can heal the sick and commune with unseen powers. Another yonder has killed one or more of the enemy and is regarded a brave man, a fierce fighter. An old wisehead has the reputation of knowing everything. Yet in none of these instances have I been able to see where the man has been lifted above his fellows (1908:5).

According to Jones and, as we will see, to Ilongots themselves, theirs is an essentially egalitarian way of life.

Today as in the past, one-room houses provide shelter for between one and three monogamous nuclear families, along with, possibly, widowed senior kin, adopted children, and occasional visiting bachelors. The family – at times called *tan tengeg,* 'one trunk,' or *matambē yek,* 'husband and wife, fellows in intercourse' – has primary responsibility for the care and socialization of unmarried children. It is often the unit of agricultural production and typically enjoys at least a hearth and a corner of the household structure where adults and infants sleep and personal goods are stored. The relations among families within a household are shaped by a universal rule prescribing uxorilocal postmarital residence – so that with very few exceptions, coresidents may include married sisters or parents and one or two married daughters, but not married brothers or sons. When daughters are newly married or when senior kin are very old, the household may be a unit of agricultural production. But even when individual families cultivate and store their rice in private granaries adjacent to their fields, households, not families, are units of consumption. In the home, all able-bodied persons work; raw produce is pooled for cooking, and cooked and equal portions of rice and viands are distributed to all inhabitants at their, minimally, diurnal meals.

Households, called (like families) *tan tengeg,* 'one trunk,' *tan bubungan,* 'one roofbeam,' or *tan 'abungan,* 'one home,' are joined in loosely organized and unnamed units I designate "settlements" or "local clusters." Denoted by the names of rivers or other striking features of the immediate environment, these groupings of related houses are often fragile, united largely by the cooperative efforts of men who distribute game among their clustered dwellings and collaborate in collective hunts with dogs. The boundaries of a settlement are not always clear, as individuals move, guests come and go, and not all affiliated households join consistently in meat distribution. But in each there is at least a core group of closely related families who are apt to share a history of common residence, having lived in close proximity over years of intermittent movement in search of fertile lands, abundant forests, or freedom from the lowland law. It is this history of coordinated moves, through times of inward-turning 'concentration' and then 'dispersal' toward the lowland margins of Ilongot lands, that lends a settlement its viability as an ill-defined yet generally recognized and cooperating social group.

Thus, Kakidugen, the settlement where we chose to live – largely because of its traditional appearance, and, in particular, its social and physical distance from established mission sites – had as its core two aging brothers, Lakay and Tagem, who lived with their married daughters. It also included two married nieces who had been raised in the home of one of the brothers and the families of two married 'sisters' (one, a first, and the other, a second cousin) of the old men. Their identity as a unit dated from at least the year 1923, when ancestors of the present people of Kakidugen were living with a large 'collection' ('*upug*, 'to gather, collect, concentrate') of their kin in the interior region known as Keradingan (see Map 2).[3] In revenge for past beheadings from the Keradingan area, the Ilongots of Payupay had led lowland troops to the interior, where Lakay – one of the aging Kakidugen brothers and the man whose house we shared   and a number of his fellows were arrested for killings they had not, in fact, performed. Freed from prison some months after his arrest, Lakay, a bachelor at the time, was told that he must live within the range of government surveillance. He therefore settled near the town of Kasibu, then partly Ilongot and now the lowland center of the municipality of which Kakidugen is a part. Finding himself among potentially antagonistic strangers, Lakay had the good fortune to encounter men whose great-grandmother was reputed to be a kidnapped bride and kinsman of his parents. Pleased to so 'discover' himself in the company of long-lost relations, he urged his closest kin in Keradingan to join him on the margins of Ilongot territory, his new home. Lakay married there, and there saw born all of the children whom we knew during our visit. His wife died as a result of complications that followed on her last child's birth. Shortly thereafter, he married again, to a young woman living as a 'visitor' in the home of nearby kinsmen. His brother, Tagem, married a traveling companion and first cousin of Lakay's new wife.

As it turned out, the 1920s were dramatic years for Lakay's fellows left behind in Keradingan. In fact, those years seem to have had similar

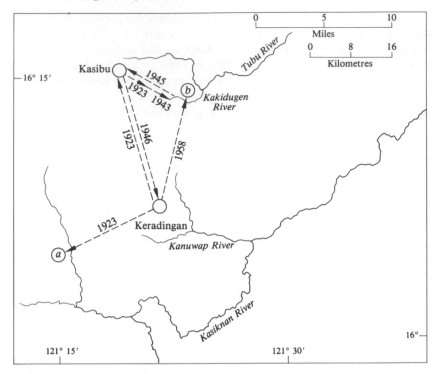

Map 2. Lakay's movements of 'concentration' (toward Keradingan) and 'dispersal' (toward Kasibu)

> *a*–Persons who moved, in 1923, toward *(a)* have tended since then to move to the area west and south of Keradingan, although they rejoined their pre–1923 familiars in the period of 'concentration' following World War II.

> *b*–The area north and west of point *(b)* was settled by Ilocano, Ifugao, Ibaloi, and Kallahan farmers in the period between World War II and the present; in 1974, there were firm indications that these newcomers would continue to settle lands to the east and south.

consequences for the Ilongot population as a whole. Headhunting forays from and against distant Ilongot settlements *(ngayu)*, internal killings 'by deception' *(ka'abung)*, and repeated raids by soldiers all encouraged the dispersal of once dense and 'concentrated' internal clusters, some of which then moved to other margins and began, by the end of the decade, to send their children to the new, American-sponsored schools. In consequence, the period from 1929–35 appears to have been one of relative calm for the Ilongots, who recall that they were worn out by violence and attracted by the promise of a useful education. Killing was therefore virtually abandoned – some say because they feared that youngsters would let their teachers know of headhunting forays by adults. In this

Lakay in 1974

period of relative quiet and, subsequently, of relaxed control, Lakay and his family moved closer to the interior, to near the Kakidugen river.

But by the mid-1930s the Depression and administrative changes associated with the 1935 Declaration of Commonwealth in the Philippines ended state-supported schooling, and late in the decade killings were resumed. The early 1940s saw intense violence, and Ilongots killed even those people recognized as kinsmen, taking them

A tatoo fashioned after American military "stripes" keeps alive the memory of World War II.

'by deception' in their homes. At much the same time, Japanese troops landed in Manila, and rumors of fighting and disruption in the lowlands led to a partial recongregation of the people of Keradingan. Lakay's family therefore found themselves increasingly involved with kinsmen they had broken with some twenty years before. But when, in 1945, American troops swept the then starving and defeated Japanese toward the presumably "uninhabited" hills of Nueva Viscaya, the group was forced to separate again. Hunger, illness, and murder at the hands of desperate Japanese cost Ilongots close to one-third of their population in the subsequent months of crisis. And although some Ilongots survived the onslaught of Japanese stragglers by hiding in the forests, Lakay's family, acquainted with the lowlands, fled toward familiar margins. There, American soldiers promised safety, friendship, and much-needed medicine and food.

After the war, Lakay remained close to the lowlands as his eldest daughter, Wagat, married an Ilongot from the area where he himself had first wed. But once again, a development in which they had small part – the rise of the Communist-oriented Hukbalahap movement in the 1950s – stirred Lakay's kin to movement. Lakay's daughter left her husband (she is one of the very few Ilongots I know to have experienced divorce) and followed her father's family back toward the interior, where she and her brothers married into another cluster of Keradingan families, people who were associated with the settlement of Pengegyabēn in the years of our research. Intermarriages and headhunting raids directed primarily toward lowland settlers marked this final period of 'concentration' in Keradingan, which lasted until 1958. Then, internal conflicts, renewed killings, and rumors of settlers laying claim to previously cultivated lands led Lakay, his brother Tagem, and some of their fellows to again move outward toward the flat lands around the Kakidugen river. Additional families joined them there, while others left to 'follow' closer kinsmen. But Lakay and Tagem managed to stay in Kakidugen, where they continued to be the central figures in a settlement that was barely resisting incursions by displaced Kallahan, Ibaloi, and Ifugao tribesmen at the time of our arrival in 1967.

Such histories of coordinated dispersal and concentration are shared by the core inhabitants of all Ilongot settlements – some of which are composed of several family clusters; although others, like Kakidugen, are clearly dominated by one. To the outside investigator what this means is that although local residential bonds are influenced by uxorilocal preferences after marriage, settlements – unlike households – are quite diverse in composition and rarely have a fixed or constant shape. A history of related moves, interpreted within an idiom of bilateral kinship[4] and reinforced by bonds of marriage, permit most members of a settlement to construe themselves as kin, who (as Ilongots express it) share a 'body' *(betrang)*. But accident, death, and – more significantly – the shifting orientations of young men and women when they marry, make local groups more fragile than the nuclear families of which they are composed. What continues over time is not a stable group but a tradition of relation. Those people who have shared in hunts, along with kin in other settlements with whom they have been wont to live at times of 'concentration,' will tend to see themselves as members of a single *bērtan*,[5] a largely endogamous 'bilateral descent group,' or, to use a more general translation, as persons of a single 'kind.'

Bērtan, unlike settlements, are seen by Ilongots as timeless and discrete collections of related persons who share an origin from unknown common ancestors who once lived together 'downstream,' 'in the lowlands,' 'on an island,' 'near a mountain' – in short, in some environment from which the *bērtan* takes its name. As the largest units of the Ilongot social system, *bērtan* are composed of all persons who choose to reckon their descent group identity through either parent.[6] They are typically associated with a discrete locality, and though theoretically unbounded, a strong tendency to endogamy, clear regional affiliations, distinctive dialects, and an inclination to give *bērtan* members unique personal appellations mean that membership can be treated as clear and unambiguous in those contexts in which a *bērtan* label is important: visits, marriages, and other interactions with unrelated *bērtan*, and in the determination of potential victims in intra-Ilongot feuds.

Thus, most of the people who once lived together in Keradingan see themselves as members of the Rumyad *bērtan*, a label that they use in visiting adults of other 'kinds,' in organizing support for covenants with one-time enemy *bērtan*, and in explaining why disputes among themselves should not occasion major confrontations, being the petty differences of kin. Historical evidence suggests that in the past, *bērtan* have split (new segments acquiring as their *bērtan* name a feature of their new environment) and it appears as well that severely ravished populations have merged, at times, with *bērtan* of their conquerors or kin. The Kakidugen people, for example, are associated not only with Rumyad but also with a presently nonlocalized and reduced group known as Peknar, and it is the latter identity label that they invoke when wishing to dissociate themselves from the activities of more distant Rumyad fellows. Furthermore, the fact that almost every Ilongot can trace ancestry from some foreign *bērtan* means that individuals from Rumyad may, for example, affiliate themselves with Tamsi, Pugu, Be'nad, and a number of other *bērtan* when such assertions of relation are politically desired. But whatever the empirical flexibility of *bērtan* designations, Ilongots speak as if their world were readily divided into a set of at least thirteen enduring localized descent groups, whose present residential foci are indicated on Map 3.

Like concentric circles, the Ilongot social world can, then, be construed as a set of ever more inclusive units – family, household, settlement, *bērtan*. Each of these units "physically" contains the others and each is composed of related persons who may or may not be able to calculate strict genealogical connection, but who nonetheless experience their bonds in terms of the cooperative orientations that unite them and lend substance to the claim that they are kin. Flexible in composition, all of these units change through time, as does the reckoning of kin ties that connect them. And kinship itself, like other aspects of Ilongot social discourse, tends to minimize acknowledgment of enduring differences, permitting people who – for whatever reason – come to see themselves as related to express at once equality, independence, common interests, and cooperative concerns.

Terminologically, the Ilongot speaker distinguishes related persons primarily in terms of generation, as 'siblings' *(katan'agi)*, 'children' *('anak)*, 'mothers' *('ina)*, 'fathers' *('ama)*, 'grandparents' *('apu)*, and 'grandchildren' *(maka'apu)*; optional terms mark distinctions with reference to consanguinity, relative age, and sex. Affines of the same generation call one another *'aum;* and parents- and children-in-law use the

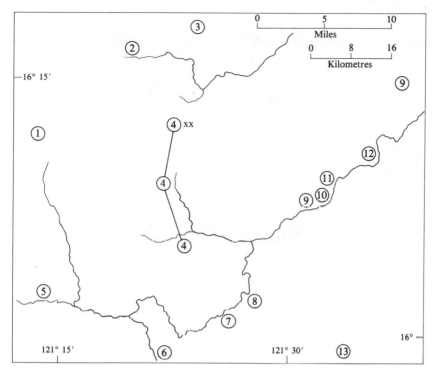

Map 3. Ilongot bērtan

1. Bēlansi (including Butag; see text)
2. Dēnabē
3. Payupay
4. Rumyad (including Peknar; see text)
5. 'Abēka
6. Taang
7. 'Aymuyu

8. Dekran
9. Tamoi
10. Pugu
11. Kebinengan
12. Sincbran
13. Be'nad
XX The settlement of Kakidugen

same term – *'apu* – that young children use for second generation seniors in their parents' homes (see Figure 1). An additional term, *bidēt*, denotes the spouse of a spouse's sibling – a person who, because of an inclination to "sibling exchange" in marriage, is likely to be a kinsman of one's own. Further, the distinction between kin and affine is underlined in a prohibition on using the 'true' names of the close relatives of spouses – a rule that marks the often strained, 'outsider' status of an in-married man.

But here as elsewhere, Ilongot practice tends to undercut such separation, and affines are apt to choose reciprocal names for one another – such as 'fellow crocodile,' *kabuaya;* 'fellow entrance,' *karenep;* 'fellow bachelor,' *kabuintaw* – in commemoration of experiences they have shared.[7] Over time, a statistical tendency to marry within a range of

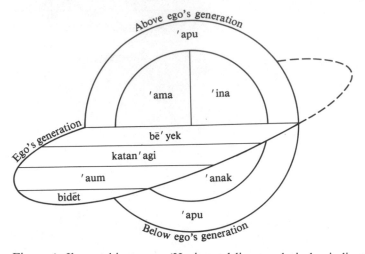

Figure 1. Ilongot kin terms. (Horizontal lines and circles indicate number of genealogical links removing prime kin types from ego.)

Obligatory Kin Types (P = parent; S = spouse; C = child; m = male; f = female):

'apu (PP, SP, CS, CC (also, *maka'apu*))   *bē'yek* (S)
'ama (mP)   *katan'agi* (PC)
'ina (fP)   *'aum* (SPC)
'anak (C)   *bidēt* (SPCS)

Optional Kin Types (e = elder; y = younger; x = cross-sex [all with reference to ego]):

tā'u, 'uita'u (PPmC)   *gu'nek* (mC)
'ikit (PPfC)   *'upet* (fC)
maka'uita'u (PmCC)   *bēkur* (PxfC), 'woman'
maka'ikit (PfCC)   *raki* (PxmC), 'man'
'eka (PeC)
'agi (PyC)

Reciprocals:

matan'apu (PP/CC or SP/CS)   *matambidēt* (SPCS/SPCS)
matan'ama (mP/C)   *matan'uita'u* (PPmC/PmCC)
matan'ina (fP/C)   *matan'ikit* (PPfC/PfCC)
matambē'yek (S/S)
matan'agi (PC/PC)
matan'aum (SPC/SPC)

second or third cousins, impressive marital stability, and the practice of reciprocal naming all help to reinforce a sense that those adults who live together are, for certain purposes at least, true equals in relation. The requirements of politics and of everyday cooperation mean that names used by affines will come to have a general circulation and that in many contexts affines will be viewed and will construe themselves as kin. Thus, although marriages appear initially as a source of strain and in-married grooms from distant groups may always feel that they lack the trust and firm support enjoyed by local fellows, the overall tendency in Ilongot life is toward a recognition that affines are also 'siblings' – a tendency to deal flexibly with such distinctions as could promote a sense of strict dependency and obligation, provide the grounds for hierarchy, or undermine the autonomous posture of adults who must cooperate in day-to-day affairs.

Aspects of fieldwork

For William Jones, this flexible Ilongot world was full of puzzles: "I haven't got the relationship of Panipagan and the Ifugu people straight in my mind. Kanta told me that Panipagan were enemies of Ifugu, yet I've seen Ifugu people at Panipagan. I believe they are friends" (Diary, Book 9, 28). Decidedly sacrilegious in cosmological discourse, Ilongots seemed to "have a way of changing custom to suit . . . convenience" (Diary, Book 10, 7). And although Jones felt certain that "warfare among the wild men of Luzon is rapidly being checked," he would recognize that "this is practically the only territory where the mice have free play" (Rideout 1912:189), and so continue his investigation among a people whose indigenous taste for violence recalled to him his native Wild West.

   Like Jones, we were at once attracted and perplexed by the fluidity of the social world that we encountered. Missionary advice led us, by a complicated route, to the settlement of Kakidugen, but we did not know why our guide – the settlement's present captain, Bangad – took us not to his own house but to that of Lakay and his son-in-law, Tukbaw, Renato's future Ilongot 'brother.' Soon, we were again puzzled. After making preliminary arrangements, we went to Manila and returned, this time accompanied by an armed guard of perhaps a dozen men who darted around rocks with rifles ready, calling out, 'Don't shoot, you Butag men; we're with Americans!' Strangely, our hosts proceeded to deny impending trouble and in fact behaved in subsequent days as if no challengers were known. It was not until nearly a year later that we learned that members of the Butag *bértan* were about to enter peace negotiations with our companions and had threatened to take a head to equalize a history of killings before forswearing grievances in a binding oath.

   Our early months in Kakidugen were marked by the slow and frustrating effort necessary to learn a language among strangers. As attentive friends who yet continued skeptical of our purposes and goals, our hosts were gratified when we cured the sick, appalled to learn (through my ridiculous mistake) that I took pills to keep from having children, and relieved when, assisted by the kind translations of a passing lowland guest, they arranged to have us pay them five dollars every other month for food and lodging. They taught us of the medicines and goods they hoped we would bring as gifts in the same tones in which they named varieties of rice for us and corrected our dull efforts to speak their language. And we felt, almost from the first, that there was a good deal to recommend the warm and casual style of the homes where we were uninvited guests. Though puzzled by an apparent lack of formal rule, pattern, or "structure," we found ourselves quite comfortable among people who – like us, it seemed – explained their deeds by reference to the private inclinations of their 'hearts,' and through their generosity managed to accommodate two questioning and clumsy anthropologists as 'equal to us humans' with whom they would share food.

At the same time, having come, in part, in search of an exotic world that would unsettle our conventional understandings, we were initially distressed to find that Ilongots did not tell nightly myths, make intricate plans for ritual feasts, or in their daily lives reveal concern for detailed webs of ancient wisdom. When we probed to learn of wild exploits in which men took heads, our hosts insisted that beheadings had not been practiced since the time of *our* enemies, the Japanese – and asked us how, when they had been so kind to us, we could think they were the sort of men who would kill their 'equal humans' without cause.

Thus, when some nine months later, this people's proud yet fearful revelations emerged as nervous testimony to a slowly growing trust, we were, quite simply, overwhelmed with what we learned. Jones had thought himself the witness to a dying breed of killers. And yet, in 1968, we found that some sixty-five of seventy Rumyad men over twenty years of age had beheaded human victims. Headhunting continued to be important as an aspect of Ilongot memory, myth, and song. Furthermore, most young men – like the "young bucks" of Jones's notebooks – still nurtured hopes of killing before accepting the constraints of married lfe. Novices were seen as dangerous men, bent on beheading; parents nurtured aspirations for the forthcoming triumphs of their unaccomplished sons.

Yet whatever the similarities between our observations and those of Jones, the violent tenor of the world where he was killed had clearly faded. Ilongots were still the lively and expressive folk Jones described:

The Ilongot easily gives expression to his emotions. He is a loud talker and is fond of animated conversation. . . . They use much gesture and exclamation, and follow it up with facial and eye expression. When these seem inadequate in telling of an incident considered interesting they will act it out in pantomime (Rideout 1972:171).

Women pausing for a rest from garden work find a chance to chew betel nuts and engage in "animated conversation" in the shade beneath a granary.

In the late 1960s Ilongots were still fearful on their trails and still alert to enemy challenge, but we did not experience anything equal to the tension, fear, and anxious expectation Jones had known:

You see the weather is growing more torrid everyday, and the sun can now shine for a whole day at a time. As a result every Ilongot house is on the watch for prowlers looking for heads, and ambitious youths are off looking for the same in other districts (Rideout 1912:188).

What had changed since Jones's time was not in any simple sense the "opening" of a previously "self-contained" and "timeless" world to modern ways and progress, for Ilongots had known contact with colonial administrators and Philippine lowland populations since the early years of Spanish rule. In the eighteenth century, Ilongot families had been "resettled" in the vicinity of Spanish valley priests, much as they had moved toward their margins to the sites of lowland schools in the 1920s and 1930s. And, in both cases, hopeful "civilizing" agents had been slaughtered when the Ilongots found occasion to move inward toward traditional upland homes. Reports from as early as the 1880s tell of Ilongots bringing forest goods to lowland traders, and though Jones suggests that before his visit lowlanders bearing matches, knives, and cloth, had feared to enter Ilongot lands in trade, his diary provides ample evidence of enduring contact between Ilongots and settled Christian groups. One might even speculate that much as Ilongots escalated violence among themselves in reaction to upheavals caused by the arrival of the Japanese in the 1940s, so some of the killing Jones found difficult to understand was an aftermath of the considerable slaughter and displacement of colonized Filipinos that followed the Spanish American War.[8]

Crucial changes in Ilongot life must have begun with a smallpox epidemic some twenty years prior to Jones's visit. Then, in the early part of this century, Americans opened and secured old Spanish roads, making Ilongot territory more accessible to government agents, settlers, and trade than it had been before. But a proper examination of the shifts that have determined their present lives probably does best to concentrate on a period that for Ilongots constitutes a sort of psychic Great Divide: the experience and consequences of World War II. For Ilongots, all time before the coming of the Japanese – be it the time of mythic heroes, Spanish priests, or American lowland schooling – is known as *pistaim,* 'peace time,' and Ilongots date most significant changes in their way of life from the radical reduction in their numbers and subsequent onslaughts of settlers that followed the chaotic months of 1945. After the war, Ilongots, equipped with abandoned Japanese guns, turned violence outward, killing lowlanders and ceasing to take heads among their fellows. Wartime displacement may well have been a factor in the Ilongot readiness to attend American missionary efforts that began in the mid-1950s. And postwar economic developments in the Philippines were responsible for the great expansion, first of low-land Ilocano, then of tribal Kallahan, Ibaloi, and Ifuago settlers onto sparsely populated flatlands – including those once held by Ilongots – throughout Northern Luzon.

These shifts had several consequences that were evident by the time we initiated research: A Filipino from the New Tribes Mission had married into Ringen, the central Rumyad settlement; missionaries elsewhere in Ilongot country had become relatively fluent in the local language and encouraged such shifts in custom as the abandonment not just of killing, but of what they saw as sexually revealing forms of dress, and even betel nuts – traditionally chewed as oral lubricants and mild stimulants that were exchanged in daily rituals of sociality. In addition, game, though still plentiful, was not nearly as abundant as it had been in Jones's time; and the flatter reaches of what was once Ilongot territory had been cultivated by peasant settlers bound politically and economically to a developing capitalist state. When we returned to the field in early 1974, an apparently irreversible movement toward conversion, the abandonment of killing, improved local communications, a changed subsistence base, and a much denser pattern of settlement left an Ilongot world with small resemblance to that of the prewar era. It was, of course, to these developments that the young, integrative leaders of The New Bugkalut Nation referred when they declared, as others may have in the past with less reason, that Ilongots were now Christians with little interest in taking heads.

Given this, it seems inevitable that my traditionally oriented Ilongot friends would look to their past with a feeling of nostalgia – just as it is certain that their postwar marriages, moves, and, in particular, acts of violence, being aspects of a radically altered context, were associated with somewhat different meanings and motivations than were outwardly similar actions at the time of Jones's stay. To kill in vengeance after one has seen one's fellows killed must surely have been a different act than the anonymous assaults on innocent settlers that were waged by Lakay's sons and those who 'followed' them in the early 1950s. Similarly, to present game to the parents of a desired bride is one thing if one hunts with guns and bullets probably obtained with the help of senior kin, and quite another if the arrows used in hunting were manufactured, as was likely, by the young man himself.

But cultural forms endure through time. Meanings persist, themselves shaping the future. And a variety of circumstances since Jones's time – the inability or unwillingness of American administrators to recruit Ilongot labor; the upheavals caused by wartime struggles with the Japanese; the fearfulness of settlers – has combined to permit Ilongots to maintain a relatively self-sufficient and traditional form of economic life, and a cultural system which, however changed, continues to encourage men to kill.

Thus, in reading earlier accounts of Ilongot life, it is easy to discover continuities between the practices of Ilongots I knew well and those reported for their predecessors almost one hundred years before. One extraordinarily precise nineteenth-century text tells that Ilongots used spoons of coconut shells with wooden handles. And though contemporary Ilongot spoons are carved of wood, they yet preserve in form a prior substance. the coconut shell provides a model for the wooden ladles on most Ilongot serving spoons today. The text also gives a detailed and still accurate account of raiding, including, for example, the fact that Ilongot headhunters wear whitened bark headbands – as did the men of Kakidugen in 1972 – to prevent mistaken slaughter of their fellows, and that "they toss the head into the air and rush to catch it, counting as most brave the man who succeeds in taking hold" (Jordana y Morena 1885:77). Yet more telling, Jones's diary notes suggest a number of themes that will be central to my interpretations of Ilongot emotional life and patterns of motivation in the remainder of this book.

Jones indicates, for example, that Ilongots depend upon the efforts of firm adult men to tame the wild energies of young bachelors:

The eager, inexperienced youths went ahead, the reliable older heads in the middle and the women with a few men brought up the rear. Some of the youths were indiscreet; they whooped defiantly. Inamon reproved them severely, told them to go slower, keep watch of an ambush and had the more reliable proceed ahead to keep a lookout for signs. . . . It was a good talk, just what I wanted him to say, because it produced the moral effect I wanted the men to have, especially on the youths (Diary, Book 9, 20–1).

He records their sense of emulation and their desire not to be outdone by others:

The Kagadyanan party balked when I told them how faulty their grannary (sic) was. I told them to quit if they desired, that I would get Tamsi to do it. But later in the day they went back to the task and have accepted my criticisms (Diary, Book 10, 7).

He notes an inclination to find in an affront a cause for violent deeds, to resolve differences by something Ilongots see as the 'exchange' of 'angry' acts for one another's 'anger':

I was waked about midnight by a loud voice in the room. I found it was Mundai paying her respects to Kanyan. It seems that he went to her house and tried to lie beside her, but she objected. She came over to the house where I live . . . but he followed. . . . She tried to get out several times, but he would head her off, and refastened the door. . . . Once he tried lying beside her. With the whittling knife she cut an ugly wound across the index finger. He walked to the door and by the light of the moon squatted to look at what she did. He groaned and complained. She stood up, walked to the middle of the floor. He quietly rose and struck her a blow on the nose. She went to one hearth, lay down, and broke further into another stream of words. . . . He made no reply but went over and sat down beside her. The last I saw of them she was asleep and he was beside her (Diary, Book 10, 10–11).

And finally, Jones shows an awareness of the Ilongot view that killings ought to follow deaths and that celebratory songs that mark beheadings are incompatible with a vivid sense of loss:

I've tried to get the Kagadyanan people to sing the [headhunting] song in my machine but they say that they can't; that many of their kin have died and they have not taken a head and therefore singing would sadden them (Diary, Book 9, 45).

In the following chapter I recount how I too learned that singing saddens men who have not killed, but neither Jones nor any of the earlier reports helped me to understand the reason for this. What is "sadness" for the Ilongots? How is it linked to song? And what connections might these bear to the warm and friendly atmosphere in Ilongot homes, to closeness among kin, to competition, to 'anger' and 'exchange,' and to the enduring romance that Ilongot men appeared to find in killings?

The Ilongots we knew did not appeal to social rule or cosmic law in explaining their continued interest in beheadings; neither gods nor claims to land, not politics, health, fertility, or a desire to excel was seen by them as reasonable cause to raid. A popular lowland myth – that the Ilongot youth must give a severed Christian head to the father of his desired bride, and therefore kills when fire tree blooms arouse his desires to "mate" in springtime – was not itself invoked by Jones nor, interestingly, was it known by our informants. The myth reflects the facts that Ilongots hope to kill before they wed, that fire tree blossoms may in fact spark men to 'angry' thoughts, and that most men prefer to raid when trails are dry and therefore hide their footprints. But it betrays a most un-Ilongot concern for "natural" and evil drives in casting killing as a sort of payment for the young groom's spring-born lust. Ilongots do not "mate" in spring, nor do they give a "Christian head" to affines; and though the bright red flowers of the fire tree in bloom are said to taunt the novice with the knowledge that he has not killed, they are not themselves an acknowledged cause of raids.

But when we asked Ilongot friends to tell us why they killed, their answers did not seem to convey a sufficient or fitting "reason." Instead of an exotic tale of scarlet trees and maddened youths, Ilongots explained themselves in terms that seemed too bland and common for us to make sense of what appeared to be an unintelligible – and unconscionable – love of gore. Men went headhunting, Ilongots said, because of their emotions. Not gods, but 'heavy' feelings were what made men want to kill; in taking heads they could aspire to 'cast off' an 'anger' that 'weighed down on' and oppressed their saddened 'hearts.'

Unable to appreciate much of the pattern in Ilongot life through the more "normative" and "structural" approaches traditional in anthropology, I had for some time been reluctant to isolate as a subject for research a single "symbol" which, like headhunting, appeared as an exotic fact that lacked exotic (*or,* it seemed, pragmatic) rationale. My first writings, on Ilongot styles of speech, gave short shrift to beheadings. And so it was with the compelling and unsettling surprise that comes of unexpected recognition that I began – during our second field trip, in 1974 – to construct from Ilongot talk of 'hearts' and feelings the outlines of an account that could illuminate not just killing but some apparently enduring features of the social world of which it was a part. To know what Ilongots meant in declaring that the wishes of their hearts led them to kill required a grasp of words like 'heart' and 'anger' as they were used in a variety of different contexts. To understand the order in Ilongot social lives, I had to hear what was implied by the things Ilongots said, and in particular, to "interpret"[9] or discover the broad sorts of concerns that lay behind their explanations of their acts. Whereas other anthropologists have been inclined to work "from outside in," first describing a patterned social world and then asking how individuals are "socialized" to work and live within it, I found it more illuminating to begin from the other pole of the analytical dialectic and ask how personal and affective life, itself "socially constructed," is actualized in and orders the shapes of social action over time.[10] This required an investigation of Ilongot words concerning hearts and motivations – especially, their words denoting 'energy/anger/passion' and civility, or 'knowledge' – and, at the same time, a discovery of local assumptions about the persons, relationships, and events to which such words were characteristically applied.

Theoretical considerations

My concern in this book is with a particular sort of relation between "words" and the "world" – not the conventional one of reference and demarcation, but rather the less formal sort of bond that connects habitual ways of talking about experience to the organization of that experience itself. My data, like that of most anthropologists, consists overwhelmingly of the things I was told – in the form of stories, tales and meetings captured on tapes, bits of gossip shared, responses to my questions. Yet whereas some have sought to specify the presumably "real" events to which collected native terms bear witness, my interests tend, more narrowly, toward an exploration of the meanings and intentions embodied in the utterances I once troubled to record.

That anthropology is, at least in part, an exercise in translation; that understanding another culture is much like the learning of a foreign language; and that, furthermore, acquiring competence in the speech of one's informants is itself a sort of initiation into the ways they view their world, is as old a set of ideas as its analytical ramifications have been various. An awareness of the cultural relevance of language has motivated everything from the sensitive ethnographies of men such as Evans-Pritchard to the descriptive tomes of Bloomfieldian linguistics and the suggestive but poorly specified claim, associated with the names of Whorf and Sapir, that language underlies forms of perception and of thought. More recently, British and continental anthropologists have shown an interest in "symbolic" aspects of ritual expression as these reveal the logic, strains, or values of a presumably "underlying" social system, and Americans interested in "ethnoscience" have examined ways that linguistically coded systems of classification lend a rudimentary cognitive order to the natural and social worlds. What these newer approaches share is much more than a concern with cultural form, language, and meaning. Though more or less aware of their connections with the dominant philosophies of this century, all tend to build on the logician's view of a distinction between language as an ordinary vehicle of reference, logic, and cognition, and "symbolism" as a unique sort of discourse, rooted in emotion and nonpragmatic – either meaningless or endowed with "hidden" meanings; either lacking reason or governed by a logic that is discontinuous with our daily sense.[11] This distinction, as Firth has indicated (1973:16–30), is found in common usage: We speak of the "symbolic gestures" of, for example, politicians, to imply that some things they say should not be taken literally, and, in particular, that there is a gap between observable behavior and its underlying, "real" intent.

"Symbols" as used by these contemporary writers[12] refers to utterances, acts, or objects that stand at one remove from the "real world" that they refer to: Like the red blossoms of the fire tree which, Ilongots say, can stir their hearts to 'angry' violence, the "symbol" points to something other than its referent alone. In contrast to the "symbol" so defined are the more ordinary, strictly referential terms of daily language – words, perhaps, like "anger," "red," or "blossom," the understanding of which requires little more than an ability to recognize the discrete emotional states, plants, or colors that their names conventionally denote. Ordinary language is thought to be straightforward, and as such, does not require a special effort of interpretive reflection. The "literal" contrasts with the "symbolic" much as "cognition" may be opposed to "affect," and as the "pragmatic" rationality revealed in the technology of grain among the Azande (Evans-Pritchard 1937) can be contrasted with the less consistent and more problematic vagaries of "primitive" or "magical" thought. These distinctions depend ultimately on a view that holds that certain meanings are, in some quite simple way, transparent – and in particular, that referential acts, much like pragmatic ones, are straightforward ways of classifying and acting upon an "objective" and universally "given" world. Mention of fire trees might well engage the interest of "symbolic" anthropology. But an Ilongot who tells me that 'We go headhunting when the rains stop,' or 'We kill because of anger,' or for that matter, 'We divide the game we catch on a collective hunt,' could – by our accustomed lights – as well have spoken to me in English: His remarks, lacking "symbolic" intimations, are descriptions on the order of the sentences of this text.

But I fear we are betrayed by our conventional distinctions. Whatever the appeal of a divide between two "kinds" of meaning,[13] I now would argue that it leads us in the wrong directions, at once impoverishing our understanding of common discourse and imputing to the "symbolic" both more and less importance than any isolated mode of expression is apt to have. For social anthropologists interested in "symbols," there is a tendency to assume that underneath a culture's nets of problematic and distinctive rituals, rules, and myths, we find our homely, but in some sense universal, next-door neighbors. And so, in ferreting out the "hidden" sense of odd expressions, they often come upon a set of terms themselves familiar, terms that fit too neatly the assumptions of the analyst's common sense. Thus, we might learn that fire trees "symbolize" anger for the Ilongots (or perhaps, that hair knots "symbolize" the penis, or that gods can serve as "symbols" for society) but fail to learn the sort of things that Ilongots mean when they speak of *liget,* 'energy, anger, passion' – just as Leach (1954), who finds that Kachin use their myths to rationalize claims to precedence, fails to tell us why such precedence is desired, what it means, in Kachin life. One may find beneath peculiar social and symbolic forms such purportedly universal terms as "the quest for power," "worldly passions," "Oedipal conflicts," or "self-interest," but in every case the status of such terms within the culture thus reduced to our discourse remains unquestioned. Having distinguished what appear to be symbolic terms from the transparent commonsense on which to found translation, such analysts prove incapable of appreciating the ways in which apparently foreign and peculiar deeds may by themselves have commonsense interpretations. And at the same time, their approach ignores the fact that common sense in other cultures is ultimately as demanding of interpretation as is apparently obscure "symbolic" form.

The classificatory lexicography of American ethnoscience (e.g., Conklin 1955, 1964; Frake 1961, 1969), because it is concerned with specifying the ways that speakers order daily worlds through the distinctive referential biases of their language, appears, in part, to answer this deficiency. It alerts us, for example, to the fact that although the Ilongot word *liget* overlaps significantly with the English word "angry," it belongs to a unique semantic field, describing violent men but also striving youths and energetic hunters, and so is opposed to words like 'passive,' 'dull,' and 'fearful.' The English "angry," on the other hand, probably enters a contrastive field that includes notions like "well-meaning" and "at peace." Similarly, Ilongot kinship terms do not distinguish 'children' of one's own from siblings' 'children,' and Ilongots use the word for 'weed' to speak, in general terms, of 'plants.' I learned something important about Ilongots the day I asked for an example of the use of *dē'ri,* 'to help,' or 'pity,' and was told to consider the sad and 'pitiable' condition of a domestic pig that lacked both shelter and companions – a remark suggesting that Ilongots in their daily life are wont to speak and act in terms of classificatory schema equating animals and human beings, a classification which for me was limited to the fantastic childhood world of a once favorite tale of "very human" pigs and spiders, E. B. White's *Charlotte's Web*. Such insights recall Hallowell's classic plea (1954) for an investigation of the culturally organized "behavioral environments" of the self. Like Hallowell, ethnoscientists discover culture not in modes of speech, but in referential "maps" that are embodied in vocabulary; human groups are seen to differ largely insofar as they use different "lenses" to discriminate among already given objects in the objective world.

And yet, what both of these approaches lack is a clue to how we are to understand straightforward native statements that cast 'anger' as a reason for beheadings. By treating lexical items as classificatory markers in an "objective" referential field, the ethnoscientist may recognize that referentially related terms in different languages include nonisomorphic sets of denotata. But in attending just to words and not to sentences and styles of speech, such an analyst fails to grasp the cultural shapes of what semanticists might reckon "connotation," and thus inevitably ignores the implications of what look like "metaphoric" turns of phrase for an illumination of the more "ordinary" ways that words are used. Social anthropologists, on the other hand, are all too likely to bemoan their ignorance of "psychological" detail, their inability to describe "real" motivations. Or – as has in fact occurred in classical interpretations of headhunting rites (see Needham 1976; M. Rosaldo 1977) – they may force native exegeses into a utilitarian causal framework and conclude that Ilongots go headhunting in search of "soul stuff" which promises them fertility and health. The difficulty, in short, is that in viewing lexical items either as crude tools for "cutting up" the perceived world into a set of discrete classes, or alternatively, as exotic "symbols" that disguise a more familiar psychological or pragmatic sense, anthropologists have failed to capture the sorts of things we need to know in order to understand the comments, texts, and even the explanatory accounts of our informants. Separating the symbolic from the everyday, anthropologists quickly come upon such "universal" facts as correspond to their assumptions,[14] and fail to see that common discourse as well as the more spectacular feats of poets and religious men requires an interpretive account.

Victims of the proverbial Occam's razor, we confuse ourselves with a false clarity when we fail to recognize the ways in which "symbolic" and interpretable[15] concerns in fact pervade our daily conversations. And we ask the wrong things both of common talk and ritual when we forget the work of such theorists as Freud, who saw that psychic needs, and Weber, who recognized that the historically specific orientations anthropologists call "culture," lend a distinctive and problematic cast to any human utterance or act. Their observations should make us cautious in assuming that "symbolic" acts or statements are distinct from and distortions of the more pragmatic stuff of common sense. Culturally specific nuances and themes enter language less by way of classificatory grids than through habitual modes of speaking.[16] Thus, if we would understand why Ilongots say that *liget* is what makes men kill, we need to ask about the sorts of discourse in which *liget* and related terms are used: Why do Ilongots see *liget* in the perspiration of a person hard at work? Why do they boast of 'anger' when engaged in graceful dancing? And why, again, do they invoke an imagery of focused *liget* in magical spells before they harvest rice? "Figures of speech" like these need not be parceled out in order better to reveal the "literal" meanings that remain "beneath" key terms and obscure phrases. Instead, these different figures must be linked and situated within the lively discourse of which they are, of course, a central part. Culturally patterned discourse, common things that people say, derive not just from rules of use that tell the names of players, moves, and tools, and outline games of conversation; they also embody a sense of *how* and why to play, a style of action and understanding. And human actors, pursuing ends with means as culturally defined as are their ultimate aspirations, must – as Gilbert Ryle saw – display a competent grasp of "how" as well as "that."

What all of this amounts to is a need for anthropology to come to terms not simply with the ubiquity of symbols, but, even more importantly, with the implications of this fact for our assumptions about the brute, pragmatic, "given" terms assumed too universally to sustain our possibilities of making sense. Formal strategies that would attempt to translate by showing first what a word denotes, or how peculiar actions fit a "rational" scheme of motivation, seem equally unable to come to terms with the fact that the realities in and for which people live their lives are themselves endowed with "meanings" that derive from the activities that people are engaged in and the ways that they describe the things they do. We can learn about Ilongot life by using words like *liget* as an initial text, not because Ilongots "classify" a person wild with rage in terms that, unlike ours, refer as well to energetic farmers – but rather because a proper understanding of what *liget* means requires us to look beyond the word itself to sentences in which it is employed, images through which it is invoked, and social processes and activities that Ilongots use it to describe. By so "interpreting" the meanings presupposed by certain terms, one can, I think, begin to translate cultures, and in particular, come to grips with motivational patterns that are to be discovered neither in classificatory nouns nor in outlandish "symbols," but rather in the various forms of discourse and activity that, of course, are constituted by a set of "symbols" all too rarely recognized as such.

More specifically, analysts who distinguish peculiar and "symbolic" meanings from readily translated everyday meanings have been forced to ask why human beings who are thought to be as "rational," or pragmatic, as they often see themselves, are yet engaged by bloody ritual acts, like taking heads, which challenge the analysts' pragmatism and morality. The generally accepted answer is that through ritual and symbolic forms, people represent – with more or less success – the structure, norms, distinctive "interests," or ideals of the "society" that binds them. Furthermore, because true "symbols" can invoke both sensory memories and emotionally laden thoughts, it is thought that they are useful vehicles of socialization, good not only "to think" but also to encourage participation in such "sentiments" of mutual concern as in fact are necessary for the reproduction of an orderly social world. The symbolic forms of ritual are thus assumed to be "effective" in reorganizing people's understandings and heightening their commitments to their fellows: Though their method may be touched by what an outsider sees as madness, their end is the pragmatic and intelligible one of providing for order and cooperation in daily social life.

Because we know that ritual participation quite often moves people to tears, and sometimes to conversion, joy, or cure, we must assume that "symbols" can serve a very special function as the potent and "effective" vehicles of affectual change and deep emotion.[17] But it is also true that fundamentalists win converts by distributing leaflets on the street, that people change through talk with friends – and, at somewhat the opposite extreme, that Ilongots who readily proclaim that tossing off a victim's head lends "lightness" and new vigor to their tired limbs do not seem disenchanted when acknowledging that no marvelous transformation in physical demeanor occurred that last time they killed. Such observations will be problematic if – assuming that the sole point of ritual participation is a sort of experiential "high," a psychological state inducing solidarity, health, or change – we fail to see that rituals are at best but moments in a "sentimental education," rich but never wholly unfamiliar lessons in *how*, or what it means, among one's elders, peers, and friends, to entertain certain goals and dispositions, to induce, indulge, explore, and often to reflect upon the things one feels. It seems to me that if one starts by recognizing the ways in which symbolic form in fact pervades the everyday – as world view, ideology, or more simply, "culture" – then the questions one is wont to ask are not just "how" or "why" symbols "work" at special times, but rather how people's feelings and understandings are organized, or actualized, both in ritual and more mundane or practical pursuits. Rather than seeing "symbols" as the vehicles through which "external" social forms acquire "inner" meaning, one can investigate folk views of human action – views given content through the practices of daily life and talk and organized in particular ways in rituals, but views whose coherence depends ultimately on continuities people experience among the things they do, the organization of what Wittgenstein calls a "form of life."

In the ethnographic account that follows, I try to illustrate this approach by considering the use of certain Ilongot words, first in sentences and as they contrast with and are bound to one another, and then in relation to activities they are used to order, evaluate, and describe. Proceeding in this way enables me to recast a number of issues which, I think, have previously been limited by a tendency to distinguish the socially organized "symbolic" from the individual's daily speech – and so to reckon culture as mere icing on a more substantial cake, instead of as what I believe it is: the intelligible form one finds, not just in sets of "symbols" narrowly construed, but in the contradictory, multistranded, and complex assumptions, actions, memories, and talk of people who communiate with one another and who are alert to commonalities in the conduct of their lives.

My starting point is a set of Ilongot terms for what Westerners conventionally cast as emotional states and inner feelings – in short, with words that Ilongots use in explaining human action and construing the experiences of "the self."[18] My focus has as its precedents not only Mauss's plea (1938) for studies of the "notion of person" as it varies with distinctive social systems, but also the work of such ethnographers as Lienhardt (1961), whose explication of Dinka cattle sacrifice was based on an understanding of Dinka views that "identify" man and cow, and of the Dinka inclination to interpret problematic experience by "separating" and "imaging" it in a supernatural guise. American cultural anthropologists – notably Lee (1959), Benedict (1946), and Hallowell (1967) – have also shown an awareness that a grasp of culturally specific notions of "the self," of personal goals and orientations, is necessary to a proper understanding of the things that people find compelling – Japanese notions of hierarchy and obligation being central, for example, to an appreciation of the popular story, "The Forty-Seven Ronin" (Benedict 1946:199–207). More recently, David Schneider (1968) has argued the relevance of culturally grounded person concepts to accounts of kinship, and Clifford Geertz (1973b), in "Person, Time and Conduct in Bali," has offered an exemplary discussion of the mutual bearing of styles of action, temporal orientation, and the classification of persons among the Balinese.[19] For all of these, social and ritual practice is interpreted from the point of view of self-conceptions – accounts of how and why to act – that must inform the social lives of actors. For all, the intelligible, compelling, and significant nature of such "symbols" as the Dinka cow, or perhaps, American marriage, has less to do with their ability to play on hidden psychic cords than with commonplace assumptions that are bound up with daily use.

In my own work, I assume that we can learn about the meaning of Ilongot headhunting raids and rites by focusing not simply on the organization of such events themselves, but instead on the emotional language Ilongots use in explaining how and why such violent deeds engage their interest. Given their interpretations of the reasons that they kill, it seems clear that the meaning Ilongots find in taking heads is inseparable from their ideas of 'heart' and 'anger' – notions that suggest not just a set of "hidden" psychic states that words like *liget* only partially describe, but a range of contexts in which this and a variety of related images and words have a conventional application. To comprehend these, we must ask not if 'anger' and 'lightness' are in fact things that a headhunter is apt to "feel," but rather how such terms inform his recollections and accounts and so provide him with a way of understanding the significance of disturbing feats of force for daily interactions. Thus, rather than probe the possible uses of Ilongot terms for illuminating facts of individual psychology,[20] I concentrate on the meanings such words acquire through their association with enduring patterns of social relationship and activity in Ilongot daily life.

Order in Ilongot life does not exist in "structures" bestowed mythically by ancestors or gods, in social rules or strict taboos, or in a firm sense of tradition. Nor can we say that *liget* consistently orders present life, because, as Ilongots are all too well aware, it can as easily make for strain. A more appropriate sort of claim is that emotionally oriented images and themes maintain for Ilongots a sense of consistency in things that people do, thereby permitting them to see over time that people act in more or less familiar ways for more or less well known reasons. And these reasons, reflected in (as they are patterned by) the organization of their social world, lend an aura of continuity and coherence to the activities that they, in turn, explain.

For Ilongots, the *liget* that beheaders know is both similar to and different from the 'anger' of a drunken man, the heat of illness, 'passion' in a tropical storm, and the intense activity described by harvesters and hunters. Neither good nor evil in itself, *liget* suggests the passionate energy that leads young men to labor hard, to marry, kill, and reproduce; but also, if ungoverned by the 'knowledge' of mature adults, to engage in wild violence. Ideally, 'knowledge' and 'passion' work together in the 'heart.' But in fact the young lack 'knowledge' just as the old lack 'force,' and women, considered fearful and thus inclined to stay at home, cannot attain the heights of wisdom or of *liget* that are enjoyed by men. In so describing differences in human hearts in terms that link the things they feel to diverse facts of health, fertility, labor, storms, and social status, Ilongots create an idiom that provides a systematic, if not flawless, gloss on what is constant in their world, a way of understanding those activities through which forever fluid social bonds are given sense. More particularly, 'knowledge' and 'passion' describe not only motions of the heart, but also the relationships of men and women and of old and young. And finally, these relationships, as I will try to show, are central to an understanding of both marrying and killing, institutions which, for Ilongots, epitomize what is beautiful and orderly in their social lives.

To speak, as I will here, of "meaning," "order," "pattern," or "form" in Ilongot social life is, of course, to make a claim concerning the relevance of connections that the anthropologist first perceives and then, perhaps, confirms – much as a Freudian analyst might – in subsequent talk with an astute informant. It is, in short, to offer an interpretation which, like psychodynamic ones, assumes that certain sorts of pattern are likely to obtain. "Cultures," like "personalities," are descriptive tropes, lent conviction by their power to illuminate the activities of individuals or groups and organized by our assumptions concerning people and societies. Although some might view the individual's life as so many unrelated acts – and for every analyst who sees culture as a "functionally integrated" whole there is another who insists that cultural "forms" dissolve into a heap of "shreds and patches" – my own view is that social life and interaction require that people recognize, along with pattern in the natural world, a sense of what they share with one another, and that that knowledge of related selves must itself be in accordance with the quality of the social world in which they act. Cultures are not uniform and "integrated" wholes, but universes of conventional discourse whose coherence, however partial, problematic, and incomplete, enables recognition of connections among the things that people do – connections that make activities not just "appropriate" but intelligible and fraught with sense. Thus, I find it difficult to imagine a human world in which people did not see any relation between, for example, their labor and their social bonds of trust, affection, and obligation; their rituals and their daily lives; their motivations and acknowledged patterns in their society. Coherence in a cultural scheme reflects connections human actors themselves must make between their times of effort, joy, surprise, and disillusion – and these connections will not be organized by an abstract scheme attaching either to "society" or human "brains," but by ongoing processes of cooperation, conflict, and relation in their common world.

In investigating words Ilongots use in talk 'about the heart,' this book attempts to show how Ilongot views of the experiencing self themselves provide the iodioms that order and connect. It also tries to demonstate the relevance of these indigenous views for an under-standing of both pattern and change in Ilongot society. My interest in emotional terms was influenced both by the ethnographic situation I encountered in the field and by a more general conviction that one reasonable point of access to the cultural ordering of any human "form of life" might well be such words and images as people use in their accounts of human action – descriptions, reflections, and explanations that give testimony to local understandings of "the self." If order in a cultural scheme derives from (as it is reflected in and yet sheds light upon) the practices of daily living, then it would seem that folk accounts of things that people do – their motives, feel-ings, reasons, goals – would lead to an appreciation of the processes by which relationships are forged and reproduced in their society.

More specifically, my selection of 'knowledge' and 'passion' (*bēya* and *liget*) as focal analytical terms is based on the belief that these describe not only attributes of individual 'hearts' but also experiences, activities, and patterns of relation that encompass both civility and strain – the various forms of Ilongot sociality. Interest in these words began with a concern to understand elaborate styles of speech which, for Ilongots, epitomize the heights of *bēya*,[21] and a hope to grasp the sense that Ilongots found in taking heads – a feat of glorious but 'angry' hearts. Attracted to these first as ethnographic facts that were as culturally complex as they seemed troubling and exotic, I grew convinced that both killing and the elaborate formal talk Ilongots use when they negotiate the 'anger' caused by murder and the pursuit of wives derive much of their cultural significance from the way that they display the interdependence of 'knowledge' and 'passion,' both in social life and in the human heart. Other words as rich and distinctive as *liget* and *bēya* – such as *dē'ri* and *dimet*, which are associated with 'pity', and *ruyuk* and *sipē*, which relate to 'happiness' and 'elation' – would, I am sure, have lent a different cast to my discussion, but both in interviews with infor-mants and in reflections after leaving the field none seemed so widely ramifying, culturally profound, or socially revealing as those considered central here.

In the chapter that follows, I introduce Ilongot emotional discourse by focusing on the uses of the word for 'heart,' and the dynamic imagery that characterizes its motions, while exploring some of the relations among these images themselves. The movements of the 'heart' are largely those of *liget*, 'energy/anger/passion' – and a consideration of the various forms of *liget* introduces us, more generally, to Ilongot views of human motivation as these illuminate the ways that human feelings are bound up with taking heads. Chapter 3 explores the individual's affective life in a variety of more mundane contexts, focusing in particular on the complementarity of *liget* and *bēya,* 'passion' and 'knowledge,' as these develop with the acquisition of civility and productive skill in the course of an Ilongot's growing up. Because of the divergence in the childhood experiences of boys and girls as they approach the years of marriage, Ilongot youths are seen to have distinct affective dispositions, and these, in turn, are readily linked to men's and women's "needs" for one another, and to differences in their activities and goals.

After exploring the grounding of affective terms in individual experience, I turn in subsequent chapters to a more explicit consideration of the social processes that are associated with Ilongot views of how and why emotions work. More specifically, I analyze emotional life in terms of the assumption that Ilongot "selves" are forged within a social world where almost everything turns on marriage, and in which relationships are organized in terms of salient contrasts between, on the one hand, men and women, and, on the other, married and unmarried men. Thus, in Chapter 4, I explain the sense of the Ilongot claim that 'men have higher hearts than women' by relating stereotyped views of the sexes to their social relationships in production. Chapters 5 and 6 explore Ilongot views of personhood and feeling with reference to the development of *bēya* and *liget* through the adult life cycles, particularly of men. Chapter 5 considers headhunting as an epitomizing realization of *liget* by young bachelors, and Chapter 6 investigates *bēya* as it is displayed in public oratory meetings in which youthful *liget* is subordinated to adult 'knowledge' and control. Finally, in a concluding chapter I raise a number of comparative questions, developing yet more fully the general assumptions that are reflected in the organization of my account.

Because my text draws heavily on the data of Ilongot language use, I have included as an appendix a detailed glossary that makes available many of the linguistic materials that inform my discussion. Within the text itself, single quotation marks are used for translations of Ilongot materials; double quotations signal more conventional quotations, theoretical references, and the like. Materials set off in block form from the text are summaries of supportive and supplementary case materials which, although important to my arguments, would, I fear have overburdened an already detailed text.

2. Knowledge, passion, and the heart

Anthropology conceived in part as discourse on the theme of human cultural differences necessarily confronts the irony Lévi-Strauss introduces as a basic theme of *Tristes Tropiques:* As strange and "primitive" worlds become more accessible to our inquiry, they also become less foreign, more like us, and more deeply shaped by their relation to our own world. Lévi-Strauss, of course, was speaking of the fact that colonial expansion was what made modern anthropological fieldwork possible in the first place. But his reflections on South America point to yet another sense in which the irony holds true: In dialogue with informants, both parties accommodate one another; in making their lives open to our questions and to a form of discourse that begs for system and reflection, the natives who "inform" us construct what are always situated and necessarily partial interpretations of more complexly textured modes of life.

So our accounts are shaped not only by the concerns of the observer, but, at the same time, by the sorts of simplifications through which our interlocutors give order to, as they reflect upon, their times and lives. Summary and system are moments in cross-cultural dialogue and analysis – in my case, they emerged from talking with informants about how they used their language, and about the sense of words with which they characterized and explained the nature of human action, and the interest of activities as diverse as killing, gardening, and hunting. But when my Ilongot friends tried to explain their ideas of jealousy and anger, energy, well-being, knowledge, and the opacity of one another's hearts, they never "just" answered my questions. They constructed an account of things they did and said that could stand up to their contemporary reflections – in part, at least, they were engaged in picturing a way of life they saw as lost.

Early in 1974, when Renato Rosaldo and I returned to the central Ilongot settlement of Kakidugen where we had lived for two years in the late 1960s, we were besieged with memories. Our notes bemoan the vivid signs of change: the endless talk of Christian ways, the ugly schoolhouse, the tattered clothes, and the omnipresent settlers. But at the same time, our diaries give witness to a special kind of learning made available because Ilongots – themselves aware of the extent to which their lives had changed – found in us a resource and an occasion for reflection on the values of the past. People who at times would speak with scorn of prior violent days, and intimate that before they learned the 'word of God' their lives were filled with fighting, yet described and analyzed their history with impressive care, and asked – almost as soon as we arrived – to hear headhunting songs recorded in 1967–9.

It was not until midsummer that I had the opportunity to answer their requests. Late in June, we moved with a single Ilongot family into a new house just large enough, it seemed, to accommodate our belongings – and yet our household, like a magnet, never ceased to draw countless guests. One night, a meeting with the teacher of the Kakidugen school collapsed into our house, surrounding us with long-lost 'kin' whom we had barely seen since our arrival. Aroused the following morning with the festivity that enlivens a household full of guests, some of our closest friends then urged that it was high time that we unpack our trunks of tapes and papers and play the songs that they had hoped to hear some months before. Of special interest (and, at the time, rather difficult to find) was a tape of the only headhunting celebration we ever attended – a noisy, vibrant, hour-long recording of gongs, boasts, and choral singing occasioned by Burur's murder of a lowlander late in 1968. More than slightly overwhelmed by the restless crowd of friends and many would-be companions – all interested in the medicines and gifts we were unpacking – it was with some impatience and a sense almost of obligation that I sought and finally produced the hoped-for tape.

I knew, of course, that Ilongots loved music, elaborate speaking, all varieties of performance. During our previous fieldwork, they had come to view our tape recorder not simply as a vehicle through which we could learn their language, but also as an instrument for their own self-assertion, and – because of the very nature of song and formal speaking – for the creation of certain moods. For them, the sound of song and oratory on our tapes had a compelling and aesthetic force surpassing that of narrative or myth. Stories were, to them, mere words that they could dictate and see us write down; but all Ilongots acknowledge that no written text could capture what they loved about the stirring musicality of true verbal art. The tapes thus occupied a special place, and people loved to play them. Some claimed that our recorder, by itself, was a deterrent to the spreading 'word of God'; yet most Ilongots would, in fact, take pleasure in what was in many ways as much their instrument as ours.

This time – to my surprise – they could not tolerate it. A crowded house, including men I later learned had stayed the night in hopes that I would play the tape, became silent when the song began, as if suddenly transported. Immediately I thought to listen with them, to share their memories, moods, and thoughts. But 'Insan – one of our most loyal friends, and an insistent pleader for the old recording – snapped brusquely at me to turn the tape off just moments after I had turned it on. No eyes explained themselves as I obeyed – and found myself annoyed, perplexed, and even angry. I felt at once responsible and confused by a new awkwardness that filled the room as people turned – quite suddenly, it seemed – away from an intensity that I had barely sensed and all too clearly failed to understand.

For the Ilongots in the room the tension quickly vanished. I was still fumbling with the rejected tape when one of our friends proposed a hunt along the trail as a most fitting way to bid his guests farewell, and others silently agreed and packed their bags. Like them, I turned to other thoughts, reflecting on new ways to use our old recordings. But later in the day, when guests had gone and we were alone with people we considered our true friends and 'kin,' I asked 'Insan to recall the morning's drama. I found that I had spent the day with feelings of indignant hurt – and so demanded an account of his abrupt command. Just what had happened with the tape? How could supposed friends impose like that, then seem to scold me? Was I the butt of someone else's fun?

As 'Insan braced himself to speak, the room again became almost uncannily electric. Backs straightened and my anger turned to nervousness and something more like fear as I saw that 'Insan's eyes were red. Tukbaw, Renato's Ilongot 'brother,' then broke into what was a brittle silence, saying he could make things clear. He told us that it hurt to listen to a headhunting celebration when people knew that there would never be another. As he put it: 'The song pulls at us, drags our hearts, it makes us think of our dead uncle.' And again: 'It would be different if I had accepted God, but I still am an Ilongot at heart; and when I hear the song, my heart aches as it does when I must look upon unfinished bachelors whom I know that I will never lead to take a head.' Then Wagat, Tukbaw's wife, said with her eyes that all my questions gave her pain, and told me: 'Leave off now, isn't that enough? Even I, a woman, cannot stand the way it feels inside my heart!'

What were they saying? Once again, I was distressed by the great gap between my superficial understanding of their words and the significance their simplest phrases seemed to carry. Slow and measured, Tukbaw's words to us took on the aura of a gift, a formal offering; he might have prefaced them with the formula he often used when exercising his subtle skills in oratorical debate: 'I lay down my heart before you; it is open for you to see.' Yet for us, nothing seemed 'open.' In the time that we could talk about such things directly, Ilongots had said that they went headhunting because of their emotions, because grief, envy, or humiliation had laid a weight that they would cast off from their hearts. And shortly before our return to the Philippines, an old and powerful kinsman had died suddenly; his loss *was* weighty, and the fact that his curses could be heard above the singing chorus on the tape was a sad reminder of men's present impotence in the face of death, upset, and emotional strain. This sense of impotence was, in fact, acknowledged as a motive for conversion to Christianity:

> Radu, some months after the event reported here, lost a child, his fourth to die in a period of five years. People in our household expected a traditional burial and period of mourning, and planned to show their 'respect' for bereaved kinfolk by abstaining from labor in their gardens for the days of traditionally prescribed taboos. But instead, 'Utup, father-in-law of Radu, called on Christian kinsmen to perform the burial, and on the afternoon following the ceremony, we were surprised to see Radu's son, along with the Christian leaders, playing volleyball on the airplane landing in front of our house. Puzzled, we asked our hosts if these men thought that the Christian God would not let children die from illness, and were surprised when we were told that no such naive motive had informed 'Utup's choice. Rather, our friends insisted, 'Utup turned to Christianity because he could not, as in the past, 'cast off' his grief through killing; by placing faith in the Christian God, he knew that death would no longer pain him. And because this God removes all cause for mourning, the new Christians thought to demonstrate their freedom from bad feelings by engaging in a game of ball.

But at the time, our friends insisted that it was not simply grief, not the old man's voice on the tape, that had disturbed them. It was, they said, the song itself that made their breath twist and turn inside them; it pained them because it made them want to kill. Tukbaw, 'Insan added, had stepped outside when the tape was playing so that the young boys who had never taken heads would not know of the intensity of his reaction; he had wanted to cry and felt ashamed.

In other moods, these same men would tell me that even in the old days, grief rarely led to killing. In the past as in the present, intense and disturbing feelings only occasionally knew a headhunter's catharsis; more often, they were lost in the distracting claims of daily life. Yet this time, they insisted on something different; although the *buayat,* the celebratory song, might be 'just a song' to us Americans, and even missionized Ilongots (who themselves deny this) might listen to the chorus without pause, my friends had grown up Ilongot. God had not changed them, the choral celebration could not help but deeply stir them – in short, they not only thought but felt things in a traditional and distinctive way.

Surely, the recent past had given my friends cause for something like nostalgia. For Ilongots, a small group of some 3,500 horticulturalist-hunters living barely 150 miles from Manila, the impact of World War II – in the form of death, disruption, the spread of guns, the rise of Philippine capitalism and so of population and a demand for land, and finally the development of small aircraft that permitted the establishment of an effective Protestant mission – had been dramatic. But so too were years of indigenous population movement on Luzon, two centuries of contact with Spanish officials, and the prewar experience of American officialdom and schools.

Ilongots allude to a time 'when we were really Ilongot,' when game abounded in the forest, no relation was reliable, and life was stirred by violence. For some, what was abandoned as recently as 1972 was a mood of beauty and a spirit of fine tension that they associate with killing. For others, a conversion to fundamentalist Christianity (a process initiated by the New Tribes Mission in 1955) meant that all passion they had known was tinged with sinful violence, and the question that most concerned them was the development of a less passionate way of life. But adult Ilongots also knew that in this century, headhunting had stopped for as much as a decade and then had begun again; they knew that a variety of magical techniques had been invented and forgotten, and that certain traditional institutions, like shamanism and oratory, had long been declining unaccompanied by an equivalent sense of loss. In short, the past gave no transparent clue to my friends' interest in the tape or to their deep and contrary reaction to it. Before I could understand the feelings Ilongots attached to our artificial reproduction of their history, I had to learn more of what the tape recording meant.

As it turned out, "feeling" and "meaning" were intimately linked. It had been easy for me, as a modern Westerner, to be impressed and puzzled by the focality of headhunting in Ilongot accounts of past experience, and the incident with the tape was one of many that confirmed my inclinations. Anthropological tradition tells us that strong emotion is a sign of social import, because cultural practice generates such affects as will guarantee the constraining force of social norms upon the self. But a functional view that renders "sentiments" the servants of "society"[1] has made us inclined to view affective life more as a "sign" that points to social rule than as itself a sphere of meaning that is as public and socially significant as are the names of kin. Unable to participate directly in the emotional worlds of our informants, we have failed to see that personal life is shaped by terms with social implications, and correspondingly that "persons" are themselves "constructed" in terms of shared understandings that inform the ways they act and feel.

My discussions with the Ilongots suggested that for them (and, I imagine, people elsewhere) talk of the emotions provided such "constructions" – a set of images through which they understood at once their world and themselves as particular sorts of beings in it, fitting "persons" with whom they were familiar to the activities in which they were, of necessity, involved. Not cosmology, but action and response, energy and anger, were what concerned them. Neither inward-looking nor oriented to the unique and individual, Ilongots spoke of feelings (and used an imagery of feelings) in describing the relation of their past to a rapidly changing present, and of themselves to social processes and to the natural world. Order and discontinuity, sense and contradiction, were things that they described, in part, through talk of the human heart and its reactions. And so, following my own theoretical inclinations and their lead, I came to see my task as one of understanding Ilongot experience through attention not to "headhunting" per se – as violent deed or cosmic feat with significance bound to deities or demography – but instead to the ritual forms and everyday reflections through which Ilongots communicated something of how, or why, activities like killing make good sense. The key here was the 'heart' that Tukbaw and Wagat said had pained them – an organ which, for Ilongots, unites concerns for thought and feeling, inner life and social context, violent anger and such desirable consequences as fertility and health. Attention to the ways that 'heart' is used in ordinary Ilongot discourse will provide an introduction to Ilongot construals of human "persons" and their society; and these, in turn, will suggest a way of understanding my friends' disturbed reaction to their tape.

The heart

Ilongots explain themselves – how they feel and why they used to kill, what they see as beautiful, admirable, effective, what odd or dangerous or dull – by reference to a symbol that for an outsider evokes the privacy of interior experience and for them does that and more. *Rinawa*, or 'heart,' is cognate with the Proto-Austronesian **ñawah*, 'soul,' and Proto-Philippine **Rehinawa*, 'breath.' It is related to such words as Tagalog *ginhāwa*, 'comfort,' 'ease,' and *'unhāwa*, 'understanding'; Malay *nyawa* and Ifugao *linnāwa*, 'soul'; and Samar-Leyte *ginhāwa*, 'bowels.'[2] For Ilongots, 'heart' is at once a physical organ, a source of action and awareness, and a locus of vitality and will. It provides a ground that links thought, feeling, and physical well-being, and ties natural and social processes to the development of the self. In different contexts, 'heart' can be equated with words for 'life' *(biay)*, for 'shade' or 'spirit' *(bēteng)*, for 'breath' *(niyek)*, 'knowledge' *(bēya)*, and 'thought' *(nemnem)*. Minimally, the 'heart' is a vital organ that animates the body; without it, there is no life.

To Ilongots, all growing things have hearts, and people – as they mature, reproduce, 'sprout forth,' and 'send out shoots' – are among them. The dried and shriveled skin of old age, like dried-out rice stalks, suggests a loss of heart, and so, of life. The heart can leave the body gradually, and in different ways, in a variety of kinds of illness; it can leave it absolutely, when one dies. A plant that lacks a heart is not worth keeping; pounded rice, I have been told, is good only for eating, because it is heartless and so cannot reproduce. With heart loss, human victims turn as thin as a strand of hair, as flimsy as dried grasses – and just as rain brings life back to a rice field, so water can be used in magical spells to recover a patient's vitality, his heart. If stolen by an enemy or spirit, the heart can call the body forward to a blind destruction. Coaxed on by magic, rice hearts may desert the fields where they were planted to contribute to the bounty of some envious harvester's yield.

In certain contexts, heart is identified with *bēteng*, one's 'shade' or 'shadow,' or the 'person' people see in vital eyes when one is living, which turns into a spirit that stays to haunt the living after the body dies. As *bēteng*, hearts may leave their bodies during sleep to heed the call of dead or living hearts that think of them or name them, permitting bachelors and maidens to grow 'used to one another' *(tagde)* and 'desiring' *(ramak)* through the progress of their dreams. But if in sleep our hearts are drawn to eat with shades of people who, in life, we loved and cared for, we are then likely to become accustomed to the company of dead *bēteng;* thus when, in dreams, we share a meal with vanished *bēteng*, our living selves withdraw and start to die. Fortunately, most hearts know better; 'startled' *(dikrat)* by what is always a temptation, they will jump back into their bodies – and so awakened, we survive.

Heart as *bēteng*, as something that can leave the living body, is an aspect not only of human persons, but also of animals and plants. But if, possessing *bēteng*, humans are related to inanimate life in nature, the 'hearts' of humans also 'think' *(nemnem)* and 'move' *('enu'nu)* with conscious 'breath' *(niyek)*. Ilongots say 'You have no breath' to indicate either ignorance or exhaustion; and they speak of the 'flow' or 'coursings' *(kurut)* of the 'breath' or 'heart' when alluding to depths of feeling and supposedly hidden thoughts. To be a man 'of breath' *('uniyek)* is furthermore to be a man of *liget* – a word suggesting 'energy, anger, passion,' which is related to a variety of physical processes realized in people as enthusiasm, agitation, passivity, and violent action, and as motion or stillness, opening or closing, splitting, spinning, rising, or falling of the heart. These motions of the heart are our emotions; and just as, according to my informants, people's *bēteng* do not differ, so the dynamics of human feelings, although they may vary in their intensity, are similar, no matter one's personality or situation in life. Further, as I will suggest below, our 'breaths' are shaped by and similar to processes that extend beyond those we see as determinate of a human personality; the passions are paralleled by processes that bring coherence to a social group, bounty to a rice field, or health to a person who is ill.

But 'heart' is associated with more than life and passion, and even though Ilongots admit that people's hearts are quite similar in many ways, they also recognize that no two hearts are the same. The hearts of people differ from those of plants and animals, and among themselves (according to age, sex, and personality), because of differences in experience, in the things that people know. *Bēya,* or 'knowledge,' is what gives form, sense – and consequence – to the motions of the heart. *Bēya* is like the body in that it develops through a lifetime; and like a body which, in age or illness, resists impulse and desire, 'knowledge' of how to talk and how to feel – particularly in cooperative dealings among kinsmen – gives form to passion, assigning meaning to the motions of the heart. Thus, babies, lacking 'knowledge,' can lose their hearts through fear because they do not 'know' that they have fallen; children must be told to work or fetch things because they do not 'know' what work to do; adolescents are too quick to 'anger,' lacking 'knowledge' of their relationships with kin. The richness of most men's experience, the fact that men gain 'knowledge' through their travels, accounts for their having passions more 'intense' than any woman's; a particular person's selfishness is explained by 'lack of knowledge' of what he owes to kin; wild violence may be excused as the 'fading' or 'relaxation' of heart or 'knowledge,' accompanying heart loss or excessive drinking; and conversion to Christianity means that one has taken a 'new' and soothing 'knowledge' into a previously impassioned heart.

Thus, talk of the heart is, much as we would expect, talk of "interior experience," but it is also talk of social life and public situations, describing not unconscious process but such qualities of consciousness as inform the ways that people act. In stories, the heart does not desire, reflect, or otherwise oppose itself to events that stand outside it. Narrators comment, 'My heart said "shoot it," and I shot it'; 'My heart said "he is coming," and he came'; and they do this by way of orientation, describing persons with reference to their 'knowledge' of activity in the world. Because 'knowledge' is associated with speech, thought is always cast as words the heart has spoken.

> In accounting for our cleverness in 'catching on' *('abet)* to his language, a friend once said in casual conversation that Renato and I must

have good 'head marrow' – suggesting that Ilongots, like our selves, believe that thought is something that happens in the head. But when I probed, he quickly rejected my inference, insisting that his allusion to the head had to do with the proximity of the ears, which are, in fact, the channel through which one learns a language. As to thinking, he said, it happens in the center, where the pounding is – and he pointed to his chestbone – in our hearts.

Breath and heartbeat are explained as air that flows when the heart is thinking/talking – and just as 'breath' is linked to movements in the heart that may be experienced as disturbing, the word for 'heartbeat,' *pedupedu*, appears to be related to *pedupdu*, a common word for 'pain' *(pedupdu)*. Reflection is conceived, then, not as a passive joy but instead as a complement to action; and so the heart reflects, 'I want that!', 'Why should he have more game than I?', 'I ache for her!', 'If only I were strong!', 'What's that I see?', or 'I must get working!' as it moves.

In a similar way, affective states are characterized in terms that stress inherent continuities between the self and social action, between emotional leanings and the things that people do. Thus, explaining joy, a friend once said, 'Your heart is gay *(sipē)* as if to say "thank you," and it smiles.' Of both 'heart' and 'breath' one says they 'have' *(si-)* such affects as 'fear' *(kayub)*, 'shame' *(bētang)*, 'pain' *(takit)*, 'unpleasantness' *('uget)*, 'anger' *(liget)*, and less often, 'happiness' *(kesipēran)*. But far more commonly, one describes the way they move. Both 'heart' and 'breath' may 'spring up,' 'quicken,' 'be industrious/energetic,' 'burst,' 'bounce,' lengthen,' 'prance,' and 'unfold' when they are 'gay' and 'thriving.' *'Engruyuluk ma rinawam (ruyuluk* being an emphatic form of *ruyuk,* 'long, expansive, to make expansive'), 'Your heart gets very long,' means you are happy, or as one informant put it:

'Enduki 'alimbawa 'ubēa 'eng tuy ma 'empa 'yakenmu 'away kıpaget rinawam,
'It lengthens, for instance, you are able to see for a long distance, there is nothing blocking your heart.'

'Your heart "unfolds" ' *(beklag)* suggests, again, a stance of openness and pleasure:

'Umbeklag ma rinawam 'eruyuk,
'Your heart will open out with joy.'

And in a related vein, 'Your heart "springs up" ' *(tenggal)* describes the complementary facts of happiness and health:

Nu pumiyaka 'untenggal ma rinawam 'entunged,
'When you get better, your heart will spring back up, to sit.'[3]

Other heart states point to less pleasant sorts of movement. If 'angry' *(liget)* and 'intent' *('ipget)* on action, our hearts may 'tense' and 'knot' themselves, displaying 'hardened' strength and purpose. And when unmediated by 'knowledge,' a person's 'anger' leads the heart to 'run,' to go crazy and lose conscious control. Angry hearts may 'spark' *(burur)* like fire:

Ma 'emburuburur ma rinawatu 'away 'edtu kaligesi ta'en nu 'atun 'ungkaat dēsi, ta'en nima 'emburur nima buur nima kaat nu 'apuy,
'One whose heart is sparking, there is nothing he isn't angry at, like a dog biting us, like the sparking from the 'bite' of the fire';

or 'move wildly' *(busiteng)* with furious frustration:

Tuy ma 'umbusiteng 'away suttun 'apitan nima ligettu 'enligēliget 'engretaret,
'One who is wildly angry has no fitting object for his anger, he gets furious without purpose.'

One phrase for raging anger – *'adub,* 'constrained fury' – may characterize as well the force contained when taut and parallel ropes are pulled together, or then again, the way that the wind within a narrow passage is empowered by restraint.

When heartfelt wishes are denied, we are 'preoccupied' *('alimet)* with the disturbing thoughts that grow of 'shame,' 'anger,' 'envy,' 'illness,' and 'desire'; and so distressed, our hearts may well withdraw and slowly 'dwell upon' *(ngelem)* unrealized plans:

'Enngēngelem ma rinawatun ma pen'iraptun ma 'amumura namutur,
'His heart dwells inwardly when he sees one who, unequally, has killed.'

Siyay ta 'enngelemin ta nemnemku ta bēkura 'iman,
'That's what is engaging my thoughts, that woman.'

Ma 'enngelem gēgē' tē ma rinawatu ten 'ed nambē' yek,
'Someone who dwells on things, her/his heart itches because she/he is not married.'

Not surprisingly, this sense of *ngelem* was portrayed, at once, as something sweet and as a delicate but fearful worm.

As feelings of disturbance grow, distracted hearts will quickly come to seem 'confused,' 'trapped,' and 'surrounded.' They twist with 'dizziness' *('alimudeng):*

Nu manngired kisi 'amunga men'alimudeng ta rinawasi,
'When we are sick, our hearts are somewhat dizzy.'

They will turn back upon themselves *('alinsukun):*[4]

Tuy ma 'en'alinsukun 'away raksiyat rinawatu 'en'uri nud 'iman,
'The distracted person can't get his/her heart out, it turns back on the same issues.'

and find themselves unable to 'let out' a sign of life. And as hearts 'itch,' 'chip,' 'clutch,' and so intensify preoccupations, they may be compared to 'plucking' *(kelding)* strings on local violins, which can themselves make men's hearts 'dwell' on yet unrealized violent goals:

Kēkeldingan nima rinawak tuy ma nampiyala ma'idengēksun gisada,
'My heart is plucked at, stirred, tormented, as I hear the lovely violin.'

Alternatively, like sticks of sugar cane or narrow plots of land, 'torn' and distracted hearts may well simply be 'destroyed' and 'cut into small squares' *(ditek):*

'Amunga nanditek ma rinawak nu 'irapengkun ma batling nima sit,
'My heart is as if cut into small pieces when I see the headhunting earrings worn by others.'

Finally, feelings of 'fear,' which cause the heart to 'startle,' 'jump,' 'rise,' and then 'fall quiet,' may – like illness or 'frustrated anger' *(kesiran)* and 'disappointment' *(kemnu)* – cause the heart to 'flop' and 'swoop,' 'keel over,' 'fall,' 'stop still' *(pedeg),* 'grow dull' *('aleng):*

Nu kumayubka 'amunga 'umpedeg ma rinawam 'agube, away 'enu'nutu,
'If you are frightened, your heart will stop and lower, it has no movement.'

Nu si ligetka 'un'aleng ta rinawam,
'If you have anger, your heart will grow dull, passive, bored.'

Phrases like these are particularly current in talk of health and ill-ness, because, for Ilongots, health, happiness, and sociality are all in-timately linked. Thus, Ilongots describe illness in terms of *'uget,* or 'bad feelings' in the heart that discourage eating. Similarly, *'uget* applies to the sense of resignation and withdrawal that leads an angry or insulted person to 'hold on' to a disturbing grievance and refuse to speak his thoughts. And just as illness may affect our thoughts and leave us sullen and distracted, so a severe disruption – occasioning fear, grief, or anger – may induce passivity and even illness because the heart cannot 'think through' *(tuntun)* what it should do:

Nu manngiredka 'awana 'untuntun ma rinawam 'awana ta'et nima
pempiyapiyam pengruyuk nima rinawam kumpude nemnementmu rawanmu,
'If you are sick, your heart doesn't make sense; it isn't as when you are well and your heart is happy and anything you think about you can go and do.'

To feel empty, as if one has 'no heart,' to feel the heart 'scattered,' 'dark,' 'heavy,' or 'turned upside down' – all these words suggest 'anger,' but they may also describe the onset of an illness; and people say the heart will 'lengthen just a little' or 'get lighter,' growing happy – like the floating leaves and sparkling grass invoked in magic – when illness is eased.

> Teged compared a sick person's heart to one's feeling in a rainstorm: *'Uget ma rinawam ten mentētegigiwka pu,* 'Your heart is bad because you huddle up with shivers.' And he contrasted this feeling to a

> healthy one associated with clear skies: *'A nu me'ugu, 'i'aa nima rinawam 'ipawa, 'iruyuk,* 'When the rains stop, your heart grows open, it lengthens.'

In social life, a feeling of confusion, of contradictory impulses and demands, may itself suggest a form of illness:

> Visiting one day in an Ilongot chapel, I heard a woman tearfully protest that she could not 'fit' or 'make coherent' *(tepek)* the demands of God because her husband laughed away her prayers. The chapel leader declared that she was 'distracted' *('alimet)* and refused to discuss her problems. Afterward, he explained himself by comparing her to a sick person who could endanger him by 'transferring' her 'clutching' *(ngalemkem)* anger and 'disturbance' *(pa'nun)* to his heart.

And sickness is, in turn, experienced as a 'dull' and 'dizzy' state inhibiting activity, a state of deep *'alimet,* or 'distraction,' in which the heart cannot 'make sense' *(tepek)* of things and knows no reason because the body cannot move. As we will see in Chapter 3, patients are very much like little children; distressed by illness, their hearts withdraw from social action and responsibility and do not display the 'knowledge' of adults.

Not only, then, can feelings affect one's physical state and can health shape the emotions, but the two are conceived in parallel terms. Further, the heart's emotional gymnastics, although providing a vivid way of talking about feelings, are not the stuff of memories, excuses, accounts of motives, or the explanation of one's plans. Rather, talk of hearts characteristically raises questions about the continuity between one's "inner" life and thought and one's capacities for action. An acrobatic imagery is used to talk of feeling primarily in conversations where healthy, light, free, energetic movement is opposed to heaviness, tension, and passivity – discourse that implicitly or explicitly connects good feeling with action, health, and 'knowing' sociality, and associates illness with anger, chaos, and withdrawal, a failure to 'make sense' of action and relation, a lack of 'fit' between the self and its immediate milieu.

An additional, somewhat related use of the word *rinawa,* or 'heart,' is to label an independent will: *Rinawak ma. . . ,* 'my heart that I. . . ,' means that I want to do something, that my reasons come from myself alone. *'Ininalugku mad sadin rinawak* tells that 'I thought it up in my own heart,' and so requires no further explanation. *Rinawa'antu,* a progressive verb, suggests 'He set his heart to, is determined,' and cannot be swayed. A failure to cooperate, an untoward show of violence, selfishness, scorn, vanity, dishonesty, or self-concern are attributed to *rinawan ma sit,* 'the heart of the other,' the perpetrator of the offenses. Finally, in expressions of disgust with their fellows and resignation to the fact that in a society without organized sanctions no agreement need be enforced, Ilongots mourn, *Nariwariwa ta rinawasin tu'u*, 'As people, we have such different wills/hearts.' In a related vein, hearts can be used when speaking of actions characteristic of a group or individual, as when one says, 'It is our heart, as Ilongots, to headhunt,' or 'It is our custom, nature,' or 'our invention, something that comes from us alone' *(betar)*.

Such references to the heart suggest not only will and purpose, but also individuality and apartness: We cannot see the hearts of others; we hear words spoken by strangers but fear that these come only from the surface, not from the inner motions of their hearts. Hearts may enter an agreement, but only because they can always be antagonistic. 'Your heart' may resist recognition of our kinship; 'my heart' may wish you well but fail to please. Hearts can become 'used to one another' *(tagde)* and learn affection; they may 'know' that we are kin and should be kind. But talk of hearts suggests the possibility of breaches. Hearts can take things badly, be offended, shrink from talking, 'hide' their discontent. Because a 'knowing' speaker can 'disguise' his heartfelt thoughts in pleasant phrases, orators will protest that in the 'coursings' *(kurut)* of their hearts run no ill feelings, and ask their interlocutors to search out hidden 'anger' where the heart is 'deep' and 'dark.' Although a good-willed heart does not 'hold on' to insults, a heart bent upon revenge has taken rage into itself. Of lovers, one says, *Nan'irinawade,* 'Their hearts are reciprocally related'; of parties to a political agreement, *'Ing-kasisitde ma rinawade,* 'They made their hearts as one'; and converts to fundamentalist Christianity distinguish two sorts of believers: those who simply take the word of God as true, and those who, changed in all demeanor, have let God remake their hearts.

Ilongots speak of 'hearts,' then, not to explain behavior by reference to character, motives, or a well-imaged personality, but to indicate those aspects of the self that can be alienated – or engaged – in social interaction. Through talk of hearts, Ilongots characterize the relation between the self and its situation, in terms of whether hearts are closed or open, light or heavy, itching or at ease. What matters in such talk is not "psychology" as we understand it, but the "passions" generated in a self that can always be in conflict with its environment. Concerned less with "motivation" than with action, Ilongots are interested in feelings because affective life has consequences for health, cooperation, daily labor, and political debate. Their talk of hearts has less to do with histories that give reasons than with the fact that hearts that stand apart are 'moved,' 'turn in upon themselves,' 'itch,' and 'grow distracted'; and although such hearts may well engage in stunning deeds occasioning celebration, the heart that is 'weighted down' with illness, grief, or disappointment is apt to forsake 'knowledge,' becoming unreliable, un-healthy, and capable of unwonted shows of force.

For Ilongots, bad feeling, bad health, social withdrawal, and disruption are all, as we have seen, related. They are associated with *liget* – 'energy,' 'anger,' 'passion' – and opposed to such cooperative dispositions as are associated with 'knowledge,' ease, and health. But if 'anger' may be criticized because it leads to wild acts or illness – and the dangers of another's discontent are often all too clear – Ilongot attitudes toward violence, threat, and 'anger' are ambivalent, combining fear and disapproval with a marked aesthetic interest, appreciation for the headhunter with dislike of men too quick to fight. Bound cooperatively by *bēya,* or 'knowledge,' Ilongots consider themselves dependent on a *liget* that energizes as it divides them; and though stimulated by *liget,* the individual requires 'knowledge' to give affective impulses intelligible, social form. 'If it were not for *liget,*' Ilongots say, 'we'd have no life, we'd never work.' But at the same time, they say, 'We don't do everything because of *liget;* sometimes our hearts are quiet and we speak with knowledge in our breath.' Everyone has had experiences epitomized by such statements as: 'Because I knew he was my kinsman I decided to forget my anger'; and missionized Ilongots debate as to whether their new 'knowledge' has done away with angry 'envy' as a motive force in work.

What is clear in Ilongot talk of hearts is, in short, a sense of dialectic or dynamic tension between a state of sociality and one of opposition and withdrawal, between a self at ease with its environment and one that stands apart. Both, in the Ilongot view, are as inevitable as they are necessary facts of individual life and social interaction; and so, their talk is less concerned with introspection and the "inner life" than with the affective quality of a world where social bonds themselves depend upon potentially divisive founts of 'energy' or 'anger' for their continued life. The two terms that are the subject of my text – *bēya* and *liget,* 'knowledge' and 'passion' – capture well this tension between civility and unrestrained vitality, bespeaking the dependence of cooperative life and reasoned action upon potentially disruptive force. These words are among the most significant in Ilongot talk of social life and feeling; they are related not as "cultural" rule to human "nature,"[5] but instead as complementary aspects of life in a society in which both civility and violence are understood with reference to the motions of the individual 'heart.'

The dynamics of emotion

My grasp of Ilongot ideas of the dynamics of emotion grew through a series of interviews in which I addressed myself to questions about the use of *liget, bēya,* and related words. I knew that the importance of heart and feelings in Ilongot accounts of action had more to do with general notions of vitality, conflict, and cooperation than with a "psychologistic" sense of persons, but had little understanding of how Ilongots thought emotions worked. The net of senses associated with emotion words was my introduction. By asking informants, "What are other words like *liget?*" and "What words resemble *bēya?*" I found, first, that of words characterizing the heart, *liget* was by far the richest in its associations; and in exploring ways that words like 'difference' *('apir),* 'strength' *('eret),* and 'quick' *('awet)* resemble *liget,* I began to see in a term that I had understood initially to mean no more than 'anger' a set of principles and connections with elaborate ramifications for Ilongot social life. So, for example, *'eret,* a seeming homonym that means at once 'to tie' and 'to be strong,' was explained through a revealing metaphor by a young man in his thirties. Strong things, he said, turn in upon themselves, are tight and focused, like a knot, like something twisted. It is for this reason, he went on, that people singing the celebratory song *(buayat)* for killings will shout, *Maka'eretkan buayat,* 'May you be knotted up, *buayat';* in these words they voice their hope for strength in celebration, for voices that will 'circle around' and 'dizzy,' 'tie up tight,' and 'fill' a crowded room. 'Circling,' 'focus,' 'dizziness,' and 'strength' were confirmed, in other interviews, as having important links to *liget.* And so, building from families of terms and contexts, I developed a grasp of certain Ilongot metaphors, and of the loose conceptual scheme that underlies them and describes the principled working of 'energy, anger, passion' in their world.

People, spirits, and certain objects, like wind and rain, liquor, illness, chili peppers, and fire, can be described as 'angry' *('uliget),* 'intensely angry' *('uligēlet),* or as 'having anger' *(si liget)* – *liget* here used as a noun or adjective suggesting potency, energy, intensity, the irritating heat of chili peppers, the rush of rapids, or the force of wind. Objects as well as people can 'cause anger' *(paliget); storms* may grow intense or 'become angry' *(limiget).* But only people can 'be angered' *(meligetan),* 'get angry' *(enliget),* or 'act excessively angry' *(qenligēliget).* Most verbal and adverbial forms of *liget* thus evoke not only energy and irritation, but also a sense of violent action and of intentional shows of force.

For people to *si liget,* or 'have anger,' means that they are neither shy nor fearful, not unduly quiet or reserved. *Liget* points in human life to a readiness to be 'different' or take offense *('u'apir),* to stubbornness and conviction, but also to the fact that one is quick-moving, youthful, active *('u'awet),* and 'tied up tight' or 'strong' *('u'eret).* In contrast to the verbal and adverbial uses of *liget,* which are applied largely to humans and always hint at passionate extremes, *liget* as an adjective – *'Uliget 'imana tu'u,* 'That is an angry person' – describes a quality often admirable and desirable. To say of someone, *Nantagal,* 'What force!' is to give praise for *liget* manifested in hard work, fine ornaments, or forceful speeches; it is to recognize a passionate vibrato is a fellow's singing, a show of muscular grace and tension in a dance. Such *liget* generates a 'redness' in the self that wards off certain kinds of illness; it makes for 'energy' and is associated with a sense of 'focus' that encourages industry and success. *Liget* is not associated specifically with sexuality, but male initiative in courtship is understood with reference to the view that men have both more 'passion' and less 'fear' than women, and, as several informants told me, that babies are the product of male *liget,* 'concentrated' in the form of sperm.[6]

Although Ilongots realize that some people – and some kinds of pepper – have more *liget* than others, they tend to talk of 'anger' as something that attaches not to selves but to their interactions; it can be transferred from one object to another and is generated in the confrontation of things that are opposed. Storms, for instance, may get *liget* from tobacco smoke, which makes both storms and people dizzy; appropriately, tobacco gives desired *liget* to the yeast that people use in making wine. Winds grow fiercer when they bump into a fence or an obstruction; an irritating whiff of ginger revitalizes 'passion' in a killer; chili can give *liget* to a stew.

In social terms, *liget* derives from insults, slights, and other intimations of inequality. Typically born of 'envy' *('apet, 'apa'apa), liget* grows through the heart's reflections on the successes of an 'equal' *(qanurut, qamumur)* and 'clutching' *(ngalemkem)* as it notes that 'I have less.' In a world in which equivalence is order and social precedence and domination constitute an inevitable source of strain, *liget* is the natural response to the vagaries of fortune, the ups and downs of social life and fate. Thus, the pain that strikes a youth who has not killed, when he sees headhunting earrings on a fellow, makes him feel naked; as if 'chipped' and 'plucked at,' his heart quickly 'takes offense' *('apir).* A woman is made envious and angry when her neighbors finish planting long before her, or if they reap a more impressive yield.

> Talin, a new Christian, once said of my close friend, Duman, that her heart 'goes beyond its limits' because she is in constant quest of admiration for her hard work. On my questioning, Duman agreed with Talin's characterization, saying that she is 'angry' and works hard in her gardens so that *Katyak ma mengadenana kimedeng,* 'I will be the one who is named for finishing,' and furthermore, that if others finish planting rice before her, she feels envious and disturbed: *'En'uget puy ma rinawak qenta'en 'anin nima 'amurura kimedeng,* 'My heart will feel bad and say, "oh dear," for those equals who are finished.'

Similarly, a man's heart rises with *liget* when he notes that other men, in every way his equals, outdo him on their hunts. One person's boasts,

news of another's happy fortune, may stir the heart with 'angry' musing – as can severe misfortune, which leads people to wonder why they
alone must suffer loss. The things that people strive for and desire are
things they want because other people have them; in fact, informants
told me, if men were not envious of one another's exploits, no Ilongot
would have enough 'anger' to want to kill.

When stirred with *liget,* a person's heart withdraws and stands
opposed to its offender; 'holding on' to its desire, it 'itches' for satisfaction and dwells in a sort of brooding self-absorption on its plans.
Passionate, expectant, energized with desire, primed to act but yet
constrained – Ilongots describe this state as *ngelem,* and with a sort of
pungent pleasure indicate that the *liget* that underlies it, although disturbing, may also be desirable.

In fact, it is a good deal more. The ambivalence surrounding *liget*
derives from the fact that it can lead in a variety of directions. Born of
insult, disappointment, envy, and irritation, *liget* is the source of motions in the heart that may, unfocused and unsatisfied, produce no
more than wild violence, social chaos, personal confusion, and an ultimate passivity and loss of will. But a lack of such motion means a lack
of will and purpose – and has much the same result. 'Without *liget* to
move our hearts,' Ilongots have told me, 'there would be no human
life.' It is envy, they explain, that stimulates industry and spurs people
on to labor, and it is *liget* that is revealed when, in work, we pant and
sweat. The energy that is *liget* can generate both chaos and concentration, distress and industry, a loss of sense and reason, and an experience of clarification and release. These various possibilities are imaged
in terms that link the emotional dilemmas of individual human actors to
certain general conditions of human existence – what I shall call chaos,
concentration, and satisfaction. At the risk of doing systematic violence to thoughts far more inchoate for the Ilongots, I would claim that
these constitute a system that embodies not only the core of Ilongot
emotion, but also the stuff of life and human effort as Ilongots in their
reflections know them.

Chaos

Liget is associated most readily with a variety of words suggesting
chaos, separation, and confusion, words that point to the disruptive
qualities of 'anger' uncontrolled by 'knowledge' – 'anger' that derives
from someone else's fury or success. Red ornaments, signifying the
liget of a killer, can irritate the unaccomplished members of his audience; boasts testify, as they give rise, to *liget* among 'equals'; red in the
sky at sunset is a form of *liget* that can make people ill. In fact, Ilongots

believe that most disease is caused by intrusive acts of spirit 'anger' (they slap and spit at, lick, shoot, or urinate upon their victims) or by *liget* that is released from potent and contagious plants.

Affliction in these instances leaves one ill, distressed, or helpless, humiliated but unable to redress imbalance, sick but too weak to cast off a disease. Like a person dizzy with heat, wild from itches, or unsettled by a rush of conflicting demands, the attacked and 'angered' heart finds itself *'alimet,* or 'distracted.' Impotent to act, it dwells on its deficiencies. 'Plucking,' 'twisting,' 'chipping,' it refuses to 'make sense,' fails to find a reasonable course of action, feels torn, unfocused, and confused. The 'weight' of grief or envy, the 'dizziness' one experiences if one tries to stand in sickness, and the 'clouds' that cloak the hearts of young men who have not taken heads are examples of such intrusive *liget*. Paralyzing and confusing, such *liget* can prevent the heart from thinking clearly; it leads to withdrawal and passivity, or else – especially in youths who lack not only the prestige of killers but also the social 'knowledge' of adults – to sporadic bursts of basket-slashing, knife-waving violence.

> Teged recalled that in his bachelor days, before he had taken a head, he got angry at the slightest annoyance, would jump to slash baskets and water containers, and in sullenness refuse to work. 'The only thing that made my heart lengthen,' he said, 'was when they brought me food.'

Just as drink and heart loss can, by depriving people of their 'knowledge,' make them 'run and fight,' so 'anger' and distraction, fights, and frustrations confound 'knowledge' and make it hard to think. In each case, what is unleashed is energy run wild, a chaos without shape or limit, a collapse of sociality into dizzy incoherence and unreasoned conflict.

Like the fury of a windstorm, the chaos of a distracted heart knows no direction, sense, or purpose. Vague, pointless, repetitious,and overdone, the motions of unruly *liget* have an almost iconic representation in the Ilongot grammatical device of reduplication: To *ligēliget* is to have excessive, pointless *liget;* to *'upu'upu* is to *qupu,* or to talk wildly; to *kuwakuwa* means to walk, or to *kuwa,* in circles without cease.[7] Lacking sense, such action suggests madness; lacking boundaries, it can occur within one's heart, in public speech, in collectivities, or in the natural world.

Because hearts can talk like people and move like music or the wind, Ilongots conceptualize "inner states" and "objective happenings" in terms that equate and interlink events we tend to see as independent. For them, a loss of sense, whether in private reflection or in public discourse, inside the heart or in the center of a crowded room, is, in descriptive terms and consequences, much the same. A room of angry people cutting off each other's speeches, casting words in all directions, making no coherent point, makes people dizzy; in the same way, a sudden, wild wind disrupts the heart. What matters in such moments is a quality of pointless and unnecessary movement, a collapse of understanding, and a sense of tension and anxiety that is generated when words, bumping into one another, miss their marks. In fact, Ilongots find noise and senseless movement disturbing in their essence: Loud talk may lead to fighting; wild play in fields or in the forest may upset the local spirits who then make people ill; and because chaos and distraction breed distraction, children who play loudly when it is storming are scolded for 'agitating the wind.'

Concentration

Opposed to the chaotic energy of a distracted heart is *liget* that is given form or focus, an 'energy' shaped by 'knowledge,' and directed to some end. 'I am full of *liget* when I hunt,' a man says, 'because I do not fear the forest'; 'I am moved by *liget* at the thought of eating game.' Unlike wild 'anger,' such 'energy' is creative, and whereas unfocused *liget* breeds distraction, *liget* that is concentrated toward a desirable object transcends the challenge and irritation at its roots. Concentrated *liget* is what makes babies, stirs one on to work, determines killers, gives people strength and courage, narrows vision on a victim or a task. Good *liget* is affective energy organized by 'knowledge,' and it is realized in activity and purpose, in a willingness to stay awake all night and travel far when hunting, in a readiness to climb tall trees or harvest in hot sunlight, in an aura of competence and vitality. It is loosed when many people work together and all do well because each, in quiet competition with the others, is careful not to be outdone.

Whereas chaos is experienced as frightening, ugly, and disturbing, *'upug* – the word for focus, collection, or concentration – characterizes a beauty that is forceful and intense. People note with admiration the skyward glance, arched back, bent knees, and outstretched arms that constitute a dancer's suspended poise and concentration; they laugh at straight-legged dancers, who, they say, 'move vaguely,' and comment that men dancing evince more 'focus' than do women, whose straighter legs follow from their alleged lesser knowledge and less intense passions. Red blouses and bandannas (but not red skirts or loincloths) are beautiful because they 'concentrate' *liget* in the wearer's face; acute angles on a knife sheath or an earring, symmetrical designs on woven pouches and embroidered cloth, have an aesthetic 'focus' that mirrors the intense pleasure of a well-dressed person's heart.

Concentrated things 'make sense,' have form and purpose, unity and order. A heart with 'focus' knows what to do and how to be effective, and a collectivity united is like an individual focused on a task. It does not lose the thread of argument, get vague, confused, distracted; it does not argue in a circle, move senselessly, repeat itself, talk wildly, or twitch. Hearts that *'upug* are one, united by agreement; they follow one another, make their points in thoughtful sequence, express themselves with care and through a single person's 'pointed tongue.' In fact, a collection of kin and friends united in an oratorical confrontation is like a single person; its collected strength is honored in the orator's conventional use of singular pronouns – 'I' for 'myself and my supporters,' 'you-singular' for 'all of you' – to characterize the collectivities for which they speak and those to which they are opposed. Finally, the same theme occurs in Ilongot historical reflections, when people contrast their periods of diffusion – *Nasiwak kami pu,* 'We were all separated' – and vulnerability with those of concentration. When the Kakidugen people lived with kin in Keradingan (see Chapter 1 and R. Rosaldo 1980) they knew such strength and focus: *'Ukegkeg kami ten 'adu kamin na'upug diman,* 'We were strong because there were many of us gathered together, concentrated, there.'

Liget can, then, be either focused or chaotic, associated with either a sense of knowing purpose or such confusion and paralysis as accompany a loss of sense. These poles describe, as we have seen, a good deal more than private feeling; the contrast between a focused and a distracted heart is paralleled by a contrast between health and illness, a 'knowing' self and unexplained disruption, elegant dance and senseless motion – or again, an opposition between one and many voices, unity and disorder in a social group. A harvester in her magical spells – to cite one last example – asks that rice hearts from distant gardens cluster and 'collect' around her, with stalks so thick and fruitful that she will find herself 'dizzied' by the vitality of her crop. Predictably, the other side of such intensity is chaos; the spirits who bring rice hearts quickly 'anger' and readily cause illness if noise, play, or even a rush of helpers disturbs the 'concentrated' energy in the magician's field.

Because energy is born of attack and challenge, the 'theft' of rice hearts and the threat of conflict, it is always problematic. Ilongots use the vagaries of *liget* as a frame for understanding their experience at the same time that they experience it as difficult to control. Unfocused *liget* is a burden, creating chaos and confusion – and although it is rarely manifested in daily life, Ilongots see the possibility of radical disorder in the form of illness, fights, and quarrels, as intensely real. Life may depend on *liget,* but life must rule it; old men, calm with 'knowledge,' must give direction to the 'passions' of the young. Only by subordinating energy to knowledge, by ordering and focusing initially confused reactions, can 'anger' be made to serve life's goals.

Finally, what is desired of focused *liget* is not conquest, violence, or domination, but rather celebration and vitality. Born of opposition and social pressure, intensified and focused 'anger' ideally transcends them – leading to an experience not of *liget* but of well-being, not of constraint and tension, but of freedom and release.

Satisfaction

Health, long life, and wealth, Weber suggests (1958:277), are the "sacred" values of most of the world's religions. For Ilongots, the imagery of happiness, health, and well-being completes and complements their talk of *liget,* illuminating its necessity and its roots. Just as *liget* for Ilongots characterizes the potentially divisive consequences of energy that at once confounds and animates human effort, so *sipē,* 'happiness,' 'joy,' or 'satisfaction,' suggests much more than passive pleasure and touches on wider concerns. Ilongots speak of happiness as the opposite of *liget* – a state of loose, free energy and sociality as opposed to one of turbulence and strain. But at the same time that they recognize that 'anger' can inhibit happy 'industry' *(kui)* and action, they speak of people who are 'energetic' in their labors as displaying *liget* when they sweat in 'angry' concentration while at work.

If *liget* is associated with weight, confusion, illness, effort, and frustration, to be happy for an Ilongot is to be light, clear-headed, healthy, and free of constraint. The happy heart is 'weightless'; it is 'fluttering' and 'vibrant,' like the stems of upright plants:

'Anggen santu nu manngasingasiyak 'un'adang nima niyekku,
'Even nowadays, if I am healthy, my breath rises (with ambition, pride).'

'Unngasingasi ma pagi nu man'uden 'amunga 'ungruyuk ma rinawutu,
'Rice plants thrive in the rain, as if their hearts were lengthened.'

Active and capable of endless, 'joyous motion,' such hearts are apt to be industrious and energetic, and willing in their work; 'like the sky when mist has lifted,' the happy heart feels 'lengthened' and 'unbounded' – as wide-reaching in its movement and its vision as the airplanes that Ilongots celebrate in song.

And yet, when asked what makes them happy, Ilongots speak not of comfort or fulfillment, but rather of successful 'concentration,' of an end to worry and of the birth of an expansive sense of self: for men, a mound of bullets so great that one can hunt without fear of wasting ammunition; for women, a harvest such that one can feed and entertain an endless flow of guests. Sitting by a fire on a chilly day is not happiness; but one's heart grows gay if, shriveled up from rain and cold, it sees a fire and knows that it will soon be warmed. Not seeing guests, but learning that they have no upsetting news, can make you happy; the joy of working comes from finishing a task.

> I asked Tepeg if his heart 'lengthened' when his wife gave birth to a child. Yes, he said, because he knew that she was out of danger, and he added that having children made him happy because it did away with worry, promising that there would be 'energetic' youngsters to care for him in his old age.

Blowing off the weight of illness makes the heart feel long and easy; killing game and so destroying the sense of deprivation that sent him to the forest makes the hunter's heart grow light. Finally, for the headhunter, there is joy in 'casting off' his burden; not murder or vengeance, but the loss of weight he feels in severing a human head and tossing it to the ground is what clears clouds and brings his heart new life.

What these instances suggest is that for Ilongots, happiness exists in the thrill of transcending what are felt as weights, constraints, and limits; in overcoming a confining *liget,* hearts open out to a new sense of possibility, footsteps lighten, and the self experiences a rush of energy and relief. As with the 'focused' *liget,* there is purpose here, and motion: The loose swinging and light shine of mother-of-pearl baubles Ilongots use as ornaments reflect, they say, the easy, open movement of a happy heart. Unlike the heart withdrawn in heavy 'anger,' a heart that is content will feel expansive; light and energetic, it wants to move, to sing, and to explore. Lively and at one within, poised, confident, and perhaps inclined to show off and parade, the happy heart looks outward, and its subjective feeling of potential is mirrored in a reinforcing public aura. At the same time that the self expands, the open heart is 'lengthened' through the social fact of reputation: In harvest spells women ask for crops whose fame will travel widely, and headhunters boast that word of their successes will carry their names to new places and previously deaf ears.

Happiness, in short, suggests activity and sociality, and has little to do with quietness, tranquility, or peace. Born of *liget* and agitation, *sipē* cannot itself give rise to *sipē;* nor, for traditional Ilongots, is happiness associated with passive pleasure and content. When missionized Ilongots claim, by contrast, that the 'happiness' in their hearts is 'quiet' *(meted),* ruled by 'hope' and confident 'relaxation,' they lead others to reflect that Ilongot Christians work less hard than do their unconverted fellows. And one Christian woman told me that she is less active than she once was, because her 'lowered' heart does not respond with angry *liget* to the accomplishments of 'equals' and instead waits for God to stimulate her work. Her 'happiness' is, she said, quite 'different' from the vitality of youths engaged in mutual emulation. Like the 'knowing,' 'quiet' old, who become 'lazy' *(kidēt)* when they lose concern for reputation, she doesn't 'force herself' *(pasi'ut)* or 'focus' effort – placing confidence not in her labors but in the 'pity' *(dē'ri)* of her God. But if new Christians look beyond their social world for happiness and satisfaction, those Ilongots who (as they themselves express it) have 'not yet accepted' Christian doctrine associate vitality with the stimulating and potentially divisive force of *liget* that is born in conflict and emulation; for them, life feeds on social 'passion,' which alone can make them move. The Ilongot version of Christianity in fact confirms their view that, lacking God, human joys depend in part on social tensions – without which the multiple and distracting claims of everyday cooperation would preclude such 'concentration' as breeds energy, satisfaction, and renown.

This is, of course, the rub, the point, and a new beginning. Just as *liget* is born in social ife, so – for traditional Ilongots – 'satisfaction' is as much a matter of public notice as it is of personal accomplishment or feeling. The heart's motions are the motions of the social world writ small. If *liget* is a response to the triumphs of one's equals, and if, in transcending and casting off the weight of *liget,* the self expands – and in expanding treads on other people's turf – then happiness is an agitator, generating more envy and passion that contentment. One man's *sipē* may be experienced by another as an insult; women will deny success in harvests, lest others hear in happy boasts a challenge, grow 'angry,' and intensify their efforts in a desire not to be outdone. The movements of the heart, whether inward-turning, tense, and constrained, or as loose and free as happy footsteps, are intimately related; well-being, born phoenixlike from *liget,* is also what creates it; one man's successes are, almost inevitably, irritating to someone else. The apex of what turns out to be a vicious circle, the happy heart transcends, only to generate life's motions again. And although the realities of daily life mean that people work, cooperate, and care without experiencing 'focused' *liget,* success in fact occasions envy, and happiness and celebration tend invariably toward new 'anger' and a new, potentially disruptive, sense of conflict. Joy and satisfaction require effort and concentration. And concentration, in the Ilongot view, is born of *liget* and so of the conflicts that one's triumphs may create.

Of songs and tapes

One can make too much of pattern. Although the relationships described in the preceding pages pervade Ilongot talk of life and feeling, their world has other patterns, structures, and assumptions, and the Ilongots I knew best neither lived nor saw themselves as living in a vicious cycle of self-reproducing energetics – the only escape from which would be passivity, illness, and withdrawal. 'Knowledge,' which gives shape to the movements of their hearts, also dictates daily living; and the *bēya* that is required to focus *liget* in the heart points as well toward routine skills and tasks, calm habits of cooperation, and patterns of sharing among kin. As Ilongots were quick to tell me, a hungry man is not an 'angry' man, though hunger can well make the heart as 'dull' as can disruptive *liget* – and consideration for the stomach rather than for one's more successful neighbors is their more mundane but ever present stimulus to work. *Liget* does not always matter, nor, as I hope to show in later chapters of this monograph, are its workings always the same.

At the same time, talk of *liget* makes connections, in describing the ways in which affective life can take on 'focus' and 'make sense.' What Ilongots have in the patterns and images described above is a particular, wide-ranging, and deeply rooted way of organizing their responses and of granting intelligibility and significance to things they do and think. In daily speech, a matter for occasional thought and otherwise pat and unreflective metaphor, the motions of the living heart – of 'dullness,' 'flutter,' 'knowing focus,' turbulent disruption – have a privileged place in Ilongot understanding because they link the world as it presents itself to them as actors to the very form and feeling of their customary acts. A standard view of human nature, construed in terms of hearts inclined to *liget,* provides Ilongots with an interpretation of their experience. In particular, their talk of hearts captures the ways that the frustrations and complex demands of daily life acquire purpose and transcendent meaning, and it tells why they, the envious sons of headhunters – and not missionaries or Christian settlers – want to kill. In the section that follows, I will suggest that, at least in part, the importance of headhunting to traditional Ilongots, and the intensity of my friends' reaction to the tape, have to do with the fact that killing and its celebration, explained in terms of *liget,* present Ilongots with an image of themselves that confirms the value of those understandings. By demonstrating an order in their 'anger,' headhunting at once displays the things that people feel and shows their virtue, portraying *liget* in its most lovely, systematic, and deeply intelligible form.

The short and heavily rhythmic lines of the *buayat,* the celebratory song mentioned at the beginning of this chapter, have no linguistic "sense" of which Ilongots are aware. They are sung during an all-night sacrifice that celebrates a killing and, through a series of progressive 'strengthenings,' or "purifications," guarantees that neither headhunters nor their families will suffer from the curses of their victims or fall victim to the 'angry' smell of blood. Only after sniffing ginger to restore their anger, taunting young boys to behead a chicken tethered to a stick, and strengthening wives and daughters by rubbing them with brass, do the men gather around a cluster of seated women to begin – with the women joining in choral counterpoint – the celebratory song. While singing, the men shout boasts of their past exploits: 'I went to where the sun sets and fell upon a giant'; 'Downstream on the great river I came upon a maiden, she kicked, but I am here to tell the tale'; 'I would not sing your lines, *buayat,* had I not tossed a Christian's head far down a muddy path.' The song goes on for hours, building until, as Ilongots say, the *buayat* 'ties up' ('*eret,* meaning both to 'tie in a knot' and 'to be strong') the room and all the people in it. The intense volume may give way to songs, more boasts, and 'focused' dancing, and these cede again to song, which lasts until all are hoarse. But if, as often happens, there is cane wine or store-bought gin for drinking, the boasts tend to grow beyond the bounds of tact, recalling slights and insults long forgotten. A distant kinsman killed by someone present is remembered; male guests who were not on the last raid may come to feel themselves affronted; carelessly, one man shoves or urinates on another; and with heightened sensitivity to the growing tension, the women slip away with any knives, guns, spears, or arrows – leaving the men to fight it out.

> At the celebration that followed Burur's taking a head, his uncle Kadēng boasted that he retained 'anger' toward one of the guests who, years before, had killed a distant kinsman. The guest responded with a threatening gesture, leading some of the others in the room to reach for their knives. In the next moments, we were rushed outside by women, who grabbed us, their children, and whatever they could find of knives and guns. We heard shouts in the room, and a squeal when one man, in fact, urinated on another at the ladder, but were instructed to wait quietly until those inside calmed down. In the morning, Kadēng gave the guest three bullets in reparation for his insult, and the guest reciprocated by paying a few pesos for the kinsman he had killed.

In accounts of actual celebrations, Ilongots often recall such drunken fighting, but when telling more generally of their raiding, the whole adventure is recounted in idealized form. A man (never a woman) chooses to go killing, talks to kin, and plans a raid because his heart is 'heavy.' Although he may have hopes to kill within particular kin groups or localities, the raider does not care about the personal identities of his victims or limit violence to opponents of his age or sex. Grieving for lost kin, envious of past beheadings, angry at an insult, and bent upon revenge, he and his fellows are concerned, primarily, to realize their *liget.* All feel a weight that is 'focused' and intensified as they progress, slowly and quietly, through wakeful nights, scant food, and unknown reaches of the forest, to an ambush whose general location is isolated in advance.

Moving with tortured care and quiet, they talk only in whispers, and play reed flutes to set their hearts on edge. Once near the place of ambush, they pound their heads to heighten *liget;* their vision dims and narrows toward a future victim; their eyes are burning red. After shooting, the raiders will rush upon their wounded and dead victims, slashing wildly with their knives. The men who will get credit for beheadings need not themselves kill or even cut off the heads of victims, but simply hold a head as it is severed and 'toss' it – the weight each killer would be rid of – on the ground. This accomplished, they shout in triumph, and others toss the heads and shout. Tense, intent, and cautious until that moment, the gay victors then abandon both the severed heads and the bodies. Purged of violence, they will seek out flowery reeds to wear like feathers signifying lightness, sweet-smelling leaves whose scent recalls the lives they stole. Finding these, they hurry home.

Most raiding stories end neither with beheadings nor the ensuing sacrifice, but rather with a report that 'we came home and sang and sang.' Women, like men, enjoy the singing and explain that through their participation in the celebratory *buayat,* they cast off distress and grief. When *buayats* were sung more often, I was told, bodies were light and men were always red and healthy; work came easily because women sang *buayats* in their fields.

No mystical power, no new privilege or wealth, only a joyous song accompanies beheadings. Beautiful in itself, the song typifies intensity – creating for all participants the "magical" sense of power and control that comes with deep emotional involvement (see Sartre 1948), a sense which, for the Ilongots, suggests the reproduction of an unconstrained and vital life. Rent with boasts and booming echoes, stirred with an intense vibrato that Ilongots find unequaled in any other song, the *buayat* is at once a celebration of *liget* and the source of its renewal. Hearing the *buayat,* youths who did not share in triumph are moved to think of killing; the boasts, the mood, the tremor that permeates the chorus encourage men who did not participate in the celebrated beheading to meditate upon a future raid. When asked what a beheader gains from killing, Ilongots say he gets an *'amet* – a word that I can translate no better than as 'spirit of the beheaded.' To have an *'amet* is to have the privilege to wear a headhunter's hornbill earrings; to have it, one Ilongot told me, is like having a name or an office – so that people everywhere know that so-and-so has 'reached his manhood,' much as they know who bears the title 'captain' in a particular locality. In short, *'amet,* like the celebratory *buayat,* has less to do with mystery and sacred power than with the display and celebration of accomplishment – a name that is bruited widely, an aura that creates new *liget* and makes more men want to kill.

From the weight of envy that spurs killing to the expansive joy of triumph and the energy that, through envy, a celebration recreates, the experience of killing and its public climax in a strong and vibrant choral song at once present to Ilongots the problems of dealing with 'anger' and intense emotion, and give these problems form. In celebrating killing, the *buayat* indicates, first, that by directing envy stimulated within a kin group to a violent catharsis far outside it, *liget* can be transcended; and second, that such transcendence is a source of communal strength and joy. The 'energy' that was 'anger,' inward-turning and distracting, is unleashed in health and industry; the *buayat*, symbol of triumph, moves its singers from one success on to another.

But the song appears to have a further message. Not only does it "resolve" the problem of intense anger, it also shows anger and satisfaction to be intimately linked. The joy and end of victory lies in an aura that is experienced simultaneously as self-expanding and affronting; stirring other men to anger is, it seems, the stuff of triumph. Although Ilongots do not intend that their *buayats* end in fighting, such fights do not surprise them. In the choral celebration, 'chaotic' squabbling and thoughts of a 'focused' future raid are presented as inevitable, if problematic, consequences of a *liget* that was sought. The point seems to be a simple one: The *buayat*, through which *liget* is transcended, depends upon and recreates it; the form that best organizes *liget* also provides for its reproduction. Feelings that in daily life seem accidental and disturbing, violations of the norms of kinship and an ideal equality, are here recognized as necessary, meaningful, and desirable. Envy, anger, and confusion are cast as moments in a cycle that includes transcendent satisfaction. And the *buayat*, celebrating energy in all its modes, sustains, illuminates, and clarifies a quality of agitation, which – though it may fade with time and daily social interaction – remains for Ilongots the very stuff of life's vitality.

These comments barely outline the meanings Ilongots attach to killing, but they do suggest an interpretation of my friends' reaction to a tape recording of several years before. Hearing the old *buayat*, and recalling an experience of beauty and excitement they considered lost, my friends must have felt (what we would call) nostalgic. More important, however, and as they themselves insisted, in attending to the beauty of the song their hearts were pained and stirred with *liget*. Itself a realization both of happiness and focused 'anger,' the song distressed them with a vitality that could produce no more than tension and frustration because impassioned listeners did not look forward to a time when they, in turn, would focus *liget*, raid, and kill.

At the same time, because several of the men in the room had, in fact, been raiding a few years after the recorded celebration, the grounds for their reaction were not obvious. Not the actual event, or even its memory, but the tape recording itself was what moved them – not an actual ceremony, but "ceremony," detached from any context and presented, textlike, in its recorded form. Ceremony, song, and other formal aspects of a culture tend to be experienced by actors as having sense and significance independent of their particular situation; because they can be performed at different times by different people, they occasion understandings and responses that are, like Ilongot talk of hearts and anger, reflective, and relatively speaking, context free. This is why, without instruction or previous experience, my Ilongot informants understood that song, magic, and formal speech were appropriate objects – in a way that casual talk was not – for tape-recording and transcription. It also helps us to understand why Ilongots were upset when I played the old recording.

For Ilongots, not only the *buayat,* but all varieties of performance may be moving; song, in particular, reflects and – in ways to be explored in later chapters – has consequences for the state of people's hearts. In commemorating events, describing feelings, formulating significant desires, songs are, like reputations, things that travel; and the tape recorder captured Ilongot imagination because it carried words faster and farther ('even to the navel of America,' as they put it in their songs) than anything they had known. Thus, performance on the tape became, for them, an occasion for a speech act that does not accompany casual singing. After playing a flute, reciting a spell, or singing of their experiences or goals, Ilongots would conclude with an elaborate boast of prowess: 'This is the song of Pekpek who has traveled in all directions, and even though the word of God has outlawed killing, Pekpek still thinks the violent thoughts of old.' In these boasts, performers named their homes, celebrated their crops, claimed familiarity with law and government, or identified themselves as people who had taken heads or who intended to 'go walking to where a victim waits.' Through boasts, the tape became a vehicle for spreading the performer's name and reputation, communicating a vital aura, stirring others – a way of 'lengthening' one's heart.

Thus, when my friends found themselves upset by the tape-recorded *buayat,* they were reacting, at once, to a form of celebration that was intended to stir *liget,* and also to a vehicle which, bespeaking lowland ways and therefore an end to killing, was associated at the same time with an abandoned *liget* to which it gave undying voice. If the *buayat* itself was experienced by Ilongots as a beautiful and significant formulation of an otherwise unruly 'anger,' the fact that it had been taped added a new – and relevant – dimension to its force. Utterly "decoupled" from their contexts, taped performances were at other times dismissed with the cynicism that recognizes disembodied form as simply form and therefore playful. But the first time they heard their old *buayat,* a variety of circumstances – the voice of a dead kinsman, the memories stirred by our return, and the fact that, since our departure in 1969, most Ilongots aside from our closest friends had converted to Christianity – all combined to make the medium extend and reinforce the message, and to turn something my friends had thought to treat as play into a presence that was disquietingly real.

Neither anthropologist nor native had expected that the tape would be upsetting. But, unlike myself, my friends immediately understood the import of what had taken place. What for them must have been a poignant reminder of issues which – through converting, starting schools, irrigating once dry rice fields, and learning English songs – they were confronting daily and in a variety of ways, was for me a complex revelation. Their reactions to the recording – strange, powerful, and utterly surprising – at once confronted me with the "otherness" that, as an anthropologist, I had thought that I was seeking, and, at the same time, dramatized the sense in which my husband's and my presence – our tape recorders as much as the new Ilongot Bibles – would shape the ways in which Ilongot culture could be experienced, and so, described. Typifying their sense of the contrast between old and new and the conflicts of transition, the incident with the tape alerted me to the Ilongot concern for hearts and *liget;* it showed that through their talk of hearts and feelings, Ilongots linked past and contemporary experience – while pointing to the complex and ambivalent frame of mind in which emotions Ilongots associated with past practice would subsequently be discussed. In short, I found a set of problems illuminated and discovered as well the contextual constraints on any understanding I might gain.

These observations bear on what I hope the rest of this book will accomplish. All understanding is ultimately contextual and, as I suggested at the beginning of this chapter, the perception of culture as "system" comes and goes with new contexts and new knowledge. Having explored the systematic view of heart and feeling that underlies and is formulated in headhunting narrative and the experience of the *buayat,* I will, in the rest of this monograph, look at the use of concepts like 'knowledge,' 'heart,' and 'passion' in a variety of relationships and contexts – in situations where their application is often contradictory, and certainly problematic and complex.

The concentrated 'anger' of the *buayat* is beautiful for Ilongots because it illustrates – for them as well as for the more or less naive observer – the sense and purpose that can be found in problematic feelings, private grudges and recurrent experiences of disappointment, loss and social strain. Headhunting creates these experiences as much as it resolves them, and it would certainly be misleading to suggest that Ilongots depend on killing to order their emotions or to cope with social stress. Rather, headhunting and its celebration at once intensify and order, acknowledge and give meaning to experiences that would not be the same without them. As we will see in the next chapters, related experiences – bound both to *liget* and to *bēya* – have a very different sense and consequence in the less dramatic but not less significant or compelling flow of Ilongot daily life.

3. Knowledge, identity, and order in an egalitarian world

Just as ritual is, by definition, a nonordinary sort of activity, so the understandings facilitated through participation in and observation of ritual activity bear a problematic relation to the ordinary organization of everyday life. The shock of "otherness" that I experienced in witnessing Ilongot reactions to a tape of a headhunting celebration is paralleled by the fact that Ilongots themselves only sometimes and in special contexts experience violence and disruptive 'passion' as a source of beauty and strength. For the fieldworker, equally puzzling and perhaps more disorienting are the things people say and do when neither anthropologist nor native sees the moment as marked or peculiar. It was precisely when life seemed most familiar and my friends and I appeared to share unself-conscious perceptions of our common world that the tone of a remark or its content called forth naive and confusing reflections on my part as to whether the people I was studying were or were not "like" myself.

So it was when we decided that I had a cold and should spend the day resting and warm. The very commonness of my symptoms, as well as the Ilongot insistence that Vicks VapoRub was the only medicine that could guarantee me any relief, seemed, at the time, to testify to the universal and objective nature of my complaint. There was some awkwardness about my wanting to eat fruits (whose acids were considered irritating) and more than a little distaste for my wasting and soiling of tissues in clearing my nose; but only later in the day, when Wagat saw me toss a dirty tissue into the fire, did I learn of a deeper mistake. Wagat, never cautious, always right, and far more maternal with me than the fact that we called one another 'sister' would lead an outsider to expect, named my folly. Did I, she scolded, want to make my cold worse? Couldn't I simply discard the soiled tissue, say, in the thicket? Did I want my nose to 'throb' or 'burn' like my mucus, scorched in the fire?

Anthropologists, confronting and trying to make sense of such statements, once puzzled about "primitive mentalities" and the partial understandings and inconsistent and metaphorical logics of not-quite "scientific" minds. More recently, they have sought out semantic patterns in systems of taboos and asked whether natives themselves really follow them. And, borrowing a recent query of Needham (1972:3), they have wondered if "the men in New Guinea" – and, by implication, natives anywhere – really "believe" what they say. My concern in this and the chapters that follow is related to all of these questions, but the direction of my discussion will be different. I am less interested in whether Wagat "believed" that burning tissues would aggravate my symptoms – at best, she had "guessed" that that would be the case – than with the facts that she *meant* her statement as a warning, that she found my actions disturbing, and that she characterized her disturbance in a particular and presumably "reasonable" way. My problem is, in short, to characterize the sense in which Ilongot statements "have meaning" – the assumptions that they draw on, the activities they refer to, and the contexts in which they are used.

In this case, what I had done was wrong and upsetting not because Ilongot tradition reckons such behavior taboo or definitively marks it as dangerous, but rather because my burning the tissues violated – in a small but significant way – an element of Ilongot common sense. *Liget*, force, and energy, as discussed in the last chapter, are always potentially disruptive; fire has *liget* that can (in well-executed magical spells) be turned against spirits or symptoms, or (as in my case) aggravate the patient herself. By a similar logic, Ilongots object to burning the hairs that come loose in a comb while shampooing or grooming; they say that the 'angry' red countenance of a successful headhunter disrupts other men's hearts and makes them want to kill. Illness comes from the 'anger' of spirits or nature; an 'angry' enemy or wind makes people 'frightened'; drunkenness comes from the *liget* of sugarcane wine. And in church, I have known Christian Ilongots to refuse to engage in discussion with a weeping woman who cried that her husband mocked her attempts to pray and act like a convert; they shunned her for fear that the 'clutching' *(ngalemkem)* and 'passion' in her heart would 'pour into' *('akin)* their hearts and their thinking and disrupt their sense of content.

In the last chapter, I stressed the ambiguity in Ilongot attitudes toward *liget*, and discussed some ways in which the experience of disruption comes to be understood by Ilongots as necessary, creative, and even fulfilling – the source and consequence of all success. Here, my questions are different. I would like to examine in detail some of the practical bases of Ilongot attitudes toward 'knowledge' and 'passion' by exploring the activities and social relationships that make them at once problematic and desirable. In this chapter, I will explore the complementary and positive relations of *liget* and *bēya* in the developmental experience of Ilongot *individuals,* showing in particular how Ilongot understanding links affect to characteristic sorts of activity that change through the life cycle, differentiating children from adults and women from men. In contrast, subsequent chapters will focus on the *social* occasions for feeling, and the ways in which affective idioms are used to explain and interpret not only personal experience, but also the patterns of cooperation, dependence, and conflict that order the Ilongot world.

Disruptions and the unknowing child

Ilongot babies 'know' nothing, and, lacking *bēya,* they are extremely vulnerable to experiences of disruption and shock. One day, I saw an infant of some three or four months fall, without apparent harm, from a low-hung cradle. Not pausing to feel the child's head for bumps, scrapes, or bruises, the mother took the infant to her chest, spat at her forehead and chestbone, and in a soft, steady voice, called over its whimpers, "Come, little girl; come, come back here.' The baby's heart, she explained to me later, did not 'know' what had happened, and so needed her voice to prevent it from starting and jumping or fleeing in fright.

Ilongot 'knowledge' develops slowly over the course of a lifetime, just as, with age, one's experience of 'anger,' disruption, and challenge grows deeper and more intense. Neither 'knowledge' nor 'passion' is viewed as a "natural" capacity of infants; both grow in response to one's social life and relations, as the undifferentiated reactions of children become, on the one hand, occasions for *liget,* and on the other, the source of experiences that adults, through *bēya,* can organize and control. My purpose in this chapter is to illuminate this interdependence of *liget* and *bēya* by examining the application of these terms to the developmental experiences of children, showing, in particular, how the acquisition of skill and civility is associated with capacities for 'concentration' and conflict: As 'knowledge' grows, so does 'passion,' permitting at once the 'focusing' of myriad affects in successful endeavors and the chaos of social division and strain. Although it considers the lives of both sexes, my discussion will highlight experiences that differentiate male from female development, following the Ilongot view that women, though 'equal humans,' cannot attain the full 'knowledge' and 'passion' of men. Comparative evaluations of the sexes will be seen here and in chapters to follow to acquire their significance with reference to men's and women's roles in production, and to shifts in

activity, affect, and status associated with a male life cycle that distinguishes unmarried and 'angry' male youths from their more 'knowledgeable' seniors – and reckons women, primarily, as the complements
to men who attain adult status, their fellow producers and wives.

From birth, Ilongot children are distinguished by gender. The question: 'What is its name?' leads to the answer, 'A boy' or 'A girl.' But
differences between the sexes are relatively unmarked in the early years
discussed in the first half of this chapter. These differences become more
pronounced in the second decade when youths of both sexes acquire a
sense of social responsibility along with productive skill. Because
neither ritual nor myth provides ready texts for the early phases of this
development, I will invoke Ilongot views through a series of anecdotes
that tell what it means to 'lack knowledge'; in the remainder of this
chapter, I go on to discuss aspects of social relationship, linguistic skill,
naming, and productive activity through which the sexes are progres-
sively differentiated – as both 'knowledge' and 'passion' are, unequally,
acquired.

Few Ilongot households lack children, and in spite of current governmental pressure for nucleated residence, most young parents share
a home with the wife's kin. This means that an Ilongot baby is born into
a world of multiple caretakers. In addition to the mother, there are
other children who fondle and carry the baby, and often a father or
some other woman whose lullabies quiet its cries while the mother
works in her garden. Never leaving their babies alone or far from the
touch of another, Ilongots speak with some horror of what they know
of American missionary custom, with its bottles and isolating cribs.
Whether tied in a sling on the back or swung in a cradle, the Ilongot
baby wants sound, motion, and usually, feeding. Its cries are upsetting
to adults and, if unattended, conducive to disruption, heart loss, and
illness in both the parent and the child itself. Lullabies plead that the
infant 'take pity,' as its tears, suggesting frustration, can reflect or induce greater ills. In fact, Ilongots view infants much as they do people
who are sick – something I learned when, confined to the house with a
serious boil, I found myself assigned the company of a teenage girl who
should have been helping her mother clear weeds from their garden.
Forced to lie prone or sideways, I was considered to be – like an infant
– weak, disorganized, and spiritually vulnerable; like babies in
folklore, I was open to attack by the spirits should my companion be
lax in her care.

Not infantile bliss, trust, and comfort, but vulnerability and *kayub*,
or 'fear,' born of lack of awareness, are what Ilongots see as characteristic of the most primitive stance of the self toward its larger environment. As with the baby whose heart didn't 'know' it had fallen, or

Father and child

another whose angry tears make it ill, all Ilongot infants are subject to fright which in turn becomes heart loss because they lack 'knowledge'; they cannot speak or make sense of their worlds.

> Sick and unknowing infants were never set down but always held in the arms of an adult caretaker. And if I asked what was the matter, adults typically responded as if my question were foolish. 'How can we know what is wrong?' they would say, looking distressed and cuddling the child. 'Do you think the baby can talk?'

Like infants, adults may be 'frightened' when, failing to understand a disruption, their hearts 'stop,' leave them 'breathless,' and experience a crisis of orientation, a sense of impotence, and a loss of will. This is what happened to my 'brother,' Tepeg, who, when caught unawares at his work in a sudden windstorm, rushed into our house and immediately dozed off into tranquil oblivion – in order, as he said much later, to quiet or 'diffuse' *(ringring)* his 'fear.' Infants, because they know nothing, need others to comfort or calm them; lacking 'knowledge' or understanding, they are particularly vulnerable to disturbances that they are unable to grasp.

This is how I interpret the Ilongot idea that a child who cannot speak or recognize a name should not have one. Although no informant said as much, I imagine that the custom is rooted in a sense that a 'named' but not yet conscious heart can be called away by spirits or controlled by forces it can neither recognize nor ignore. Such an account would be consistent with the fact that 'naming' friends brings their hearts near one's own during dreaming, and naming or thinking of a lover is a way of influencing his or her heart (see Chapter 2). The infant, unable to 'know' or reflect on the forces – like naming – that move it, is too much their subject. Only when the child acquires understanding (usually in the second or third year) will a name, made up in play or the more serious reflections of senior kinfolk, enter habitual usage, becoming uniquely his or her own.

One way to think of the development of the self is in terms of this progress of awareness. The infant does not recognize names or even faces; it does not 'know' what it needs or why it reacts as it does. Adults like Tepeg can *ringring* – 'ease off,' 'cleanse,' or 'diffuse' – their sense of anger and upset by sleeping or working, setting off to the forest to avoid and forget a domestic disturbance, or dozing at home to dispel the 'bad fortune' *('uget)* that met them in the form of an omen on the morning's trail.

> We were visiting 'Insan's house when he decided to go work in a distant garden, disappointing our hopes to interview him during the day. Shortly after leaving, however, he returned and immediately fell asleep without speaking. As it turned out, a snake had crossed before him on the trail, foretelling bad fortune, and so he had slept to *ringring* his *'uget,* 'bad feeling, bad luck.' Sometime after waking, he set off again for the field.

To *ringring* can mean to 'clear up' or 'cleanse' a blemish or sign of disturbance. Waxy plants are described as *'uringring* because they shed water and so stand, in medicinal magic, as metaphors suggestive of health. Sick people may sleep in a field house to *ringring* internal disruption. And older children leave their houses to play and so *ringring* such feelings as had made them envious or angry just moments before. But infants and children – when hungry and sad or distressed that their parents appear to have left them – need others to ease their anxiety; not the child himself but a caretaker is ready, through lullabies and gentle distraction, to *ringring* disturbance and fear.

> Often, on encountering someone walking in a houseyard with an infant, I would inquire as to the location of the child's parents. My queries would be immediately silenced with words to the effect that my addressee had taken the child to *ringring,* hoping to distract it from impending parental exit from the house. When children did get upset by the exit of parents and no one was able to calm them, adults usually decided that inconvenience was preferable to unknowing tantrums – and took the insistent youngsters along.

By the time they are three or four, these children begin to have 'knowledge.'[1] They 'know' names, recognize and respond to language, speak a bit, and attend to informal commands. They learn simple tasks but do not 'know' what to do without direction, and can barely tell truth from falsehood or enemy from playful kin. Buy, a child in our first Ilongot household, must have been about five when his mother would coax him to eat by saying that soldiers were coming to catch him, and his grandfather could drive him to tears by insisting that he had had intercourse with 'Ibir, a coresident uncle's adopted daughter. Similarly, the four-year-old 'Ibir would dissolve into sobs when people claimed that her settler father was really her lover, or worse yet, that her mother was known as Buy's spouse. Trying to respond, these children were inevitably overcome by a failure of wit and a simmering protest of sobs that replaced their attempts to answer. If Buy called his grandfather impotent, the latter would wave his gray ponytail and comment on the youngster's supposedly ancient and balding, but actually scabies-ridden scalp. The child's tentative, 'You sleep with your mother,' would be drowned by the grandfather's taunt that Buy was probably too old and feeble to sleep with anyone at all.

After some such defeat, Buy was in a corner, crying softly, when an 'uncle,' Pukka, entered our house. Wild-eyed, Pukka said that he would not stand for the child's inelegant 'music'; he lifted Buy roughly, put him down, and pretended to look for a gun. Pukka threatened to bag Buy and toss him in the river, stab him if he could find an arrow, drop him in the freshly stoked fire, behead him if there were a knife. Buy's tears turned to hysterics when his mother, barely rising, called him to her side. She told him not to listen to outsiders, that his mother was there to comfort and protect him, and she pleaded with Pukka to take pity and forgive her poor sobbing son. To me, she explained that Buy didn't 'know' that Pukka was really his 'uncle'; he didn't 'know' the threats could not be true.

Buy's older brother, Sangpul, and his cousin, Kerisan, both close to fifteen, do 'know' something of the principles of everyday social relationships, but they still lack a sense of the continuity and commitment entailed by ties among kin. Both 'know' too much to be deceived and too little to be trusted; they 'know' the names of their kin groups, and enough about verbal repartee, challenge, and insult to move from an exchange of boasts about reputation to a near exchange of blows. One afternoon, the question of whether Sangpul (through his mother) or Kerisan (through his father) had more in common with a group of distant but ill-reputed and highly acculturated kinsmen had roused my attention – and their wrath. At first, Kerisan's mother, who happened to be looking on while the boys' taunts were mounting, ventured no interference; then she snapped out, to no one in particular: 'These boys "work" at nothing but "play" and so only make trouble.' Turning to me, she said that even though the boys 'knew' how to work, they were too young to know that they *should* work, and that they were – and should act like – close kin. In her view, their childish words turned toward violence because, like men whose drink has dulled their awareness, the boys lacked full consciousness or adequate *bēya*. As with drunks, there was nothing that could be done.

'Lack of *bēya*' is used by Ilongots to explain why unmarried youths who kill game and butcher it cannot be entrusted with its distribution; it characterizes, for physically competent and often courageous young men in their late teens and twenties, the difference between them and more verbally poised, less self-absorbed, and far more reliable mature adults. 'Knowledge' of how to act and speak, of 'where to go' with one's feelings and what is due to one's kin, is the culturally recognized basis of adult authority; lacking it, children fight and youths are understandably wild.

So, when Burur, the nineteen-year-old subject of the headhunting celebration we witnessed, slashed a footbridge that his aunt had to cross to fetch water, his mischief (which could have killed her) was dismissed in familiar and stereotyped terms. Burur meant to do harm, but whatever his actual motives, the adults agreed that the youth did not 'know' the weight of his actions; the boy still lacked 'knowledge' of how to behave among kin. Youths of Burur's age are in fact seen by Ilongots as dangerous; if they have not taken heads, they are probably intent upon killing, and even successful young headhunters lack the ease, self-respect, and aura of confident autonomy that is enjoyed by mature married men. In this case, Burur had already taken a head, but because his lowland victim lived near the district of only distantly related Ilongots, his father feared that their annoyance at having to face the authorities would, if they heard of the offender, lead to the arrest of his son. By slashing the footbridge, Burur, still unsung for his achievement and, in any case, inclined to sullenness and withdrawal, may have been protesting the failure of his parents and kinsmen to celebrate and proclaim his recent achievement.[2] But, when we stopped at the aunt's house on our way to go visiting elsewhere – and learned of the event and her justifiable rage – the question of Burur's motives did not temper the popular response. Immediately, we were struck with horror. It was all too clear that if the aunt had stepped with any weight on the damaged footbridge, it would have collapsed with her into a gulley several yards deep. And even though nothing had happened, the 'threat' in the action remained. Some in our company felt that the youth should be fined and punished. For others, the proposal was senseless – how could an aunt ask her nephew, a mere boy, to pay her? Would she kill him if he refused?

For reasons I clarify later, it turned out that the aunt had no choice but resignation. Burur was her nephew, and, people claimed, still a child, who could not tie knots to secure his own houseposts, let alone deal with feelings of 'anger' or act dependably toward adults. He did not yet 'know' about, or understand, indemnatory payments, and she, as his aunt, could not think of revenge. Tukbaw – the boy's mother's brother – took Burur aside and gave him a lecture on kinship: The aunt was his mother's first cousin, a woman who listened to Tukbaw; she 'held hands' with Burur's parents, helped them with their harvests, moved with them, and often shared food. In the end, not guilt or intention, but sheer 'lack of *bēya*' was invoked to explain the event and resolve it. Burur was not asked to apologize, but simply to acknowledge connections; he was instructed to 'know,' and so order his actions in terms of the ties among kin.

Following adults

The early development of 'knowledge' is associated, for Ilongots, with an ability to 'hear' and so 'follow' one's elders, thereby displaying awareness of kinship and rudimentary physical skill. By the time they reach the age of Buy, the five-year-old child whom Pukka threatened to kill, children will 'know' how to sit, stand, walk, and climb the houseladder – skills that Ilongot recognize as acquired by children in turn. Like others of his age, Buy now has younger siblings; he no longer sleeps with his mother, but lies instead with his father, another coresidential adult, or some of the older children who also live in the house.[3] In speaking of children of this age, Ilongot adults note that they 'hear' and 'understand' what is said to them, but do not yet 'know' what to do. Their hearts and their bodies are moved by the things adults tell them – they can be 'commanded' *(tuydek)*, 'frightened' *(kayub)*, and 'shamed' *(bētang)*. When upset, they must be 'fooled' and 'persuaded'; not knowing proper behavior, they must be 'led' or 'directed' *(bukur)*, 'dissuaded' *(tukbur)*, and 'warned' *(tengteng)* of the consequences of their acts. Children like Buy are seen as understanding the links between words and persons or objects, but, unable to make new connections, they cannot plan or conceive of activities on their own. Whereas adult hearts will say, 'I must hoe' and start working, the child is stirred into action not by his or her own heart, but by another's requests and commands. 'Knowledgeable' hearts dictate the activities of the selves in which they exist, but children, lacking *bēya,* are regulated by words and threats from outside.

Of all people in an Ilongot household, young children are most subject to direction by others, and – because of taboos on naming affines and a tendency to use kin terms (see Figure 1) for parents and other adults of their age – are most likely to be called by their names. In casual speech, Ilongots say they 'name' *(ngaden)* others when they mean that they 'shame' or 'command' them:

'Enngadenanmuwak bēt,
'Do you think you are naming me, commanding me?'

'Awana rawentaka qengadeni,
'I am not going at you to name you, shame, fault you.'

And they explain that obedience to the demands of another grows from 'fear,' or *kayub,* and from *bētang,* a word whose sense includes aspects of the English "respect," "embarrassment," and "shame." What this means, for young children, is that a name or social identity and an attitude of 'shame' toward the adults who now can command them are learned at the same time that they 'come to know' *(bima'bēya,* 'he came to know a little bit') the rudiments of certain skills. 'Fear' and 'shame' in the child are understood by adults as the conditions of obedience and so, of acquiring *bēya;* for children, they appear to be linked to an unknowing and partial control of spoken language, and to the experience of being 'named.'[4]

Children who are 'named' can be mocked, commanded, or scolded; they can be cajoled and dominated by those more adept than themselves. Accordingly, in 1908 Jones reported Ilongot children's reluctance to say what their names were, and I observed that children's names – often composed of reduplicated syllables that gave them a silly and singsong tone – were the subject of word play and verbal abuse. Sensitive to this possibility, Dulay, Buy's younger brother, once cried at my mention of the English word "July," because the unintentional rhyme suggested that I had 'named' him and that he was the butt of my fun. To be named, as I suggested for infants, may be frightening and disturbing; as children grow older, naming becomes associated with demands for obedience, with submission and feelings of 'shame.'

Certainly, for adults, these facts are connected. Adults say they do things for 'fear' of their senior kinfolk; ungenerous people 'have no shame,' whereas good hosts will share food out of 'fear' of or 'respect' for their guests. One listens to and cares for aging parents because one 'fears' and 'respects' them; and people avoid naming parents and siblings of spouses – just as they avoid naming dangerous spirits – out of feelings of 'fear' and 'shame.'

> People often said that they worked with us in interviews because they 'feared' us, and on questioning explained that they felt *bētang* or 'shame' in their hope to comply with our needs. Children who hesi-

tated to request the candy they knew we had among our belongings were said, similarly, to be inhibited by 'fear' or 'shame.'

Tepeg, my thirty-five-year-old 'brother,' once told me that the very 'essence' *(pu'un)* of 'fear' is 'the parent' – because, as children, we are frightened of beatings for failing to listen or for doing things wrong. But this is a complicated matter. Ilongots readily threaten their children with taunts about soldiers or monsters who seek them, and with hints that the youngster who urinates while sleeping may have his or her genitals stitched closed. Yet at the same time, beatings are rare, monsters laughed at, and soldiers almost mythical figures. Children are threatened and more rarely punished, but not for disobedience; rather, noise and disruptive behavior occasion reminders of their lack of 'knowledge' – as when Pukka attacked Buy for his tears.

Furthermore, for children of Buy's age, 'fear' and 'shame' are genet ically related. The diffuse 'fear' of a child toward senior kin who taunt and threaten becomes linked to more complex and positive sanctions associated with 'respect' for one's elders and a desire to avoid disapproval, to emulate, and to please. Youngsters learn to silence their sobs or their play because 'there are visitors' who will 'think we are bad' and 'be angry' and 'shame us' – or more simply, because noise is chaotic and dangerous, spiritually disruptive, and socially conducive to stress. With time, most children are said to learn 'out of shame' to 'follow' *('unud)* and 'accede to' *(tebēr)* their seniors' directives; and they note that adults' verbal parries are not only frightening to youngsters but also amusing to parents and kin. For them, 'fear' itself becomes an occasion for *bētang,* and shame and defeat lead to 'admiration' *(dēglw),* 'humility' *(tu'ngan),* and a desire to learn and excel.

It is clear to Ilongot adults that the frustrations of youthful incompetence induce rage as much as they teach children to control and direct it, and that the experience of verbal taunts, threats, and contests is generally more intense for boys than for girls. But these consequences are not viewed as serious, or as destructive of the real affection that children and their parents clearly share. By adult account, 'fear' and 'shame' lead ultimately to obedience and an inclination to 'follow' *('unud)* one's seniors – to respond with 'respect' *(tu'ngan)* rather than with 'anger' to people who 'know' more than oneself. Because children are 'shamed' and 'frightened,' they can be persuaded – to stay at home when their mother goes off to her gardens, to help with small tasks in the household, to follow a senior sibling, or even to eat a meal. What actually happens in early childhood, as Ilongots see it, is that children start to learn about *bēya* by experiencing and responding to their ties to a number of adults.

Language, skills, and commands

Central to this process is the child's ability to respond to language, and
language, for Ilongots, is in many ways epitomized in *tuydek,* or 'commands' to do petty tasks. The interior of an Ilongot house contains a
large sunken floor space surrounded by a raised platform where adults
sit, sleep, chew betel, eat meals, or work individually at crafts. In the
center, children play, dishes clank, and food is prepared and apportioned. Whereas edges of the space are quiet, the center tends to be
noisy: In formal debate, antagonists sit on opposite platforms, casting
their words, as they put it, into the middle of the room. Activity in the
'center' *(bengri),*[5] involving food preparation, play, and commotion,
concerns women more than it does men, and young children (who often
eat from pots with their mothers) more than their seniors. And patterns
of *tuydek* reflect this hierarchy of place. Mature men, the people whom
Ilongots say are most 'feared' within the household, are also, in this
context, most 'lazy' *(kidēt),* depending for movement and service on
the efforts of children and wives. Relaxed in the light of a window or
the dark privacy of a corner fire, adult men are most apt to issue
tuydek, and are also least likely to move. Inside the house, men *tuydek*
women, who in turn pass their commands on to children, and children
are quick to *tuydek* those who are younger than themselves. The
dynamics of *tuydek* tend ultimately to permit all adults the orderly
poise of the platform – while requests for betel, food, tools, and water
set children in almost continuous motion across the relatively unor-
dered floor.

But *tuydek* are more than assertions of dominance that rank ages and
sexes and demand a submissive response. Ilongots are quick to point
out that no speech is truly coercive; refusals to obey do not, by themselves, lead to discipline; and even young children must be coaxed and
persuaded to follow the will of adults. Parents plead with their children
to stay at home when they go off to the garden or forest; they beg them
to go out for water, fetch wood for a fire, or attend to some other
command. But no *tuydek* is experienced as binding, and youngsters
may balk or ignore them without being punished or harmed. Rather
than building character in a Western sense, Ilongots say that *tuydek* are
necessary to inform those whose hearts still lack knowledge of work
that needs doing and those relationships that ought not be breached. In
attending to *tuydek,* children acknowledge their love and commitment
toward the adults who bore and raised them and who became
'exhausted' in providing a new generation with life. Parents say they
want offspring because they need someone to *tuydek,* and children of
Buy's age or younger may be 'adopted' by married but childless

kinsmen for months or even years at a time. What is crucial here is not the work done by youngsters but rather their gaining new 'mothers' and 'fathers': In becoming 'used to' *(tagde)* the care and commands of additional elders, the child develops an attitude of responsibility and commitment that guarantees support for the aging and provides those whom Ilongots call 'big' or 'old' ones *(mesiken)* the help and consideration of youth.

Of children like Buy one says, 'he listens,' for example, to his name; he 'knows' his mother, his father, and probably a number of their kinsmen; and finally, he 'understands' minor *tuydek,* or commands to fetch things inside the house – first betel pouches that are passed between adults, then objects like dishes and knives. In time, he will accompany children a year or two older when they go to fetch wood and water, and gradually, he will come to respond to *tuydek,* 'on the outside,' by himself.

Tuydek, epitomized in sentences of the form, *Rawmuy ma "X,"* 'Go for the "X,"' or *Man-"X"-ka,* 'Go "X," you' (no matter what is being requested), are, for Ilongots, a sort of prototype of all language (just as, one imagines, the declarative sentence is for us); they are also seen as the primary means through which children acquire the linguistic and technical 'knowledge' which, as infants, they lack.

> One day, early in fieldwork, my Ilongot 'sister,' Wagat, asked a child to bring her betel pouch from across the room. Wanting to please and be helpful, I jumped to the task. Wagat laughed when I handed the pouch to her, and told me I was like an unmarried maiden, who fetches objects when told. But when I looked hurt, she went on to assure me that I, like a child, would learn to speak by being commanded – and by fetching what she had asked for, I had demonstrated that I 'knew' its name.

When schoolboys were asked to compose sample sentences for our vocabulary cards, close to fifty percent were cast in the imperative form of *tuydek;* similar results emerged when adults were asked to explain a word's use. Most dialogue in Ilongot narrative takes a command form, and stories of hunting or killing almost universally begin by reporting: 'I said to my sister/wife/mother, "Pound me rice, for I am going off."' Through *tuydek,* Ilongots claim, children learn how things are called and they show that they know what a word is. In hearing and attending to *tuydek,* they learn something of what work and talk are; they learn the meaning adults give to action, and come to participate in the rhythms of life in their homes.

Although children of Buy's age can respond to *tuydek* only 'inside' the house and with their familiars, they soon learn to fetch water from wells, bring tools from the house to the gardens, and carry small shares of meat or betel to nearby homes. By the time they are eight or nine, children 'really know' *tuydek,* and are ready to learn, through imitation, some of the skills of adults. Ilongots describe these subsequent stages of children's development in terms of the skill they acquire, the distance they travel beyond their own households, their movement from 'inside' to 'outside,' and their ability to work, travel, or assume responsibility on their own. As children 'come to know' more, they move ever farther, and their hearts, no longer requiring care or external direction, come to think 'by themselves' of people to visit and of work that needs to be done. Neither fearful nor lacking awareness, they gradually acquire the 'knowledge' that makes the self an autonomous actor, its heart independent of others – the determiner of its own moves.

Girls, in the Ilongot view, will now come to 'follow' their mothers, acquiring their skills and sharing their obligations and concerns; but they are rarely inclined to move as widely as their male agemates. 'Fear' keeps girls close to home and their thoughts far from travel. And, failing to explore and to voyage, they never develop the sort of 'knowledge' that permits men to 'focus' disruptive experience as creative 'anger,' to move easily in new environments – or, by a circular logic, to overcome 'fear' itself. At the same time, the young girl learns the skills that will make her admired as a woman: to hoe and to weed, then to pound rice and winnow, to cook, plant, and harvest the grain. Boys, as they approach their teens, are too young to participate in older men's heavy agricultural labor or 'suffer' *('adug)* the cold and leech-ridden forests where their fathers commonly hunt. Instead, they learn aspects of those agricultural activities that men share with women – like hoeing, shooing rice birds, gathering firewood, and clearing debris from a garden; they play and watch older boys fish in smaller rivers; and with miniature arrows, they 'hunt' for rats in their houses and gardens and shoot at moving targets of fruit that they roll through their yards. 'Restless' *(kalikal)* and 'lazy' *(kidēt),* boys and girls of this age 'come to know' the rudiments of a variety of tasks, but lack the *liget* required for consistent labor; outside of the house, they would sooner be 'playful' than join with their parents in work.

> I visited Sawad in her garden – perhaps half a mile from her house – in time for a rough lunch she was preparing for the three children (all under fifteen) in her care. She had been hoeing all day and was tired with the details of meal preparation, but when she called on an eleven-year-old son to fetch water, he looked up at her and said 'No.' She then asked a girl, somewhat younger, and again got a negative response. To my surprise, she did not repeat her *tuydek,* but shrugged in disgust and – before I could offer assistance – went off for the water herself.

A boy watches his uncle check the alignment of a fishing spear shaft.

Young children will 'flee' the commands of their seniors, and adults are continually complaining about having raised such youths to no purpose – because they do not 'know' what needs doing and refuse to attend to commands.

But the 'knowledge' that permits independence, self-direction, and true self-control develops much later. A boy will have entered his second decade before accompanying his father into the forest, and he will be fourteen or fifteen before shooting and killing a wild pig or a deer. In his late teens he ventures alone, and on night hunts, far into the forest, and at the same time he shows that he has learned, through years of watching, to butcher an animal, stretch a deerskin, and cook the meat he has bagged. Girls, as they move into their teens, show a similar progress in competence. After learning the various and individuated skills associated with agriculture and food preparation, they manage to light a fire, roast a sweet potato or manioc, and, by their tenth or twelfth year, prepare small and generally watery pots of rice for a midday meal. They are in their late teens, however, before they can be trusted to think of tasks – such as pounding rice or fetching water before mealtime – when no one commands them, to select vegetables from those growing in the garden, or cook quantities of rice that are dry but not hard and raw. Although in speech and social relations their youth continues to be apparent, the young adults who attain these productive skills also 'know' when to use them; serious labor is now part of their technical 'knowledge' and their hearts incline them to show off their energy and skill.

Youthful peers

Most aspects of the production and preparation of foodstuffs are learned by children from their same-sexed parents, and the sequence in which skills are acquired is a matter for stereotyped cultural account. Until girls start to pound rice and boys to play at shooting targets, the sexes learn things together, moving from inside to outside the house. After that, their skills will differ; girls cook, fetch wood, food, and water, while boys begin to move through the forest – a process culminating, as I suggested, in the late teens, when girls can be entrusted with meal preparation and boys with moving through relatively unfamiliar territory by themselves. Young teenagers, like Sangpul and Kerisan, the two boys who fought when they should have been working, fall somewhere short of this competence. They can follow their fathers on hunts, pollard (cut high branches off) trees, and move freely on tasks and in search of companions through a settlement of five to ten houses; they can help to clear thickets and gather edible ferns and the tasty hearts of rattans. But they are still young and fearful, and lack the 'knowledge' to govern their movements and the skill, perseverance, and confidence that enables men to work alone. Because their labor is still marginal, these children – in recent years – have been encouraged to go to school.

At the same time, they are no longer youngsters. Relations with elders have more of humility and 'respect' *(tu'gnan)* than the rage and 'shame' *(bētang)* that Buy suffers; no longer concerned with outdoing their senior kinsmen, teenage youths boast of the exploits of fathers and uncles, and take pride in their mothers' rice yields. If early childhood taught lessons of shame and obedience, the meaning of *tuydek* and obligation, and the necessity of acquiring skills, the teenage years – for boys in particular – become fraught with a concern for balance and fairness, a desire to show themselves to be the equals of their age-mates, and ultimately, of knowledgeable adults.

These are years in which a youth will learn that one must work to eat and that work requires cooperation, sacrifice, and sharing, hardship as well as the occasional reward. Unlike infants and even youngsters, who are fed whenever they are hungry and often find cold rice or freshly cooked taro to meet their morning cries, teenagers learn that food awaits their pounding rice or fetching wood and water, that all consumption is collective – and that even the wild berries they cull from thickets by the river should be distributed in equal portions to all who are in sight. When food is inadequate, they no longer nibble at their mother's servings, but find instead that everyone from adult to youngest sibling must receive and be content with equal shares. The howls of a youngster who is unintentionally slighted argue powerfully that failures to *bēret*, to divide all food in equal and individual portions, produce anger and disruption, shame and social stress.

The word *bēret*, which means at once 'to divide' and 'to distribute,' 'to contaminate' and 'to revenge,' is one of the most complex and central words in Ilongot social discourse. Epitomized, perhaps, in tidy rows of individually apportioned plates of rice and chunks of meat that constitute the meal following the return of lucky hunters, *bēret* captures both the defining features and essential strains of Ilongot conceptions of an orderly social life. It involves a distribution that is indifferent to age, sex, or any other attributes of status, and defines a group of equals who are expected to cooperate and share. So, within a home ut mealtime, it is thought that cooked food should be provided to all (including children) who happen to be present – though a woman who fears her rice supply is inadequate may feed her guests while nibbling by herself on sweet potatoes in a corner, 'ashamed' that her deficiencies will be subjected to the public view. Similarly, meat, uncooked and freshly butchered, is distributed to the households of cooperating hunters, ideally reaching all the residential units of which a settlement is composed. Because reception of a *bēet*[6] or 'share' is an acknowledgment of collective ties and interests, able hosts are always anxious to feed a passing guest or neighbor; travelers are called to stop and eat whenever passing friendly households, and told, 'Go then, and don't blame us if you are hungry,' should they happen to refuse. And finally, because patterns of food distribution define and alter social units, the woman who cooks her breakfast in a lonely fieldhouse, or the man who hides and hoards his game for sale, is acting out and activating emergent lines of social cleavage, signaling the collapse of a presumed field of equal and cooperating kin.

> The people in our household considered Bēgtek to be the worst offender in Kakidugen. He rarely joined their hunts, preferring to go into the forest only with his sons. Further, everyone knew that he did not bring shares of game acquired to other households, and all found themselves increasingly reluctant to share their game with him. Because one of his sons was married to an Ifugao settler, and his wife – the reason for his membership in the settlement – was long dead, people speculated that he planned to move, perhaps toward Ifugao neighbors. Certainly, people noted, it was with them that he engaged in cooperative garden work.

Bēret, like our word "division," suggests strain as well as balance, and for Ilongots, the other side of 'sharing' is 'anger' and 'revenge.' I imagine that Punlan, a middle-aged father and the first man in our settlement to convert to Christianity (and so proclaim his loyalties not to local families but to more distant Christian kin), was reflecting on the social consequences of his decision when he explained why 'one name,' *bēret,* can refer both to vengeance and to the cooperative business of apportioning equal shares. Himself increasingly excluded from settlementwide collective hunts, and less apt to receive or to distribute game, he said that the diverse uses 'held together' because a person denied a 'share' *(bēet)* of what has been 'divided' *(bēret)* will feel 'shamed,' excluded, torn with *liget;* such a person wants a 'share,' a chance to *bēret,* 'in revenge.'

> Visiting kinfolk often made requests for the medicines and goods of hosts, and hosts found it virtually impossible to deny them. People might attempt to hide from view desired goods, but when guests spoke of bullets, cloth, or pills they knew their kinfolk possessed, the latter were constrained to 'share.' So, for example, individuals to whom I gave pills sufficient for an extended treatment of malaria or tuberculosis almost always found themselves constrained to give away the bulk of their medicine before completing a cure. As with food, people felt that a failure to 'distribute' goods was tantamount to an insult – inexcusable among presumably equal kin.

In other words, the distributive impulse that defines units of sharing and cooperation also operates in terms of shame and insult; all distributions define boundaries between cooperating equal kin and those who are excluded, and persons who are denied a 'share' to which they feel themselves entitled are apt to *ki'bu,* or 'return a selfish gesture,' to show that rather than accept a slight they can grow 'angry' and reciprocate 'in kind' *('amumur).* Just as *liget* is experienced positively by those who can participate in 'focused' joy, but causes a 'distracted' and disturbed response in those who stand outside it, so *bēret* suggests at once the positive equality of a cooperating group and the imbalance and disruptive tension accompanying 'selfishness' and denial. In all its senses, *bēret* speaks, in short, to Ilongot concerns for balance and the disturbing consequences of slights that will occasion, as they may in turn be answered by, an 'angry' move – the necessity and dangers of equality.

In later chapters, there will be cause to look more closely into the uses and applications of the Ilongot word for 'distribution,' but here I would like to turn again to the question of its implications for the developing social attitudes, or *bēya,* in Ilongot children as they reach their teens. Having seen their younger siblings rant when denied a share of sugar cane or fruit that older children bring within their sight, they know that the distributive equality that governs ordinary sociality involves the risk of wildness and violence in its breach. Furthermore, from talk or more immediate experience, they are apt to know of kin ties dampened and resentments born through failures of meat sharing and distribution; and they may have lived through claims and counterclaims of selfish interest in terms of which adults (and women in particular) articulate the strains that lead a household to divide. Attuned to the importance of cooperation – through the experience of being 'lent' as laborers to their parents' siblings, and through familiarity with the habitual generosity that exists between most consanguine kin – they recognize at the same time the fragility of its bases. Distributive norms give meaning to the barest hint of rejection, and slights recognized can rip apart the ties on which one's play, support, and sustenance depend. When Sangpul and Kerisan fought about their kin affiliations, they must (as the mother who bemoaned their lack of 'knowledge' seemed to be suggesting) have been learning just this lesson: Their feeble imitation of adult modes of boast and verbal challenge would give way, in time, to a sense of when such behavior is appropriate, and correspondingly, to the knowledge that it is painful and disruptive to insult or try to dominate the people with whom one works and lives.

But there is a further sense in which the teenage youth finds himself or herself confronted with the problems of sameness, balance, and equality – and that is in a new consciousness of peers.

> Renato Rosaldo and I, consistently impressed with the difficulty of giving different kinds of gifts to friends who did not see their favors as having different value, were particularly struck by the expectation among adults and youths alike that most of our goods intended for distribution should go to the unmarried. And although each maiden and each bachelor might claim to need the cloth, beads, and metal wire with which to ornament themselves and publicize the facts of their youthful beauty, we would be told that so-and-so had not yet received an 'equal' gift; that one brother or sister would become 'envious' or 'angry' toward more favorably endowed siblings – in short, that all unmarried teenagers in the settlements where we were working could and did expect to receive equal 'shares' of our goods.

In the Ilongot language, none of the early phases of a child's development are matters for strict lexical differentiation. *'Anak,* or 'child,' used primarily for infants, is also the kin term for referring to one's 'children'; similarly, *'upet,* 'girl,' and *gu'nek,* 'boy,' can in some dialects be used to distinguish the sex of youngsters but name as well the kin positions of a 'daughter' and a 'son.' The first differentiated age grade is that of 'quick' *(me'awet)* unmarried ones, the 'maidens' *(madēkit)* and the 'bachelors' *(buintaw)* – idealized as a class of youths from middle teens to twenties whose strength and energy, ruddy cheeks and weightless stride make them at once the perfect type of Ilongot aesthetics and also the most valued laborers in local social life. Used for all unmarried people from their midteens onward, *me'awet* will be followed by *mesiken,* 'mature,' 'big,' or 'old' ones, and then by 'old woman' *(bi'al, baket)* and 'old men' *(lakay)*.

For youths, the shift to 'quick' unmarried status, though gradual and ritually unmarked, is accompanied by a shift in orientation. In the early years, Ilongots see themselves as learning individually, 'out of shame' and in imitation of their parents; but once some basic tasks of food production have been mastered, they say they learn 'with others' and as members of a group. So Talikaw, an aging 'bachelor,' gave the following account of the growth of a boy's knowledge:

He tried to look for food to eat; he went abroad to search for food. But he got nothing; he didn't know how to get his food because he was still a child. Let's wait and see what he will come to know. He'll manage when he knows a little more, but we can't expect too much, as he is still a child . . . Well, look at that! He really did stand tall and step with certainty. He got himself an arrow to practice with; he shot with blunted arrows at a rolling target. And he managed to hit the target. He learned *(nan'adal)* what to do when he felt hungry. He knew how to go into the forest for the hearts of the rattans. Now, *he would learn (naki'adal) with others.* He'd learn to make himself a bow and arrow, and with others he would hunt . . . (italics mine)

The key here is a shift in verbal prefix from the simple past, *nan'adal,* he 'learned' or 'practiced,' to a form, *naki'adal,* which implies reciprocal or collective acts.[7] Unlike the rudiments of productive skills that are acquired while 'still a child' and from one's seniors, there are things that youths now learn through the added stimulus of interaction with their peers. Tawag's text names 'making bows and arrows' only after casting learning as collective; and it moves from 'learning hunting' to the claim that 'now he learned to arrange and beautify his body,' 'he looked for necklaces, shell baubles; he learned to make these goods.' These concerns are born in youths from orientations that will focus ever less on parents than on those 'fellow' *(kasi-)* bachelors and maidens with whom one 'moves together' and who are now seen as 'reaching' the various marks of adult status one before the other – like hikers who file out into a clearing from a narrow trail. Whereas children's hearts are stirred by the commands of seniors, the youth's heart learns of effort and intense desire in envy and emulation of the accomplishments of peers. No parents tell their teenage sons and daughters to learn embroidery, song, or shellcraft – or undergo the painful but cosmetic filing of their teeth. Nor are thoughts of killing said to come so much from adult taunts as from the envious and twisting motions of a young man's private musings; aware and covetous of the feats of would-be equals, he encourages his father or some other senior kinsman to 'care for' him and take him on a raid.

Energetic young maidens pounding rice

Once youths like Sangpul and Kerisan 'know' the full rage of sex-linked productive tasks, they become what Ilongots call 'true' *(pìpiya)* bachelors and 'true' maidens, a generally willing crew of energetic offspring who permit their parents, aunts, and uncles to relax a bit and 'taste' the produce of their untiring 'hands.' Not only valuable as laborers, but also keen to show themselves the equals of fellows of their age, they experience and have the skill of focused *liget* born of envy, and turn competitive strivings to happy and productive use. Their 'quickness,' absent in young children, comes both of technical competence and a desire – as they pound rice, step through the forest, pollard treetop branches, or harvest sun-browned fields – to make their prowess known. Healthy and hard-working, abjuring solitude and pitying those friends who have to spend their time alone, they seek out other 'equals' *('anurut)*, 'fellow quick ones' *(kasi'awet)*, and 'companions' *(kabuintaw)* – whose presence makes work easy, gay, and stirs the heart with hopes to win one's 'share' of recognition and 'reach' the feats attained by others like oneself. As pollarders, youths sing from treetops; as travelers, they seem unburdened by sharp rocks, steep climbs, and heavy loads tied to their backs. Dressed up in earrings, beads, and delicately embroidered skirts and loincloths, they bring with them an aura of enthusiasm and communicate a will to be admired.

> Talin commented that youths' desire to 'command admiration' makes them poor converts; dressed up in finery to go to chapel, they demonstrate that their hearts lack the 'quietness' necessary to thoughts of God. When I asked a boy of about ten if his teenage brother were a Christian, he said, 'No, he's a bachelor *(buintaw)*' – suggesting again that the *liget* of youthful emulation (and more specifically, perhaps, the *liget* of boys who hope to take heads) made 'quick ones' most resistant to Christianity. My own impression was that teenage girls were likely to be attracted to Christianity – in part because the spheres of church and mission household provided an opportunity for intense contact with their 'fellow maidens.' But boys, who had much richer opportunities for peer group communication (and who, as novices, still harbored hopes of taking heads), were, in fact, reluctant to accept the Christian faith.

A youth who may seem inconsistent, shy, or sullen in responding to the wishes of a lonely parent becomes a very different sort of person when, on travels or in the company of kin or friends who visit, he or she experiences the vitality that is born in groups of peers.

> Visiting the mission settlement of Kawayan, I had a conversation with a girl in her late teens who asked me to name the maidens in the Kakidugen area. When she realized that there were few, she saddened

A bachelor rests alone.

and said that the 'quick' years of girls there must be 'wasted' because
they are unable to enjoy the company of peers. Bĕgtek's daughter, the
sole 'true maiden' in Kakidugen, and – since her mother's death some
years before – the key provider in her home, was far too busy to
accompany senior kin on visits elsewhere; and people described her as
'a maiden become aged' *(bimi'ala madēkit)* because she had no opportunity for the emulation born in groups.

Because settlements rarely exceed a total population of one hundred,
gatherings of more than two or three bachelors or maidens require travel
– and so tend to be less available to young women than young men.
Youths of both sexes orient to their agemates, fashion ornaments to
show off to them on visits, copy songs from one another, and look
forward to the arrival of those they call their 'equals' as their guests. But
where true bachelors hunt and travel unaccompanied by senior kinsmen
and learn to move abroad in groups of 'equally unmarried men,' young
women have less freedom. Whether kept at home, sent to homes of
kinfolk where they help the senior women, or traveling in the company
of 'fathers' for whom they carry loads and cook – these girls remain, like
children, the recipients of *tuydek,* or 'commands,' from people older
than themselves. They may see agemates and friends, find time to play,
parade, and demonstrate their skill and prowess – just as young men
may receive commands and do a lot of work – but between the sexes
there is an important difference. Boys move relatively more frequently
in peer groups and are freer from adult supervision, whereas girls are
tied to elders and their *tuydek;* their compliance, stimulated in part by
the 'angry' energy of competition, is based largely on an attitude of
submission, a stance that – as for children – combines both 'fear' and
'shame.'

In short, the 'quick,' unmarried years, exciting for both sexes and a
time when youths who have transcended the dependencies of childhood
can enjoy a sense of freedom and potential that marriage and responsibility do not yet undermine, are at the same time most fully realized in the
experience of youthful collectivities, enjoyed by bachelors on the move.
The fact that men 'lack fear' and are inclined to travel permits them to
acquire 'knowledge' and to conquer hesitation; to expand familiarity
with new people and new places; and finally, to enjoy the *liget* born in
the intense and competitive equality of a peer group, while escaping the
contexts of shame, fear, and subordination that bind a woman to her
home. Eventually, these youths will move into their wives' homes when
they marry: For Ilongots, uxorilocality is consistent with the fact that
women 'stay' *(pedeg)* and receive *tuydek,* whereas men 'walk,' 'circu-
late,' and 'go afar.'

Knowledge, identity, and order

All of this has further consequences for *bēya* – the developing attitudes and identities of youths. In tracing the early development of a child's social knowledge, I spoke of the Ilongot view that those who cannot speak are vulnerable. Fearful and utterly dependent on the care and consciousness of others, they lack understanding and so cannot be named. Naming, in fact, reflects the progress of a person's identity and awareness; the variety and distinctiveness of an Ilongot's repertoire of appellations indicate a good deal about the extensiveness of his or her experience and social ties.

So *'umel,* 'little girl,' and *dungi,* 'little boy,' are universal[8] names for infants. But as children learn to speak and to respond to *tuydek,* they are further differentiated, receiving names that may last throughout their lives. Often marked by a distinguishing sense or sound – a simple repetition, as in Mimi and Pengpeng; or as in Buy (English "boy") and Bibi (English "baby"), a semantic link with youth – these first names tend to be transcended by what will be a 'true' name sometime before the child reaches the second decade of his or her life. 'True' names tend to be unique within a *bērtan* or extended local kin group of between 100 and 300 persons. Anyone can give these names and chance determines whether names acquired through play or casual talk 'become familiar' *(tagde)* and take hold. Some 'true' names have no meaning. Some – like Watil, from the English "water," or Natu, a name acquired because the parents heard and liked Renato Rosaldo's 'American' appellation – are chosen because an adult likes their sound. But probably some fifty percent of people's names are said to 'climb on' senses that concern details of killing, formal talk, or marriage – and these are generally understood to reflect upon the social character of the child's father. They may be names like Burur, 'flame,' or Si'rat, 'to light a fire,' which bespeak a parent 'hot' with 'anger,' or, like Kerisan, 'disappointment,' a name commemorating the failure of a father's rival to win the woman who became Kerisan's mother and his father's wife. Mayat, a woman we knew well, had been named in thoughts of oratorical indirection: *pengimayat mad purung,* 'to make riddles in oratory,' suggesting verbal art.

> Sili, 'chili pepper' – from my name in English, Shelly – indicated to Wadeng that my father had been a man of 'burning' energy and strength. When I protested that it was I who 'burned like chili,' Wadeng said that all names 'climb upon' the father, and as my name suggested 'anger,' it could not have been a woman that was implicated by its sound.

Although not all 'true' names have meaning, all tend to be interpreted with reference not to the child, but to those adults who give and use its name.

With age, the relation of a person to the names that he or she is called by will be altered. To hide from spirits or from soldiers, a person fearing illness or arrest may invent new self-appellations:

> Takiwag was called Tagdēy, the name of an object used in headhunting celebrations, until illness led him to change his name in hopes of *tengkiwag ma ngired,* 'doing away with illness.' Nguyek's original name, Tappeng, was similarly abandoned in a period of illness; out of hope to deceive spirits that pursued him, he was renamed after the words of oratory: *nguyeknguyek 'ita 'upu,* 'the abundance of words.'

In youthful years, 'true' maidens and bachelors who dislike their childhood titles will often think up new ones to copy friends or signify such attributes as fierceness, youth, and grace – or, more recently, the salvation promised by the Bible – which correspond more closely to the reputation they desire.

> Dungi had been called Tungan, from *Si tungan ma ra'nupsin namasi,* 'The foreheads of those who killed bear ornaments,' but when in bachelor years he found no opportunity to take a head, he insisted that he be called Dungi, 'little boy,' and so remind his senior kin that as an unaccomplished novice he was still a child.
>
> Badil was known for some time as Tukgageng until he met another by that name and found that he didn't like him. He then encouraged others to call him Tukbaw, 'beak, hornbill headpiece for headhunters' – a name used along with his 'true' name, Badil, today.

Furthermore, as siblings marry, alternate names, or at least verbal disguises whereby, for example, Bimaru becomes Bē'ru, and Wagi becomes Paniswagiyan – become essential because of taboos on naming the consanguines of a spouse. In fact, it is through use of such alternative appellations that a bachelor who comes to work and visit in the home of a desired bride makes known to all his hopes to have her as his wife.

> 'Udi was thinking ahead to the time when a son-in-law would need to call her by an alternate name when she chose to be called Likya. She took the name from a friendly woman in a distant group because her husband's alternate name, Purung, or 'oratory,' was the name of the original Likya's husband. When she did this, the woman in question decided to reciprocate and take 'Udi's name, and her husband began to be known as 'dance' or Tagem, the 'true' name of 'Udi's husband.

Finally, as one travels and builds friendships with same-sexed agemates and companions, reciprocal names – like *kabundusil,* 'fellow bulldozer,' commemorating an attack on men engaged in roadwork; *kabuaya,* 'fellow crocodile,' for two men who have killed together and know each other to be strong; *nadēpa'an,* 'scented,' to commemorate a large deer caught by dogs while hunting; or *'inarem,* 'depths,' for two closely related women who had sworn to keep bad feelings buried in their hearts – replace one's real name with selected friends. These latter, though available to both sexes, are most common among men who use reciprocal names to keep alive the memory of their prowess; and it is through reciprocal naming that in-married husbands can avoid the asymmetrical prohibition on using the names of would-be 'equal' affines in the homes where, after marriage, they reside.[9]

Men, moving more widely, have more names than most women. But the important point, for both sexes, is that as people enter their late teens and create for the first time a network of ties to those who may be future affines, allies, and friends, they shift from being youngsters whose names and social identities were determined by the character and relations of their parents, to the 'knowing' shapers of their own biographies – in important ways, the namers of themselves. This development in the nature of identity corresponds to a shift in social attitudes, or 'knowledge,' from the infant's unknowing fear and profound dependence to the 'shamed' subordination that is encouraged in a growing child; what remains to be discussed is the last step in this progress, the movement toward an increased understanding and control of social situations, which underlies the cooperative interactions of adults. As with names and peer-group orientation, this last development is less marked for women than for men.

Earlier in this chapter, I spoke of the way in which an infant's 'fear' becomes in the young child an attitude of 'respect' or 'shame' before his elders – an attitude that accompanies his receiving names and attending to and learning from increasingly demanding *tuydek* or commands. 'Shame' and 'fear' are not identical, but in Ilongot thought they tend to go together: 'Fear' of parents inclines a child to be respectful and obedient; simultaneously, the lack of 'knowledge' that makes for 'shame' before a senior is also associated with feelings of confusion and with 'fear.' It would now appear that women, whom 'fear' keeps close to home and at the service of their elders, are more likely than men – by Ilongot logic – to retain these attitudes throughout their lives.

Although Ilongots readily remark that women have more 'fear' than men, they are reluctant to speak of women as people who surpass men in their *bētang.* In fact, many of the adults best known for 'shame/respect' or *bētang* are themselves not shy and quiet but highly respected and articulate older men. This is because the *bētang* of an adult is not the sort of thing that 'shame' is for a child. *Bētang* may in certain contexts derive from slights or consciousness of limitation – in which case, one may say, as is commonly the case for children, *'Embētang,* 'He/she is ashamed.'

But for adults, one most often speaks of 'shame' that is possessed or is lacking, and just as 'having no shame' (*'Away bētangtu,* 'He/she has no shame') points to lapses in a cooperative orientation, so 'having shame' (*si bētang,* 'to have shame,' or *'ubētang,* 'to be shameful') suggests an attitude of humility *(tu'ngan)* and 'admiration' *(dēgiw),* a readiness to cooperate with those whom Ilongots see as 'equal-to-us-humans' (*'anurutsin tu'u*) – what we would call our "fellowmen." Delicacy in interaction, the ability to avoid conflict and dispute, a sense of burning pain in the face of untoward violence, a willingness to resign oneself when it makes no sense to fight – all of these, for Ilongots, display that one has *bētang.* And this sort of 'shame' is something one acquires as much in competition with one's equals as in the fear of elders; it is learned less from obedience toward seniors than from the mutuality and cooperation that underlie successful interaction with one's peers and friends.

The experience of a peer group provides youths of both sexes with a sense of the importance of mutual emulation and the delicacy of a group's achieved equality – in part by generating an awareness of the envy, energy, and 'anger' that are born in oneself and others when equality is violated or breached. For bachelors in particular, the 'higher' *bēya* that creates their peership produces at the same time a more intense capacity for *liget* and disruptive action than any they have known. From peers, they learn to think of killing: The sight of young men 'just like others' who wear headhunters' hornbill earrings weighs the heart with vicious envy; the thought that someone 'otherwise my equal' can love and win a sister or a woman one had thought to 'talk to' may itself be the immediate stimulus to raid. Anxious for recognition and assertive in the company of fellows of their age, bachelors become sensitive as well to the lack of parity between themselves and men who are their seniors. Irked by hierarchy in the home, they sulk and rage, sing quietly by themselves or lounge in hammocks; they spend long days alone and restless, preoccupied with a flute from which they hope to sigh out music, or, more simply, remain self-absorbed. Many married men have told me that, in fury, they used to bark commands at tired sisters, break pots, tear trays, spill water, and toss out their food. And, of course, when Burur slashed the footbridge that his aunt used to fetch her household's water, his actions – though extreme and unquestionably upsetting – were seen in much this light; they had the quality of opaque, unthinking violence expected in a young man whose heart is set on killing, and possible in any 'quick,' unmarried and unsettled, envious, and still dependent youth.

For youths, the desire to be recognized as an equal and one's capacity for 'angry violence grow together. But these develop at the same time that one achieves a social identity relatively independent of one's parents and learns to value friendship, cooperation, and the company of peers. Aware that others, like themselves, are sensitive to insult, youths learn, as children never can, to 'forget' or to 'resign *(kinurud, kesiran)* their hearts to minor slights and disappointments, to 'leave off' *(kemnu),* 'diffuse' *(ringring),* or 'give up on' *('adug)* anger when there is no cause to give offense. Because they are involved in building ties with 'equal quick ones,' youths learn not only to compete and show off 'energy,' or *liget,* but also to respect the independent hearts of equals, avoid uncalled-for ostentation, and demonstrate new kinds of 'shame.'

Unlike the 'shame/respect' or *bētang* of a child, which implies compliance, the *bētang* of adults is thus identified with *dēgiw,* or 'admiration,' and with *tu'ngan,* an attitude of 'humility' that is not embarrassed but that hesitates to dominate or offend. A matter of mutual acknowledgment, and the respect that comes from recognition of another's thoughtfulness or skill, *dēgiw* is, like *tu'ngan,* a mature variety of the child's submissive stance before its seniors. But if a child's 'shame' is born of fear and feelings of subordination, these later attitudes come from an appreciation of the claims of people who can be upset or hurt and angered – of people who are, in essence, like oneself. So, *tu'ngan* keeps one from issuing commands to equals, seniors, and also – for most women – to one's husband; it makes it difficult to criticize, fault, or interrupt a peer or friend. *Tu'ngan* prevents the heart from getting 'restless' *(kalikal)* as one sits for days at the sickbed of a kinsman; and it tells members of a settlement to avoid work and follow the restrictions imposed by neighbors who must mourn a recent death.

Similarly, *dēgiw* is the sort of thing that killers and nonkillers alike should feel in acknowledging another man's beheading; it is the stance that permits a would-be husband to let a senior who is knowledgeable in oratory 'lend his tongue' and verbal prowess to the suitor's cause. To *dēgiw* is to admire not those who would 'cause admiration' *(pedgēdgiw,* 'cause *dēgiw')* – through dress or gossip, 'self-conscious show' *(mega'maga, 'agal'agal),* or the 'belittling' of another's worth *(bēngen)* – but rather to appreciate the knowledge of a person whose heart inclines to shame and balance and whose skills (in song or medicine, oratory or crafts) facilitate collective pleasure and success. Although a synonym for *dēgiw – qegē,* a word whose primary sense is 'giddiness, dizziness, as from a height' – suggests that even this sort of admiration is experienced as disruptive to Ilongot equality, Ilongots will themselves insist that adults who 'know' are capable of appreciation without envy or the shame that leads to untoward *liget;* in mature relations based on *bēya,* recognition of another's talent is compatible with good feeling, cooperation, and mutual respect.

Dēgiw and *tu'ngan* are matters of accommodation – based not on hierarchy but on a desire to appreciate one's companions, and so avoid intrusion and disruptive stress. Involving more of delicacy and resignation than active demonstrations of fellowship and goodwill, they are grounded in what struck me as one of the most poignant and consistent features of Ilongot reflection: a despair of knowing or controlling the private motions of another's 'equally human' heart. The Ilongot world at once denies all claims to precedence and yet requires nonetheless that kinsmen work together in an atmosphere of mutuality and agreement; although permitting all adults a sense of privacy and independence, it may demand as well that people act as 'of one body' and recognize a single speaker as their common 'tongue.' In such a world, appropriate forms of accommodation are both necessary and the height of wisdom. Just as, when hiking on narrow trails, people follow one another and one person takes the lead, so, in social life, well-being and cooperation demand that each participant – without surrendering self-respect or personal autonomy – 'make way' for other people's knowledge, skills, and needs. As will be clear in later chapters, the sense of balance involved in being 'shameful,' combined with the 'anger' that protects one's interests from abuse – the very attitudes that youth must learn in peer groups – constitute, in their tension, the stuff of Ilongot maturity; they are the essence of the 'knowledge' of adults.

Not hierarchy or order in the sense of a fixed model of eternal process, social precedence, and place, but a deep respect for others as 'equal-to-us-humans' and potentially cooperating friends and kin – this is, I have been suggesting, the core of the *bēya,* or 'knowledge,' acquired and internalized by Ilongot children as they are growing up. The idea of *bēya* includes a number of features of adult identity and competence: skill, strength, speech, and understanding; a relative lack of fear and a capacity to stimulate and control 'anger' and disruption; physical prowess and a lively and cooperative network of social ties. *Bēya* develops as the child moves from vulnerability to independence, from a lack of awareness to an understanding of the needs articulated by others, and ultimately to an ability to initiate and take responsibility for action on his own. It involves a shift from passivity to movement, from childlike 'fear' and 'shame' to adult 'humility' and 'admiration,' and from subordination to equality with peers. Ilongots characterize the growth of 'knowledge' in terms of physical skills – sitting, walking, pounding rice and cooking, climbing trees, and killing game – which permit a person to move, without fear, beyond the confines of the familiar; and they symbolize its progress in expectations concerning *tuydek* and the various processes by which one acquires and changes names.

Finally, Ilongot views of the ideal development of the person support their sense that 'knowledge' can, itself, be far less fully realized in the hearts of women than of men. Adult women, as we will see, are said to 'know less' than their husbands, to have seen fewer places, and to be more inclined to display their lack of knowledge in misunderstandings and rude speech. Because experience has given them less cause for *liget,* and the necessities of domestic work and *tuydek* have reinforced an inclination to be constrained by 'fear,' women seem without exception to 'lack knowledge' in the dual sense of lacking familiarity with things distant and of failing to 'know,' or act in terms of, the threat of violence generated in groups of would-be peers. For men, on the other hand, increased movement leads to ever increasing 'knowledge,' the conquest of the 'fear' that limits children and the 'heightened' *liget* that makes for personal autonomy and continued growth. As they move beyond the household, men 'come to know' the skills and self-respect that permit a severing of dependent ties to elders; and in the company of agemates they experience the birth of new names, new social attitudes, and new kinds of social bonds.

Men's *bēya* – shaped through childhood with its *tuydek* and the mutual emulation that marks the 'quickened' teens – continues to develop as they become adults. With marriage, the birth of children, and the establishment of stable affinal ties and claims, men become ever less concerned to demonstrate their 'anger' and equivalence with others, and more interested in maintaining balance and mutuality in the local interactions that make up daily life. No longer dependent on the favors of a senior (a man who, as husband or as father, can direct the women who cultivate, cook, and serve one's daily rice), the man who 'knows' can himself determine how the game he kills will be distributed; unlike the youthful hunter, he is now said to understand enough about social relationships to take responsibility for *bēret,* 'sharing' – both of food and of *liget,* cooperative sociality and vengeful strife. Cautious, 'slow' to speak, respectful – and, if wise, attentive to the silences as well as to the voiced wishes of those with whom he shares – such a man will hesitate to slight another. But although informed by 'shame,' or *bētang,* he rarely performs an act of deference, shows compliance, begs when he is lacking, or gives voice to a complaint. All of these are activities acceptable in a woman, but problematic for the man who, in preserving social balance, would not himself lose face. Ilongots assume that a mature man's 'knowledge' will distinguish him from women, youths, and children; the guardian (and, in some sense, the foundation) of his position in a world of equals, this 'knowledge' is, at the same time, the regulator of the 'anger,' 'passion,' and potential conflict that his world creates.

Conclusion: 'Knowledge,' Burur, and his aunt

What *bēya* means for adult men in their often tense relations with one another is a topic I will explore at length in later chapters. My interest here was rather to show how, for Ilongots of whatever age or sexual status, the growth of 'knowledge' is construed in similar terms. It involves the simultaneous development of understanding and of feeling, of social attitudes, linguistic competence, and technical skill. The forms and complexity of *bēya* depend, in large part, on the experience of the actor – the distances he has traveled, the challenges confronted, the relationships in which he has engaged. And insofar as these experiences are shaped by the contradictory impulses of a culture that values 'anger' on the one hand, and, on the other, prescribes an ideally cooperative and egalitarian social life, the progress of the *bēya* that will rule them is apt to be marked by characteristic sorts of strain. The important point seems to be that whether Ilongots are reflecting on the raging tears of an insulted child or discussing serious quarrels among onetime adult friends, they use the same ideas, words, and associations – the same assumptions about the nature of disruption and of 'knowledge,' of 'passion' and how it is controlled – to make sense of what is going on. What differs with variations in age, sex, and context is not, for them, a matter of human "nature," but rather the intensity and organization of human experience. What changes is not simply one's capacities for feeling, but instead the ways that feelings are themselves informed by people's consciousness of others – and, in particular, by awareness of such consequences as emerge when potentially disruptive feelings manage to escape our conscious regulation and control.

For infants, we have seen that disruptive motions in the heart may lead to heart loss. For older children, heart loss is a possibility, but so too is new 'knowledge' and an understanding of the personal limitations that caused one to be frustrated, 'teased,' or 'given over to' an unhappy contest or a fight. With maturity, however, 'disruptive feelings' *(pa'nun)* take on a new potential. Just as, for 'truly quick ones,' focused *liget* may lead to work, enthusiasm, song, and the beauty Ilongots realize when they celebrate beheadings, so chaotic forms of 'anger' can occasion competition and destruction, stress and physical violence among once cooperative kin and friends. To conclude this chapter, I would like to look again at the incident in which Burur slashed the footbridge that his aunt used to get water. Her potential death trap – the product of his youthful *liget* and still partial *bēya* – points to the real threat in Ilongot life of challenges that subject both property and persons to chaotic violence. But it also illuminates their opposite: the order that, for Ilongots, depends on 'knowledge' and through which the destructive potential of an unruly 'passion' may come to be subordinated to the requirements of an ongoing social world.

Three sorts of behavior are available to Ilongot adults as ways of dealing with severe disruptions. Each implies a slightly different view of the offense and the offender, and therefore a different use of 'knowledge' in ordering the social world. Whether the disturbance is individual, as in the case of illness, or more or less public, as was Burur's challenge to his aunt – is less important than the ways one is related to and can manipulate a recognized disruptive 'source.' Thus, *bēret*, here meaning 'vengeance' and 'contagion' – the discharge of misfortune or bad feeling by casting it outside oneself – is invoked in explaining and curing illnesses that come from plants whose *liget* was unleashed by accidental cutting; it is the principle used in spells that threaten to sicken an afflicting spirit 'in exchange' for making someone ill. Again, in social terms, Ilongot friends would often speak as though there were a finite quantity of 'evil' or 'bad fortune' *(uget)* in the world that is communicated through 'vengeance' *(bēret)*. And persons who would do away with *'uget* caused, most typically, by the experience of death or illness, were thus inclined to visit strangers, and perhaps, encourage youths to take a head – so casting their misfortune elsewhere, lightening their own hearts, and protecting the good health and welfare of their kin and friends. Ideally, *'uget* should not simply be 'cast off,' but like a curse or illness, be 'reciprocated' or 'returned' *(tubrat)* to the original offender. And so it is that people who decide they will 'reciprocate' or *bēret*, 'take revenge,' can, in effect, undo misfortune by transferring their bad feelings 'back' to their initial source. Finally, *bēret* in the form of killing and beheading is an appropriate response to insult, threat, or murder visited by an enemy on one's local group of kin.

> Typically, *bēret* takes the form of feuds (see Chapter 6). Thus Luku led a raid to kill and take the heads of members of the Butag *bērtan* because they were known to have threatened the life of his father years before. Maniling joined in the same raid with hopes to *bēret* because he held Butag men responsible for the arrest of his father. In some cases, *bēret*, or 'vengeance,' has been taken by calling soldiers to arrest people who have killed one's kinfolk. In others, in-married men have been killed or threatened because kin of theirs have, over the years, been held accountable for the death or insult of relations of the local residential group.

Because Burur was the nephew of the woman he offended, *bēret* on her part would have been possible only if she and her husband had been willing to define themselves as enemies of their neighboring relations – people with whom they were in fact closely and cooperatively linked.

The second possibility, *'aked*, 'to give' a gift or an indemnatory payment, permits Ilongots to acknowledge a breach in ties, a hint of social distance or of tension, while at the same time reaffirming the positive bases of future relations with recipient friends or kin. Distant relatives who visit are 'given' (*'ising*) money, pots, or ornaments as a way of 'making known' their kinship; husbands, in certain circumstances, will give gifts as an apology for beating or otherwise offending angry wives. Punlan, who infuriated me by spending two months at a distant sawmill when he had agreed to help me translate texts, never excused himself or said that he was sorry; rather than satisfy my desire that he admit his violation, he appeared smiling at our house as if nothing had happened, and handed me something he knew I wanted: a beautifully carved and decorated wooden spoon.

Gifts to spirits are intended to oblige their aid and effort in catching game or conquering an illness; gifts to a woman's kinfolk (*langu*) or her unsuccessful suitors help to silence any 'anger' they might feel toward the man who takes her as his spouse.

> 'Adēlpig, having 'stepped ahead' of Tukbaw and taken Biya, Tukbaw's first wife, as his own, gave Tukbaw a brass pot to appease his *liget*. Tukbaw reported years later that had 'Adēlpig been less closely related (they were second cousins) he would have sought to *bēet* and killed him instead. Slights occasioned by competition for a woman have in the past led to such violent 'vengeance,' as when Bangkiwa killed some distant kinfolk of Tepeg to *bēret* for the latter's marrying a woman he had courted. When Tupek won a bride pursued by Ranit, he satisfied the latter's hope to *bēret* by leading him on a headhunting expedition and 'giving' him a head – so reaffirming, in this case, that the two men were not enemies, but kin.

And finally, it is through gifts to victims (*bēyaw*) that enemies 'discover' (*bimaya,* 'come to know') kinship, 'dissolve' past insults and beheadings, forge covenants, and terminate old feuds. Whereas acceptance of a gift implies a willingness to forget the *liget* that was its occasion, the absence of exchanges (especially after killings) indicates that tensions remain vital beneath quotidian surfaces and external calm. In fact, for Ilongots, it was unintelligible that American soldiers could befriend the Japanese with whom they fought in World War II without indemnatory exchanges – and equally peculiar that, after accepting the spoon that Punlan gave me, I remained unsatisfied and acted moody and annoyed.

Why it was decided that Burur did not 'know' about such payments, why he was not asked to satisfy his aunt with a small gift, is something I did not explore through interviews at the time. But in retrospect, I imagine that Ilongot reasoning was twofold. First, because he was a youth, still lacking *bēya* – a boy who 'knew how' to hunt but not how to butcher and distribute game – Burur did not have the wherewithal for a significant 'gift' to answer 'anger.' And second, reliance on his father or some other senior kinsman would have turned a bit of youthful folly into a political event among adults. This is because giving, although an affirmation of positive ties, is at the same time an acknowledgment of their near– and therefore, possible– dissolution. And in the instance in question, the aunt's recent marriage to a man from a distant kin group made it likely that a gift from Burur's parents would lead to unwanted friction with her spouse. Luckily, Burur's youth made it easy for a third option– the most appropriate with kinsmen – to be invoked.

For Ilongots, what turned out to be important about Burur's challenge to his aunt's immediate environment, and potentially to her survival, was not his personality or motives, not the "causes" of his action, but rather, the youthful ignorance of his heart. Burur's lack of *beya* meant that his threatening deed lacked 'focus,' permitting senior kin to treat his violence much as they might the wild actions of a man whose heart 'relaxes' (*ringring*) under liquor – but who, when sober, is assumed to 'come to know' that he offended kinsmen and to feel 'ashamed.' Such a man is rarely faulted for his acts.

> Tepdurak, a man from the Tamsi *bertan,* had appealed to Rumyad men of our acquaintance as distant kinsmen who should display their 'knowledge' of relation by helping him procure a bridewealth payment for his wife. Decked with goods, we went with him to Tamsi, but Tepdurak's own marginality in the Tamsi area, along with a certain awkwardness about his newfound Rumyad ties, meant that the timing of the bridewealth meeting was never specified– and our arrival in Tamsi was greeted with the 'anger' of a father-in-law who claimed to be unprepared for formal talk. That evening, our initial difficulties were only partially resolved when the men started drinking. Laput, Tepdurak's Rumyad 'brother,' said something that the latter interpreted as an insult about his size. Tepdurak jumped up and hit Laput; then, thanks to the alert response of others present, the two men were quieted and pulled apart. Throughout the night, people muttered about the unfortunate and rather 'shameful' incident, but all insisted that no indemnity would be asked of Tepdurak because when sober in the morning he would come again to 'know' of kinship and find himself ashamed. When I probed to learn if Tepdurak's violence did not reflect much deeper– and probably, enduring, tensions– people said that no, it was drink that did away with *beya* and so made him wild. And in any case, they told me, it was silly to ask such questions because one never knows what 'flows' inside another's heart.

In an earlier chapter, I suggested that Ilongots rarely question the reasons for any action, and that talk of private hearts, their motions and intentions, implies either illness or a judgment of disapproval (as of an abusive soldier, a stingy trader, or an enemy who is violent, coarse, and wild) – a breakdown in once lively social bonds.

> When Pudnga, the newly married son of Begtek, an older man in our settlement, violated assumptions that in fact permit both sexual play

and physical intimacy among cross-generation kin by trying to seduce a niece when she was alone in her mother's garden, all talk of his 'crazy' (*pa'nun*) nature, his way of being 'volatile' and 'unreliable' (*simusimu, sawasawa*), was silenced almost as soon as it had been proposed. Pudnga's mother had in fact been insane when she died some years previously – and some proposed resemblances between the mother and her son. But in this case, tensions between Pudnga's father and other local kin were probably too great to tolerate either gossip or public confrontation. Decrying talk of Pudnga's 'heart' or "nature," Bēgtek's 'brothers' said that Pudnga was a young man, lacking *bēya;* they proclaimed themselves 'ashamed' to raise the matter with his father, and urged instead that the mother of the girl – who had cried out that her heart was 'torn' with horror – herself arrange a conference and, perhaps, request a gift from the erring 'child.'

To label or accuse the hearts of others – possible when people who have been cooperatively engaged 'look elsewhere' and begin to draw apart – is disturbing and inappropriate in dealing with people who, as kin and neighbors, 'lend' their care and labor and share in the concerns that shape one's local world. For Ilongots, talk of motives is an acknowledgment of distance. And so, in Burur's case, the fact of close connection with his parents, as well as the unmotivated moodiness and *liget* expected in a youth, all led to a desire to avoid further confrontation by stressing not his history or intentions, but the things he didn't know.

Given Ilongot understandings of the nature of personal development and the growth of knowledge, it was possible to find in Burur's action (however cruel and disturbing) nothing more peculiar than the 'anger' displayed by kinsmen who engage in drunken fights. Of the latter, it is said that sobriety will restore awareness of relation, giving rise to 'shame' for shows of violence that could 'serve no purpose' and to the sort of 'knowledge' that causes tensions to dissolve. Similarly, with Burur it was thought (and, having seen him some five years later, I think, correctly) that he would refrain from untoward violence when he came to 'know' and 'understand' the pointlessness of conflict among kin.

If 'vengeance' deals with disruption through the focusing of 'anger' on an object, and 'giving' subordinates past grievances to the present satisfactions of exchange – neither is appropriate to those close and confident relationships that govern daily social life. Cooperative interactions among kinfolk dictate, on the contrary, that the best way to deal with local insults and disruptions is (whenever possible) to forget them. Rather than 'cast off' one's *liget,* one ignores it – 'resigns' oneself (*kinurud*), finds 'patience' (*pasinsia,* cf. Spanish *paciencia*), 'diffuses' (*ringring*) feelings of disturbance, and avoids public dispute:

'*Unlegem kami 'umpasinsia ten 'ed mide pasiya,*
'We'll just be patient because we wouldn't kill them.'

Just as Tepeg, when caught by surprise in a windstorm, fell asleep in order to 'diffuse' or *ringring* a tormenting sense of fear, so a woman may 'diffuse' feelings of *liget* toward her husband by spending a quiet night by herself beneath a granary in her garden. So too, Ilongots abandon houses where kin have died and suffered illness – not to flee obnoxious spirits, but to *ringring* their misfortune; and sick people visit homes of friends and neighbors to 'diffuse' the internal upset that an 'angry' spirit brought. Disappointed, distressed, and tired by the conduct of a covenant that had absorbed his verbal talents for two long and noisy days, Tukbaw – a man known for his 'knowledge' – left our party and went into the forest, in order (as he told it) to *ringring* a sense of chaos born of crowded rooms and heated talking, to 'cool' his overly excited heart.

Not confrontation, but avoidance and the lessening of pressures, an 'end' to the heart's desires, and an attitude of 'tolerance' (*'adug*) toward those who may 'know' too little to avoid a fight – all of these are aspects of the ordinary stance of calm and resignation necessary in local life and interaction, and more generally desirable in the 'knowlegeable' conduct of a mature adult. When asked to give examples of the uses of *'adug*, a word that means to 'tolerate,' 'accept,' or 'bear,' teenage boys consistently wrote of 'tolerating' the cries of infants, demands of elders, and insults voiced by peers; one 'accepts' and tries to minimize disruptive feelings born of ordinary human interaction – just as the responsible and 'knowing' worker 'accepts' or tolerates the burden of steep paths and heavy packs, damp chills in the forest, and piercing sunlight in a ripened field. The point seems to be that Ilongots, although they acknowledge the value of 'energy' and 'passion,' stress motion and activity, and cast *liget* as the source of beauty and of life, are at the same time acutely conscious of the need for patience and endurance, and fearful of the disruptive consequences wrought by 'anger' uncontrolled. Their concern for intense feeling is paralleled by a cultural stress on delicacy, constancy, and resignation: the sort of 'shame' that grows with 'knowledge,' the calm that can survive a turn of fortune, and the sense of balance, trust, and mutuality that lends a gay and generally cooperative spirit to the mundane work of life.

In arguing that the core of Ilongot *bēya* involves respect for other people, a sense of care and balance, and a readiness (as far as possible) to 'diffuse' disruptive feelings, and to avoid conflict and dispute, I do not claim that Ilongot social life lacks violence – any more than my discussion of the ways in which Ilongots found sense and beauty in focused forms of *liget* made a claim for the reverse. Nor would I portray the realities of Ilongot experience in terms of a simple oscillation – with 'knowledge,' calm, and resignation at one pole, and 'angry' and intense excitement at the opposite. The Ilongot social world – like any other – takes shape for actors through an infinity of specific variations: the child's often uneasy education, crises like the one induced by Burur, Tukbaw's shows of tolerance and wisdom, the intensity of public celebration, and the joyous experience of a peer group, in which both *bēya* and *liget,* cooperation and mutual emulation, appear to be combined. As tools for understanding and guides for conduct that at once reflect the order in their lives and help to shape it, 'knowledge' and 'passion' provide Ilongots with interpretations of a world that has its share of violence, misfortune, and disruption. They describe and give significance to lives in which potentially disturbing 'passions' must be 'diffused' by 'knowledge,' but lives that at the same time require 'focus' and 'concentration,' and that encourage youthful *liget* as a source of energy and vitality.

Bēya organizes affective life; it grows along with *liget*. But the *bēya* that is supposed to govern daily ties inclines, in adult years, to minimize more intense feelings born of emulation – inhibiting 'focused' bursts of vigor and of effort which, although dangerous, are also necessary and desirable. *Bēya* makes for evenness and calm, whereas *liget* is an ever present source of tension and disruption. And though the two should work together in an ideal heart, Ilongot social life is organized in ways that limit both the 'anger' and the 'knowledge' found in women, and furthermore distinguish between the violent and disruptive hearts of youths like Burur, and the calmer, though once 'angry,' thoughts of mature and married men. In the chapters to follow, it is these differences between persons that will concern us. Having explored some of the developmental issues which, in the Ilongot view, differentiate men from women, I turn in subsequent discussions to questions of how 'knowledge' and 'passion' acquire significance – first, in everyday labor and cooperation, and then in the public, ritualized forms of headhunting and oratory, activities that link men's *liget* to their marriages, and so, again, to their relationships with women, at the same time that they illuminate both the interdependence and the inequality that characterize relationships between youths and older men.

4. Horticulture, hunting, and the 'height' of men's hearts

Ilongots says that men's hearts are 'higher' then women's, meaning that men surpass women in *liget* and *bēya,* capacities that – as I have already suggested – provide much of life's challenge and sense. Because of certain characteristics of a young man's experience – his fearlessness and his propensity to movement, his skill, strength, and contact with peers – both 'passion' and 'knowledge,' energy and the mature sort of judgment that gives energy purpose and form, are apt to find their fullest expression in the lives not of women, but of men. To label men 'angry' may not, to our lights, be surprising. But when Ilongots say that men's hearts 'exceed' those of women, they are concerned not with "natural" dictate but with the social and moral ordering of a particular style of life.

Ilongot talk about the kinds of hearts and persons in their world appears, in short, to be concerned not simply with the ways that people are assumed to feel and think, but with how and why they organize their actions. And the Ilongot equation of desired strength and wisdom in men's hearts bespeaks not simply the experience of youths, but even more the organization of adult political life, and of productive roles and patterns of cooperation in Ilongot society at large. Having traced, at least in part, the bases of men's special claims in childhood development, I turn here to a consideration of the ways in which culturally organized differences between the sexes are made salient in the activities that constitute their daily lives. Relations between the sexes are understood by Ilongots in terms of the differences and similarities in men's and women's hearts; and the emotional bents of men and women are, in turn, at once occasioned by and revealed within the kinds of work they do.

It was Duman, the productive and articulate mother of six healthy children, who first directed my investigations. 'Women,' she said, 'cannot "reach" a man's strength and "anger"'; look at the way they climb trees and carry huge logs; do you think we could garden if men did not go before us clearing the forest; do you think I understand all of

99

the twists and turns of men's talk?' Women may, she admitted, differ in skill, speech, and wisdom. Some, like herself, may be known for their 'straight,' thoughtful voices, for the size and success of their gardens – or, in their husbands' absence, they may show that they know how to hunt. But no woman attains a man's prowess; none 'goes around' all the thoughts and experiences, the curves and the depths, of men's hearts.

What Duman meant by her statement – or, more broadly, what it is about Ilongot life and experience that makes accounts like hers of male/female relations seem telling and apt – is the prime concern of this chapter. Rather than ask, as in previous discussion, how *liget* and *bēya* "work" in Ilongot talk and reflection, I turn here to a closer consideration of some relationships and activities in terms of which these concepts are interpreted and to which they are made to apply. From a consideration of some things Ilongots say about men and women, I will proceed to an exploration of Ilongot conceptions of men's and women's activities as these are represented in the imagery of hunting and horticultural magic, and realized in the organization of productive labor itself. My goal is to show that the things men and women characteristically do in the forest and garden lend notions like 'knowledge' and 'passion' much of their immediate coherence and relevance – while, at the same time, these concepts shape people's understandings and evaluations of everyday action and turn potentially problematic expressions of male dominance into the obvious and inevitable consequences of everyday life.

Duman's characterization of male superiority came in response to a question about men's leadership on public contexts. We were discussing the recent growth of Christianity among Ilongots, and I asked her, with smug indignation, why churches – with which she was not sympathetic – were unambiguously dominated by men. To my surprise, she saw nothing to fault here: She found in the Christian belief that links women to Eve – the world's first and most culpable sinner – an obvious and unquestioned sense. She claimed to understand things less readily than her husband, to depend on his 'knowledge' and judgment, and, in speaking, to be more inclined than most men to misunderstanding and unintended offense. Her view that male 'quickness' (*'awet*) and 'force' make men a group's rightful 'leaders' was echoed by others who told me that women have 'vague' (*sawasawa*) hearts, whereas men's hearts have 'focus' (*'upug*), or again, that young and recalcitrant wives who refuse to perform household chores or to follow male wishes must learn to attend to their husbands. Wives must accept the 'commands' (*tuydek*) of their spouses because men and not women 'throw boulders,' that is, because men can take heads.

Katan said that her husband Tepeg listens to her because he fears her 'words' (*upu*), but if their hearts are really 'different' (*riwa*), she will be 'defeated' because she fears his strength. When first married, she didn't like being 'commanded' (*tuydek*) by Tepeg in the household and farted at him one day in disgust. In response, he beat her, saying: 'Just because I'm younger than you, don't think you can do that.' Since then, she has learned to obey. Duman, in the room while we were talking, explained that women 'look up to men because they have killed their equal humans.'

Yet this claim, that male force and 'anger' provide grounds for mature men's authority, was contradicted not only by my own impressions of the generally intimate and accommodating relations that obtain between spouses, but also by other things people said. Ilongots say that if women are fearful of male strength and beatings, men themselves may 'fear' their wives' angry gossip; they point out that even though men can, and do, command wives to do petty tasks in the household, women tell men when to stay at home or to travel, when to help in the gardens or to hunt. When we talked about Lundi, a widowed 'cousin' who a 'father-in-law' from some distance was hoping to wed, Duman criticized her husband's efforts to support the man's suit when the woman herself was clearly against it; or again, when we discussed a visit planned to a distant settlement, Duman guessed (as it turned out, correctly) that those men whose help was needed in family gardens would obey their wives' wishes and stay behind. Because of their 'fear' and because of men's skill in speaking, women are often persuaded to accede to male interest.

Katan tried to keep Tepeg at home to clear a path around her garden when he wanted to join others attending a meeting upstream. When Maniling stopped by the house to call for Tepeg, the latter claimed that his wife was 'stalling' him and so he could not leave. To this, Maniling responded that he would never 'pull' on Tepeg against Katan's – 'his mother's' – wishes, if it were not the case that the weather was much too poor for him to do any decent work in his fields. Katan muttered quietly, 'What could I explain to you?' so indicating that she felt herself defeated; helpless before Maniling's argument, she sent her husband on his way.

But most public decisions in fact reflect women's opinions and feelings; people remember cases in which women 'spoke right out' and so turned away hopeful suitors; and in daily life, those women who – like youths whose mere whims can decide where adults will go hunting – remain unconvinced by male rhetoric can speak in their own forthright manner and enforce strong desires of their own.

In the spring of 1974, the government-appointed local captain hoped to go to Manila with a local schoolteacher in order to petition the National Government for books and supplies. His plans, however, were thwarted by the 'angry' talk of his wife, Mayana. The captain had once promised to take Mayana to Manila, so she now refused to let him go 'equally,' without taking her. 'Insan said that the captain handled things badly by getting angry at Mayana, threatening to hit her, and so heightening her rightful intransigence; he might have done better by explaining, as he should have, that he had responsibilities and lacked the money to take her along.

'Equal humans,' like men, women may ignore or resist male assertion. And public norms of distribution and sharing constrain all demands based on force. For Ilongots, adult 'knowledge' views humans as 'equals,' casting women as men's fellow laborers and enabling adults of both sexes to voice public and recognized claims. Whatever its 'height,' no man's heart – women say – has reached heaven; nor has any man's stomach learned how to live without food. To the man who makes claims based on 'anger' or 'passion,' women respond: 'You too are a human, who must breathe, eat, and work on the ground.'

Beatings, threats, and other male shows of violence, though real, are neither approved nor common features of ongoing male/female relations[1] and although all adults know that only men hit their spouses, they explain this imbalance more in terms of women's fear and men's petulance than by invoking a hierarchy of sexual "rights." Men, with their 'higher' hearts, can command, and in some contexts, silence their women. But as people whose everyday lives involve work, sweat, and uncertain consumption – who cannot hunt, kill, or travel if women do not pound rice for them – men recognize their dependence on female care and cooperative labor. And they 'know' that they should be, like women, more concerned with production and sharing than with disruptive assertions of force.

In short, men's 'knowledge' and their 'higher' capacities for feeling are, in most contexts, shaped by the practical demands of cooperative living – and the values associated with 'knowledge' and 'passion' must be understood in this light. Ilongots say they want *liget* because without it there is no labor; they say that taking heads clears the heart of distraction, that it 'lightens' the steps of the worker, and in 'opening' hearts that were 'twisted,' leads to energy, joy, and productive success. Without finding all labor rewarding, Ilongots recognize that vitality depends on production, and for adults of both sexes the real point of health and excitement, beauty, and envious desire, is not some transcendence achieved through male violence but rather the concrete sort of energy that motivates daily work.

As hunters and horticulturalists, men and women are viewed by Ilongots as complementary producers and potential equals – each contributing his or her produce to the household diet, each receiving equivalent portions of rice and of game. Similar insofar as the labor of both demands envy and 'anger,' different because men's hearts can reach greater 'heights,' the sexes are typified for Ilongots through the style and organization of their characteristic tasks.

Horticulture

Ilongots speak not of physical "nature," but of work – which turns forest to garden, garden to rice bowl, and game in the wild to meat that accompanies meals – to explain differences between women and men. Their commonsense thought regards all men as "hunters," as 'strong' ones who 'know' and make use of the forest, whereas women appear as the 'fearful' but steady and reliable producers whose commitment to local rice fields is the constant and self-reproducing 'foundation' (*tengeg*) of family survival.

As tasks that Ilongots assign solely to women are, for neighboring swidden cultivators, the cooperative responsibility of both sexes, it is clear that their patterns of labor are hardly determined by strict technological constraints. Nor is the sexual division of labor necessarily binding and firm: Men can and do help women in the house and garden, just as women may join men on hunts. Although shaped by rocks, soils, rivers, seasonal rainfall, and the availability of game, daily work has its own reason: It reflects, on the one hand, the immediate contingencies of daily living, and on the other, a set of patterned but flexible cultural expectations that dictate that male and female activities – be they wood carving or embroidery, planting rice or stalking game – be complementary and distinct. Women, Ilongots explain, are like youths who do not know how meat should be butchered; and men, we discovered on asking, cannot name and distinguish the variously colored and flavored rice varieties they eat.

In a world that looks from the air like a mosaic of forest and garden, and feels on the ground like so many islands of individual houses separated by thickets and woodlands from gardens and neighboring homes, the contrast between cleared and forested spaces becomes an image not of culture and chaos, but of the wide and interpenetrating array of daily activities dominated by women and men. Women work in cleared spaces, the house, yard, and garden, whereas men cut down trees and engage in construction; men are fishers and hunters, foragers for wild produce who transform the forest to garden and escape to the forest (as a woman escapes to her granary) when noise and dissension disrupt daily life in their homes.

> A quarrel in the house where we were living in 1967–9 culminated in Lakay's swinging a knifehandle at Wagat, his daughter, and cutting

her scalp. Wagat left the house and went to sit and sleep under her granary, where she remained for two days in sullen silence, her coresident sister bringing her food. Tukbaw, her husband, red-eyed with 'distraction' (*'alimet*) and 'shame' (*bĕtang*) for the chaos within his own home, set off to *ringring,* or 'diffuse,' his discomfort, by spending a night in the forest; but, concerned for his wife's welfare, he returned – as hunters normally do – by dawn on the following morning.

Neither taboos nor social pressure make this contrast a strict one, but everyday practice as well as the seasonal organization of labor reinforce a division that enables Ilongots to say that the work of both sexes is 'the same' (*'anurut*) as their hearts.

> Wadeng, in an interview, remarked that women's work is repetitive and 'thorough,' 'vague' (*sawasawa*) and unfocused, 'like their hearts'; he contrasted the style of women's work in their gardens with the 'decisive' (*tu'meg*) and quick-moving efforts of men on a hunt.

The early phases of the agricultural cycle, beginning in the mild late January drizzles, involve the work of both sexes (see Figure 2). Because most married couples have their own gardens, husbands along with their competent male children are likely to clear fields for their wives. Garden selection does not appear, in most cases, to be difficult. Men choose sites near their homes or prior gardens, and establish in informal conversation such agreements as will forestall conflict with their neighbors' plans. While men begin the slow process of 'clearing' (*penguma*) the 'forest' (*kabu'an,* 'primary forest,' or *kabean,* 'secondary forest, forest with stands of miscanthus grass') for planting, women 'cut weeds' (*ramun*) and dead rice stalks from old 'standing gardens' (*'inuged*) that will be planted for a second or even a third year in rice. Slashing at underbrush, vines, small trees, and low branches, men may collect edible fungi, wild ferns, or palm and rattan hearts, which they contribute – at a time when few cultivated greens are available – to evening consumption. But their main purpose is to prepare the forest for the days from late March to mid-April when, in groups of two to ten workers, they will climb and 'pollard' (*tengdĕr*) large trees.

In pollarding, the men climb as much as 100 feet in the air to slash off the leaf canopy that shadows what will be a garden. Their rather spectacular labor, which leaves no more than mere trunks and large branches still standing, combines work and aesthetic display.

> Duman cited men's ability to climb tall trees as one proof of the height of men's hearts: *'Awana tabiyenmi ma pengkayabde 'amumura,* 'We do not reach them, equally, in their ability to climb.' Men's pollarding stood for her as one example of the ways in which women depend on men's ability to 'go first' or 'lead.'

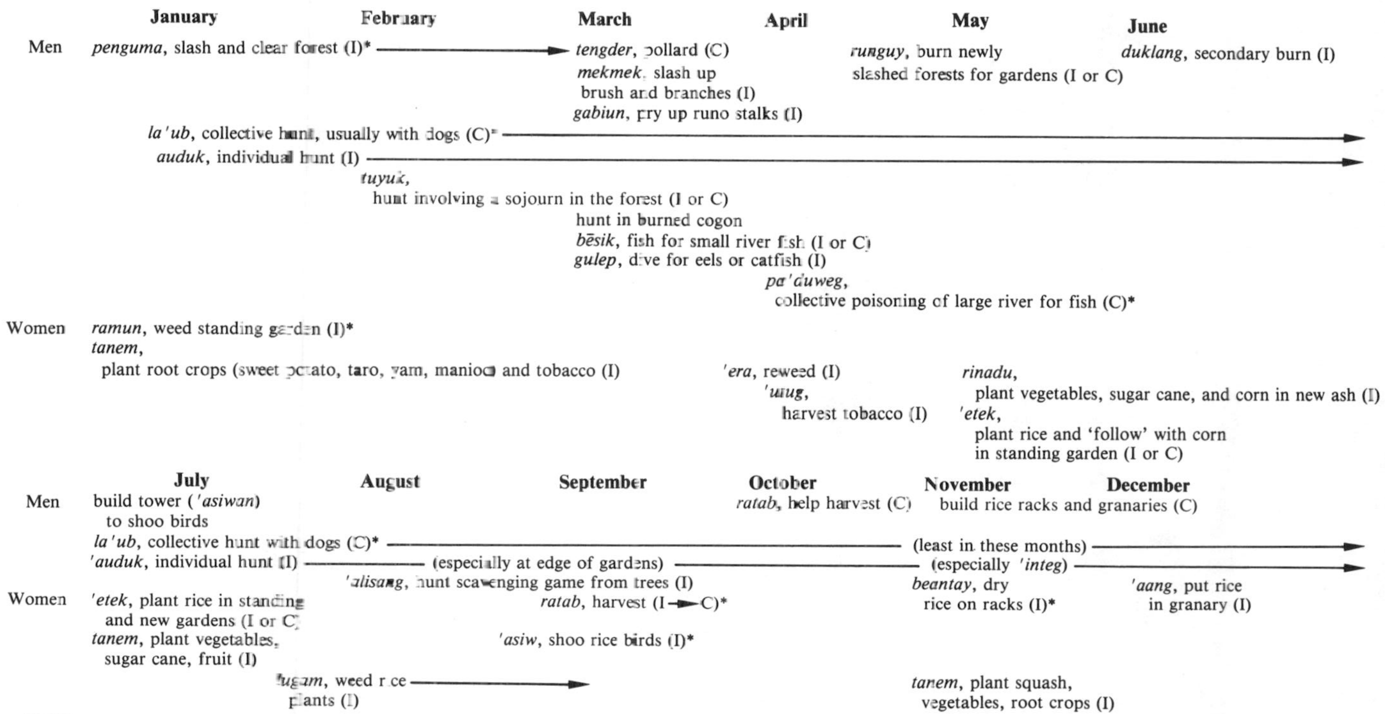

January February March April May June

Men

penguma, slash and clear forest (I)* runguy, burn newly slashed forests for gardens (I or C) duklang, secondary burn (I)

tengder, pollard (C)

mekmek, slash up brush and branches (I)

gabiun, pry up runo stalks (I)

la'ub, collective hunt, usually with dogs (C)*

auduk, individual hunt (I)

tuyuk, hunt involving a sojourn in the forest (I or C)

hunt in burned cogon

bēsik, fish for small river fish (I or C)

gulep, dive for eels or catfish (I)

pa'duweg, collective poisoning of large river for fish (C)*

Women

ramun, weed standing garden (I)*

tanem, plant root crops (sweet potato, taro, yam, manioc and tobacco (I)

'era, reweed (I)

'uug, harvest tobacco (I)

rinadu, plant vegetables, sugar cane, and corn in new ash (I)

'etek, plant rice and 'fallow' with corn in standing garden (I or C)

July August September October November December

Men

build tower ('asiwan) to shoo birds

la'ub, collective hunt with dogs (C)*

'auduk, individual hunt (I)

(especially at edge of gardens) (I)

'alisang, hunt scavenging game from trees (I)

ratab, harvest (I→C)*

ratab, help harvest (C) build rice racks and granaries (C)

(least in these months) (especially 'integ)

beantay, dry rice on racks (I)*

'aang, put rice in granary (I)

Women

'etek, plant rice in standing and new gardens (I or C)

tanem, plant vegetables, sugar cane, fruit (I)

'asiw, shoo rice birds (I)*

'ugam, weed rice plants (I)

tarem, plant squash, vegetables, root crops (I)

NOTE:

(I) indicates individual labor, with possible but not routine assistance

(C) indicates collective labor, routinely involving help from people associated with other household or gardens

* indicates occasional help from opposite sex

Figure 2. A sketch of annual productive activity

A pollarder uses his rattan tightrope as a support while 'tearing the dress' of the forest.

With rattan vines as their tightropes, the men swing from one tree to another; perched on high branches, they may pause to chew betel; and while chopping at live vegetation, they proclaim they are 'tearing the dress' of the forest, taunt youths with loud boasts of beheadings, and sing of their heights and their strength. Their grace and fine balance, the booming of songs, boasts, and dead, crashing trees – all call forth an audience of happy and appreciative women. Young girls may fetch the men containers of water to tie to a vine that the climbers hoist skyward, and when the display is finished, serve them sugarcane wine, rice, and game.

Epitomizing men's role in agricultural production, pollarding asserts male control of the forest. In no subsequent agricultural activity is their role as dramatic or marked. The laboring weeks that follow involve a far less moving (but equally trying) attempt to 'pry' (*gabiun*) heavy stumps of runo from thickets that border on newly slashed forest, 'chop up' (*mekmek*) fallen branches, and keep weeds from invading the freshly hoed fields. They must complete this work before the dry season (which began in late February) ends in mid-May. Field labor during the dry season is interrupted by fishing trips, visits, and meetings; in the past, these were the preferred months for headhunting raids. When near home, the men hunt or help their wives as they 'weed' (*ramun*) and then 'reweed' (*'era*) old gardens. With an eye to the newly cut forest, they wait for the time when the sun will have dried out dead vines and chopped branches – vegetal debris they must burn to provide an ash cover for planting before the dried refuse turns soggy with summer rains.

But 'burning' (*runguy*) itself, although spectacular to the outsider, involves neither the care nor cultural elaboration reported for other swidden populations (cf. Conklin 1957). While children toss buckets of water on the roofs of those structures that might be touched by the flames, the men call out to the Maiden, Spirit of Gardens, to flee the hot fire; then, with runo torches, they set sudden light to the dried and dead branches, leaving a flattened and ash-covered field. The short hours of fire are followed by what is probably the least pleasant aspect of men's agricultural labor. In the hot dusty sun, they clear stubble and roots from out of the ashes, sorting, chopping, and 'burning' (*duklang*) those stumps that remain from the earlier firing for a second, and usually, decisive time.

While men comb the ash, women use the charred, fertile ground to 'plant' (*tanem*, 'to plant vegetables'; *rinadu*, 'to plant in ash') sugar cane, bananas, vegetables (beans, mustard, squashes) – and cucumbers, which are intended to ripen in time to provide cool refreshment for harvesters in early fall. But with the onset of drizzles sufficient to soften their old weeded gardens, women turn their thoughts to a task that for them has something of the intensity and aesthetic satisfaction realized by men in treetops earlier in the year. 'Planting rice' (*'etek*) is a task which, for Ilongots (but for none of their swidden neighbors), is the exclusive responsibility of women. Generally unaccompanied by ritual, the planting of rice initiates a period of female dominance in agricultural activity, and invites the attention of the Spirit of the Gardens, the Maiden, who watches her sisters at work.

Planting involves, first, a 'scraping' (*mua*) of topsoil into neat parallel ridges – in order, women say, to limit the growth of weeds. Then, with 'dibble' (*patek*) in right hand and grain in the left, the gardener punches holes in the ground and 'lays the rice seed' (*'etek*). Rhythmic body control marks her slow, careful labor; carvings and bells on her dibble call the attention of spirits, and also – women playfully told me – of passing young men. In regular holes, approximately eight inches apart, the women first plant their quick-growing rices, intended for consumption in early September, when old stores are apt to be wanting. Corn and vegetables – 'following' (*'unud*) the rice but due to ripen before it – may be added to the humus-rich ridges; and, as these plots are completed, the women move on to the ashy new swiddens where slower but often more flavorful varieties of rice will be sown. The total effect – of slopes striped with ridges between which rice slowly emerges – is 'vibrant' (*ngasingasi*) and tidy, evoking aesthetic descriptions that Ilongots apply to tiny and waving shell baubles, to unconstrained energy, and gay, youthful hearts. Standing in elegant contrast to all other features of the Ilongot landscape, the fields with their new green vitality call forth the admiring comment that rice, like humanity, is 'never used up/exhausted' because it gives birth to more of itself. But if planting, in its studied regularity, captures a distinctively Ilongot aesthetic, linking the health of successful gardens to the 'energetic' efforts of women who are quick to take pride in their work, it is also a lonely activity. Because of a fear that intensified planting will lead rice to ripen more quickly than they are able to reap it, the women tend to work individually, with visits and cooperation from kin and neighbors occurring informally if at all.

Between the period of planting and harvest, women occasionally perform short magical spells to ward off small 'worms' and bad spirits; weeds must be prevented from growing (*lugam*, 'to weed in a planted garden'), and as the rice grows 'like a maiden,' 'becomes pregnant,' 'bursts,' 'reddens,' and then 'ripens,' flocks of birds – which myths claim were once lazy women – must be 'shooed' (*'asiw*) from the browning fields. Men construct towers and clappers to scare off the unwanted predators; they hunt boar that seek root crops edging on the gardens, and build traps to keep monkeys and wild chickens from damaging the healthy new grain. But midsummer is a lazy time, with food stores low and labor casual and intermittent. It is only with the onset of harvest, in late August or early September, that women are once again engaged in a constant and intensive activity; and they reap much as they had planted, slowly and, for the most part, by themselves.

Magical spells, to call 'rice hearts' at the beginning of harvest, require that women work their fields individually.[2] Noise and the presence of helpers will, they say, quicken fall's rainstorms; and if they visit their neighbors, the 'life' that they invoked in their magic is apt to 'go visiting' as well. Only after some four or five days of lonely reaping can larger parties of helpers join in the harvest, and, even then, their work tends to be slowed by an Ilongot tradition that forbids using metal to sever the rice stalks,[3] and by a habit of storing the produce in neatly tied bundles – requiring that every panicle be cut to a standardized length. As the expanses of ripened grain widen, and autumn downpours lash at the full, heady plants, men may join women to help

A planter uses her right hand to dibble, or punch holes, and then drops rice seed with her left hand.

speed the harvest. But in everyday fact and in ritual, the plants that women's efforts created remain a predominantly female concern. Lest crops rot, and their 'exhaustion' be wasted, the women rise early and rush off to their fields without eating; 'angry' with fear that their fellows will finish their harvests before them, they greet every scant stalk with despairing reflections and cry if winds flatten the grain.

Intent and 'distracted' (*'alimet*) throughout the harvest, it is hardly surprising that women say their hearts 'lengthen' (*ruyuk*) when fields are completed and harvested bundles are laid out on tall racks to dry. Radiating shades of beige and gold, the racks stand ten tiers high[4] and stretch as wide as the crops may require. And although women themselves may deprecate yields, and never boast of the 'heights' of a harvest, the rich decks of new produce provide a visible testimony to the success of each woman's gardens. Her rice racks bespeak months of hard, lonely labor, promising the successful gardener all the pleasures of guests, of a wide reputation, and of the fame that she sought in her harvesting magic, when she asked for yields known 'all around.'

After harvest, patches of old fields may be hoed for planting in root crops (particularly when rice yields appear to be slight) and tobacco. Granaries, constructed by husbands with the help of their kinsmen and neighbors, will be filled by individual women by the end of December. And a cycle of spells that was initiated when the rice began sprouting early in summer, and intensified for the reaping of thick, fruitful 'rice hearts' throughout the fall, is completed when the granary itself is 'adorned' (*'aimet*) with magical herbs and fresh invocations. These spells ask for a store of rice which, despite constant use, will stand as 'high' as a rooftop, and, grasping 'like thistles' to its place of storage, remain as plentiful as thick grasses, and as inexhaustible as grains of sand. In fact, of course, individual granary stores are reduced almost daily, but Ilongots tend to think otherwise about the factors that deplete their food. Some women suffer guests who will outstay their welcome; some find that, though rice stores were great, the grains have themselves become 'heartless,' quickly shattered by pestles and far too quickly consumed. And when several married women live together in a household and divide daily chores so that one fetches wood and another brings grain, each may suffer abuse by her fellows – so that, if some women exhaust granary stores sooner that their coresident kinfolk, their misfortune is explained by reference to faulty magic, or perhaps to the 'selfishness' of other women who live in their homes.

Although other crops – sugar cane, manioc, taro, sweet potatoes, vegetables, and corn – are all significant additions to the Ilongot diet, none equals rice as a focus of women's effort; nor is the loss of these minor crops – to dogs, storms, or predation – a matter of major concern. Like game for a man (who also fishes and traps birds, gathers honey and betel, and fetches fruits and wild greens), rice is a woman's most prized and significant product. And like game, which hunters themselves should distribute, rice belongs to the married woman who 'tired' herself in its planting and lost sleep to tend to its growth. Men, who were dominant in the early phases of the agricultural cycle, have, since the laying of seed, not entered a garden without the relevant woman's awareness and probable company; nor will they think to approach and take rice from the granaries in which her produce is stored. Because men do not pound, plant, or fetch rice – and because they rarely cook it, and then, less successfully than their wives – the adult woman knows that the rice that she worried and cared for is hers to distribute to kin or to bring forth for household consumption: All future use of the product reflects only her 'hand' and her 'heart.'

Thus, when men begin narratives (see Chapter 3) with the stereotypical, 'I said to my sister/wife/mother: "Pound me rice for I am going off," ' they are not simply asserting authority, but are also acknowledging dependence; without women to grow rice and to pound it, men could not travel or hunt. Men say they need women to prepare food and serve it; they say that women attend to their household 'commands,' or *tuydek*, because as the 'foundation' or 'trunk' (*tengeg*) of human existence, women recognize that men are helpless without female 'consideration' (*dē'ri*) and aid. But women, in parallel fashion, claim to need men to cut trees and clear forests; to realize, through force, wit, and physical prowess, the conditions of safe, happy labor; and finally, to get meat and the various trade goods (salt, kerosene, pots, knives, cloth, and wire) that the sale of meat brings. Through a variety of practices that seem distinctive to the organization of Ilongot agricultural labor – the male drama in treetops, the organization of planting, the fact that women initiate harvests, and the general expectation that only women pound rice – Ilongots reinforce a sense of both the difference and complementarity of the sexes, assigning each dominance in a relatively independent domain. Just as rice, in its growth and preparation – and no matter what help men may offer – is unambiguously associated with women, so men are linked to the forest; and although game can be killed by adults of both sexes, hunting in all its variations is an activity dominated by men.

Hunting

Hunting and horticulture are activities that typify for Ilongots the complementary contributions of the sexes – a fact revealed at mealtime, when men butcher, apportion, cook, and then serve the boar or the deer they have hunted, while women prepare and distribute the rice that accompanies the meat. Both sorts of labor are similar, Ilongots say, because both demand 'sweat' and 'endurance,' 'anger' and 'knowledge,' or skill. They are like one another in that an individual's efforts in either direction come, first, from the fear of starvation – a 'knowledge,' Ilongots have told me, 'of stomachs' – and beyond that, from the envy of those who, through effort, good fortune. or magic, may be more successful than oneself.

But, unlike the tasks assigned women, hunting, fishing, and foraging by men in the forest are not classified by Ilongots as *dapat*, or *talabaku* (from the Spanish *trabajo*), which mean 'doing/making' or 'work.' Because the hunt involves more of 'looking for/seeking' *('adiwar)* than constant care and activity, it is differentiated from the 'true work' of 'tending,' 'caring,' or 'cutting,' of transforming and slowly reshaping a landscape – not because it does not involve effort, but because in organization and style it bears little resemblance to domestic and horticultural pursuits. Whereas the gardener is 'pulled' by the demands of her rice or by weather (as are men who must acknowledge the pressure of seasons when they clear their forests for fields), the efforts of hunters are shaped less by seasonal constraints or concerns to attend past investments than by immediate wishes and needs. Characteristically born of a moment, the hunt – like all forms of 'seeking out produce' *(tukdu)* – has none of the prolonged, anxious quality associated with agricultural labor. In the woods, men confront the unknown and uncertain in search of a sudden reward.

What is more, the quest for large game leads to stories. Although their forests are rich in a variety of animals – monkeys, civet cats, crocodiles, pythons – Ilongots see most of these as taboo or distasteful; fish,[5] eels, frogs, and wild birds are, like honey, cast primarily as pleasant additions to a household's diet, and domesticated pigs and chickens are, for most traditional Ilongots, barely acceptable foods.

> While visiting Manila with Tepeg and 'Insan, we made the mistake of ordering for the former a stew that contained small bits of pork. He ate slowly, then stood up, went outside, and vomited. Pig meat, he said, was not forbidden as food, but its 'soft' quality was nauseating in contrast to the boar meat that he loved.

It is only 'true game' *(pipiyan 'atap)* – deer and wild boar – that regularly occupies Ilongot hunters. Deer and boar are the ideal complement to rice in daily consumption, and in 1967-9 they were probably the major protein source in the diet and certainly the prime object of protestations of *tabrek,* 'hunger for meat or fish.' Furthermore, their consumption, in contrast to that of small animals, always involves more than one household, and their bagging, often uncertain, lends drama to daily talk.

Unlike gardeners, who are bound to return to old fields and past efforts, hunters traverse a world where the strange is expected, and their movements give meaning to relatively uncharted space. Once at home, hunters tell of rivers crossed, hills climbed, and cliffs circumvented. With studied and stereotypical gesture, they dramatize their attitude of deep and intense concentration, their hours of seeking and planning, and then, the decisive moment – 'So I said in my heart: "Draw the bow!" and I drew it' – when they took aim. Names of ridges, trees, and valleys, and descriptions of rivers and hills, are the substance of these recollections:

So it was that I set off. I went to spend the night midway up the Ranung River. I thought, "The moon has just about set." I said to myself, "Let me go downhill just a little." So it was that I went downhill and I saw an acorn tree and decided to stalk it. But I didn't get anything and so I went on, toward the mountain, and I said, "Hey, let me go see the mountain called Penduk where the deer may be lying down." My arrow slipped and so I lost that one . . . I said, "Why don't I chew betel?" and then I set off again, once again toward the mountain and there was a deer standing there and I shot but I didn't kill it. And so I set off to cross toward the rocky mountain called Dalawan . . .

Concerned less with triumph than landscape, less with the hero than matters of accident, movement, and surprise, the frame for all stories by hunters is provided by actual travels. Radi's story of being surprised by a python captures well both the dangers of hunting and the fact that adventure is ordered by exit, return, exploration – by movement, eventful and various, through what is always significant space:

Well, the time I got carried, it was like this. So we called one another. I called to Kemmi, "Kemmi, let's go hunt the 'Asimun Mountain; the game has been eating the fruits of the *tarang* tree and the *radēng* tree; I saw them when I was hunting." And so they said, "Yes, let's go for them, let's hunt the 'Asimun" . . . And so we set off. Well, they set off toward the Nalungtutan River. And I said to myself, "I'll go toward the fork of the Nagetruwan River. And we who had the dogs spread ourselves out. And I went with my dogs in that direction. I heard my dog Woolly on the scent; surely, he was after game. And I hurried on to go to the runo grasses trampled by the game as it fled my dog, along the bank, the wide stretches toward the 'Asimun. I headed upstream. And there you coiled, snout of a loser of a python, hiding by a tree. "Hey, what's this that is rising up past my thigh?" And at that point, I said, "I don't like this. Pudnga, I'm bitten by a snake; I won't live, hurry up!" I called out to the boy, like that. And then I said to myself, "Well no, I'll slip my hand into it and stretch open the jaws of the snake." And so I stuck my hand in at that moment. Well, I'd caused my hand and my foot to be pinched together in its jaws. That's how it happened; I was like one with a twisted limb, like someone in handcuffs. And after that, I looked wildly at the snake as it twisted and turned. Well, its companion was resting just upstream. And here it was pulling at me. "Oh, so that's why it's squirming, it's trying to pull me." And I said, "It's pulling me over the thorns, and twisting as it pulls me by the thorns." Well, the young shoots of a rattan were there and we all know about how thorny that can be. Well, that's what I scratched past as it dragged me. And as for my behind, and my groin, well my groin felt it all; it was totally scratched up. And my behind burned with thorns. And as for you, land that I cleared clean in the process, well it was pure thorns that were peeled from you when the snake dragged me by. Then I really had at it. I pried my hand loose and cut at it with my bolo. And it took off with the bolo, just like that. "Hey, you know, it's taking my bolo uphill." It took it upstream; it went twisting off upstream. Well, at that I called out, "Pudnga, come here, I won't live." My blood was spurting all over and that was the last thing I said. I just passed out. Well, finally, they came to carry me. They carried me toward the 'Asimun . . . and Pukpuk came to medicate me. He said, "Imagine if it had been a man. Just think, if he had gotten at you like that . . . If a person had beaten at you, you'd be dead now." No, it really would have been the last time I ever spoke. Well, Ya'maw carried me home. And my wife attended to the three animals we had shot.

Because the hunt involves movement and uncertain action, situational diversity and distant rewards, it entails more of discovery or 'knowledge,' more intense, focused *liget,* than does the repetitive work done in gardens. But the distinct and complementary significances associated with hunting and horticulture go beyond matters of style, and reflect social organization as well. Ilongot hunts can be individual or collective, and occupy men for between a day to a week in the forest, depending on both their purpose in hunting and the habits of animals during the major seasons of the year. When the weather is dry enough for dogs to trace scents through a thicket, collective ventures involving most men in a settlement (who set up a semicircular ambush into which dogs drive the game) are frequent. At other times, individual men stalk the boar that scrounge roots in their gardens, seek game in leafy and branch-laden burrows, or wait patiently by salt licks or pools of fallen acorns where animals may come to feed.

Hunts of the first kind, called *la'ub,* peak in the dry months that begin in late January, but they are common throughout the year. Inspired by tales of game spied in the forest, by 'meat or fish hunger,' by plans or the presence of guests, the decision to hunt is informal: Any competent man can initiate *la'ub,* any can refuse to participate, question the proposed distribution of animals, or object to the choice of a site. But cooperation, although occasionally challenged, is generally taken for granted, and observations throughout the 1967-9 period of fieldwork (when game had not been significantly depleted by an onslaught of settlers in what once was an Ilongot forest) indicate that, weather and circumstances permitting, Ilongot men engage in collective hunts from one to three times per week.

Plans may be laid by casual talk or a chorus of calls that hasten the men of a settlement during the early morning; in shouts, the men name a place for their ambush and decide on a single man, usually an elder, to 'lead dogs' *('anup)* to scare up the game. This man will follow the mass of the hunters – taking time, first to feed, and then magically, to

A hunter pauses en route to his ambush.

'anger' his hunt dogs, while his fellows rush off to the business of clearing a comfortable space for an ambush, building screens for disguise and protection, and hacking at underbrush to diffuse human odors that circumscribe movements of game. Except in the case of those rare hunts in which men hike to a distance and sleep for some days in the forest *(tuyuk)*,[6] standard hunt sites – a conjunction of rivers, the narrow stretch between adjacent mountains, the curved base of a hill – range from one to four miles from a settlement and are generally less than an hour away. When possible, the men like to start early so that they can avoid afternoon rainstorms, and, depending on luck and ambition, build a new ambush and set the dogs on new courses as many as two or three times in a single day.

Game caught through everyday *la'ub* is almost always intended for immediate consumption: A large meal follows the return of the hunters, and then a distribution of 'equivalent portions' *(bēet)* of meat takes place, ideally to 'every roof beam' (or, more precisely, to each married couple) in a settlement.

> Variations in distribution reflect at once the composition of the hunting party and settlement relationships and precedents. In some areas, there is a standing, formal agreement about distribution, but in Kakidugen – the settlement where we lived – two clusters of houses, one upstream, one down, shared meat only if representatives from both groups joined in the hunting or happened to be present when the meat was butchered, or if the catch was considered large (see Chapter 6).

While their husbands are absent, the women pound rice, chop wood, and fetch water, in hopes of impending consumption; at home and expectant, they pretend not to think of the hunters, and neither stare nor ask questions when the men emerge from the forest – for fear of the Forest Lord who gives game but also disease. If there is meat, the hunters typically return to a single house,[7] where deer may be skinned and boar hide seared and then butchered. Saving the bulk of their catch for settlementwide distribution, the men designate one portion that is immediately boiled for eating by all who are present; and while women are busy with cooking, adult men may roast bits of organ and rib meat for snacks, which they share with young children who gather to witness their 'fathers'' success.

Teenage boys sear, skin, and then cook the meat, while adult men take charge of the more delicate matters of butchering and apportioning household allotments – dividing all game into chunks of equivalent value, then grouping these slowly and carefully into a predetermined number of shares. Shares will, in turn, be allotted to households in rough accord with their number of coresident married adults. At the

same time, the killer himself, or an elder, gives thanks to *'agimeng,*
Lord of the Forest – planting a bit of roasted liver in the roof or the
houseyard, and imploring 'our companion' *(bēkir)* and 'master' *('apu)*[8]
to take and enjoy the good fortune he granted his poor hunting 'sons.'
Depending on the time of day, children may be sent off with shares of
fresh game to other homes in the vicinity, or, as more frequently happens, the men carry meat shares to the various cooperating households, where there are likely to be women and children waiting to cook
their own meals.

More variable in style and purpose, the *'auduk,* or individual hunt, is
performed more by some men than others; its product can be set to a
number of uses; and its form varies depending on factors of personal
skill, age, and inclination, as well as on seasonal conditions and
change. More than *la'ub,* it is the focus of divination and magic. Individual hunters do spells to find out where game will be hiding, dispense
with all kinds of bad fortune, dull the scent and slow the pace of their
victims, or 'quicken' the hunter's firm hand.

Individual successes in this sort of hunt vary widely; during the two-
or three-month season of *'alisang,* or 'tree ambush,' when autumn
acorns and new fruits have fallen, and men await foraging wild boar in
simple platforms in trees, we found that although some men bagged
none, others might kill well over thirty large animals. But an Ilongot
insistence that luck and industry rather than skill govern success in the
forest, and an assumption that meat, unlike rice, should be distributed
and enjoyed through the entire settlement, made men reluctant to
speak of the unequal endowments of hunters, and our grasp of personal
differences came not from public discussion, but from slow and often
embarrassing interviews, in which individuals who insisted that all men
were equally able were asked to count out the animals they had killed.

> While conducting one of these interviews, Renato Rosaldo was sur-
> prised to hear Tukbuw advise him with a smug giggle that he ask
> Lakay, the old man in our household, the extent of his catch. In good
> faith, Renato turned to the old man, who until then had been silent,
> and learned to his surprise that although the two middle-aged men in
> our household had each killed over twenty deer and boar in the past
> season, the old man had caught none. As it turned out, hunting prow-
> ess corresponded closely to the age of hunters, inexperienced
> youths and failing elders doing consistently less well than married men
> between thirty and forty-five years of age.

Although it had been easy to learn the extent of each woman's harvest, questions about the extreme variation in hunting successes were
seen as potentially disruptive; protesting that all men are equal, Ilongots
revealed their awareness of difference only in nervous jokes about men

who bagged nothing, and complaints that the animals killed by good hunters had been tainted by magical plants.

The plentiful *'alisang* season, which lasts from late August to early November, is followed by months when the habits of game are less certain, and when luck more than skill or ambition governs the outcome of quests. Once autumn has passed, winter rains drive the game into burrows, which can be sought out by day (in which case the hunt is called simply *'auduk*), or at night, with the men 'hunting by lamp' *('integ)*. Spring's dry months may lead men to decide collectively to spend several days in the forest *(tuyuk)*, sharing a shelter, yet hunting without dogs and pursuing the game by themselves. During the same period, stretches of cogon grass may be burned to reveal hidden animals, and, when new grasses emerge in the fired expanses, grazing deer provide easy targets for hunting with lamps after dark. Finally, in the months of planting and waiting for young rice to ripen, foodstores are low, animals thin, and fish take the place of game as the prime protein source in the diet; but when animals, unable to feed in a dry season forest, come to scrounge for greens and fat roots in the gardens, their presence is generally welcome and men stalk them during the night.

However caught, game bagged in *'auduk* is an individual product, and its use and distribution rarely follow the same collective patterns that are associated with communal hunts. Depending on settlement precedent, local social relations, personal likings, and needs, the produce of individual hunters is, most often, divided: Part (the head and perhaps forelegs) is for distribution and/or immediate inhouse consumption, with neighbors receiving cooked portions if not true 'shares' of raw meat; and part is preserved through drying, either in thin strips *(pindang)* for sale to lowland traders,[9] or in chunks *(kulagem)* for planned festive events. Finally, game caught when men go in groups to the more distant forest can be distributed within the settlement, or, as more commonly happens, reserved in dried chunks for their collective endeavors: bridewealth or peace meetings, headhunting ceremonies, days of cooperative labor, church-oriented and political gatherings, school meetings, and holiday feasts.

Thus, whether or not the meat is distributed for immediate settlementwide consumption (and even though, as the product of individual labor, it occasionally serves private profit alone), the game caught through individual *'auduk* is – like the product of group hunts with dogs – always intended for "public" or extrahousehold use. A collective bias reflected in the organization of almost all male activities – from housebuilding and pollarding, to travel in peer groups or men's cooperative hunts – is echoed as well in the use of men's most significant product. And the reluctance of Ilongots to talk about inequality of skill among hunters is rooted in a view of game as a collective product, publicly appropriated and consumed. Unlike rice, which a woman cultivates by herself and uses primarily for relatively "private" within-house consumption, game is bound up in patterns of "public" exchange and settlementwide cooperation and conflict; unlike rice, it implicates male 'knowledge' of trade and of travel, of shared needs and public affairs.[10] Although concern for her neighbors and kinfolk may lead a considerate woman to share a few bundles of grain with those whose rice stores are wanting, women are not obliged to distribute their produce, and their fame lies not in extrahousehold prestations, but in their ability to feed all who come to their homes. For men, by contrast, the regular distribution of game involves less of choice than of flexible but public expectations: Good men do not roast themselves snacks of meat that is better divided; bad men try to hide the extent of a catch. Whereas a woman thinks first of her family and household, a man should distribute his produce, using his game to establish the unity of men in a settlement, to assert lines of friendship and mutual dependence, and to shape ties beyond his own home. This contrast – overdrawn, and as I will suggest later on, rather partial – nonetheless corresponds to what Ilongots see as women's more local and limited orientations, as against the more expansive and 'knowing' thoughts, acts and feelings that Ilongots associate with men.

'Preparations' for work

Collective effort and appropriation, distance, drama, uncertainty, and sudden reward – all of these differentiate hunting from rice and its cultivation; and, as I have been suggesting, differences in the style and organization of men's and women's productive activities are intimately tied to Ilongot views of what the sexes are like. But at the same time that they dramatize gender differences, productive tasks reveal as well the ways in which women and men both complement and resemble one another. Sharing needs for food, consideration, and their spouse's labor, women are viewed as similar to men in their fundamental quest for energy and 'focused' *liget;* both are motivated, on the one hand, by the 'anger' that breeds 'envy' and a desire not to be outdone by fellows, and, on the other, by their hopes for abundance, well-being, and good health.

One way to explore these views is to look, as we have, at the things people ordinarily do, at sex-linked activities and idealized styles of labor. Another is to examine those formal cultural representations through which recurrent sorts of action are interpreted and given sense. In the formulaic lines of a now declining (but in 1967-9, still rich and

Magical 'preparation' of hunt dogs

lively) magic, Ilongots picture to themselves a world where game and rice are bound up with human effort. They at once 'command' *(tuydek)* their 'hands,' 'rice hearts,' hunt dogs, and bows to behave in accordance with their wishes – and 'prepare' themselves for the sort of focused energy, or *liget,* that will sustain their work. Much like the 'knowing' parent who gives 'commands' to helpful children, so 'knowledgeable' hearts 'command' in spells (called *'aimet,* 'preparations') the lively and compliant actions of their human 'hands.'[11] These Ilongot spells invoke the picture of a productive world requiring human work within it; they describe the stance of men and women who, to live, must hunt and garden – and who, although 'equal humans,' are also shapers of a mode of life in which women, 'life's foundation,' cannot attain the 'heights' of men's more 'angry,' and more 'knowing,' hearts. Attention to these spells will clarify something not immediately apparent from my examination of sex roles in production – the sense in which women and men, engaged in different tasks, are yet construed as similar – as well as illuminating the asymmetry in Ilongot notions that associate both more *liget* and more *bēya* with the characteristic tasks of men.

When an Ilongot woman prepares for a harvest,[12] or a man, having fed his hunt dogs, is about to set off after game, each gathers a collection of herbs that are, typically, charred with pitch or steamed over a preheated hearthstone. An object like steam is said to 'quicken' *('awet)* the pulse of the performer, producing the feeling of 'hot' excitement that foretells a productive endeavor. The hearthstone itself is a symbol of closeness and stability, of rice so thick that the harvester stays in a single spot throughout an entire day's reaping, of game that meets the hunter near his home. The plants (indicated by asterisks   [*   ] in the following texts and discussion) have names that resemble the Ilongot words for 'meet*,' 'hasten*,' 'near*,' and 'encounter*'; they too suggest that success is available close by. Finally, the spoken spells are rich in images of plenty; they ask that practitioners be 'dizzied' and overwhelmed with the rice or the game they desire, that quantities – like stars in the night or leaves that fall in a windstorm – appear before their eyes.

Whether he steams his herbs on a hearthstone or lights pitch in the footprint of game, the hunter's words are apt to be something like the following:

You, spirit who walks by the rivers, come join my steaming here!
Here I do steam magic on my hand by the hearthstone,
Don't fail me, let me shoot, you Spirit, my Master!
They like you, hand
Hand that is steamed on the hearthstone, hand
May they be full*, hand, the wild game, hand
They like you, hand
Make it a hoard* of wild game, hand
Make them meet* you, hand, the wild game, hand
Make the eyes of the deer bulge, hand, in a clear place, hand
They like you, hand
May they be like stars to you, hand, the wild animals, hand
Don't, please, hand, go too far away, hand
Make your hunting place near*, hand
Be, hand, like the sure hand of a Negrito hunter, hand
They like you, hand . . .

Similarly, a gardener, at the beginning or end of her harvest when she wonders how healthy her plants are, or later, when she puts the harvested bundles in her granary for use through the rest of the year, will use much the same language and images, asking again and again that her rice supply be unending, that its 'fruitfulness*' collect in her field:

Here I steam you, rice, with your fruitfulness*, rice
Rice, you have a spell performed now, rice
Make it pile high, rice, your fruitfulness*, rice
Beckon* your fruitfulness*, rice
Here is the plant called beckoning*, rice
Don't please, rice, act childish, rice, don't run around, rice
Be like the rice of lowlanders, rice
Make it so people everywhere speak of you, rice
And may I be please, rice, like a spinning bug in the center of a field, rice
They like you, rice
This is the plant called hoards*, rice

Let there be hoards* of you, rice
And be full*, rice
Let your fruitfulness* flourish*, rice . . .

Though actual spells range in length from the fragments recorded here
to recitations of five or ten minutes, their form and core sense do not
change. Using similar lines and repeated formulaic expressions ('be like
hand/rice. . . ,' 'they like you, hand/rice. . . ,' 'please don't hand/
rice. . .'), practitioners refer to the plants they have gathered, and – in
the name of sweet potato vines (whose runners are thick and constant),
bugs (that sting, bite, or spin), and birdcalls (that travel like gossip and
echo like dogs on the scent) – they ask for hands 'full*' with
'awakened*' rice hearts and with beelike swarms of fresh game.

Because hunters and gardeners alike care for 'fullness*' and 'produc-
tivity,' because both find the 'angry' motive to work not only in
hunger, but also in an 'envious' and problematic desire to 'reach' the
accomplishments of peers, their spells give voice to common interests.
Of some thirty plants used in each, the vast majority appear in both
kinds of magic; they invoke related images of an organized, intense,
and 'dizzy' plenty, and, by implication, reject the fear of chaos and
confusion that figures heavily in spells concerning health. Just as the
gardener wants to be spinning amidst her inexhaustible rice plants, so
the driver of hunt dogs directs his animals to make the game rush
around and 'encircle*' his person. Both may *puipur,* or mime the 'circling' of product, by winding a rice stalk, a dog leash, or a vine around
a planted and immobile stick. Both make figurines or 'personifications'
from plants to 'embody' the 'hearts' they hope to gather; and both
speak of their 'hand' or *deyaka* (a word used only in *'aimet*), asking
that it be 'awakened*' and 'warmed' like the 'boiling' hearthstone, and
so 'cling,' 'meet*,' and 'beckon*' the produce it takes as its goal. As
they cite and steam plants whose names mean to 'equal*,' 'fill*,'
'hoard*,' and 'add onto*,' they ask for foodstuffs which 'coming near*,'
will exhaust them – so that, as if bound to a single location, they can
neither proceed through the forest nor reap the extremes of a field.

Unlike *sambal,* or spells that medicate illness and use plants whose
'contagious' *(bēret;* see Chapter 3) power can make spirits 'toothless*'
and ill, *'aimet,* or 'preparations' for gardening and hunting, invoke
positive forms of 'energy/anger.' And *'aimet* for hunting and gardening
speak not of spiritual dangers – not of chaos or threats of intrusion –
but of a life that is 'centered' around the producer, a focus that cannot
be disturbed. Whereas medicinal spells place their stress on the loss of
pain and disruption, the *'aimet* recited by workers seek potentially disruptive excess: The harvester asks to be 'dizzied' by the abundance of
rice in her garden, and the hunter may request diarrhea from eating

great quantities of game. Medicinal spells invoke images of purification and safety, of thorns that defy a predator's approaches, plants that shed water, metal resistant to scratches, tall trees untouched by grass fires, mirrors that have a 'clean' glow. These are countered in *'aimet* by notions of joining and clinging, and by the image of a virtually immobilized worker, overwhelmed by the extent of a yield. Rather than 'splash away' illness, or reverse and 'return' the contagious misfortune acquired from spirits or plants, the 'hands' of the hunter and gardener seek the 'warmth' and the fertile abundance, the intense focused *liget*, that 'equal*' humans have 'called*' to the site of their work.

Concentration and focused *liget*, on the part of both the producer and the rice or game that is sought, are the goals of both gardeners and hunters. Not surprisingly, this parallel conception of productive experiences shapes not only the lines of their magic, but also their views of the space where they work. Ilongots know and address both a Forest Lord, *'agimeng*, who is usually called *'irungut*, 'from the forest,' and a figure who some call his wife, *madēkit*, the Maiden, also known as *'i'uma*, the one 'from the fields.' In the forest, a wild chicken, *'ikaratan* ('from nature/the wilds/the forest'), parallels its unmarked opposite, *manuk*, the 'bird' or 'chicken,' which belongs to domestic contexts; plants called 'his' (or *'agimeng*'s), 'areca nut,' 'piper betal leaf,' 'root,' and 'banana,' all have their garden equivalents (although these latter are not explicitly linked to the Maiden); and *laman*, the wild boar, is in spells called *bēbuymu*, 'your' – *'agimeng*'s – 'domestic pig.'

Of both forest and garden, one speaks of a *bengri*, or 'center,' of life and productive effort, and an 'edge,' or *gelibgib*, where ancestral spirits cause their living kin pain and disturbance, where envious neighbors steal rice hearts from gardens, where weeds can bring illness, and where noisy visitors cause rain.

> Sitting one day near Banaw as she hoed weeds from her garden, I was surprised to realize that close to half were weeds recognized by Ilongots as 'contagious' *(beret)* plants, causing stomachaches and the like when cut. This suggested that contagion was a property that derived, in part, from ill-ease about boundaries, and, in particular, the intrusion of "natural" or forest-born growth on cleared fields.

On the edges, aspiring producers may perform *tugutug*, spells to 'smoke away' disruptive ancestral spirits – here using a technique common in medicine, where the goal is to 'return' or 'cast off' the symptoms of illness. For workers, *tugutug* 'fence out' those distracting forces that endanger high concentration and (by urging hunt dogs to scatter and rice hearts to wander) lead hunter and gardener to waste efforts in pointless quests. By contrast, the *bengri*, or 'centers' of rice

Rice magic in the center of the garden initiates a harvest.

field and forest, are likely sites for one's *'aimet,* or 'true preparations';
they are the homes of the Forest Lord and the Maiden, charged with the
intensified *liget* of magical 'calling*' and the expectation of productive
success.

Finally, however, it seems that the *liget* that is invoked in *'aimet* –
like 'anger' in human hearts or in social encounters – may itself harbor
dangers; and 'centers' (or *bengri*), when 'angered' by magic, are places
for caution and fear. One only does *'aimet* and invokes the Forest Lord
and the Maiden if rice crops look healthy and the forest is thought to
have game.

> People tell that, in the past, collective pig sacrifices were performed to
> recall lost 'rice hearts' after a succession of poor harvests. One such
> sacrifice involved three Kakidugen households in 1966. Women
> brought stalks of rice intended for use as seed to dip in the sacrificial
> blood (which, it was hoped, would restore their 'hearts' and vitality),

while an old man killed the pig. I gather that these sacrifices were rare in the past, occurring no more than once every decade. By 1974, people claimed to no longer 'know' how to stage such events, and furthermore, to no longer have the 'knowledgeable' ritual specialists or 'shamans' who, in the past, restored health to people sickened by the Maiden or the Forest Lord. Thus, their present caution in performing spells.

In the absence of reasonable hopes for productive successes, people fear that the *liget* invoked in their magic may well turn against human workers, who, in any case, must proceed with due caution – shunning all forms of play and distraction lest wild behavior on the part of producers occasion the fury of those 'central' spirits who can also steal 'hearts' (of both produce and persons) and cause madness or the serious and sudden fevers Ilongots know as *bēut*.

Themes introduced in the previous chapter, of the human need for 'energy' or *liget*, its disruptive potential, its ties to competition and envy, and its place – both as cause and symptom – in all mortal success, clearly underlie these parallels in Ilongot images of productive actions and spaces; and they account for the common observation that spells for the forest and garden use similar plants, gestures, and images because they are concerned, in both cases, with the food that draws guests and gives comfort, and without which there is no life. In *'aimet*, as in everyday living, Ilongot adults of both sexes portray themselves as 'equal humans' for whom work, energy, and successful labor are both the end and the source of their efforts; both seek accumulation as opposed to dispersal, and both contrast images of focused, immobile concentration with the wild and purposeless action associated with energy uncontrolled.

At the same time, however, the patterns of their daily labor serve both to reflect and confirm what Ilongots see as deep-seated sexual differences. The images of hunting and horticultural magic give voice to contrasts as well as to similarities – to men's 'heights' and women's foibles – and to the motives and interests they share. Thus, when hunters ask dogs to bite like ants, bees, and pythons; when they tell them to bark like the thunder or a headhunter's celebratory song; when they liken game to overhead growth that collapses, to rapids that rush through a channel, or to sugar cane squeezed through a press, they are speaking in images that have more to do with notions of violence, destruction, and killing than with the productive energies that inform a harvester's labor. And when gardeners compare their rice to thick grasses they plant in their gardens, to plants that 'take hold of' the rocks that they grow on, to firmly anchored bananas, and to the 'clinging' of useful rattans, they speak of a condition of growth and stability that has little relevance to the hunt. In images unique to their respective spells, gardeners and hunters speak in terms that reflect Ilongot views of their difference: the one linked to domestic and personal issues, to growth and continuity, the other to sudden and violent upheaval, to destruction – and to the headhunter's taking of life.

Thus, whereas the hunter likens the warmth of his 'hand' to *runguy,* the fire that consumes both grassland and forest, gardeners choose a more stable, domesticated imagery, and speak of rice hearts as warm as *'apuy,* the fire one lights in a hearth. Like clouds or deep pools, like motionless earth or like sand that cannot be exhausted, the gardener's rice – like her labor – is pictured as fixed and abundant. Reproducing itself, it is bound up in the annual cycles of human existence and provides every year for her fields. Hunters, by contrast, are linked (with their dogs) to headhunting songs and a bird whose beak is a headhunter's earring; they may ask for repeated successes and limited effort, but their images have more to do with sudden and uncertain drama than with stable and constant rewards. Catching hold like harpoon arrows, grasping like crocodiles, rushing like whirlpools or wind, they would cause game to fall from the woods like newly pollarded branches, to come forth like stars in night skies. And just as the hunt dog itself is equated in other contexts with the young, anxious killer, so *'agimeng,* Lord of the Forest, provides men with both game and the human victims whose death and beheading bring a kind of transcendent satisfaction, renewing one's commitment to work.

Hunting, in short, emerges in spells as involving something of the 'high' and aesthetically salient sort of *liget* that Ilongots tie to the headhunting exploits of killers; and this equation between male productive activity and life taking operates in other spheres as well. Male pollarders may boast in the trees of 'beheading' or of 'tearing' the dress of the forest. New hunt dogs and young boys who have first killed big game may – like young headhunters – be 'angered' with ginger and chilis, the 'heat' of these spices exciting their prowess and ensuring their future desire to kill. Or again, like the killer who fails, poor hunters may be called *depyang,* 'worthless,' 'unaccomplished' – a word whose challenging and disdainful connotations capture the deep sense in which men's failure and inequality are considered abnormal and deeply problematic. This word is never applied to women, whose 'lower' hearts more readily accommodate failures, and who find less to disturb them in the fact that their bad luck or sheer lack of effort becomes known through their impoverished yields.

Women, less 'angry' than men, cannot, like the hunter, be identified with life-taking violence; nor do they, through childbirth or their daily labor – through work they see as steady, repetitive, and 'painful' *(takit),* but lacking in dramatic force – display the valued strength and high 'passion' that killing is said to involve.

> When I asked if childbirth did not parallel headtaking as a show of *liget*, Ilongots said that childbirth had no 'anger' but only 'pain' *(takit)*. Mayana was amused by my suggestion that men might 'look up to' *(dĕgiw)* women for their role in childbirth, as women 'look up to' men who take heads. 'A good idea,' she said, 'but not an Ilongot one.' A general downplaying of biological reproduction in Ilongot thinking about women was reflected, as well, in the fact that Kakidugen Ilongots were appalled to learn that neighboring Ifugao couples saw cause to divorce in a failure to bear offspring, insisting that husband and wife should stay together and 'care for one another,' sharing labor, even if their youthful vitality is 'wasted' in a failure to bear young. Parallels between agricultural fertility and biological reproduction are few in both magic and daily discourse (see Rosaldo and Atkinson 1975), and Ilongot women seem more inclined to take pride in the former – their 'industry' *(kui)* and skill as producers – than in reproductive success.

Working alone and for produce that will be directed to household consumption, a woman will speak in her spells not of sudden joy – not of birth, or destruction – but of the pleasures of publicly recognized achievement, of rice that 'people everywhere talk about' and of a reputation that 'circles' her world. She calls for the 'fruitfulness*' of gardeners who live at a distance, uses plants that may 'beckon*' good fortune and rice hearts from neighbors, and fears to go visit her kinfolk lest her rice escape to their fields. Because the meat that men bag is ordinarily divided, no one household enjoys the good 'hand' of a hunter. But rice is an object of private consumption, and the harvester may ask, in her *'aimet,* for personal glory and fame. Thus, when Sibat, a young gardener in our vicinity, asked in a spell that I happened to tape, that the Maiden provide her with rice hearts that neighbors no longer gave proper care, her words were at first judged by kin as 'unknowingly' selfish. Sibat had asked for the 'fruitfulness*' of 'those who no longer do *'aimet,'* meaning to triumph at the expense of her Christian kinfolk and neighbors who had recently abandoned their spells. Those who helped me to transcribe the tape were disturbed by her unfriendly language, but in subsequent discussion, they agreed that Sibat's request was consistent with the more acceptable phrase of traditional *'aimet:* 'Call* all the rice hearts from people who live far away.'

Hunters say they know spells to limit the fortunes of fellows, and, like gardeners, they admit that their *liget* is heightened, their efforts encouraged, through envy of neighbors and friends. But, unlike the gardener, they do not envision their catch as something that grows with another's misfortune. They may care to be 'equal*' to others, to eat well, be healthy, and avoid a 'worthless' man's shame – but they do not, like

Sibat, portray their desires in terms that their fellows find 'selfish'; nor do they speak of their produce in terms stressing personal renown. Unable to 'reach' men in 'anger,' women, by contrast, look forward to the 'circling' echoes of fame that will answer their efforts. Isolated in work, they are promised a wide reputation; and, if inclined to stress their private interest, they know too that their generosity will guarantee public notice as a reward for productive success.

In what could be called a similar "frame" – an imagery based on their common humanity and shared productive goals – each sex speaks in *'aimet* in terms that refer to their difference. Women voice, among other things, their private hopes for a fame that recalls that of killers, whereas men elaborate other ties between hunting and killing, stressing, by implication, the 'anger' that makes them 'higher' than women who work in fields.[13] I have already pointed to some ways in which these themes – the individual and competitive nature of women's achievements, the heightened *liget* and drama associated with exploits of men – are themselves bound up in the style and organization of their productive experience. And I would claim that these themes are reflected in *'aimet* because they 'prepare' men and women for a life which, in any case, is theirs.

By calling their productive spells *'aimet,* 'ornaments' or 'preparations,' Ilongots in fact come very close to the perspective adopted in this chapter, in which spells are considered less in terms of their intended outcomes than the ways in which their imagery serves to order, picture, and give sense to the experience of a working life. To *'aimet* may mean 'to dress up,' or, alternatively, 'to arrange' packs or baskets for travel. In either case it suggests a sort of "preparation of self" for the activities in which one intends to engage. Similarly, magical spells can be said to 'prepare' both the forest and garden by portraying at once the *liget* essential to successful labor, and such differences between men and women as are reflected in their characteristic tasks. In the section that follows, I will review the nature of these differences, asking again about the sense in which most female gardeners enjoy less 'anger' than do their hunting spouses, and the ways in which this fact is linked to patterns of conflict and cooperation in the conduct of their daily lives.

The 'height' of men's hearts

When asked why men are 'angrier' than women, Ilongots may dismiss the question, insisting, on the one hand, that adults of both sexes must sweat in labor, or, on the other, that male *liget* is, in any case, disruptive – the sort of thing encountered, if at all, in their drunken fights. Alternatively, they may speak of prowess, of men whose strength and daring, skill and lack of fear, provide for joy and celebration, for travel, knowledge, and ultimately – because *liget* 'concentrated' as sperm is what makes babies – for human life. A third sort of answer speaks of women: women, who like men need energy for work, know 'weighty' hearts and envy, but who, Ilongots say, 'have no place to go with *liget*,' and therefore are less passionate than men.

As Ilongot talk of *liget* is less concerned with hidden and obscure internal states than with forms of motion and activity, the notion that an 'angry' heart is one that can 'go places' with its feelings does not raise the sorts of psychological questions – about repression and resentment – that their view of women might occasion in the modern West.

> For Ilongots, strong affects are associated with culturally organized opportunities for their public expression. Thus, in response to a letter in 1975 in which I reported the death of my father, Tukbaw dictated a letter to a schoolboy that explained that in the old days the almost simultaneous deaths of his mother and my father would have left *'uget,* or 'bad feelings,' in his heart. Because I was a woman, I would not, his letter said, 'hold on to *liget,*' and he himself had decided to abandon his 'bad feelings' because he knew he could not go headhunting as in the past.

Rather than regarding women as people who are limited in their opportunities for what we might see as "natural" self-expression, Ilongots consider women's feelings to be essentially consistent with the activities and experiences of their daily lives. To explain differences in male and female hearts and forms of *liget,* they look to differences in their modes of action: to the fact that, even as young children, boys move and explore more than their sisters, or that, as adults, each sex is characteristically engaged in very different sorts of work. In particular, the view that women 'have no place to go' with *liget* seems to refer not to expressive behavior in daily interaction, but instead to stereotypes associated with: (1) a *style* of labor that is constant, and lacking in decisive drama; (2) an *orientation* that is local and limited in its command of space; and (3) a form of *organization* that individualizes women's efforts, casts their work in terms that highlight competition, and makes what *liget* they give voice to a source of disruption rather than of public acclaim. Each of these points, alluded to in previous discussion, will now be explored.

First, to speak of style. By retreating to the forest or the garden when they are burdened or annoyed, men and women equally use their productive spaces as a sort of private haven, a place to 'cool' *(remna)* their hearts of chaos and hide from troubles in their homes. For both, their work provides relief from heartfelt *liget,* weight, and envy; yet they describe the working transformation of their feelings in rather different terms. A heart 'heavy' with domestic stress slows a gardener's efforts: Dulled with *liget,* she seeks, in work, no more than to distract herself, to 'diffuse' and so 'forget' or 'calm' bad feeling – recovering joy and energy with time. Men, on the other hand, can 'concentrate' their fury in patterns of 'quick,' 'decisive' motion; and a morning's temper is, they say, 'abolished' in the moment of killing sought-for game. A man's sudden joy in killing – like the headhunter's experience of 'casting off' the grief or envy that made him want to kill – has no parallel in women's 'vaguer' labor. And although all completed effort (an animal bagged, a baby born, a field just planted and about to grow) can lead the heart to *ruyuk,* 'lengthen,' as it experiences release from prior worry, only men enjoy the sudden sense of *rekwab,* 'bursting open,' that satisfies a killer's weighted heart. Because they know and can look forward to the sudden violent actions that will relieve them of un-wanted pressures, men can – more than women – indulge intense and weighty feelings; they can let their hearts get 'heavy' when confronted by an insult, or grow 'twisted' and 'distracted' with the experience of grief.

To put the matter otherwise, both sexes in their work need their share of 'knowing' skill and 'energy' or *liget,* but women's work tends to have the character of nagging obligation and inevitable routine: There are always weeds to tend, rice birds to shoo, new crops to gather – or, as women put it, their gardens exert a constant 'pull' upon their hearts. Ruled either by demands established by their prior labor (as when rice crops ripen or weeds begin to crowd a field), or by requests, 'commands,' and expectations of men and children in the home, wom-en's work admits less show of will, and so, of *bēya,* than do the far more varied and intermittent tasks performed by men. Although there is a sense in which constant domestic labor provides women, and espe-cially young girls, with an opportunity to display their industry, their 'passion,' and their 'knowing' skill, their tasks are punctuated by little of the drama, the daily variation, and the violent force associated with men's more 'angry' work. If 'lazy' when at home, men are also capable of exhilarating shows of effort; less reliable and, in recognized material terms, less important than the tasks performed by women, men's labors are, for Ilongots, both evidence and cause for women's lesser *liget* and men's 'higher' hearts.

Contrasts in style are confirmed by differences in orientation. And for Ilongots, the sheer fact that men climb higher and move farther than most women at once displays their lack of fear and heightened *liget,* and permits them all the *bēya* one acquires with new experiences and new perspectives – a sense of variation and diversity in nature and in human social life. Because women are constrained to move within a world defined by manmade clearings or the safety of a male companion, they experience more dependency, reserve, and fear than do their spouses; less 'knowing,' they are commonly unable to take command in public talk. Returning always to the same field and oriented to a single home, a woman's name and reputation may travel widely, but her knowledge and ability to discuss the new and distant remain constrained. Men, in tales of hunts and travels, may recount the places they have passed through; in headhunting songs and boasts, they name the obstacles encountered and hills and rivers crossed when on a raid. But women do not boast of their repeated daily efforts in familiar gardens; and on our tapes, when women's songs were finished, they tended to permit a man to celebrate them for their ties, as wives, mothers, or sisters, to masculine figures of renown. Or else – more rarely, and usually in laughter – the singer would proclaim herself the occupant of some particular river, or the annual provider of 'one hundred tens' (100 *pengē,* or 'columns of ten bundles') of grain.

Oriented to their families and gardens, women are more limited than men in both experience and courage – but, as is generally the case in Ilongot society, the contrast is more relative than absolute. Young girls, accompanying senior men, may travel, and so develop a familiarity with distant places that will provide them with the stuff of endless stories; and older women who have known and gardened hills as far as twenty miles distant can boast of all the slopes their hands have turned from forest into thicket – of distant plants and fruit trees that mark the world with evidence of their work. Finally, there are women who, like men, have traveled widely; less fearful of the stranger, they are seen as both intelligent and strong-minded   and adults of both sexes, in conversation, show respect for their more 'knowing' and often 'angry' tongues.

> Duman cited my Ilongot 'sister,' Wagat, as a woman of considerable *liget,* associating this with her travels to the lowlands during the time of the Japanese. That I was seen as such a woman (though never as respected as my husband) emerged in Wadeng's observation that women's hearts are likely to grow 'higher' when they go to school.

Yet the cultural importance of male movement is hardly taken lightly: Ilongots have, in recent years, begun to hire settlers to dig irrigation canals for what they hope will become permanently watered rice fields – not because Ilongot men have not begun to learn the skills required for the establishment of a stable paddy, but because (as several women told me) Ilongot men do not stay home enough to be entrusted with such labor; they are always on the move.

Distant orientations and a stunning and dramatic style provide, perhaps, the most obvious interpretations of the Ilongot claim that men have, more than women, an object for – 'a place to go with' – *liget;* they can, quite simply, travel to distant places, gain knowledge, and take life. But when informants spoke of women's lesser *liget,* they spoke not only of men's more violent style of labor and apparent need for movement, but also of the fact that women, when they fight, are sure to injure kinsmen, and that an angry woman can, in feeding her own children, make them ill. In short, informants seemed concerned not only about *styles* of action and expression, but also about implications – about the consequences of women's anger, given the form and organization of men's and women's lives. Women have 'no place to go with *liget*' because they live in spheres defined by kinship and cooperation – spheres in which heightened feelings are at once most likely to be expressed by women, and where their 'anger' leads, almost inevitably, to social division and domestic strife.

A contrast noted earlier, between the relatively "individualized" work of women, and the more "public" and community-oriented tasks performed by men, is, I think, central to this view of women's *liget* as limited because disruptive of local social life. Although a survey of some thirty-five Ilongot households indicates that in the thirteen where married women live with sisters or their mothers, most (with four exceptions) cultivate in common gardens, Ilongots view collective gardening as peculiar, insisting that it is best for every adult woman to tend a private field. Sisters will, they say, produce more if each cares for a separate set of gardens – because when women share responsibility and reputation with each other, they are far more likely to be lazy, to find themselves less 'angry' in their work. And in fact, though sisters may upon marriage cultivate gardens shared with sisters, and older women often work with daughters in a common field, there is a tendency over time for individual married women to establish separate gardens, and ultimately, to move from natal households, leaving at best a youngest daughter to remain within the household of her mother and to share food with her.

Magical prohibitions that limit collective effort at the onset of the harvest; the preference for all married women to have independent fields; as well as the fact that each independent producer stores her rice in granaries that are individually owned – all serve to mark the private and individualized nature of horticultural labor. Unlike the meat of hunters, rice is associated strictly with the woman who produced it;

and whereas male productive efforts are viewed, ideally, as collective – often engaging men from a variety of households and celebrated by their joint participation in a collective meal – women are restricted in their opportunities to help in one another's fields. Though our records of the days that individual women spent in planting, hoeing, or harvesting their neighbor's gardens indicate that networks of female extrahousehold cooperation are roughly coextensive with the collectivities involved in pollarding, hunting, and the distribution of game, women's cooperative labor is seen as casual and informal, deserving neither celebratory feasting nor other public note. Stated otherwise, female forms of cooperation – whether in collectively held gardens or informal labor in one another's fields – receive little cultural attention, thereby encouraging the view of their labor as individual and of their rice as produce that is individually appropriated and owned. Women *do* engage in socially significant forms of cooperation, and when rice is served at mealtimes, coresident women pool their labor and their produce in providing and preparing the household's staple food. But these facts are countered by a cultural view of rice as private produce, the fruit of individual effort in a private field. It is significant in this regard that Ilongots speak of times when feuds were triggered by a theft of rice or other garden produce – but never mention intrusions on a "hunting territory" or a "theft" of game.

A first and apparently contradictory consequence of these facts is that women in their daily work are assumed to be less 'angry/energetic' than most male producers. Because competition and a fear to be outdone excite the heart with *liget,* collective work groups lead laborers to strive and 'race' with one another – and so women, who tend to work alone much more than men do, are, by Ilongot reckoning, less likely to be stirred by 'angry' energy in their productive tasks. Though *liget* is occasioned by the individual woman's pride in private gardens, Ilongots recognize that in daily labor lonely workers are less stimulated by a spirit of emulation than are people who work in groups. Thus, women who work alone because they should not share responsibility with fellows find that their actual days of labor lack the added stimulus of collective effort; encouraged by individual subsistence needs and a personal pride in produce, women still do not, in daily work, experience the heightened *liget* known by men in publicly organized, collective work.

But even more significant is the cultural meaning that – given the stress on women's "private" orientation – comes to be assigned to female *liget.* I have already shown that women see productive gains as potentially dependent on the depletion of 'rice hearts' from their neighbors' gardens, their successes deriving from competitive advantage vis-à-vis people who are, or ought to be, cooperating kin. Because their work is cast as individual, women may be seen (or, like Sibat, cast themselves) as 'selfish': In spells, they ask for fame and reputation, calling 'fruitfulness*' to their gardens from all distant fields. Furthermore, because all stores of rice reflect directly on the women who produced them, women are often reluctant to use up supplies in everyday consumption. Their cooperation is not governed by the relatively formal and explicit norms that regulate sharing among hunters; and social strains developing in their communities and households are apt to be reflected in women's reluctance to lend their labor to each other, or to share, and so deplete their stores of grain. Rice, in such a context, becomes an idiom for the expression of selfish and divisive interests; and women's self-serving *liget* is readily identified as a source of social stress.

Thus, during the hungry years of World War II, grave imbalances in rice stores and failures of sharing were generally understood as the reason that people who had come to live together in Keradingan (see Chapter 1) could not continue as members of a single settlement. Fleeing Japanese troops who ravished granaries and gardens, some families were dependent for subsistence needs on kin who were already well-established in the interior area to which they fled. But women – it is claimed – were reluctant to give up declining rice stores to their kin in other households, and because of them, impoverished families were forced to move toward the lowlands where American soldiers promised food.

Similarly, in households where coresident women ideally share their produce, taking turns in going to their granaries to 'bring down' fresh stores of rice, conflicts about cooperation provide regular grounds for the splitting off of families from their residential groups. So it was that Disa, the stepmother of two coresident married sisters, was seen as the vain and selfish source of division in her husband's household. Proud of her stores and reluctant to exhaust them, her failure to contribute regularly to the daily diet was interpreted by the daughters as incompatible with their desire to live with and care for an aging father; and when one daughter moved upstream – to farmlands that, in any case, had to be cultivated if settlers were to be prevented from further expansion – Disa's self-concern (as reflected in recurrent household quarrels) was seen as the immediate occasion for the split. Similarly, Maniling's hope to move with his wife, Liya, to the settlement where her sister, Banaw, then resided – a move laden with political consequence, and a choice on his part to ally with the kinsmen of his father as against competing claims – was considered problematic, not because of the generally tense and burdened context of the new alignment, but rather because the sisters, Liya and Banaw (the first too proud, the second far too lazy), often quarreled and showed themselves unable to cooperate and share.

What these examples illustrate is that Ilongots, by casting female labor as essentially individual, make it likely that local conflicts will be blamed on women's competitive and disruptive *liget* – their unwillingness to share their grain. Pressures of a variety of sorts – the requirements of postmarital uxorilocal residence and subsequent demands of aging kin, the need to cultivate and so make claims to land desired by settlers, the noise of growing children in a crowded home – may encourage families to join or to divide their place of residence; but the immediate and disruptive consequences of such shifts are often muted by attributing them to women's limited, expectable, and selfish goals. When women fight about cooperation (as they did in Disa's household), men can 'follow' them and yet bemoan their lack of *bēya* – so guaranteeing that divisions "caused" by women will not make for permanent and destructive grudges among presumedly related men.

Or, to reverse perspectives: Because local splits are readily blamed on female *liget,* and because women, who should cooperate with coresident kinfolk, are encouraged to work alone, it makes sense that the *liget* associated with women's efforts will be held to be not desirable, but problematic, and so, whenever possible, either trivialized or suppressed. Women's hearts are not, in general, 'high' and violent – not because of women's nature, but because their lives are organized in ways that guarantee that 'anger' is the source, at once, of pride and conflict. In a world where women's goals are tied to rice and private interest, their *liget,* potentially divisive, must be limited in both experience and expression – or, as informants put it, women's hearts are 'lower' because their *liget* has 'no place to go.'

Conclusion

The ways that Ilongots talk about the difference between the sexes and represent it in their magic are bound up in the style and organization of their traditional productive tasks. That men and women, engaged in complementary sorts of labor, are seen as 'equal humans,' while, at the same time, the *liget* both desire in their efforts is associated in a special way with men who hunt and kill, makes sense to Ilongots because it "fits" a world view that insists on the rootedness of human life in human labor, and because Ilongots have, traditionally, cast labor in a particular and distinctive form. It is not, perhaps, surprising, in the increasingly Christian world of contemporary experience, with headhunting virtually abandoned, game seriously depleted,[14] and men a good deal more inclined than previously to pound rice and help wives in their fields, that even non-Christian Ilongots are adopting new patterns of production, making new use of cash in interactions with one another, and abandoning the magical spells that provided them with images of what traditional productive tasks (and so, the men and women who perform them) are, or should be, like.

Yet I speak of change not to reify the past or to predict the future, but to underline the cultural centrality of the activities with which this chapter is concerned. For Ilongots, the violent and dramatic cast of hunting as opposed to gardening; the fact that men move through the forest while women stay in clearings near the home; and finally, the locally divisive implications of women's private rice stores that emerge because of strains that are themselves a part of the organization and cultural image of women's work – all contribute to a view of women as less 'angry' and less 'knowing' than the male producer; and they do this while providing, nonetheless, for a positive recognition of women's efforts and their skills.

Because Ilongots do not elaborate upon specifically female virtues (regarding even reproduction and lactation as relatively incidental to women's productive work), I have asked in this discussion not "What do Ilongots see as different or distinctive about women?" but rather why or in what sense do Ilongots, who view the sexes as similar and 'equal humans,' come to see women as morally subordinate because less 'angry' than most men. What remains to be examined is the question of how men who do, or did once, have 'a place to go with *liget*' understand the place of 'angry' force in their lives and social relationships, not so much with women as with one another; and how *liget* plays a crucial role not only in the relations of the sexes, but also in relations among men.

5. Headhunting: a tale of 'fathers,' 'brothers,' and 'sons'

A mutual reticence prevented Ilongots from speaking – and us from asking – about topics we all acknowledge to be threatening to our slow and carefully tended growth of friendship and of trust, and this feeling kept us from raising serious questions about killing until we had completed close to one year in the field. We learned then of songs and ceremony, and gradually, of raids and living feuds, but it was only weeks before our first twenty-one-month field stay ended that we felt we could discuss with Tukbaw a matter that had long been on our minds. What we wondered was, quite simply, how people whom we liked and admired as much as Tukbaw and his companions could be killers; we thought we could understand many things they did and said, but not why people whom we valued for their open ease and generosity found it reasonable and important to take heads.

Tukbaw's answer, as pithy as it then seemed unrevealing and stark, stood for a long time in our reflections as a symbol of the very distance that our question had addressed. To our probing "Why?" he responded with a dull, 'It is our custom' – as if acknowledging, or asserting, the limits of our talk. We were all, he told us, children of one God – and we agreed with him. But at some point, he claimed, our paths had separated, our ancestors winding up across the ocean from his own. He imagined that since that time, and in every generation, most sons had followed fathers: Because the grandfathers of his grandfathers had taken heads, so did their sons; our (American) ancestors had no such custom, and so we did not understand what made Ilongots want to kill. With the care of a craftsman and a sense of problem that indicated that he knew just what it was we sought, Tukbaw spoke in terms that for years remained in our silent notes as if to mock us. Humbled by what seemed his reasonable – if apparently unilluminating – assessment, we resigned ourselves to the sense in which we never would be able fully to accept or understand a world whose values seemed as arbitrary as they were abhorrent to our own. Tukbaw's 'customs' were nor ours, nor could we hope to grasp them. I still do not know why Ilongots find deep psychological satisfaction in killing, in slashing victims, and in severing and tossing to the ground a human head. But if awareness that our friends took pleasure in their violent past continues to distress me, investigations during our return fieldwork in 1974 began to show the sense in Tukbaw's tale of the inheritance of 'custom' – and I realized that something of the "answer" I once hoped for was in fact the point of Tukbaw's earlier remarks.

What I now think Tukbaw was saying is something like the following. The *liget* that Ilongots associate with youthful prowess and, for them, with the universal agitation that makes young men want to kill, takes on reality and significance because it is bound up not in mystery or cosmology, but in three forms of relation central to Ilongot social life. *Liget* is transmitted through a hierarchical, cross-generational tie between 'sons' and their 'fathers'; it is activated in the symmetrical relations that distinguish tiers of 'big ones' or 'fathers' from unmarried youthful peers, 'quick ones,' or 'sons'; and finally, 'angry' killing delineates a contrast between Ilongots as headhunters and a disapproving outside world.

The Ilongot/Catholic lowland contrast, and the ways in which headhunting has served for both Ilongots and outsiders (though with rather different meanings and evaluations) as an emblem of their distinctive forms of life, make sense in a historical context fully explicated in the work of Renato Rosaldo (1979) and only briefly mentioned here. But the ties of 'big' and 'quick' ones, and the symmetrical and potentially competitive relations that emerge in groups of peers, were experienced by Tukbaw and others as a timeless charter, generative of motives that might at any time encourage killing – and grounded in the wide-ranging and complex significance that *liget,* as epitomized in taking heads, lends to Ilongot conceptions of everything from crafts to agricultural labor, from youthful skill and violence to marriage and the reproduction of a familiar and intelligible social world. My purpose in this chapter will be to examine aspects of 'energy/anger' realized in the traditional Ilongot practice of beheading human victims; to explicate the logic by which young men come to be the angry 'bachelors,' who – as a boy of ten once told me – 'will not accept the Christian "news" *(bēita)* because they now are "quick ones"'; and to show how a youth's concern to win a 'spirit of the beheaded' is related, first, to Ilongot conceptions of the ties between young men and elders, and then, to marriage and competition among peers.

'Fathers' and desiring 'sons'

When asked why they go killing, Ilongots occasionally mention grief and the 'bad feelings' *('uget)* which, born of the loss of kinsmen, are felt as weights and burdens until one 'reaches' the dumb body of a victim, slashes it, and tosses off its head. They may, with reference to specific situations, speak of vengeance: an insult, threat, or theft that stands unanswered; assaults on land by settlers; killings performed by Ilongots of other kin groups in the past. The loss of would-be lovers; a breach of 'word' experienced as an insult; the memory of sleepless nights when unfamiliar hosts talked, or indicated that they thought, of killing; the destitution of refugees who, in fleeing soldiers, happened to 'steal' sugar cane or corn from local fields – all of these provide accounts for killings in which the victim is selected by virtue of some tie of kinship to the perpetrator of the original offense. But at all times, and whether or not the raiders recognize a complaint against their victims, Ilongots see headhunting as the product not just of vengeance, but of desire – the goal of hopeful youths whose numbers were increasing and who, through tears and songs or constant sulking, indicated that their hearts were 'twisted up' with *liget* and anxious to 'reach' the violent feats attained by 'fathers' in the past.

Whatever their political concerns or quirks of fortune (and the factors that move individuals to join together and go raiding may be at least as various as those mentioned in the preceding paragraph), Ilongots agree that headhunting has a good deal less to do with enemies and victims than with the desire of young men to emulate their 'fathers,' the hopes of people who – because of youth or individual misfortune – have felt a weight that they would 'cast off' from their hearts. It is for 'cloudy,' crying, 'empty-handed' youths, for 'novices' *(siap)* who have not 'reached' their 'manhood' or known the pride of men who wear bright headhunter's hornbill earrings 'perched' (like victims' 'hearts,' which are identified, at times, with birds) upon their ears – it is for them that Ilongots say they tire themselves in cautious raiding. Concerned less with personal glory than with the young man's need to kill, men recognize that headhunting is an aspect of the process by which children realize in their turn the life and energy once achieved by elders, renewing, through their show of 'passion,' the experience and vitality of adults.

As children, young boys learn, and relive in their play, the headhunting encounters of their elders; they hear songs that celebrate the distances traversed by raiders; have mock duels with tiny shields and spears of local grasses; and from the 'stories' told by seniors, learn of slights and insults that they will, if truly 'angry,' avenge when they are grown. In his teenage years, the boy experiences not only the humiliating accomplishments of would-be equal agemates, but also the boasts of elders – who, in treetops when they pollard gardens, and at rituals and celebrations, taunt young men into *liget* with booming 'invocations' *('eyap)* of their prior deeds. Aware and 'angered' by their predecessors' feats of violence, alert to scorn and to the mocking claim that 'empty-handed' grooms behead their wives, these youths declare that they are loathe to court or marry 'without earrings.' Some Ilongot men in youthful 'clouds' have taken oaths *(binatan),* like those occasionally pronounced by mourners, who – to heighten their own *liget* and notify their fellows of an intention to take life – forswear the use of certain foods or weapons, or even, in extreme cases, carry whips that they have friends and neighbors use to beat them on entering into any but familiar homes. Others show their 'angry' goals by slashing baskets, yelling, or spilling water, by singing songs of longing, by being irritable and distracted, or, in public contexts, by reflecting on the unknown deeds that separate them from more accomplished elders – and sobbing softly as their tears 'drip to the ground.'

On our tape recorder, these youths proclaimed: 'Even though the word of God has permeated our country, I, so-and-so, will not forget

Flute music both expresses and excites thoughts of beheading.

the *liget* of my fathers,' or again: 'My heart is twisted and distracted and cannot let loose its weighty thoughts.' They sang of knives with lovely scabbards, decorated by 'a girl, a maid, as if to shame me' – the beauteous design serving no function because its owner, incomplete and shy to travel, finds himself condemned to 'foggy' days at work in fields. And, in 1968, a boy (who took a head in 1972) composed these songs to let his elders know his heart:[1]

> Oh dear,[2] boy, you are as a fog, and all things wait,
> dear child, for the moment when you will say the head-
> hunting spells;
> warm your thoughts for the thing you desire, that you
> may, like an airplane, fly to the spirit that you will dismember;
> go right on with your plans to kill!
>
> Ah, it is fine for you grown ones to be quiet while
> your shoot here your child is all astir;
> oh, if only he had, like you old ones, clipped off the
> red blossoms of the fire tree, and returned home from
> his travels a killer,
> looking like flowering feathery grass.

In more recent songs, youths mourn a presumed eternity of cloudy unfulfillment, their knives valued for no more than projected bridewealth giving, their lives constrained, since 1972, by Marcos and his feared Martial Law.[3]

Though men at different times have married and seen families grow without themselves beheading victims, and in the local interactions of cooperating kinfolk one encounters no invidious distinctions between the 'unaccomplished' *(depyang)* few and more successful killers of their age, most men have, in the past, managed to toss off a victim's head and most have done this before marriage – desires for killing being associated primarily with the bachelor youth.

> Exceptions are those men who reached their late twenties and thirties in years when pressure from governmental troops or hopes of school-ing led to a virtual cessation of killings in the Ilongot region as a whole. Data from early in the century suggest that perhaps one quar-ter of the men who came of age in the late nineteenth century, and until about 1915, married without beheading. Again, about one-half of the men married in the 1930s were 'novices' *(siap)*, but most of these managed to take Ilongot heads in the subsequent years of internal chaos and disruption (see Chapter 1) or else to behead a Japanese in 1945. Kadēng, for example, was a married 'novice' with three chil-dren when he was arested on false charges of beheading in 1940; but while in prison on the island of Palawan, he served as a guide to American troops and managed to behead a Japanese.

Because men who came of age in the 1950s and early 1960s had univer-sally taken heads before they married, the bachelors whom we knew in

1967-9 intended likewise. And at the time of our initial fieldwork, youth was recognized by all as a period of intense and often rash preoccupation (see the story of Burur, Chapter 3) – a time for energy and hard labor, but also for shows of shy ill-ease and erratic self-absorption, which indicated that young men, free of a 'vine-like' maiden's legs and otherwise unsubdued by family obligations, were capable of anarchic and 'unknowing' acts of self-indulgent force.

Like young plants, these youths were full of life, but also – like new knives in songs – untried and full of danger. Not only were we discouraged in 1967-9 from using such men as guides in lonely places, but I recall at least one instance in which a youth (who was to take a head in 1970) was explicitly instructed to behave himself while hiking with an elderly uncle on a distant trail. Certainly, young men, anxious to kill – and in defiance of political designs and even the sworn covenants of elders – may occasionally call friends together and, alone or with no more than one or two companions, stalk unwary victims by themselves. These killings, called *linibēt,* 'sneaked,' or 'hidden,' are much more likely to be immediately disruptive of ongoing social and political ties than those planned by older men:

> In the early 1960s, Tayeg went alone with an Ilocano lowland companion in search of beehives he claimed to have discovered – but, once in the forest, he killed the man, whose death turned out to place the Ilongot kin with whom Tayeg was living in an uncomfortable position vis-à-vis their Ilocano trader friends, and even more seriously, with the enforcers of Philiine national law. Tayeg's action had no 'cause' other than the restlessness of a bachelor. Again, when Luku, having been present on the occasion of an oath sworn by salt to ensure peace in 1952, decided in the same year, and on the basis of a variety of as yet unaddressed personal grudges, to raid against the Butag *bērtan,* the 'causes' for his action were only slightly less opaque. The raid was carried out by four young men – all but one of whom were bachelors, two novices, and none established family men – without the guidance of an elder. As in the case of Tayeg, it turned out to undermine explicit public and political relations that had been established by adults.

But far more common are the stories of boys in their late teens who, having learned to pollard, hunt, and otherwise display the skills of elders, urge fathers that it is time that they too had the opportunity to win a headhunter's ornaments and reputation. And elders, 'knowledgeable' about the needs of youths and possible avenues for beheadings, then show their sons a 'place to go' with 'angry' hearts. They may (as Tukbaw recalled of his own father) tease boys with comments on their youthful fear and inability to abide the trials of raiding, or disappoint them with indefinite pleas for patience – because, as fortune has it, 'we' no longer have so many enemies as in the past. Whether, as in

Tukbaw's youth, the coming of the Japanese; or, as in the case of Lakay (his wife's now aging father), a combination of moves, feuds, and local realignments made potential vitims of people once considered friends; or again, as happened in the postwar adolescence of the sons of Lakay, settlers, moving in on Ilongot margins, provided easy targets for a sudden flood of raids, the specific congruence of historical factors that selects the people whom one's elders see as likely victims has varied considerably in the course of this century. And the mean age of first beheadings has varied with it, from a high of about thirty-five years in the last decade (1925-35) of American colonial rule to a low of twenty years in the early 1950s.

> As already noted, the late 1920s and early 1930s were characteized by an almost complete cessation of Ilongot raiding. Not surprisingly, many bachelors married in this period without taking heads at the late age of about thirty, and, in marked contrast to postwar patterns (when almost all first beheaders were bachelors), raids before the war included a number of married men who were still novices, but who were bent on beheading. Lakay himself was married when he joined Rumyad kin in raiding against the Payupay *bērtan* and took a head in 1927.

Clustered at certain times, virtually abandoned during others, killings in different periods have tended to assume the various forms of *ngayu,* proper 'raids' on distant places, or *ka'abung,* 'in the household,' the deception and ultimate beheading of unwary guests or neighbors in a nearby home.[4]

But although the timing and style of killings differ, their place in autobiographical reflections tends to have a constant shape. Of well over 100 raids for which we have good data, none in the last fifty years has been without at least one 'empty-handed' youth, or 'novice' *(siap),* and very few have lacked the guidance of adults. Furthermore, although a minority of men have had occasion to take more than a single head during a lifetime, the presence of 'knowing' seniors has helped to guarantee that at least one novice takes a head on each successful raid. Thus, the personal and age-specific goals of youths merge with political designs and needs of elders; and just as young men hope to 'reach' the *liget* of their fathers' prior efforts before they marry, so accomplished headhunters find in grief, in their care for 'sons,' or in more enduring feuds and grudges a reason to guide young men on a raid.

In general, it is the responsibility of an older man, who 'knows' how to ambush and to flee pursuers, to call on spirit helpers, cut through thickets, 'suffer' days of short provisions, and demonstrate the mix of *liget* and due caution necessary to a safe assault. It is for such men to call together a company of variously motivated raiders. Adults will give direction to youth's 'angry' thoughts, choose objects and pursuers, and guarantee through hours of careful talk and planning that participants will cooperate with one another and help selected 'empty-handed' youths toss away the severed heads of victims in accord with a fixed plan. So it was, in 1969, that the near-blind Kugkug of the downstream region visited and gave new life to kinship ties with certain Rumyad men of our acquaintance – in hopes that they would jointly assume the role of *'anup*, 'master of a pack of hunt dogs,' in guiding his unhappy, 'angry' son, the 'young pup' Sideng, on a raid.

This process, by which older men bring together a raiding party by speaking to selected kin or friends and neighbors, and then, through formal talk when all are gathered, attempt to fix among participants a shared sense of the prerogatives of their numerous 'children' depending on the numbers that are killed, is only one of many ways in which elders emerge in raids as 'knowing' guides of youthful *liget,* the people who can show young men a focused and appropriate avenue for their 'passion' and keep the related threats of chaos and passivity (see Chapter 2) in abeyance for the period of the raid. In Kugkug's case, his skillful talk led to the formation of a raiding party of men who at the time remained non-Christian, and who had reasons of their own to recognize Kugkug as a 'father' and Sideng as a 'younger brother' needing care. Because some raiders thought of other 'pups,' of sons and nephews who were equally oppressed with weighty 'clouds,' ashamed, and 'empty-handed,' formal oratory before the raiders left their houses was necessary to guarantee sequential access of the boys to victims. And so, for each 'young pup,' one 'hunting master' was recognized as a sponsor, who would guide him through the maze of slashing and excited raiders to a body other men might struggle to behead. Victims downed can readily become the focus of a wild contest among killers, were it not carefully and formally negotiated by the elders, before departing, which children they were 'hunting for' and helping to take heads.

> In the excitement that follows killing, formal agreements are not always successful. While raiding in 1966, Bēgtek – an older man who had taken a head almost thirty years before – found himself carried away with *liget* and beheaded a victim intended for the bachelor Wagal. Bēgtek reported the event as testimony to his *liget,* but my impression was that, for other Ilongots, Bēgtek's failure to attend their cries to 'remember our oratory' proved that he lacked the *bēya* and consideration expected of adults.

These 'masters' of 'young hunt dogs' warn the boys before they leave of hardships and the difficulties they will encounter, and in their 'knowing' speech set forth for all the terms of joint cooperation and dependence and their need to act as 'of one body,' subordinating knowledge of their varied provenance and kinship to the collective trials that lie ahead. When on the trail, these older men may carry, climb, and generally work less than the young boys they are guiding. Enforcing silence and the cautious stance that guarantees the Forest Spirit's pleasure, they will instead 'command' the youngsters: first, to scout, to cook, and to distribute food while they are walking, then to pound their heads to 'raise' and 'concentrate' their *liget,* and finally, to chew the betel nuts prepared at home by wives and lovers, enjoy last thoughts of kin and comfort – then spit, and thus 'cast off,' their weighty thoughts of women left at home. Elders will, while on the trail, attend to omen birds, movements of snakes and bees, and warning calls of owls. They teach raw youths to 'purchase' betel chews with leaves called 'heads' of victims; to avoid a food like salt, that 'disappears,' or eel, that slips and makes one's grasp uncertain; to sit on thorns and suffer cold, concealing 'anxious' *('iteg)* twistings of their hearts in 'slow' and cautious movement. And, in 'coaxing' boys who would turn faint with fear and hunger, they guarantee that by the time they reach their chosen place of ambush, all participants will feel their eyes as blazes, focused only on a victim, and uninvolved with any but the thought of killing fellow humans, 'equal men.'

Once shots are fired, the raiders rush upon and struggle for their injured and dead victims in a chaos Ilongots describe with the word, *'amuluk* (probably related to the Austronesian root contained in the English expression "run amok," and used primarily for dogs who race toward meat set out before them). It is typically a 'master' who fights off competing thrusts of other angry killers. This 'master' calls out, *Rarawantu dimu,* 'So-and-so, it goes to you to act, if you would hurry and behead this human,' and then 'captures' *(dekep)* as he sits upon the body that his 'young pup' will behead. The youth himself may manage to cut through the neck or simply hold the head as it is severed: Recognition of 'beheading' *(putur)* belongs to the man who manages to throw the head directly on the ground.

> If the tossed head is caught by another before reaching the ground, the man who first threw it does not count as its 'beheader.' So it was that Gelgel, cousin to Lakay and a distant 'father-in-law' of Tukbaw, once tossed a head that Tukbaw's father caught and dropped to the ground. Tukbaw and his brothers enjoy the secret knowledge that their father was responsible for the beheading, but Lakay and his kin, never having noticed the interception, believe that the beheader was really Gelgel, and, in order to avoid conflict among affines, Tukbaw has chosen to let Lakay's version stand as public fact.

The successful beheader throws the head while calling out, *Buu, pipiriw-mu dēken,* 'Buu, you can't snatch this away from me, this head of,' for example, a 'big man' *(makutay),* 'girl' *(kepariyan),* or 'child' *(mala'eg)* – suggesting that in triumph he is singled out from his peers. Wild with what they describe as burning joy, furious, and intent on mutilation, his fellows join in tossing, slashing, and shouting after all the heads are severed – 'I grabbed you up from off the ground and tossed your head, my victim,' 'I cut so you could feel my knife as well'[5] – until one man, again an elder, brings their *liget* to its senses, calling out, 'It goes to you to act; we cannot stay here; do you think this is a feast?'

Returning from the site of death, the raiders 'taste' *(tamtam)* by picking up pots, weapons, food, or other items from their victims' persons. To keep their *liget* hot and strong, they make a point of toasting sugar cane and drinking only heated water – or, if inclined to cooler drink, they are sure to say while sipping, 'May this water chill the *liget* of my enemies in such-and-such a place.' If tense, the raiders yell and may occasionally cut off short locks of hair to free themselves of gorey 'smells of blood' *(na'nget),* which some men find oppressive. But the high and lightened spirits that emerge from a successful raid know nothing of the plodding, silent strain that characterized their approach. Alive and energized with their success, released from fear, and gay with singing, older men relive the 'anger' of their youths, while young men know that they have shed their 'clouds' and, as they put it, 'found their bodies' – having reached, through killing, a semblance of their fathers' deeds, the long-desired accomplishments of adults.

Ilongots say that they need elders on their raids to keep their *liget* 'high' and their hearts 'focused'; that without them, youths are apt to be incautious and expose themselves to pointless risks. Typically, it is for older men, not youths, to choose a time and object for beheadings, and with victims downed (when men rush wildly to slash and to behead them), it is generally the older men who are expected to remember and enforce the agreements of their prior discourse, keep youths from hurting one another, and guarantee each 'pup' his opportunity to take a head. The place of older men emerges too when, safe at home, ceremonies must be performed to ensure and give new life to youthful *liget;* to strengthen women who – for fear of ulcers, scars, and sores – must be protected from the 'smell of blood' on brothers, sons, and husbands; and, with the sacrificial blood of pig or chicken, to guarantee the killers' health and 'red' vitality in the face of curses from the kinsmen of the dead.

> 'Redness,' associated with *liget,* and therefore with disruptive phenomena such as fever, as well as with strength and health, is acquired through eating meat, taking heads, and wearing red ornaments. As most red ornaments are associated with headhunting and youthful vitality, it appears that the things that promote 'redness' are them-

selves the products of the 'energy/anger' that the color is said to reflect. Whenever we returned to the field from Manila, Ilongots commented on our loss of color – something they attributed not to urban
life and confinement, but to our failure, while in the city, to eat game.
And although associated with healthy 'redness,' meat is a tabooed
food in many kinds of illness because *liget* is, in such cases, undesirable.

When sacrificing pigs, an elder must be named to 'hold' the youths
who have, through killing, 'reached' their manhood – and if, as happened in the case of Burur, close senior kin were not the ones to guide
the youth in killing, the choice of such an elder can itself call forth
disputes concerning kinship, and arguments about which men are truly
'fathers' to which 'sons.' In every case, what is important is that 'angry'
and accomplished youths are linked in their achievement to an elder; the
fact that Burur had gone to raid with a young and distant 'uncle' (who,
though 'mastered' as a 'pup' by Lakay, a close 'grandfather' to Burur
and a more distant 'uncle' of his own, had since avoided ties with
Burur's kin) was interpreted as an insult to the closer kin of Burur's
parents – and the choice of a leading elder became so problematic that
it took our anthropological curiosity to assure that the celebration in
fact occurred.[6]

In short, the thoughts that motivate a raid, and determine its shape and
organization, are rooted in and understood in terms of ties between
young 'cloudy' boys and more accomplished seniors. The continuity of
generations is hardly incidental to the harsh facts of beheading; it is –
even when, as in Burur's case, ill-defined and problematic – a good part
of what killing is about. Youths say they kill because their 'fathers' have;
and adult men are responsible for inciting, giving direction to, then
celebrating the triumphs of, the lively and demanding 'anger' in young
hearts. Distinctions between old and young enhance and lend conviction
to adult claims to authority, while at the same time public recognition of
the unruliness of youths becomes a resource in adult political life.

> In the early 1960s, the Pugu people convinced our Rumyad friends to
> swear an oath of salt against assaults on lowland settlers in their vicinity
> at a time when the Rumyads – fearful of all oaths because of a recent
> death brought on by one apparent violation, and in any case, far from
> inclined to raid where friends might accidentally be killed – found the
> request insulting and absurd. The Pugus won their point when a young
> man of the Rumyad group, known to feel some private *liget* against
> Pugu, left the site of the discussion. His exit proved that he harbored
> thoughts such as the Pugus feared, and so, when Pugu leaders argued
> that 'whatever your intentions, youths are more inclined to heed an
> oath than a mere elders 'wishes,' the Rumyads felt themselves obliged
> to join in an oath.

But although the image of youths' violent and unthinking wills can serve political designs of elders, the 'quick' and 'angry' thoughts of boyish hearts belong to a significant world that old and young must share: a world where *bēya* and 'slow' caution in adults depend upon the *liget* realized in youthful glamour, and where elders will themselves find satisfaction not in power or the reverence people elsewhere grant ancestral figures, but rather in the reproduction of their way of living, in the accomplishments and vitality of the young. Taking heads is something youths desire because it promises equality with seniors; for adults, it is an aspect of the self-renewing cycles of 'energy' or *liget* that operate, as we have seen in Chapter 2, in individual motivation, but also in the ties of generations, and in projected hopes for sons.

Lives cycling: liget and age

Headtaking, as a moment of great emotional release and expansive and transcendent satisfaction, represents, for Ilongots, the point in the human life cycle when vitality is at its fullest, limited neither by childish constraints of 'fear' and lack of 'knowledge,' nor by the deterioration of 'energy,' skill, and independence that accompanies marriage, childbearing, and age. The 'heightened' health and energy that killers feel epitomize a 'passion' that will, at other times, stir one's heavy limbs to work, call forth the 'hearts' of rice and game, draw guests, and ultimately contribute to an unconstrained and lively reputation. With plentiful food and stores of rice, both men and women think of entertaining untold guests and enjoying in their homes the helping hands and gossip of near strangers; but even more, by taking heads, young men revitalize the working rhythms of their homes and think as well of fame that will keep 'shame' and 'fear' from limiting their voyages abroad, of ornaments that communicate to all the new and forceful *liget* in their hearts. Thus, much as gardeners invoke the 'hearts' of rice, and hunters 'heat' their bows and 'hands' in preparation for their efforts, so headhunters, while still near home, give offerings to a Forest Lord who provides them with the hearts of future victims. And the aspiring killers, thus endowed, cannot but find the 'dumb' and fated victims who will wander, much like lovers, in search of hearts now destined to become an aspect of the fame of men who take their lives.

Commanding distance, calling hearts, cutting others while remaining safe from danger. headhunters typify Ilongot ideals of potency, productive health, and beauty – and in their songs, ornaments, boasts, and dance, they show that, 'angered' and renewed by a fresh victim's life, men can turn disturbing facts of daily worlds into the substance of a collective and transcendent joy. 'Hardened' with sacrificial blood, they have the potent 'redness' which, if challenging to other men, is for themselves a sign of well-being and protection; and wearing the sweet-smelling leaves that signify the spirits of the dead, they bear reminders of the fact that joy acquired must be renewed if it is not to die like long-cut leaves and grasses – that human effort has no point if not to recreate itself in time to come.

Thus, if headhunting exemplifies for Ilongots the way in which a *liget* socially induced can be the source of collective health and pleasure, it also links collective interest to the activities of envious peers and of the striving young. Aspiring headhunters, as they appear in story, myth, and casual talk, are almost always cast as bachelors; and killers, proud with earrings, ornaments, and strength, are recognized, in recollection and in song, as well-equipped to tempt unmarried teenage girls:

> Here, here they are, these men who have taken heads,
> Wearing earrings, they have taken heads,
> Here, here they are, all lined up, the girls,
> Wearing new red blouses, all the girls,
> Ah, like a twisting vine, the thighs of killers and the girls.

Not surprisingly, the imagery associated with successful killers is itself bound up in Ilongot views of youth and aging – of cycles whereby *liget* is inevitably lost and then renewed by children in their quest for satisfactions that their elders have acquired.

For Ilongots, to be young and 'quick,' unbound by family claims and undiminished by the wearing facts of sex or reproduction, is to be energized, 'alert and anxious' *(ngelem)* with desire. The unmarried of both sexes acquire 'knowledge,' grace, and skill in seeking the recognition of adults and peers, a personal sense of competence and control, and the admiration of future lovers. Stirred on by maidens' taunts or songs, inspired by bright red tufts of wool – the 'berries' that a girl has stitched upon one's loincloth, belt, or scabbard – young boys sing songs which, in Ilongot phrase, are said to 'climb upon' the aspirations of their 'bodies' *(betrang)*, indicating their sense that they are unfulfilled, dependent on, and so demanding of, the senior kin who shaped and gave direction to their hearts. They sing of hopes to marry and to kill, to make good use of the food that they were fed as babies. Desiring to 'shed clouds' and grow, they cast themselves as crying infants who, though limited by age and skill, seek light and fame in which to thrive:

> Oh, now, for you, bachelor.
> Oh dear, it seems that your body finds itself sad and aban-
> doned, that no one will help you chase your clouds away.
> Sadly, those who bore you, young bachelor, are no longer with

us, and so, bachelor, bachelor, you go on hoping for
someone who cares.
But alas, as from spite, your fog will not leave you, since
the New Law, from Marcos, forbids you to realize your thoughts.
O dear, then, poor bachelor, still crying and still the tears fall, still they fall.
But there is nothing to do since, in spite, it is forbidden,
ruled out.
Forbidden to you, by the offspring of God.
Pointless, even if you take care of the shine of your knife,
you are doomed to be sad forever, ceaselessly cloaked with fog . . .
Ah, it would have been fine if right off, when a babe in the care
of one who bore you, you had died in her arms; since now
she has wasted her pains.
And your song, when it travels, when it goes far and wide,
will shrink, will withdraw, like your cloudy heart . . .
Ah, maybe a skirt, a blue skirt will distract you;
maybe you can turn to a woman . . .
Who knows what will happen to this bachelor who sits by
the river and waits.
Farewell.

But if youths see themselves as limited and incomplete, they know
that at the same time they are healthy, strong, and lively. Hardwork-
ing, they are desirable as guests; and lacking obligations that confine
them to their homes, they seem to love to travel.

> In 1974, after 'discovering' kinship with his Rumyad kin, the Tamsi
> father of Pagad 'lent' his bachelor son to labor with and live for some
> weeks as a 'follower' of a Rumyad 'brother' who promised to make
> the father a gift of arrows. Pagad wound up staying with his Rumyad
> hosts for several months, and, despite 'gossip' that told that he was
> expected in his father's home, he continued to enjoy the opportunity
> to hunt and visit in a strange locale and learn crafts from his still
> youthful 'uncle.' Though he occasionally voiced hopes that Rumyad
> kin would one day lead him on a raid, and there were rumors of
> romantic interest in a local maiden, Pagad's visit turned out, in the
> end, to have no special purpose; my impression was that the uncle
> never managed to complete the promised arrows because he so en-
> joyed the young man's company and labor in his household. And like
> many an unmarried youth, Pagad himself seemed content to have a
> chance to live away from home.

Like airplanes, songs, good names, or fame, these youths are light and
mobile. And when Ilongots speak of endless, stirring, youthful songs;
of maidens' voices that move men to kill; of pure vibratos which, like
quivering earrings, touch the heart, and which, like youths themselves,
will travel widely, their talk of light and energetic voices evokes images
of potency and expansion, qualities associated with youthful freedom
and the real prowess of young men who boast of crossing mountains,
fording streams, and even 'traveling to the sunset' in their quest for

human victims and the fame of taking life. Capable, alert, still 'looking for' *('adiwar, gēlasagēt)* new forms of 'knowledge' and satisfaction, the youth who is not 'slurred' or 'tainted' *(bēngen)* by a lover's name – not bound by 'vines' born of romantic promise and attachment – is called a 'shoot' or 'sprout,' a young plant 'pushing' upward; and this image of potential growth recalls the headhunter who, returning home, relieved of weight and 'reddened' with the spirit of a victim, will warn that doorways can no longer hold his new-found size, nor houseposts bear his strengthened body.

Again, like headhunters, who will cut and 'steal' or 'snatch' *(piriw)* a life, but themselves gain in vitality, grace, and presence, so 'quick ones,' undiminished and unscarred by age, are often said to 'steal' *(piriw)* the life of elders. Ilongots who saw photographs of me dressed up in Western clothes, relaxed and 'looking pretty,' declared that such pictures must date from my more youthful years, when I was still a 'maiden' – much as my good friend Duman claimed that I had missed a glimpse of male perfection in never seeing my 'brother-in-law,' Tukbaw, as a graceful and unmarried boy. Marriage and reproduction are, for Ilongots, a 'cutting short' or 'clipping off' of healthy growth and motion; and if victims are literally cut in two and equated with the lovely plants that headhunters clip and kill to wear in armband decorations, so the old are seen in opposition to their living 'branches,' 'shoots,' and 'sprouts' – the children who deprived them of young strength. Their life, like that of victims, has been diminished in contributing to the substance of a still growing generation; and, like victims who, in heart at least, are thought to be attracted to their killers, so adult men and women speak in songs with longing for the energy and mobility of youth:

Ah, to travel like the airplane that goes spreading
God's word to people everywhere, covering the globe.
But this girl must be patient now and stay at home.
Oh, dear, it is no longer as it was when she was grow-
ing and her song flowed forth in all directions.
Sadly, she is changed now, and her shoots have grown big.
Cut short, she must limit her play and stop her singing.
Oh dear, it is not as it was when she would spend her days
arranging her skirts to go walking along river banks and
open paths.
Oh dear, she is faded now, because her shoots themselves have
grown.
Farewell, fly away, farewell.

Oh dear, alas, no longer a bachelor, you poor boy.
It isn't as it was when you were growing up and thinking
thoughts, making plans of all kinds, when your playful song

knew no limits and cast itself far and wide.
Because now, all has changed, and your footsteps have aged,
like water, bogged down with mud and dead leaves.
Sadly, your heart must submit.
Oh dear boy, you have lost your youth.

Their voices weak, their skin turned soft from having given life, their thoughts constrained by obligation, adults experience a sharp decline in the desiring and expansive ease that they enjoyed as growing children. Our skeptical friend, Tepeg, remarked that men should marry only after taking heads because with family and responsibilities to attend, a man is no longer free to plan extended absences from home, and so is not inclined to think of killing. 'Weighted down' and ill-equipped to walk or cast their voices far, most married men will say they must cut short their songs because their bodies, having sent forth 'shoots,' are scarred, reduced, and 'toothless'; the loss of teeth, in dreams an image of forthcoming death, in childhood a promise of development, is itself bound up in Ilongot views of bodily imperfection and of change. But where a child's tooth, tied to a runo sprout, is – like the plant itself – full of potential, the aging singer can look forward only to failures of 'energy' and strength, to dessication, illness, and decline.[7] When listening on our tape to Tedining – an older woman whose vibrato even then could make men pound their chests and declare that were her voice as full as it had been in her young, 'sprouting' days, it would overwhelm their hearts with thoughts of killing – our friends bemoaned the fact that we could only hear her 'toothless,' 'broken harp,' the product of a 'dried-up plant,' a fading and diminished body. And, when reflecting on the attributes of physical beauty and of grace, Ilongots insisted that small waists, light steps, and red, firm cheeks belong especially to the young.

Age is lacking in the lovely force realized in youthful song and stance, then lost through shedding teeth or bearing children. And if youths' songs address their desires to take a life and their hopes to cast off clouds, gain stature, and marry, so adults speak longingly of a vitality and fullness that they have been denied. Varying words to what are common tunes, the songs of both bespeak a sense that one is incomplete, and – whether as a 'quick' and beautiful, but 'clouded' boy, or a 'slower' but more 'knowing' elder – ultimately dependent on another generation's sensibility, sense, or 'passion,' its form and style of life. Bound up in one another's fates, young men must look to older ones for the *bēya* that will give their *liget* point and shape, for experience and guidance; whereas elders, having 'reached' and gone beyond the beauty of youth's more 'passionate' days, look to the young to realize and recover their former vitality.

What this means for Ilongots of all ages is that even though one's growing old begins with the entanglements of marriage, the loss of substance associated with creating children, and, for women in particular, the lesser strength and 'anger' manifested in the pain of giving birth, life itself is wasted if it is not, through youth, renewed. Aging and death are, of course, inevitable aspects of the human situation. And for Ilongots, the existential knowledge that all pleasures fade means that one's youthful glamour serves no purpose if it fails to reproduce itself in new and youthful 'shoots.' Realizing that even the unmarried age, they say that children are an 'exchange' *(ta'rat)* or a 'remembrance' *(tawid)* for the life of aging parents – the word 'remembrance' being associated with open, horizontal lengths *(ruyuk)*, with joy and wide expanses, as opposed to vertical breaks, which suggest a 'cutting short' of vital passion, an 'anger' blocked and turned to harm. And just as children are extensions or 'remembrances' of declining adult prowess, so, in one form of divination, where finger lengths of rattan are placed in alternating vertical and horizontal sequence along a blade (Figure 3), those people whose good fortune ends with a horizontal piece at the knife tip are said to have a *tawid*, or 'remembrance' – in this case, to still have within them the stuff of further life.

This sense, that human life seeks length and continuity, and that children – the realization, in new and vital form, of fading energy or passion – are themselves a 'lengthening' of an otherwise declining life, is demonstrated even further in the Ilongot claim that the fetus is a product of a man's concentrated *liget*, and again, in the fact that children's names are said to reflect upon the passion in their fathers' hearts.[8] Acquiring bodily vigor from adults whose reproductive life is thought to age them, children are – through sperm and names – made repositories of an energy and beauty that their predecessors enjoyed when they were 'quick ones.' In hearing boasts and tales that move their hearts toward violence, they are charged to recreate the *liget* that can 'lengthen' hearts, enhance young growth, and ready youths for marriage – to kill and so recover a vitality that adults would not see wane.

Thus, youths and adult men are tied by bonds of longing and of

Figure 3. *'Iteng,* a headhunting knife

common aspiration, the one seeking to realize an elder's feats and boasts of violence, the other to recreate and so sustain a vaguely re-called experience of intensified and heightened life. And this cycle – by which youths desire to emulate, and adults to reproduce, a 'passion' which, like life itself, is always fading – has, like life, no ultimate goal, and within the constraints of traditional Ilongot experience, no conclusion.

> The logic of such cycles once led Tukbaw to comment that if Ifugao settlers in his region had once – as rumor had it, and was in fact the case – been headhunters like the Ilongots he had known, then he doubted that, short of conversion to Christianity, they could truly have abandoned killing and given up their thoughts of old.

Realized in movement, ornament, and song, in productive industry as well as in killing, a hoped-for *liget* is what leads women who lack offspring to bemoan the absence of a younger voice to 'relay' or 'pass on' their playful footsteps, 'bouncing' songs, or well-famed gardens; and it drives the man with only daughters to sing with some resentment of the fact that his declining 'anger' will not be fully realized in the 'shoots' that 'stole' his youth:

> Oh dear, old man, it isn't as if there were a shoot, a
> child of yours, who could be a killer, grab for a victim
> as you did when you were young, old man, oh dear.
> But, old man, it's just that, unfortunately, your quick
> youth was snatched up by a female child. I like that.
> But it's a fact, old man, something to cut short further
> thoughts, the knowledge that you no longer are as you were
> once, when you were young.
> Now, old man, you must content yourself with seeking tasty
> meat in the great mountain valleys. You were not made for this,
> oh dear . . .

Accounts of when decline begins, and how a 'passion' acquired through youth diminishes with aging, will vary with the context and the point of the discussion. But whether one focuses on the 'quieting' of chaotic hearts, which men say follows on beheading; on the fact of marrying, or 'sitting down,' suggestive of an end to motion; or again, on the birth of children, who in 'multiplying' will 'diffuse' the sub-stance of one's youthful strength, the general contours of an opposition between young and old remain the same. Unmarried youths and novices alike are *gēlasagēt*, 'anxious seekers'; they are opposed to those who, satisfied with a victim or a bride, find that their bodies 'lose their tension' *(yated)* and concern themselves, quite simply, with the quest for food. Thus Talin once described *gēlasagēt* as 'the feeling when our bodies grow and our hearts are "confused" *(sawasawa)* with longing; but when a man takes a head, his body "loses its tension" (*yated*), he gets lazy, and his heart turns quiet and looks for nothing but food'; and 'Insan commented that '*gēlasagēt* is like a child whose body is not warmed by contact with a woman, not yet full of thistles; like a maiden or a bachelor who has not touched a lover and whose body has not "lost its tension" (*yated*) because still "looking for" ('*adiwar*) a victim or a spouse.'

In Ilongot thought, the young 'explore' ('*adiwar*), and age 'cuts off,' confines, and limits youths' much freer and more mobile musings; whereas the joy of youths involves a sense of competence, expansiveness, and ornamental splendor, the happiness of elders is typically described in terms of 'stillness' (*meted*), 'stopping' (*pedeg*), and 'contentment' (*sipē*), words used as well by converts to describe the bliss of faith. Youths' more varied and chaotic thoughts, their love of movement, and their 'quick' propensity to what can always be disruptive shows of 'angry' violence, at once disturb and give new energy to the slower and more 'knowing' impulses of their seniors; and adults who, though 'stopped,' enjoy the gifts of family, respect, and reputation, reflect with quiet longing on the stirring, vital *liget* of the young. Like 'knowledge' and 'passion' in the heart, old and young are necessarily incomplete without, and complementary to, each other. Bound by need and what might be called a reciprocity of desire, both are ultimately united in their concern that young men grow into adulthood, and in particular, that – through killing – youths win for all the violent joys their elders realized in the past.

Of course, in daily life, unmarried youths are the subordinates of their established seniors. Though free to move and to resist requests that contradict their plans and wishes, young men lack wives and gardens of their own, and so are subject to 'commands' (*tuydek*) by senior kinfolk in whose households they reside. Adult men may decide among themselves to 'lend' the labor of their sons, and thus affirm their ties of kinship and concern with their adult fellows. And furthermore, though young men often 'follow their own hearts' in choosing a prospective bride, adults will guide the romantic aspirations of their sons, and youths in turn depend upon approval and support from senior kinfolk in the negotiation of their marital ties. But if in daily fact unmarried youths are not the equals of their married elders, the spirited joy that follows a successful raid treats young and old as complements and peers. In celebration, the young headhunter joins his senior kin in songs and boasts that are enjoyed by all who, 'equally,' have killed;[9] and they are differentiated both from women, who are their counterparts in choral song, and from the younger 'empty-handed' boys who do not sing but who are encouraged to look forward to the time when they will win the *liget* of adults, by rushing to behead a chicken tethered to a stick outside the house.

Songs cited earlier in this chapter, 'true songs' *(pipiyan piya)*, which speak of age and insufficiency, desires to marry, kill, grow older, or recover youthful force, are forbidden in the period of victorious celebration – when men give voice not to their all-too-human longings, but instead to stirring boasts of prowess, self-sufficiency, and pride. As killers, men experience themselves as persons who are complete, enriched, beyond desire – as in ideal, if not in practice, all raiders are 'equally' peers in their achievement, having had the opportunity to hold a human head as it was severed and to cast it on the ground. Rather than flute and violin, whose music mimes the twistings of a heart moved by unrealized strivings, they play gongs and zithers;[10] they dance and sing the choral songs *(buayat;* see Chapter 2) that are the stuff of celebration; and, in boastful songs called *tarapandet,* they tell the spirits of their victims (now bound, like earrings, to the singer) the story of a fleeing voyage across mountains, streams, and great expanses, from the place where young men cut and tossed them, back to their killers' happy homes:

Oh dear, he killed, now I want to tell where you come from.
Isn't it, Sir, the mountain, 'Alatang as they say?
They went there, and he plucked you, like a banana shoot to
plant, the boy that you came to love.
And the very mountain they climbed with you, Sir, the river Pinali,
there they broke off a leaf for your memory – a charm to
wear upon their arms.
And now Sir, over there, the mountain Pengaditan, and the
Dingiliyan river, he led you on, the boy.
He ran wild, out ahead of the others; he
ran after you, poor thing.
On then, by the flow of the
Sangbẽy, on and on, Sir, like a spirit.
It was your doing, Sir, to let yourself be called.
Now, you call
another, like yourself – just as, with a young shoot
of cogon grass, the boy beckoned your heart in his spells,
you poor thing.
You are stamped, soiled, adorned by me now, all those I have
cut or killed.
Yet, I like that, for they carried you farther, past the foot of the
Kabikab, with him who ran to you, struck you – poor thing – onto
the place where you stay now, by the flowing 'Atanay.
Feel his blow!

It's good now. Where were you from?
Oh, maybe from the foot of the 'Asimun mountain – there he killed.
From there, you traveled on.

You wore pants, didn't you? Oh dear!
Yes, I like that, since you dared to pass by when the boy came
to you, when he threw your head, you were waiting.
And your body will continue there, there where the dust from
the road always blows. There he killed.
You, Sir, be with the boy now, alive like the lively turning of
a good fish – a charm, to beautify the arm of the man who
made you a spirit.
Feel his blow!

These singers, having traveled far, acquired new life, and 'reached,'
or found the measure of, their 'anger,' would seem to be beyond all
limitation. Because headhunting provides a form through which desire
can appear to be transcended, and through which the 'anger' occasioned
by one's daily life and situation loses its disturbing cast, the men who kill
are as if detached from the cycling and impermanence of young life, old
age, and passing generations. Though Ilongots do not make the explicit
claim that through their killing men suspend the toll of time, it would
appear that headhunting serves momentarily to dissolve pragmatic differences between married and unmarried men by casting all as 'equals'
in their *liget* and vitality. Joyful, energetic, and creative, the killers
cease to be aspiring youths or fading and nostalgic 'fathers' – and become, in ways that Ilongots were barely able to articulate and I could
only partly understand, something like Yeats's half-crazed but fantastic
singers, who, self-contained and satisfied, can dance upon a fellow human's burial plot, as if deriving life from death.

This view of headhunting celebrations suggests a way of understanding the otherwise quite puzzling fact that Ilongots recognize death and
mourning, along with youthful aspirations, as a common cause for
raids.[11] Though Ilongots insist that spirits of the dead do not themselves
inspire killing, they say that death of kin makes hearts grow 'heavy' and
distraught – and that through killing, men 'cast off' the 'weight' that
comes of grief and pain.

> Kangat was anxious to take a head and had insisted that he would not
> marry as a novice, but it took his father's death to stir his kinsmen to
> take him on a raid. When the father died, Kangat's older brother made
> clear his intention to help realize Kangat's hopes, and at the same time
> 'cast off' grief, by placing his dead father's gun in the latter's hand and
> pulling the trigger; he then 'swore' *(binatan)* that the gun would not
> again be fired on a wild animal until it had cast a bullet on a human
> victim.

When confronted by a kinsman's death, Ilongot men may swear to avoid
the use of objects linked to the departed; a gun, a knife or arrow, a pot or
granary full of rice may be 'tabooed' *(binatan)* until the mourner cuts
into a human victim, and then – enlivened by the fact of conquest –

returns to sing a celebratory chorus on the lost kinsman's grave. In fact, in recent years, Ilongots who for political reasons (fear of schoolchildren's tongues, the eyes of settlers, scorn of Christian neighbors, or the force of Martial Law) have been reluctant to go killing, identify the death of kinfolk as a major motive for conversions – not because they think a Christian God will do away with death and illness, but rather because His faith is said to quiet hearts that once were twisted, torn, and heavy, and to remove the need to find a 'place to go' with painful feelings born of loss. For traditional Ilongots, by contrast, it is killing that will 'lighten' weighted hearts, and it is headhunting that clears away disturbing and distracted thoughts associated with mourning. For them, a sense of collectivity, destroyed through death of kin and broken by a series of taboos that limit visits, eating, and communication with the relatives of the departed, is recaptured in the celebration that follows taking heads.

Diminished by a loss of kin, weighed down by grief and by the dead man's deep reluctance to abandon human ties, the headhunter turns his pain into another person's anguish; he lets his dulled and twisted heart burst out with celebration, and discovers through the loss of life new potency and joy. Traditional Ilongot rituals for death require the bereaved to build a separate fire for their lost kin outside the house, then sweep away, lock out, and sit in wakeful watch against the dangerous and lonely 'spirits' *(bēteng)* of the deceased. The names of dead kin are but rarely and reluctantly pronounced; and during the period of ritual 'taboo,' mourners call utensils by the name of *rupa (Laporta luzonensis)*, an allergic and 'contagious' *(bēret)* plant, because they hope to frighten and deceive the dead, thereby abolishing their presence and their claims.

But if the names and spirits of dead kin are weighty facts that burden hearts, bring sickening dreams, and threaten illness,[12] killing as a response to death not only does away with grief but also turns a victim's anguish into a source of joyous life. The beheaded victim does not, Ilongots say, become a *bēteng,* dangerous to all, but turns instead into a harmless, often beneficial power (*'amet;* see following discussion) who will contribute *liget* and vitality to the men who called its heart. Like the gardener who can 'steal' and 'beckon forth' rice hearts for harvests, the killer takes a life to win a *liget* that sustains, enhances, and lends continuity to the human experience of unending change and constant striving. Affirming strength in face of death, the headhunter thus appears to stop life cycles. And because, in killing, life and energy are recognized as things that men must sacrifice themselves to recreate, it seems likely that for Ilongots taking heads is an experience through which one can forget, but more importantly, reinterpret and in some sense understand the painful 'weight' of mourning and the inevitability of loss.

Thus, if, as was suggested in Chapter 2, the celebration of beheadings is itself a sort of commentary on the experience of 'anger,' show-ing private and disruptive feelings to be part of a larger process that provides for an intense and satisfying collective life, it is also the case that headhunting provides Ilongots with terms that link the vagaries of *liget* to the facts of youth and aging, the changes of a self through time. Aging is, like envy, a disturbing but unavoidable aspect of the human situation, responsible at once for suffering and effort, death and life. And because there is, for Ilongots, no passion and no pleasure without some real frustration; because most satisfactions (a gain in rice hearts, loss of illness, reception of a share of meat) follow a 'distributive' logic (*bēret;* see Chapter 3) that demands that one man's triumph is someone else's loss, a cultural form that binds the facts of death and age to promises of life and reproduction is apt, for them, to be as deeply grip-ping as its significance is clear.

That young men should kill human victims – because their fathers did so – makes sense because it fits a pervasive cyclical pattern in Ilongot understandings of human social life and development; that tak-ing heads relieves one's sense of loss, renewing pleasure and vitality, is at one with their observation that 'without *liget* there can be no human life' (see Chapter 2). But if these cycles have for them a very general application, and if headhunting, as a symbol of social continuity, links collective needs to recreate and give new life to *liget* to the relations between older men and youths, most young men find a more immediate cause for killing in their bachelorhood and hopes to marry, and in their competition with acknowledged peers. Informed by stories told by older men, inspired by 'angry' fathers, the headhunter is, in cultural lore, defined not so much by age as by his drifting, mobile, and unmar-ried status, his orientation toward his fellows, and his hopes to 'reach' a human victim before 'sitting with' (a euphemism for *bēyek,* 'to marry, to have intercourse') a wife. Why killing is connected in this way to peers and marriage will now be explored.

Lovers and peers

In everyday discourse, social life, and lore, Ilongots picture youthful 'quick ones' as the people who are most attentive to the presence, friendship, and accomplishments of equals; and they say that youths' propensity to violence is bound up with their concern to win the hearts of women, and with their desire to 'reach' achievements claimed by fellows of their status or their age. The models, equally, for mutual friendship and for competition, the young are inclined to travel, work, preen, compete, and strive in groups made up of agemates. Locking legs and arms with handsome and excited 'equals,' they combine the closeness born of ease and friendship with a desire to *patabēr,* or 'excite admiring anger,' among peers. At work and play they glow with mutual and enthusiastic emulation – a spirit described by Ilongots as *mega 'mega* and *'agal 'agal,* words indicating elements both of healthy liveliness and distracting self-absorption, 'energetic action' and gratuitous 'showing off.' And it is not, perhaps, surprising that although bachelors are the ones to mark encounters among unrelated kin groups with 'angry' wrestling and dueling contests, it is, at the same time, the ties of *buintaw,* or 'bachelors,' that provide a sort of paradigm for enduring formal friendships, called *kabuintaw,* 'fellow bachelor' (though engaged in by men and women of all ages), and affirmed through the exchange of gifts or names with peers away from home.

The importance of peer groups among youths in their teens and twenties – as a source of energy and education – was suggested in an earlier chapter. And their cultural significance emerged as well when youths in settlements we were visiting would ask, time and again, for us to tell them 'all about the maidens' or 'the bachelors' in the Kakidugen area where we lived. Youths who, at any given time, are 'equal quick ones,' will tend, in spite of variation in their ages, to see themselves as constituting a tier or balanced group of equals – a fact encouraged by a kinship system that differentiates not descent lines, but generations, and by a form of domestic organization that casts all unmarried people as in some ways free but still dependent, lacking either a fixed residence or the private rice stores that come from gardens tended only by mature, married adults. And finally, if historical contingencies are such as to permit a particular cohort of unmarried men to act on what is seen as natural peer group envy – and so 'follow' *('unud)* one another in accomplishment and growth – their beheadings will tend to cluster and they will tend to marry 'in the same direction' (related men marrying, or, in marriage, exchanging related women) and at roughly the same time. This is, for example, what happened in the years following World War II – when in the Kakidugen-Pengegyabēn area alone, a cluster of some ten men, whose ages ranged from early twenties to midthirties, took heads in sequence (three in 1945 and seven more from 1950-4) and then married, 'one after the other,' within a period of approximately four years (1955-8; see Renato Rosaldo 1980).

A vision of unmarried youths as peers, potential equals, and so, companions capable of disturbing or creative strife, is reflected too in song and story, in which only the unmarried are named as friends or paired in contests. By contrast, married men, always cast within the contexts of their family relations, are almost never parties to a fight.

Young men display their *liget* in a ritual duel.

Thus, in one old song, a bachelor is encouraged to see his bragging
fellow as a 'monkey,' here called *miyungki,* from the English "monkey": The word used is a wry allusion to the Ilongot *me'amet* (or 'male
monkey'), which, sounding like *'amet* ('spirit of the beheaded'), points
perhaps too clearly to the fact that challenge and insult can lead to
taking heads:

> Oh dear, for your fellow bachelor, why should he get
> to brag and talk?
> Make your shoulder like cement, because he's bigger than
> you and his knife has a reputation that crosses mountains.
> Well, it will just be a matter of trying, slashing at one
> another, and with luck, you'll say, "he's just a 'monkey';
> that's what his body is like."
> Go on, curse your fellow bachelor; he's as easy to hit as a
> banana trunk.
> You'll manage to curse that big body, that big "monkey."

And, like bachelors, young girls too can be competitors, as indicated in
this song in which one friend berates another for disguising her romantic ties with a desirable young man:

> Oh, dear, oh dear, why do you hide from me the fact
> that a bachelor went and brought you betel nuts at home?
> Oh dear, oh dear, what do I have to hide from you,

as if there were a bachelor who had gone to bring me
betel nuts at home.
Oh dear, oh dear, why do you hide from me the fact
that a bachelor went and brought some lovely gifts
to your home?
Oh dear, oh dear, what do I have to hide from you,
as if there were a bachelor who had gone to bring
back lovely gifts to me at home.

But even though young maidens can compete, the vast majority of
stories, songs, and ballads address the lives and situations not of wom-
en, but of the men they are attached to – touching quite directly on the
trials of mutual emulation among youths who are, as peers, potential
enemies or friends:

Go ahead and fight with your shields, and if you give
up on shields, have at one another with knives.
Because a man just like you will get the young girl, and the
one who spoke to her first may well be defeated and die.
Give up the knives then, and use spears, with hard shafts
and bright copper ornaments, lined with woolen tufts and
strips of bark cloth from your girlfriends.
May you be strong.

Similarly, this story of two friends who called one another *kasibuk*,
'fellow breath' (which suggests that they had once shared 'breaths,' or
thoughts, of killing), highlights something of the affinity between male
friendship and disruptive strife.

Two friends who shared the friendship name *kasibuk* decided one day
to go together into the forest, where they would make a rattan ladder in
order to climb a *masina* (unidentified) tree in search of fruits. But after
one had climbed, his fellow severed the ladder, leaving the first to live
deserted (and probably die) without companionship, and with no food
to eat but leaves. Finally, a civet cat came and carried the first boy
down the tree on his back. But in the meantime, the deceiver turned out
to have taken a head and married the girl to whom the climber had been
betrothed. At the ceremony celebrating the deceiver's killing, the first
boy, thought dead, appeared and killed both his deceiver and the un-
faithful girl.[13]

And when, in 1959, Bangad was outsmarted by a fellow bachelor's
show of *liget,* his fate resembled that of the young men in the *masina*
tree; much like his mythic counterpart, he had to prove himself by killing
before he could continue to pursue a wife:

Bangad and Punlan were both courting Tanul, Lakay's niece, in the
late 1950s, when their 'uncle' Pawig, organized a raid in response to
his daughter's death. Among the novices in the party were both
suitors, and in lieu of prior agreement, Punlan rushed ahead of Bangad
to behead their single victim – Bangad losing, through a moment's

hesitation, not only the opportunity to 'cast off' his novice status, but also the desired Tanul, whom Punlan shortly wed. It was not until the mid-1960s that Bangad managed to behead a victim, and shortly afterward he married Mayana, his present wife.

These examples show, first, that youths, whom we know to be the most concerned to prove themselves with peers, to take heads, and to wear, like other men, the emblems of a headhunter's violent triumph, are, by cultural account as well as personal situation, inclined not only to be close, but at the same time bound in competition to their equals. And second, though in a variety of ways still to be examined, they indicate that competition among young men concerns not only shows of prowess but also thoughts of love and marriage and the conventional notion that before 'sitting with' a woman, it is desirable for a youth to take a head.

Marriage, competition, and beheading are related, Ilongots say, because most 'empty-handed' youths would prove themselves 'as men' before they think of courtship – and equally, because once 'quieted' by marriage and obligation, men are apt to be preoccupied with their families and so less likely to spend their time on 'pointless' raids. Both marriage and beheading are named as moments that transform the heart and silence youthful longings; both prove one's *liget* and guarantee that the youth attains the material independence (assured through wives and private gardens) and unchallengeable presence (won through killing) of competent and respectable adults. In both, youths' 'passion' must be shaped by an adult's less energetic 'knowledge'; just as, in both, achievement of one's end provides for the independence born of accomplishment and experience – and for the youth, a set of social ties that will permit him to become a relatively autonomous actor, free of his father, and engaged in relationships of reciprocity and cooperation with his 'equal men.' And although Ilongots are aware that men occasionally grow old and wise without the benefits of either, they also know that aging bachelors command but small respect in local dealings, and married novices lack the ornaments and pride required to address an opposite in oratorical encounters, or to command the status and admiration enjoyed by more accomplished family leaders in their middle age. Thus, young men, as we have seen, declare themselves reluctant to enter marriage while still 'in search' and 'empty-handed.' And young girls themselves sing songs that voice intentions to 'stay young' until mere boys have 'reached their manhood'; and by decorating ornaments and weapons, they encourage youths to turn their thoughts to raids. In farewell dirges *(mina'naw),* women seek to stir the hearts of killers; and men say they are 'ashamed' to return 'unaccomplished' *(puat)* from distant raiding when their lovers bid farewell.

But if young men have hopes to kill before they wed, their preference has less to do with women's wiles than with the ways in which a marriage can itself be seen as a challenge, and a cause for *liget* among presumably 'equal' fellows. And though marrying, for Ilongots, need not occasion contest (and marriages with close kinfolk, often second cousins, are at once most frequent and least likely to give rise to violence or to 'angry' words), Ilongots will demand that future grooms display their *liget*. They see in marrying both an ideal sequence to beheadings and a potential ground for insult and consequent shows of force. Much like anthropologists, who traditionally have ignored the consequences of marriage for the experiences and relationships of women, so Ilongots reckon marriage as a male achievement and a potential source of conflict, because, in making claims on women, men make assertions about their status and their relationships to their fellow men.

Unlike taking heads, the facts of marriage include no unique ceremony or climax, no single moment marking one's maturity or success. The bachelor visits, courts, gives gifts, and shyly offers betel nuts to his beloved; depending on his luck, local custom (which varies considerably with *bērtan* and region), affinal circumstances, and goodwill, he may begin by tending fields and eventually come to lie beside the woman he desires; her kin may set demands for trials, gifts, and formal meetings. Or, in rare instances, his parents may, through formal talk – and long before he thinks to 'speak with' any maiden – have publicized their preference for a particular young woman as his bride. But if marrying is, in every case, an arrangement both processual and uncertain – fixed more by talk and by repeated practice than by the clear sort of acknowledgment entailed in formal ritual acts – Ilongots describe and will negotiate a marriage in terms that highlight not its temporal ambiguities, but instead its structural relation to the more stereotypical and decisive facts of taking heads.

Thus, the would-be groom, much like the 'empty-handed' youth, is cast as a 'seeker' *('adiwar, gēlasagēt),* and people say he enters his wife's home (and never the reverse) because it is for men to travel, move, and in so doing, show their *liget* when they wed. Betrothals that occur without a parent's knowledge are (like headhunting raids lacking an elder) described as 'sneaky,' 'hidden' *(linibet),* and the product of 'excessive' *('iteg)* passion. Ideally (and as is the case with raiding), young grooms should play the 'pups' to senior 'masters'; and elders, through their knowing talk at bridewealth meetings, should be the ones to organize the 'anger' wakened by youth's hopes of marriage in a constructive plan of gifts and work. Again, like headhunters who commemorate their triumphs in reciprocal friendship names (like 'fellow-bulldozer,' 'fellow-crocodile,' 'fellow-anger'; see Chapter 3) that mark a shared experience for a lifetime – so youths on marriage enter into, and in altered forms of naming reconfirm, new patterns of relationship and new kinds of social ties.[14]

And, finally, much as through taking heads a man acquires the prerequisites of an 'angry' reputation, the confidence to answer boasts with boasting, and the sort of presence that gives opinions weight, so marriage is, in other ways, a source of social standing, self-confidence, and voice. Indebted to no other man for female care and labor, the married man stands with his wife as an independent social unit; and whereas unmarried men and youths do not receive a share of meat in settlement distributions, the married (though residing with their in-laws) are likely to be counted on their own. Marriage provides a man with wife and fields; a hearth from which guests can be fed; the 'knowledge' that permits him to distribute game; the needs that form a basis for cooperative exchanges – all attributes of independence that the unmarried of whatever age[15] appear to lack. And it is this fact – that marriage, like beheading, provides young men with the experience, relationships, and 'knowledge' through which youths' limitations are eventually overcome – that makes marrying, like taking heads, a mark of status and a proof of *liget,* and that underlies conventional forms of discourse that assume the two events to be related in the process of growing up. With marriage as with beheading, the youth transforms his social self by demonstrating that he is an 'equal' – dependent on no other man, and equivalent, in 'angry' force, to all.

Because marriage involves young men in status change, and so in potential contests, male relatives of a desired bride may find a cause for umbrage in an 'equal's' sexual interest in their 'daughters' or 'sisters.' And again, because (in a system of uxorilocal postmarital residence) the suitor is always an outsider, in fact displaying *liget* by the very act of entering and unsettling another family's home – it is easy to see that a man who marries at some distance can, by simply showing courage, cause offense. Whether driven by adventurous will, romantic love, or (what is far more likely) the political designs of elders, the man's approach is readily cast as irritant, boast, or challenge; his deepest thoughts are hidden in a heart that lurks behind the words that he puts forward; and the kinsmen of his would-be spouse, confronted by a suit they see as insult or deception, will oppose affront with shows of stubborn *liget* – demanding further proofs of worth and courage from the prospective groom.

When building roofbeams for their houses, Ilongot men may carve two hornlike arms – 'headhunting knives' or *'iteng* – to protrude from and so ornament the thatching; and these 'knives,' crowning the housetop and proclaiming to all comers the *liget* of the men who live within, are paired with 'maidens' breasts' (*rinapa,* as opposed to *tutu,* 'breast,' but especially 'mature breast, breast milk'), which are carved on the interior face of the roofbeam and indicate the presence of a marriageable sister in the house. This juxtaposition, as it were, of 'angry' men and young girls not yet married, had left me puzzled – until I recognized a connection between the rooftop's boast of strength and *liget*, and Ilongot views of what it means for men to enter one another's homes in hopes of marriage, a view that links heartfelt affection to peerlike tests of poise and strength.

Thus 'Insan, in playful fantasy, had carved a head transected by a knife to place atop his house in Pengegyabēn, intending, as he told it, to try the mettle of any youth who dared to 'come up to my threshhold' and court his energetic eldest daughter (then nineteen years old) as a wife. And though conceived in fun (and with reference to his daughter), 'Insan's innovation was in fact taken as a more serious sort of challenge when, in 1973, the Dekran people came to ask in formal oratory for a union with his niece. On entering his house to speak, the Dekrans found themselves confronted by the taunting and reluctant words of 'Insan and his fellows; they construed the rooftop boast of *liget* as a threat they could not answer, and so intimidated, withdrew. Reporting this event, 'Insan would laugh, and others told that 'no man dies from his attempts at marriage.' They recalled an occasion in the past when kinsmen of a desired bride shot threatening bullets in the air, yet failed to daunt the party of an 'angry' and committed would-be groom. And in one instance which, for them, epitomized the way in which aspiring bachelors are required to show their *liget,* the brother of a sought-for bride shot arrows at her suitor, while the latter, pollarding in a treetop, maintained his calm and called out, ''Brother-in-law, I didn't know that you had come.' Thus, my friends insisted, the Dekrans lost their suit because of 'cowardice' *(depyang)* and hesitation; they failed to show the *liget* and conviction that is expected of a successful groom.

At other times, the lover shows his fierce intent by helping his beloved's kin at work in house and garden. With gifts of game, he demonstrates his *liget* in the forest; and swearing to pursue his love above the clouds and under rivers – to offer presents to her kinsmen though they greet his gifts with pointed spears or guns – he may agree as well to give expensive bridewealth payments, even promising to provide his affines with true proof of his prowess: victims for them to behead. Extravagant shows of hunting skill as well as victims were required of the mythic Bugēgiw, a fearless suitor whose courtship is recounted in a ballad that a man from Tamsi knew:

> Bugēgiw wants to marry, to go have a look at a maiden whom he knows to be as tall as a bamboo. His sisters worry that she will feed him no rice and he will have to eat the sap of the papaya, but he answers that he has

already seen her granary, which is stuffed full of rice and made of wood.
Bugēgiw then tells his sisters, "Pound me rice and fix my ornaments, so that
when I travel, I will look feathery and grand."
Then off he goes with Lugkaking, his brother . . . to where the maiden
fetches water.
And so they reach her waterhole, and the brother asks, "What is this wind I
feel pulling at me here?"
And Bugēgiw replies, "It is my heart that beats because of the maiden whom
I love, the maiden who is fetching water here."
The maiden sees them and jumps back in fear, and then the brother says,
"Young maiden, don't be frightened; look now, men don't go headhunting with their dogs, and we have dogs here, dogs for hunting, crouched
at the base of the tree."
And Bugēgiw says, "Young maiden, I have nothing to hide, I've come to
marry, to bring my bow into your house."
To this, the maiden answers, "Ah, you brothers, don't be hasty; my brother,
who is the namesake of Lugkaking, will make quite a contest; he'll ask
for wild carabaos[16] and he'll ask for people to behead, as many as the
dried leaves of the *'abaka* plant."
Bugēgiw then says, "Even if he makes a hard contest, I'd be as soft as a
youth who is still a novice if I could not do the things he asks."
The maiden begs, "Have pity, then, and give me time to reach the house, so
that my brother cannot guess that we have spoken, that all I did was
fetch some water at the stream."
. . . She goes then to her house and as Bugēgiw approaches, she says, "Oh
brother, why should I hide from you that Bugegiw and his brothers have
come to bring their bows into our house?"
The brother then shuts all his windows, and closes the house against the
coming guests.
But when they come, they laugh to see the house closed up and call, "Well,
namesake, if you don't open your door, we will stomp your house open,
we brothers who have beheaded huge men who wear beards: Your
house will crumble with our weight."
They force the doors open, enter, and the brother's eyes are wild with fear.
Bugegiw laughs and says, "These dogs are for hunting. How can you fear
them?"
And then the brother speaks and asks for four herds of wild carabao, and
Bugēgiw laughs and says, "All right, but all the ties[17] that hold your
house are weak and will collapse when we bring home the heavy game."
. . . The suitors say then, "Look at our wife, the maiden, she is cooking for
our hunt dogs as our sister never has.
She's cooking for them and feeding them in the middle of the night, by the
light of the fire."
And so, again, the brothers grab the leashes of the dogs and Bugēgiw calls to
his affine, "Brother-in-law, you come along, and help us kill the
carabaos you asked for."
. . . Once loosed, the dogs set after four herds of carabao.
. . . Bugēgiw then calls, "My brother-in-law, come help; the dogs are tired
and hoarse from chase; come help us cut this game here."
And he laughs, and says, "It looks as if my brother-in-law is frightened;
there he is climbing a *ba'wat* tree, climbing to its highest branches and
looking like a shrinking worm."

. . . Then Bugēgiw says, "Maiden, lover, make a betel chew for me and my brother; say farewell, in case we are hit by the horns of the carabao your brother has requested, your brother who is afraid and still a novice who has yet to take a head."

. . . Then Bugēgiw crawls toward the animals; he runs, but they don't move; they stand and wait.

And the tip of his bow hits the horns of the carabaos, and he walks around the animals and when he finds the place to strike, he lets loose his arrow and it goes through the body of the first on to the others and then four herds fall over dead.

He is happy as he sees the hair on the animals' neck shake while he slashes at them, and he catches live a carabao cub, but still his affines shrink back and are afraid.

Then he beheads the cub and laughs and tosses off the head

. . . And so they carry the game back home.

. . . In the morning, Bugēgiw, says, "Pound some rice, some sticky rice, for we are off to kill, to lead your brother who cannot wear a headhunter's hornbill ornaments, who has asked us to offer up some victims to behead."

The headhunters set off.

. . . And they reach the house, but stop to wait for the slow affine who appears to be afraid.

And Bugēgiw says, "Why are they afraid? We'll storm the house and kill them all."

They go and walk around the house, pronouncing spells against misfortune. They eat.

. . . And then they set off, the brothers holding their affines' hands, like dogs that line up for a hunt.

They reach the house, the base of the ladder, hands drop, and Bugēgiw rushes into the house, delighted as the bodies fall like poisoned fish.

He calls to his brother-in-law who stalls, and hides, and is afraid.

. . . They cut one body across the chest and toss the torso to the affines; they move the knife for the fearful brother who is helped to take a head.

Bugēgiw's knife bends from his efforts and it cuts his leg, which swells so that he cannot walk, and so the affine helps to carry the suitor home.

. . . And then the maiden comes and cares for her new spouse.

Like Bugēgiw, young suitors have occasionally been asked to lead their affines in beheading, and satisfy the *liget* of a woman's kinsmen by demonstrating *liget* of their own. Though our records show that 'gifts' of victims have been rare throughout this century, new and prospective affines often manage to raid together, kin of the groom displaying *liget* in helping to secure the young man's claims in his affinal home. But even when a man has married, moved, and 'brought his bow' into the household of a woman, his status may be challenged by unruly shows of *liget* on the part of her still edgy kinfolk. And bachelor youths who marry at a distance will, with reason, fear the mythic fate of Lefty, who was killed by his wife's brother, leaving a son to 'remember' and, in due time, behead his father's murderer – who, interestingly, had cared for the child and his mother when the boy was still quite young (see R. Rosaldo 1968). In-married men from distant regions may, like Wadeg of the Kakidugen-Pengegyabēn area, be reluctant to go on headhunting raids with affines; or they may, as happened in the case of Iddung early in this century, find themselves threatened with beheading – unless they prove their loyalty to affines by guiding them to households where their own unwary kinsmen can easily be killed.

> Tension among affines is most likely to lead to violence when men marry at some distance – especially in cases in which marriage is used to bind a covenant or 'discovery' (*bimaya*, 'coming to know') of kinship between once strange or feuding demes. Thus, Pawig of Rumyad married a Tamsi woman when the two groups, once enemies, had moved together and 'discovered' kinship ties. But Pawig's character reinforced tensions developing in the difficult context of coresidence, and led to his temporarily deserting his wife to have an affair with a Rumyad woman more closely related to his family. The Tamsi response of righteous affinal 'anger' led to threats and counterthreats of killings, culminating with Pawig's waiting in ambush for a Tamsi man who had married a Rumyad woman – and the separation of the two groups. Some years later, Pawig returned, in peace and with gifts, to his Tamsi wife.

The point is not, of course, that marrying in any sense requires such shows of violence on the part of affines, but rather that marriage provides an occasion for men to give voice to hidden tensions, to prove themselves, and to test their peers. Potential spirals of insult and challenge are generally forestalled by shared experience, gifts, and by the 'knowing' talk of elders; and a preference for marriage with close kinsmen makes it likely that affines will be 'ashamed' to challenge affines with excessive diffidence or threatening demands. But at the same time, marriage permits a woman's kinsmen to act 'angry' and insulted, and so encourages desiring lovers to demonstrate the serious and vital 'anger' that lends conviction to their suits. And because such shows make sense only where male parity is in question, Ilongots tend to see the most severe affinal contests as limited to men of a single generation – lovers and brothers – who are in the potentially competitive situation of opposed and 'equal' men. Thus, several women recall fearing their brothers more than their fathers for the 'anger' they expressed regarding marriage; and ballad songs recount demands voiced not by fathers, but angry brothers – and fulfilled by passionate lovers who then overwhelm and even shame their girlfriends' kinsmen with their show of skill and strength.

But if, as 'equals,' brothers readily take offense at any would-be lover's daring, the tension between same-generation men regarding marriage has even deeper roots: Because marrying, like beheading, provides young men with terms that will define their adult status, all men of a cohort may find themselves caught up in fights concerning women – and it is not, perhaps, surprising that Ilongots (like many tropical forest peoples; see Siskind 1973), often allay the *liget* sparked by marriage with an 'exchange' *(tubrat)* of maiden 'sisters' to be the 'brothers'' wives. In fact, the ballad song that Ilongots find most moving is a story that suggests that any brother's anger vis-à-vis his sister's marriage is rooted in the ways that a young man's command of sisters is related to his acquisition of a wife. Its verses tell of two girls, 'heavily' pregnant, who are left at home to rest in quiet when their brother leaves to hunt. The girls remain, only to be beheaded by their lovers who, mistaking pregnancy for unfaithfulness, murder the girls when they go walking in the woods. The brother, in a tale that forms a sequel to the ballad, meets betrayal with unheard-of violence, killing whole households of people related to the men until his heart is sated by the return gift of two women. One he murders, the other he accepts as replacement for his sisters, as the tender of his gardens, and as his future wife. Because, in Ilongot experience, a wife may be 'exchanged' for a lost sister – exchange serving at once to balance or 'distribute' *(bēret)* insult, and to encourage, among affines, a reciprocity of concern – the overwhelming nature of the lovers' violation (they not only compromised but also killed the women who provided their brother both with care and the promise of a happy marriage of his own) is, for them, extreme enough to make the brother's wild vengeance seem appropriate. But at the same time, a recognition of the young man's need for female love and care – along with victims – was essential for the feud to be resolved. A related case, in which one man's sexual abuse of another man's sisters called forth reciprocal abuses and demands, came to our attention at an angry public meeting in 1968:

> Rebpak had intercourse, first, with one of Tupdek's sisters, only to abandon her for a second who, in dying, left a third for him, eventually, to wed. After Rebpak's marriage, the bachelor, Tupdek, considering himself personally affronted, felt called upon not only to demand one of Rebpak's sisters as his wife and an 'exchange' for the sister lost in marriage, but also to sleep with (and impregnate) a second, and finally (at the meeting we attended) to threaten vengeance unless he received a substantial 'payment' for Rebpak's sexual interest in the third.

Finally, if 'equals' can, as kin and suitors to a single woman, find themselves opposed in contest, Ilongots recognize as well that threats and shows of violence may be occasioned by the competition of two 'quick youths' for a girl. Because the loss of sought-for love implies a failure of the *liget* which, maintaining parity in groups of 'equals,' permits the 'empty-handed' youth to reach the status of adult, defeat in courtship is, like insult among affines, an inevitable source of tension. As is the case with divorce, it can produce a radical break in social order, leading to feelings Ilongots see as wild and often violent beyond control.

> In the early 1950s, Tepeg's wife Midalya, was being courted by Bangkiwa – a man who, though related, was unacceptable to Midalya's mother because of a still too-lively incident in which Bangkiwa's brother killed an uncle of the desired girl. Tepeg, inspired by a rash of marriages in the Kakidugen-Pengegyabēn area (1955-8; see p. 160) decided to 'step ahead of' Bangkiwa and seek the woman's hand. Bangkiwa, insulted and defeated, but reluctant to kill in vengeance people as closely linked to his own family as was the family of Tepeg, then joined with friends to raid against a settlement of people distantly related to Tepeg's father. Thus, though 'angered' by the loss of a desired lover, he managed to let his victor 'see his hand.'
>
> At much the same time, 'Adēlpig's sleeping with and eventually marrying the first wife of Tukbaw was the occasion of one of the very rare divorces in the last fifty years of Ilongot experience. A second cousin of the man who 'stepped ahead of' him, Tukbaw wanted, but was dissuaded from attempting, to kill 'Adelpig, and let himself be satisfied instead by the gift of a large pot. Such use of gifts, to satisfy the often violent *liget* of those who, for whatever reason (as former suitors; fathers or – more often – brothers who would see their daughters or their sisters marry elsewhere; wives and husbands irritated by the adulterous dealings of a spouse) find themselves insulted by a woman's sexual relations is very common; in fact, as we have seen, most bridewealth payments are cast as recompense for *liget* on the part of the young girls' recalcitrant male kin.
>
> When, in the 1970s, people from Pugu managed to 'step ahead of' a young man from 'Abēka, and marry a Rumyad woman the youth had thought to wed, vengeance was out of the question because the parties concerned considered themselves Christian. But when the defeated suitor, Tubeng, asked in a formal meeting for recompense from Pugu to cover all the gifts that he had given the desired girl and her close kin, his request was viewed by many as tantamount to vengeance, and criticized in those terms. In response, the frustrated young man's father argued that the youth was not, as in the past, demanding a 'return' for *liget*, and to highlight what he saw as the most Christian motivations of his son, he told a story designed to contrast the boy's requests with those of a 'fellow bachelor' who had lost a woman to him years before. The father, the successful groom, had 'paid' his failed competitor a kerchief for his 'wasted feelings,' but this was not sufficient; the defeated man was not satisfied until he wore the kerchief on a headhunting expedition (led by the offender's kinsmen), and broadcast his heightened *liget* by dipping the kerchief in a human victim's blood.

Or, to put the matter otherwise: Marriage and beheading are related to one another in Ilongot conceptions of the lives of growing bachelors in a way that is consistent with the fact that brothers of young maidens

A young married couple dressed in their finest for visiting; the man's earrings and the cowry shells on his legbands indicate that he has taken a head.

may, before permitting marriage, demand a show of 'anger' on the part of hopeful suitors; with the actual vulnerability of in-married husbands; and with the fact that competition over women can itself occasion feuds. Although recognizing that all insults are not sexual, and that 'anger' has other causes than the struggles of young men for women's hearts, Ilongots can (with accuracy) maintain that fights over women were, in the past, a most frequent source of (intra-Ilongot) feuding – just as their traditional tales and songs connect beheadings with the competitive desires of young bachelors to 'sit' and settle with a wife.[18] Killing as an aspect of, and commentary upon, the relationship between young men and elders is culturally bound to competition among youthful peers and to hopes to 'sit' in marriage, because all concern the *liget* that young men must demonstrate to fellows in order to enter into and enjoy the 'quieter' wisdom and authority of adults. Ilongot men – whether as husbands, lovers, or brothers – experience sexual ties with women as facts that have immediate consequence for their presumed 'equality' with others. And in a world where *liget* comes of violations of a presumed equality and balance; where bachelors, anxious to become adult, are jealous of those peers who, having taken heads, have then removed themselves from youthful groups by marriage, it is hardly surprising that historical experience as well as cultural stereotypes confirm a view connecting marriage and male shows of anger, love and taking heads.

Marriage and beheading are related, then, as terms for youthful competition – significant to young men because they promise the autonomy and experience that make a man adult. But we can go one step further: If marriage, like headtaking, provides the youth with proof of *liget* (and it is for this reason that Ilongots associate thoughts of marriage with plans for taking heads), this makes sense because the *liget* that stirs youthful hearts to growth and effort is for Ilongots a good deal more than public testament to one's private worth. The reputation and stature won in marrying and killing prove a *liget* that is at once the stuff of private gain and social reproduction – a vitality through which human beings in their actions can appreciate and maintain a world they know.

Conclusion: 'Amet and 'anger'

The point of severing and tossing human heads, as opposed to merely killing, is, informants say, the acquisition of an *'amet* – what I have called the 'spirit' of the beheaded. And the reason youths aspire not just to shoot or slash, but specifically to hold and toss a head as it is severed, is that only as beheaders do they acquire such a 'spirit' and so 'enhance their lives' (*'Usiken ma 'ara'antu mad sadilin biaytu*, 'Something big is what he gets in his own life.').

But, when pressed to speak of *'amet*, Ilongots insisted that these 'spirits' bear small resemblance to more conventional spirit powers – and that, though 'hardened' by the experience of beheading and the sacrifices that subsequently 'redden' and preserve the men who kill, the lives enhanced by raiding are in most respects no different, no more powerful or healthy, than the less glamorous but otherwise quite tolerable and productive lives of 'empty-handed' youths. To have an *'amet* is simply to be able to boast or curse by naming one's successes; it permits the man who first has cut and killed, and then in sacrifice been 'hardened' against the damning words of equals, to curse and bring to harm the foolish boaster whose experience of blood and gore is more confined. Yet this, my friends insisted, is not a truly 'spiritual' sort of power; nor are *'amet* very different from a lively reputation or a 'name.' Damning curses only work in face-to-face encounters – because an *'amet* is essentially an aspect of the killer's social personality, empowering him (much as a governmental office grants authority, and as age empowers adults to give commands to youths) to engage in boastful talk. Unlike *'ayug,* or 'spirit familiars' (though, like them, compared to birds), *'amet* can, informants say, 'do nothing.' Unlike ordinary human *bēteng* – our 'shadow souls' or 'hearts' that voyage in the course of sleep and dreaming and become 'ancestral spirits' after death – the *'amet,* being headless, does not reside with deceased fellows, roam on earth causing disruption, or, in longing for still living kinsmen, bring them unwanted harm. Though associated, like *bēteng,* with human hearts, life, and awareness, *'amet* lack autonomy and substance; they have less to do with something we would recognize as "spirit powers" than with "spirit" in our related sense of "vitality" and "will."

Before the deaths of victims, *'amet* are an aspect of the human hearts prospective killers ask the Forest Lord to give them – as they provide him, in a tiny rattan basket, an offering of rice that promises larger, pig-meat offerings should they be successful and have the opportunity to enjoy a sacrificial meal. These hearts, encouraged by the Forest Lord, answer the raiders' birdlike calls by 'perching' on the earlobes (where hornbill earrings later mark the triumphs) of the men who will eventually behead them; and once 'accustomed' *(tagde)* to their destined killers, they are said to call upon the 'dumb' but as yet lively victims from whose bodies they were drawn. After decapitation, the hearts, now known as *'amet,* are directed to 'stick to' and so enhance their killers' persons – the word *'amet* being used as well to characterize the seasoning effect of salt which, if mixed with meat while it is cooking, will enhance its taste. In boastful songs called *tarapandet* (see p. 156), the *'amet* learn the story of their fate and travels, so as (it seems) to fix their memory for killers – or, as Ilongots put it, so that they will 'stay with us' *(pedeg)* and not find themselves 'confused' and 'lost' *(sawasawa).*

Hanging onto beheaders' ears, the *'amet* play with, and permit the use of, hornbill earrings;[19] sweet-smelling, lovely, and attractive, they are associated with ornamental, pepsin-scented ferns (*tagēngitang*, uniden-tified) called *'amaya,* or 'magical charms for binding hearts and making healthy,' which are inserted into bracelets on the killers' upper arms.[20] And whether in the form of red and quivering earrings, full of *liget,* or of ferns whose lovely perfume quickly fades – the *'amet,* while still fresh, are thought to seek companions, invoking by sheer powers of attraction the hearts of future victims who will add new leaves and new vitality by providing lively objects for the killers' 'angry' peers.

At times when *'amet* were renewed by frequent raiding, Ilongots recall long periods of energy, well-being, and abundance. But the sense in which these 'spirits' won of violence could contribute to a general atmosphere of healthy triumph had, by their account, much less to do with an accumulation of spiritual or mystical sorts of power reported for headhunters elsewhere (who have been said to seek "soul substance," see Needham 1975) than with the pleasure people find in ornaments and endless choral singing – the killers' own enlivening experience of celeb-ration and success. Though the availability of *'amet* makes bachelors glamorous and lovely, Ilongots deny ever seeking victims as a source of such specific benefits as fertility, health, or strength. Rather, Ilongots say that they sought *'amet* so that their dress could be complete – so that they would not be 'lacking' hornbill earrings. And they tell of wanting earrings because they envied peers; desired the opportunity to excite the emulation of other youths who were still 'empty-handed'; sought a name or 'life' of wide reputation; and hoped, if cautiously and shyly, to win the respect and admiration of certain lovely and unmarried girls. In short, the much-desired 'spirits' of the beheaded were significant as tokens of an experience of well-being and renewal – in contexts marked by youths' desires to 'reach' the feats of elders, and by the trials of competi-tion among peers.

Because young men experience themselves as socially limited, inex-perienced, and incomplete, they seek a wife and *'amet* – in each case, desiring a companion who will complement and transform their social selves. Attaining them, the youth acquires the autonomy born of a loosening of dependent ties to elders; a sense of self-sufficiency that neither fears nor suffers challenge; and the 'reddened' and invulnerable presence that permits a man to boast. The youth without an *'amet* is like the bachelor, physically deformed, whose body shows the signs of weakness that will inhibit him from marriage; incomplete, ashamed, and silent, he cannot enjoy the confident sense of pride that comes of having proved his 'angry' heart. And though Ilongots are aware that neither marriage nor beheading can by themselves make youths grow older (and that the full benefits of maturity come not simply with accomplishment, but with age), their experience, and – even more importantly – their recollections, suggest that these events define a deep and enduring change in the bachelor's social status and in his sense of self. As a married man with *'amet,* he begins to lead and guide the wishes of young men who are his juniors; released from the immediate demands of youthful competition, he can be trusted to support and reinforce ideas of social order that are, in formal talk and in more casual patterns of cooperation, the ongoing responsibility of mature adults. And finally, just as marriage and *'amet* are, alike, the proofs of realized *liget,* so both provide in different ways for a continuation of the life of 'angry' youth. Much as *liget* concentrated in the form of sperm is what creates new human beings, so *'amet* as ornament, song, or fern – excites the lively envy through which the killer's 'anger,' energy, and vitality are eventually reproduced.

The place of *'amet* in Ilongot thought must, then, be understood by reference not to the power of souls or magical virtues acquired through beheading. Its force lies rather in its ties to a form of generativity that is both social and concrete – a *liget* born in youths' desires to 'equal' peers and 'reach' their elders, and transcended through activities that at once provide the young with the prerequisites of a 'completed' adult status (described as 'lacking' nothing, or as 'having reached' one's manhood) and permit older men to recreate the vital energy that makes for life and effort, the enthusiasm and passion known in youth.

6. Negotiating anger: oratory and the knowledge of adults

Marriage and killing are seen by Ilongots both as proof of and occasion for 'anger.' Young men display *liget* in taking heads and winning the favor of the kin of the women they marry. But in proving themselves among peers, youths will move, make new ties, cause offense, and occasion reflection on ongoing social alignments. For elders, the *liget* called forth as a boy becomes an adult requires not only direction but also discussion. Either casually or in the formal context of an oratorical confrontation, adult men show themselves to have the *bēya* that permits them not so much to regulate social life as to negotiate its interpretation; speaking well, they may clarify, change, or affirm what is 'known' about kinship and social connection, giving explicit form to inchoate and shared understandings on which the diffuse reciprocity of daily living depends.

My purpose in this chapter is to explore this 'knowledge' of older men as it relates to stability and continuity and also to changes in social relationships over time. What do adults 'know' and how does it relate to youthful 'anger'? What sort of *bēya* constitutes the frame for everyday cooperation and how does it differ from the oratorical stances adult men may adopt when shared expectations cease to be viable? Ilongots do not conceive of a "social world" or see their situation as one in which individuals must conform to, and reproduce, a differentiated and enduring social order. Rather, their very notions of what gives order to their personal lives include the possibility of violence. Ideas of 'shame' and 'admiration' toward one's more accomplished peers and elders, of groups of men who 'follow' one another, and of communities wherein close kin will 'help' and 'pity' one another as they 'distribute' valued game suggest not only sociality and cooperation but also an inherent possibility of strain. 'Distribution,' we have seen, may be related to 'contagion'; 'respect' and 'dizziness' are homonyms; and the idea of 'following' one another becomes problematic when certain people never take the lead. Activity in their social world is understood by Ilongots as a sort of actualization of emotional states, an enactment of

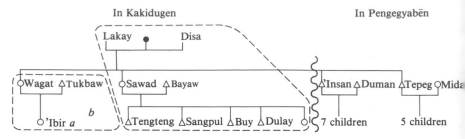

Figure 4. Lakay's family and household, 1974
Notes: a–'Ibir is an adopted daughter born to Kallahan settlers.
b–in Lakay's household 1967–9; moved upstream in 1970
c–moved to Kakidugen as an independent household in 1974

the heart's directives. Yet Ilongots are quick to recognize the difficulties that beset attempts at mutual coordination and say that 'people's hearts are not the same.' Do they, then, worry about social anarchy and chaos? Or, more to the point, when and why do Ilongots identify problems in informal cooperation and what is revealed about the nature of social experience as Ilongots understand it when adult men acknowledge strains, discuss them, and so set forth the terms on which their subsequent relations may proceed?

Local cooperation

It was only days after our return to the field in 1974 that Tukbaw, Renato's Ilongot 'brother,' the most respected local orator, and probably our most important friend, called a meeting of the people in Kakidugen. Some two years before, Tukbaw had taken the initiative to arrange a trip to Baguio, a city with which most local settlers were familiar, where he managed to record for us a taped message requesting our present visit. But since then, he had moved upstream, out of the house we had shared in the late 1960s with him, Wagat (his wife), Lakay (her father), Sawad (Wagat's sister), and Wagat's brother-in-law, father's wife, and sister's children (see Figure 4). And though he wanted us to join him, Tukbaw feared that we would choose to live in Kakidugen proper, near the airplane landing we had cleared on our last trip.

The real issue, however, had less to do with housing than cooperation. Would we be guests of everyone in Kakidugen? We might stay, for the time being, in Lakay's well-built house along the river, but would all think to feed us and tell us stories, and would we give everyone gifts? When we first entered the captain's house – the first house that one reaches on the trail from the mission settlement where we had arrived by plane some days before – there was not only cane

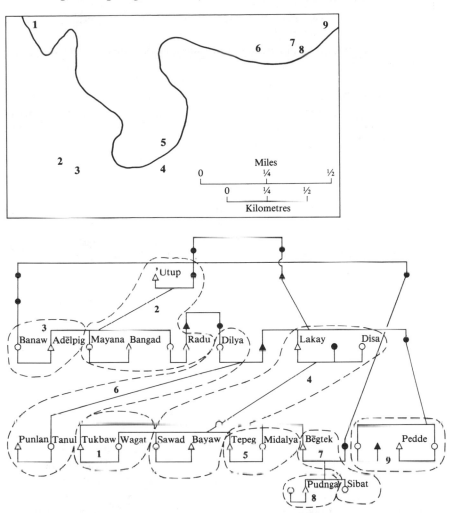

Figure 5. Kakidugen map and genealogical diagram, 1974
Note: Household 5 was built after our arrival to house us.

wine and meat, but also tearful warmth, an overwhelming welcome from remembered friends and neighbors. Did that mean that we were everybody's kin?

It did not take a man of Tukbaw's insight to be aware that differences in our commitments and bestowals, never explicit, had caused considerable resentment during our prior visit. But this time Tukbaw called on all, hoping through his formal talk, or *purung,* to avoid the tensions that our presence, goods, and curiosity had called forth in the past. Men from all local households heard and echoed Tukbaw's wishes. Those present (see Figure 5) were: Bangad, the local captain, and

Radu, his wife's sister's husband, the two still living together with their father-in-law, children, and wives, as they had been in 1969: 'Adēlpig – son of Bangad's father-in-law and husband of a distant 'granddaughter' of Lakay – a newcomer who had built a house in Kakidugen in our absence, and been joined there, temporarily, by Maniling, his wife's sister's husband and Tukbaw's brother's son; Punlan, once our neighbor, now living downstream by the Ifugao settlers, son-in-law to an old woman whose husband, Lakay's brother, had died when we were gone; Pedde, whose wife was also a distant granddaughter of Lakay and who lived with her newly widowed sister among the settlers downstream; Bēgtek, Tukbaw's brother, and his son, Pudnga, now married to an Ifugao and living with her – in most un-Ilongot fashion – next to his father's home. Aside from deaths and 'Adēlpig's rather unexpected presence, the settlement population seemed much as it had been during our prior visit – yet, we were to learn, much had changed.

At the meeting, Tukbaw proposed that the people of Kakidugen, together with their kin in Pengegyabēn, together clear the now overgrown and deserted airstrip and build a house for us at its base. All would work equally, all would give us food, visit us, and tell us stories. We in turn would keep them supplied with kerosene, salt, and medicine, and further – in response to Tukbaw's comment, 'Look at us from head to toe and know that we are naked' – give a lump sum of something like 150 dollars for them to divide among themselves. All local contributions would be equal; no outsiders could share their profits by joining labor on the landing or the house.

A month later, however, and well before our house was near complete, we knew that Tukbaw's plan had failed. Our presence in Lakay's household and our special ties with Tukbaw never ceased to be a problem. We learned, for instance, that the men of Bangad's household had become 'bored' (*'aleng*) with work for us because they felt that Lakay's housemates resented their requests for medical attention. Punlan's efforts turned increasingly erratic, and we heard from his mother-in-law that his commitment to us waned when beads we had left in Wagat's charge in 1969 were sold by her and not distributed to our local friends. Tukbaw worked on the house, as did Tepeg and 'Insan, Lakay's sons from Pengegyabēn, and to a lesser degree, we could count on help from Bēgtek (Tukbaw's brother) and his son. Disturbed, we tried to speak with captain Bangad, a relatively young in-married man who had been named the captain not for his skill in local ways but rather for his facility in the trade language, Ilocano. Bangad bemoaned the fact that Ilongots are not responsive to authority, indicating that even though he himself was busy he had delegated tasks in what he thought was a satisfactory way. Meanwhile, the older Tukbaw – close to the end of his physical prime but recognized for his graceful talk as something of a leader – sulked and mourned the 'breaking' of his *purung,* the discussion he had held when we first came. Yet neither man would call another meeting, and work on our house proceeded most haphazardly, led by those already mentioned with grudging and, at best, occasional assistance from the other men.

At the time we wondered if in fact we had been welcomed. Seeing strains, we blamed ourselves, but puzzled too about the vulnerability of what we had known as a cooperative and integrated community to what seemed a minor stress. The problem clearly went beyond considerations of our presence. We were struck, for instance, that the incidence of collective hunts, or *la'ub,* was much lower than we recalled for the late sixties and that men now seemed inclined to hunt as individuals – a fact that they attributed to the loss, with Martial Law, of guns and bullets at the same time that increasing numbers of settlers had cut down their hunting forests and depleted available game. Daily, our housemates muttered among themselves, made clear their sense that Bēgtek hid his meat, and that the captain gave out only scraps and traded the best part of his catch for cloth and liquor. And when Sibat, Bēgtek's daughter, tried to leave her uncle Tukbaw's house while meat was being butchered, people said she was 'shamed' by the thought that any share she carried home would not be reciprocated with a distribution from her father's hand. Around this time, the middle-aged bachelor Talikaw, who had moved in with his brother-in-law, the captain, suggested that Tukbaw call a public meeting to encourage local men to hunt collectively and truly share their meat among all Kakidugen households.

Like Talikaw, I too hoped that Tukbaw would use his verbal skill to set our once cooperative lives in order. Elsewhere, Ilongot communities appeared to respond with a good deal more resilience to land pressure, game depletion, and – with the declaration of Martial Law in 1972 – a loss of guns.

> In the missionary settlement of Ringen, reduction in available game in the early 1970s led to the decision to distribute catch from individual as well as collective endeavors. If the catch is too small to permit a reasonable distribution of raw meat for household cooking, cooked morsels will be brought to individuals for immediate consumption as a snack. And in the downstream area, where population density makes settlementwide distribution problematic, men frequently go in groups for several days of hunting in the forest; unlike the Kakidugen men who bemoaned their loss of bullets, they have proudly renewed their traditional skill with bows and arrows.

But in Kakidugen, nothing happened. Nor in retrospect does it seem that the situation was peculiar – an unhappy product of external pressures on an otherwise cooperative way of life. Rather, what I would suggest is that for a variety of reasons – including the presence of anthropologist and settlers, but also having to do with the immediate histories of Kakidugen's residents (their ages, marriages, kin ties, and recent deaths) – local relations were, in fact, unstable. People were planning moves and negotiating new alignments in a way that happens periodically in the lives of Ilongot local groups and has manifold consequences for a man of Tukbaw's standing. And yet, for Ilongots, the vagaries of local ties are not matters that one can readily and publicly address.

An Ilongot adult is not inclined to 'orate to his body'; kinship is not debated; and tensions that emerge among close relations are more likely to call forth withdrawal and 'resignation' than a full-fledged political exchange. Public oratory and formal speech concern the deeds of 'wild' youths, their marriages and killings; but one does not, in oratory, address real failures of cooperation or competing claims for precedence among adult men. Why this should be the case – or rather, how it is that difficulties like the ones we saw in Kakidugen did not lend themselves to explicit formulation, and that orators were inclined to deal in wives and heads but not in local cleavages and power – will become clear in the course of this chapter. The answer, which can be gleaned from the brewing conflict in Kakidugen, has to do with certain problematic aspects of *liget* and *bēya* as these are construed in dealings that concern relationships between youths and elders, and among adult men.

In Ilongot life, ideally, local ties are regulated by shared *bēya* concerning kinship – a 'knowledge' of shared needs that is exemplified by collective hunts and settlementwide norms of equal 'distribution' *(bē-ret)*, but reflected too in displays of respect, concern, assistance, 'shame,' and emulation that are required by daily work. To 'know' of kinship means, in large part, to be inclined to visit, offer food, give care, and contribute labor; and although none of these is rigidly adhered to or prescribed, frequent and informal shows of a cooperative orientation constitute both a display and an acknowledgment of ongoing kin-based ties. Thus, Punlan's mother-in-law would stop and visit at our house because she cared to 'look out for' Lakay's wife, her 'sister'; and she showed her special fondness for a 'brother,' Radu, by helping his wife garden and finding time to spend the evening in their home. Wagat brought Sawad rice from her fields because 'we all must feed our children'; reciprocally, Sawad's children often helped her sister hoe, pound rice, or chase rice birds because their 'mother' needed aid. Tukbaw called on Pudnga, his brother's son, to help him lift a rice rack torn by wind because, he said, 'He really is my child,' but would at other times request a hand in pollarding from Radu, a distant cousin; from Tepeg, his affine; or from Punlan, a cousin's son. On visits, we would be told that we were treated well because our host or hostess, Tukbaw's 'sibling,' was 'fearful' and 'respectful' of his or her 'brother's' *liget*. And even Lakay, eighty years old in 1974, proved himself a vital father by slashing underbrush to help his son clear forest for a field.

Because they lack gardens of their own, unmarried youths work in others' fields and help in others' homes more than their married seniors. In fact, the most frequent cooperative exchanges involve loans of a 'quick' child's labor to people whom their parents reckon kin. Thus, when a hunter's daughter stops by a neighbor's house to present a share of meat, she may well stay to help pound rice for her 'parent's' forthcoming dinner. And a bachelor son, restless at home, may find an uncle who will teach him to make arrows while he spends a week harvesting and joining the uncle on his hunts. Similarly, Lakay and his daughter Wagat can enjoy the help of Katu, 'Insan's daughter, in their gardens, and Tukbaw asks his sister, Katan, to send her son, Burur, to assist him when he needs an extra hand. Sawad's sons may spend a day assisting Punlan as he builds a house, or visit with and help their uncle 'Insan in his fields. And when Gimmu, from faraway Nalungtutan, 'discovered' (*bimaya*, from *beya*, 'to know') kin ties with some people in Pengegyabēn, he signified his understanding of relation by 'loaning' them the services of his bachelor son for several months (see Chapter 5). Of course, the reverse is also true, and when people choose to 'forget' or 'cease to know' kinship, labor exchanges come to an end:

> Over the years, Disa, Lakay's wife, had come to expect an annual visit and perhaps a week's labor from Lunik, her dead sister's daughter. Unfortunately, the girl's father – a distant relative of Lakay – had grown increasingly distant from the people in Kakidugen, and when Lunik's brother died in a logging accident, there was no responsible person left to inform her of her obligations to her 'mother.' She ceased to visit and when she married, failed to inform Disa – a symptom, Disa thought, of the girl's father's estrangement from Lakay and herself. Absent from the marital negotiations, Disa said that Lunik's father apparently considered her an unrelated, 'other person,' as he did not count her as kin deserving of a bridewealth gift.

Through their cooperatives moves – their visits, work, and labor of their children – adults can, then, signal understandings of relational ties, build up lines of support, and indicate divisions. Casual, unspecified, and diffuse, their bonds may be contained within or reach beyond the boundaries of a settlement, crosscutting and potentially undermining a sense of closeness presupposed by residence and the distribution of game. But it is most often locally coresident kin who visit one another for short meals and share not only meat but also liquor, betel, rice, medicinal skill, a morning's work, and in particular, the labor of unmarried children. And it is through such interactions that a sense of mutual commitment is maintained.

Effective kinship of this sort survives through unreflective give-and-take, which ranges over meals proferred, requests or playful 'thefts' of betel chews, and supplies of corn or vegetables from neighboring gardens. A lack of public calculation makes it difficult to denounce abuse, and a sense that violence grows quickly from complaint promotes a willingness to ignore offense rather than let *liget* lead to *liget* among kin. Thus, for example, Tepeg once said that he 'abides' *(kinurud)* faults in his wife because he 'knows' that peoples' hearts cannot be 'forced' *(pasi'ut)*, and because he would not kill his wife *(ten 'edēksu 'anuwed pasiya,* 'because I wouldn't really kill her'), he must have 'patience,' show 'endurance' *('adug),* and accept her. Similarly, when Burur broke his aunt's footbridge (Chapter 3), we saw his prank interpreted as a 'lack of knowledge' rather than as a serious 'threat' because of the constraints of kinship. And in a related vein, when Disa, Lakay's wife, responded to a rumor that she resented sharing meals with Dilya, her own 'sister' and her husband's brother's wife, her distress was shrugged aside. Disa wanted to clear her name by plunging her hand in boiling water (a traditional ordeal wherein innocence is equated with an ability to endure the heat unscathed); but her brother-in-law laughed and said that people everywhere would mock them if it were known that such close relatives had been forced to fight. In fact, complaints of a variety of sorts – including our suspicion that one of Tukbaw's 'cousins,' living downstream in 1969, had stolen a rather expensive round of brass wire – were quite intentionally suppressed because of a feeling best expressed by the query, *Rawenmu pa'ugiyat katan'agim,* 'Would you abuse a sibling?' or, more simply, because one does not quarrel with one's kin.

But if ongoing kin-based ties require a denial of dissension, difficulties in cooperation are hardly well disguised. A woman's 'selfishness' with rice supplies may, as we saw in Chapter 4, be readily identified as a source of strain – as may her children's noisy clamor. Less noted, though often more profound, are the competitive and disparate impulses of men of the same generation who make division a likely outcome in the absence of senior figures who can enforce their bonds. Young men who have left their homes upon marriage may hope to move with their wives to the locale of closer kin upon their in-laws' death or dotage; others may look forward to a time when they can call a net of loyal children, siblings, and affines to themselves. Family needs

– care of one's children, garden work, a leaky roof – provide a ready excuse for men who would avoid collective hunting, and the in-married man who finds the circle of local kin inadequately supportive spend a good deal of his time away from home.

In 1967-9, two aging brothers, Lakay and Tagem, could – as 'parents' who had cared for, fed, and housed adults from every 'roofbeam' in the settlement – still manage to inhibit shows of difference in Kakidugen. The vital and concrete foci of cooperative ties, they seemed to define for all their various 'children' a 'knowledge' of connectedness that made it shameful to show anger and sensible to share. Adults like these make kinship real and through their presence forestall conflict – much as when, years before, Lakay himself had thought to kill a man who had slept with his then new wife Disa, his father had dissuaded him by indicating that the rival was himself the father's 'son.'

But even more, those elders who have lived to see their families grow, and furthermore outlived those peers with whom they might engage in conflict, can through humor, generosity, and good sense provide a context wherein defensive *liget* has no place and one assumes bonds of affection. Because the old man 'knows' who can be counted 'one of us' and who to reckon 'other,' he freely criticizes his own, and, with his 'children,' gives and accepts challenge. Thus, Lakay could tell Tepeg, his son, that he preferred the company of his more energetic, older child, 'Insan; and with equal and affectionate ease, his sons could 'silence' *(tukbur)*, scorn, and mock their aging father. Even obscenity, a serious delict among same-generation kin,[1] does not cause concern for 'parents' and 'children.' Playful, mischievous, loving, and involved, the efforts of these senior men are viewed with a mixture of indulgence and admiration. No longer bound by selfish and familial needs, and probably no longer very 'angry,' an aging parent may work to keep up his fields, continue visiting distant kin, insist on hunting – and yet refuse to roast a private piece of meat in order that meat be shared.

But in 1974 Tagem was dead and Lakay nearing dotage. Punlan, now the senior man in his mother-in-law's home, had thoughts of moving closer to the settlement of his father and brothers. The captain wanted to stay where he was, building on ties of 'siblingship' that linked him both to Lakay's children and to his place of birth, but his father-in-law seemed inclined to bring his family elsewhere. Tukbaw, childless but still the leading figure in Kakidugen, had hopes of 'calling' on close kin who lived in or near the settlement of Pengegyabēn – a brother, his two sisters, and perhaps some female cousins – and using his powers of persuasion to draw a net of kinfolk toward his home. Meanwhile, Bēgtek strengthened his ties with Ifugao affines and Pedde found himself ever more involved in hunts with 'brothers' living faraway than with his

Kakidugen kin. In short, the crucial kin-based links defining settlementwide cooperation were open for revision. Differences previously suppressed took on, increasingly, a tone of calculation, and failures of cooperation, ever more frequent, appeared to lead to little but despair. People clucked when Tadi, for example, spoke of 'Udi's owing her a 'return' *(ta'rat)* for the pig she had contributed to a sacrifice to cure the latter's son of illness; and Tepeg was openly dismayed when Bēgtek threatened to charge the captain for damages to his rice fields caused by a carabao that broke loose, just once too often, from the captain's land. To charge, to ask for an 'exchange' *(ta'rat),* is not, Tepeg insisted, behavior one expects of kinsmen:

'Amung den sita tu'u nu rawende pata'rata,
'It's as if they were "other people" if they ask them for an exhcange.'

But these differences, foreshadowing moves and realignments, were, I think, related to the difficulties Tukbaw encountered in his hope to engage everyone from Kakidugen as our hosts.

What was happening was that the decline of a senior generation in a settlement had opened the possibility of a realignment of cooperative and residential ties. When old men die, there is a tendency for young and middle-aged adults to divide among themselves in their attempts to guide, and so define, the future. What is at stake for all is the difference between an adulthood and an old age surrounded and supported by the 'children' that one 'raised,' and a more marginal situation. Because Ilongots experience kinship as the basis of cooperative support – and frequent contact is considered a prerequisite of true kinship – no man wants to live further than is necessary from his relations.

> Tukbaw's ties with his three sisters nicely illustrate this point, as two live in relative proximity, in Pengegyabēn, and one of these, following her brother's 'call,' showed her willingness to move with her family to Kakidugen in 1974. Sons of both are regular visitors and helpers in Tukbaw's home, though the second sister, now a Christian, has shown increased interest in moving to her husband's family, in a settlement where mission influence is strong. The third sister, 'Undiya, because of a number of coincidences in Tukbaw's youth, when his father was still alive, married and moved to an even more distant settlement, following not her brother but her husband. When she has not visited for some time, Tukbaw complains that she has 'forgotten' their relation, 'as if she didn't know that we are siblings.' Her son, now married, rarely visits Tukbaw, and never comes to help him; in fact, the one visit I witnessed was treated more or less like an encounter between related men who had only recently 'come to know' of kinship and to establish a sense of relation. 'So that he will know I am his father,' Tukbaw says, he gave the visiting nephew several gifts. Tukbaw now fears that if the second sister follows her husband, she will become equally strange to him as well.

Faced with a multiplicity of competing kin-based claims, individual men thus try to coordinate residential plans with those of kin, and in the process often find themselves in conflict. And it is precisely this dissension born of men's concern, not to marry and become adult, but rather to secure their situation in adulthood, that a reluctance to have arguments with kinfolk seems to hide.

In what follows, I will suggest that Ilongots distinguish the cooperative arenas of daily life from situations that are defined by public conflict in an effort to sustain a daily world wherein most married men can treat one another, reasonably, as equals. Masking differences, they promote a view of local life in which all, equally, are 'children' of some one or two key 'fathers.' And so, although limited in their grasp of difficulties like those we saw in Kakidugen, Ilongots maintain a rhetoric, and in important ways, a practice, of cooperation without dominance or the denial of mature autonomy. The unifying position of a senior man lends reality to the claim that people who call one another 'siblings' share a common 'body' *(betrang)* or 'blood' *(matrem);*[2] and the needs known by their common flesh form obligations recognized by all. Thus, although some within a settlement may benefit more than others from the proximity and support of local kin, there is no acknowledged hierachy. Distributive norms secure for all a 'share' *(bēet)* in the collective life; grown men who have not taken heads can yet enjoy an 'equal' voice in plans for local moves or hunts; and the absence of distinctive statuses or privileged claims to goods prevents successful men from dominating or indebting 'equal' fellows. Striving to maintain a quality of activity appropriate to youth, a man like Lakay knows no special privilege because of age; he expects no reverence as an "elder." Rather, as Tallkaw, in outlining the life cycle, once said of the old: 'An old man ought to listen to the "quick ones" as they answer back because he no longer has bounce in his body . . . and, well, we will silence him because he no longer is the sort who confronts his fellow man with *liget* in his voice.' At the same time, the captain, as he appeared to be aware, commands almost no respect in local life. And though Tukbaw may enjoy the prestige that attaches to his skill in public speech, he is in most respects the peer of other adult men and has no real prerogatives. Tukbaw might have spoken out, and in so doing helped to check the tensions in his local group, but I was wrong to think he could have bent, against their wills, his neighbors' minds.

Or, to put the matter otherwise: Cooperating kinsmen are constrained by egalitarian norms (which, as we have seen, are presupposed by the distribution of game) to minimize conflicts among themselves because to do differently would suggest that some men give, or need, more than their fellows. Ilongots say that no man will fault another's failure to distribute meat lest it be thought that he himself does not know how to hunt, and is required, like a woman, to go begging. Inequality, as we saw in Chapter 2, is what breeds 'anger' and therefore *liget* has no place among those married men whose everyday cooperation is organized on the assumption that they are peers. But if the 'knowledge' that defines their kin-based bonds suppresses *liget*, equality and cooperation among married adults is based in part upon the inequality of unmarried men who are inclined to 'angry' shows of force. The male adults who join as equals on a hunt assume that in their not-too-distant youth each proved his *liget;* and by attributing comparable motivations to their 'sons,' all can – as 'equal,' 'knowing' men who hope to shape the moves and marriages of 'angry' children – at once sustain equality and express dissent in a present discourse that concerns the wild young.

Thus, if Ilongots would not debate the moves of individual families to or from the Kakidugen area, adult men can manipulate their fortunes and relational ties in a somewhat different context. When men confront one another not as coparticipants in a cooperative life but as rulers of young 'angry' 'pups' who must negotiate divisive facts of death and marriage for their 'shoots,' they are less shy of calculation, strict exchange, domination, and the threat of violence. Men will acknowledge and work publicly to resolve divisions in their social world when youthful hopes to marry and to kill provide a recognized source of *liget*. And so, for Ilongots, the *liget* of men's youthful years is significant not only as a response to qualities and experiences that bachelors lack, but as a potential that mature men keep alive because it offers an occasion for the explicit formulation of relational norms, an excuse for public oratory and debate, a way of understanding and addressing social opposition. Good orators have both 'knowledge' and 'passion' in their speech; they wear ornaments and taunt their opposites with witty words, and in so doing, prove themselves established men of 'anger.' But at the same time, their goal in speaking is to establish that, in *liget*, opponents ultimately are 'equal men' who, through exchange, may forge a sense of kinship – and so bring under the compass of their kin-based ties, or *bēya*, the necessary but disruptive *liget* of the young.

What is oratory?

Purung, or public oratorical debate, involves a style of speech, and correspondingly, of social interaction, that Ilongots recognize as different from that encountered in ordinary working life. Thus, people say, 'One should not orate with one's kinsmen.' And so too, several adults in Kakidugen said that they had married close kin, their second or third cousins, in order to avoid the arguments and prestations that accompany an oratorical exchange. Equally, I have been told by some that marriage with close relations is *undesirable* because it precludes the oratorical working through of 'angry' thoughts that are engendered by a union; because marriage is, of necessity, a proof and an occasion for shows of *liget*, some Ilongots feel that is is best to marry at a distance so that the inner motions of the heart can be made public through the course of a formal and stylized debate.

In *purung*, but not in daily talk, there is a concern for hearts that hide their deepest thoughts, a use of language that is intentionally indirect, a drama of revelation and deception. *Purung* deals, as local life does not, in the explicit invocation of kinship norms, and in idioms not of diffuse reciprocity and loosely wrought cooperation, but of exchange, accounts, and calculation. A consideration of the form of *purung* will tell us a good deal about what Ilongots think is accomplished by public speech. Why do Ilongots orate? And, in particular, why is *purung*, which can be held for almost any cause – the arrival of anthropologists, a sale of land, negotiations for a bride – associated primarily with the moments in which a boy becomes an adult, with marrying and killing, which Ilongots describe as the affairs, respectively, of 'women' *(bēkur)* and of 'hands' *(rima)?* Ultimately, we will see that the form of Ilongot political discourse is itself bound up with its contents. The social relations between unanchored youths and adult men provide the subject matter of *purung*, just as oratorical style involves at once displays of *liget* and of the heightened *bēya* of adults.

In our years of fieldwork, we attended and taped large segments of some nine major *purung*. One was a *bēyaw*, or peace meeting, which ended a feud of close to forty years between the Rumyad people and Butag enemies who our Kakidugen friends had thought were in the forest planning an attack when we first began our fieldwork in 1967; several were *langu*, or bridewealth transactions; and a number of others were marriage negotiations in which preliminary consent was sought or payments arranged for a forthcoming betrothal.[3] In addition, friends described at length and simulated on tapes several *purung* we were unable to attend. Each a major, scheduled event, these meetings typically involved a festive meal of rice and game that followed hours of highly formalized discussion. At each, one saw an accumulation of men and women from several settlements and, in every case, the key encounter was preceded by a period of informal talk and planning, during which allies conferred and called on kinsmen, clarifying differences as they agreed on contributions of meat, rice, or liquor and specified predictable demands.

Because, in *purung*, all is public, and most adults affiliate unambiguously with one of two opposing 'sides,' it is the business of the period of preparation to create, from daily ties combining both affinity and difference, an explicit sense of shared commitment, common enemies, and agreed-upon goals. Before the peace meeting, for example, Rumyad men from Ringen won the support of kin in Kakidugen by inviting Lakay and Tukbaw to visit and be paid informal compensation for a distant relative of Lakay's whom Ringen men had murdered six or seven years before. Because the residents of Ringen and Kakidugen were recognized by some as equal members, and therefore kinsmen, of the Rumyad 'people' *(bērtan)*,[4] this offense had not previously been addressed in public oratory. And in fact, in the course of this preliminary encounter, it was established that men of *each* place had killed relations of the other, offenses that – as 'siblings' – they could 'rub away' *(redred)*[5] immediately with a mere exchange of knives.

Once grudges had thus been forsworn, Luku, the man who killed and now wished to make peace with the Butags, managed 'as a son' to slip an extra gift to his Kakidugen relatives, so affirming their shared identity as people of a single *bērtan* who would be equally vulnerable to vengeance killings by the Butags and should, therefore, participate equally in the peace meeting to come. This set of exchanges was followed, on Ringen's part, with a number of others designed to augment their backing of kinsmen. Ringen men made clear their plans to contact relatives to the south and east, leaving Tukbaw with the responsibility of urging all individuals in Kakidugen and Pengegyabēn to participate in and assist the forthcoming peace. Winning support meant, for Tukbaw, persuading various local kinsmen to forswear their grievances toward the Butag 'enemy' as well as toward the people in Ringen who, though closely related, had killed and otherwise offended fellow Rumyads in the past. In particular, he had to make clear that it was the Ringen people, and not he, who had taken the initiative in asserting their shared relation. And, as a token of his own unfailing *liget* and willingness to speak out for his kin, he called to mind the fact that Luku's killing had itself precipitated the accidental death of Lakay's father, who, because of prior covenant with the Butags, had 'dissolved like salt in water'[6] when a person of his 'body' shed the Butag blood. This loss, Tukbaw explained, gave him the right to a 'return' peace meeting, or *bēyaw*, from the Butags and considerable deference from the erring Ringen kin.

Such exchanges and recollections are likely to accompany preparations for any *purung*. Before they orate, people 'let out' what they know of the past, 'hiding' differences they are concerned to 'hold' while 'making known' those past events that present politics seem likely to resolve. In preparation, adults *tadēk,* or 'tell stories' – which may consist of little more than an account of predecessors who once lived as kin alongside a particular hill or river – through which they document and make explicit the historical foundations of their kinship. They evaluate shared claims on their opponents, and in casual interchange, resolve interpersonal differences which, having occurred among men recognized as relations are, by definition, of small account. Thus, during the preliminary arrangements for a peace, longstanding differences among allies may (like Lakay's with the men of Ringen) be revealed and quieted. And, en route to a negotiation for bridewealth, one learns of claims and damages of some history, so that if 'they' dare ask too much or prove unnecessarily stubborn, 'we' will be able to reciprocate with mention of 'their' delicts in the past.

> In the course of preparations for the formal *purung* to accompany the marriage of 'Eget to Dili, Tayeg's sister, I learned a good deal about grudges previously suppressed. Tayeg, it turned out, was a Rumyad man who had once lived among 'Eget's kin, but then took the head of a settler whom they considered an ally, fled with goods stolen from his relatives, and eventually married into the Tamsi *bertan* as an 'exchange' *(tubrat)* for the marriage of a Tamsi man to a Rumyad woman. Because Tamsi people are known to demand more extensive bridewealth than do the Rumyads, it was rumored that Tayeg had adopted the expectations of the people with whom he lived. En route to the confrontation, Tukbaw, who was to speak for 'Eget, his 'brother,' made it clear that inordinate demands from Tayeg would be met with demands for compensation for troubles caused by the latter's prior deeds. As it turned out, Tayeg demanded little – by his account, because he was a Christian who had abjured *liget* in relation to marriages, but, according to Tukbaw, because he was afraid of the history he knew his opposites could bring to light.[7]

Finally, a man like Tepdurak of Nalungtutan – who was supplied with game, a kerosene lamp, and arrows by his recently discovered 'brothers' from Pengegyabēn – may use the excuse of a bridewealth transaction, or *langu,* to establish that he has 'come to know,' and intends to work and visit with, potentially supportive and hitherto unfamiliar kin. At the same time, his 'kin' in Pengegyabēn can, through their decisions as to who would work to help him, indicate lines of solidarity among themselves.

Through this period of preparation, the past comes to be 'made known' and relational bonds may be adjusted and asserted. As events that demand an unambiguous formulation of what are usually flexible sorts of ties, *purung* occasion reflection on inchoate grounds for daily conflict and cooperation, permitting interested adults to make political use of feelings that ordinary dealings encourage them to set aside. The 'knowledge' that is called forth when men turn daily life into the 'sides' of *purung* is, then, discontinuous in important ways with daily living; it presages, in a less formal style, the interactions of the oratorical event itself.

Once preparations are complete, both 'sides' convene, one group performing as 'the one who stays,' or host, the other as the 'jumping frogs' who have 'stepped out from the shade of quiet dwellings' to give gifts, request a woman's hand, or in the case of *bēyaw,* ask recompense for killings. On their way, participants stop to gather friends and recount relevant stories; and as they near their meeting place, or 'center' *(pambengriyan),* they preen and deck themselves in ornaments suggesting youthful energy and strength and indicating the numbers of their company who, wearing red hornbill earrings, are thus known to have taken heads.

A man like Tukbaw who had led preliminary negotiations and is likely to be a dominant figure in the oratory to come may be addressed respectfully by youths as 'grandfather' or 'old man' instead of as 'father' or 'uncle'; and, in affirmation of his now unquestioned role as leader he may give 'instructions' *(tengteng)* to his fellows, reminding 'quick' ones in particular to follow stereotypical norms for good behavior when they are away from home. So, for example, before the meeting with the Butags, we were 'instructed' by a man from Ringen to stay calm because the myriad Rumyad kin there mixed together could easily confuse gestures of friendship and start fights among themselves. Young men, aspiring grooms, immediate kin of victims, and atoning killers (who at a *bēyaw* are, I believe, seen as the equivalents of youths) will be 'ashamed' *(bētang)* to take a public role in the forthcoming discussion. But they are likely to play an informal part in preliminary arrangements, coordinating the timing of arrivals, and bearing word and rumor of intentions and demands. In fact, before the peace meeting, a Rumyad bachelor was sent to Butag as an official hostage in the thought (ultimately rejected as unnecessary) that the Butags, on nearing Ringen, would be secured against an ambush if, brandishing a ready knife, some one of them could hold the young man's loincloth by the tail.

Of course, overt displays like these of the imbalance between old and young, and then, among adults themselves, between a silent grouping of supportive kin and those few who are most likely to perform as speakers, may themselves be problematic when – as often happens – persons with diverse interests are uneasily united on a 'side.' In the past, young men have stepped out of the room when senior kin swore peace, and then have 'dissolved' their elders' oaths through subsequent beheadings. And at the bridewealth meeting in Nalungtutan, our plans were almost ruined when Tepdurak, who was giving gifts, began a drunken fistfight with some of the Pengegyabēn 'brothers' who had traveled several days to speak for him. Again, our friends resented Ringen dominance at the Butag meeting, and after the terms of peace had been decided, they found cause to challenge the presumption of goodwill with people who, they said, could easily be construed as enemies rather than kin.

Tensions may, then, barely be suppressed within a 'side,' and unity within a 'side' may virtually dissolve during the conduct of a meeting. But if and when two parties meet, there is no question as to who, as 'tongue,' will be the first to speak; and even though no formal features of the setting mark beginnings, the opening of most oratorical events is standard and predictable in form. A routine 'greeting' *('imanu)* that acknowledges the gathered public – 'So you have come here, and can you tell me why you came, so that our fathers and brothers may hear it all?' – may be elaborated, in the case of a *bēyaw,* into an exchange of opening boasts and, in the past, a period of violent dueling. Further, for *bēyaws,* taboos that prohibit sharing food with 'contaminating' *(bēret)* members of a 'people' *(bērtan)*[8] who have shed one's body's blood must be 'rubbed away' through the prestation of strengthening metal gifts before opposing parties can exchange so much as betel nuts with one another – a necessary prelude to any interaction with a guest. But, for all *purung,* the first order of business involves an identification of parties as, for instance, 'parents' and 'children,' as those 'whose name is Butag,' 'who live upstream at the river's source,' 'who come from beyond the mountains,' or, in yet more glowing terms, as 'navels to whom all weeds are blown.' And such identification is accompanied by preliminary questioning as to why, and on what terms, the 'sides' will talk.

Thus, Tayeg, called to *purung* by an 'uncle' – who hoped through oratory to forestall 'angry' and surprised demands by Tayeg for a sister with whom the uncle's 'brother' had already come to live – started by saying 'Well, whatever it was you called me for, I came to hear; alas, I can't speak well, but I said to myself, "Maybe there is some reason he commanded me, so I will go and hear its name."' At another meeting, Tukbaw, speaking as 'brother' to a woman his wife's kinsman hoped to wed, began by saying, 'Before I take a betel chew from you, I think that I should ask why you are here.' Similarly, before 'rubbing' can initiate a *bēyaw,* guests expecting gifts in recompense for killings are apt to ask why they have been called out from their homes. Such openings are so familiar that a playful rehearsal that I taped of a bridewealth *purung* turned out to be virtually identical to the first hour of the meeting itself!

At the same time, these questions have no simple answers. To

Tayeg's query came the reply, 'Oh, if you are finished speaking, then may our brothers and our fathers hear it all. I will not hide the true reason I called you. The true reason that I called you is something that the wind brought, a bit of gossip that came and touched my ear. And so the reason I, your father, sent for you, is that when it reached me, I did not know if I should take that gossip to my heart.' So too, when Tukbaw hesitated, in his 'sister's' name, to accept first betel and then liquor from the men who sought her favor, he was told that they had come with gifts because they wished to join him in conversation and to share liquor; they were visiting, they said, in quest of 'news' *(beita)*. Even in a more 'modern' *purung,* at which the educated Christian captain from 'Abēka began by 'instructing' people of both parties to speak clearly and to follow 'direct' norms of lowland law,[9] clarification was slow in coming. The captain's remark was answered with a query, 'Why did you call me?' which was followed by a response to the effect that before anything could be said, one had to 'answer' the captain by acknowledging that all had, equally, been 'hit' by the impact of his peaceable discourse, and then by a rather long explication of the speaker's desire to start 'where things left off' and not return to 'name' the painful 'origin' of the dispute in question. And these comments led in turn to a reply in which the questioner indicated that words were 'missing their mark' because he still failed to understand why he was called.

Eventually, of course, the speakers for potential grooms let it be known that their 'young pups' can hardly be restrained since they first 'sniffed' the honey in a nearby forest; or alternatively, that their kin lack rice and so would like to join their present hosts in planting grain. And although the hosts may well, in feigned surprise, respond that 'rice' and 'honey' are locally in short supply, all recognize these metaphors as conventional ways of talking about a wife. Eventually too, the Rumyad men found themselves ready to say that they had hopes of sharing food on a single leaf with upstream Butag men, 'as brothers.' And in the confrontation that the 'Abēka captain chaired, the 'callers' were finally constrained to give an account of gifts they wished to see returned, as it was clear that a woman they had thought their 'son,' Tubeng, would marry had been 'snatched off' by the woman's brother's friend.

Even mission Ilongots, who are critical of the 'crookedness' of their oratorical tradition and declare themselves committed to 'straight' and simple speech, do not wish to seem 'anxious' and 'speak out' their hearts in *purung,* and hesitate to give a precise 'name' to things they want or fear. Trained in elaborate and metaphoric turns of phrase, all orators are 'slow' and cautious in their use of speech; they allow time for words to 'reach' their points and avoid direct statement. In *purung* as in daily talk, the overt mention of offense may be disruptive. And although the orator hopes his phrases will excite an opposite's response, he knows that insults suffered may give rise either to violence or to new and difficult demands. Speech alone seems to provide a neutral ground in terms of which one can negotiate relations; thus, orators devote more of their talk to commentary on the style and nature of discourse – 'I will add feathers to my tongue,' 'I lay my words out flat before you,' 'Hand me a share of your thoughts,' '. . . but I wonder if there is something, some pit in your heart, that you are hiding,' and 'Are you speaking from the coursings of your heart?' – than to concrete details, demands, or points of fact.

In Tayeg's case, for instance, the night-long *purung* centered largely on questions of identity and relation. Would he – asked the speaker for the man who wed his sister – behave as an outsider who had forgotten kin ties and taken on the customs of his bridewealth-hungry neighbors? Would he make himself his uncle's "affine," or in his speech display a proper 'knowledge' that he was the uncle's 'son'? And when Kama of Butag was reluctant to enter Rumyad homes before he was repaid not only for his severed 'body' but for a gun taken from the dead victim's hand, he never once said, 'I want you to return our firearm,' nor did he have difficulty in clarifying allusions to something 'tasted' (see Chapter 5) by Luku in the raid so many years before. Instead, once 'rubbing' was complete, Kama indicated his reluctance (sustained for several hours until the Rumyads came up with an acceptable weapon as a return) to enter into what he considered a particularly compromising situation, the shelter of already crowded Ringen homes:

Well, if we are to be friends, let me say I know the flesh, the humanity of other men; I know what it is to enter my equal human's home. I have a spleen *(bēsit)*,[10] and though I am a child facing you, I have knowledge enough to give you a share, so I will gossip; I will let you in on my thoughts. And listen to me, too, I who belong upstream on the Kasiknan River, there where everything reaches me, there where all points converge. Well, what I am stirred by, what I don't know, is why you have called so many, beckoned even the weeds of the Ilongots, summoned all these people to the biting roofbeams of your home. Isn't that something to be criticized? . . .

And later, he indicated that the Rumyads, who had known his demands beforehand, were pleading for sympathy when there was a more direct way to placate his wounded heart:

I am a child, oddly, by a turn, a child to you, but you know now and you knew before the target of my thoughts, as I have already told you what is in my heart. If only it were over there, in my own place, and there were something, some sharp point, you thrust at me, in a sense, well, I would satisfy you when you came to my place . . . Truly, the words falling from my mouth are better, as I let you see, I speak so you can see my thoughts. But look, you who I call Rumyad, see how you are doing things; it is no more than tears that you are feeding my requests. And, oh dear, I can't like that, and that's why we keep adding words on words without a meeting of the things we know and that's why we can't come together in our hearts. You beckoned all the weeds of Ilongots, but there is only one thing that I asked . . .

His talk, in short, concerned itself with who said what and when, the form and the development of the *purung*. Factual details – in particular, his decision as to whether particular weapons offered in the course of the increasingly cold and uncomfortable night could be accepted – received only summary address.

There are no "judges" in *purung*. Though mediating parties may – especially in the case of *bēyaw* – arrange encounters, no jury stands ready to decide the virtues of competing arguments and determine outcomes by allocating praise or blame. One may, in *purung,* state one's claims when all recognize with whom the responsibility for an action lies, but it is virtually impossible to accuse an unacknowledged offender.

> In 1969, I was in the company of Kakidugen friends when we met with a group of people from Payupay who were to join us in a festive fishing expedition. Some among our group had been on a headhunting raid in which lowlanders were intended victims, but a Payupay man happened to be one of the roadworkers our friends attacked and killed. The Payupays, suspecting our group as their murderers, indicated that they thought there might be some reason that we should not eat together (i.e., they would be ritually endangered because we had shed their blood), but Kakidugen speakers insisted that they did not know what was being referred to, that people from Kakidugen were, as all knew, distantly related to the Payupays, and so the accusation was absurd. The Payupays, reluctant to accuse us directly for fear of inciting an incident, gave in and joined us. Later Tukbaw said that at some time, the Kakidugen guilt would probably become known, but hopefully it would occur so far into the future as to reduce the hurt feelings and, therefore, the demands for recompense on Payupay's part.

One may phrase hopes in terms of friendship, or the sorts of cooperative behavior people would expect of 'sons' or 'siblings' – pleading kinship as a grounds for 'pity' *(dē'ri)* and the reduction of demands – but there are no rules or expectations that govern every marriage, death, or friendship, no norms whose application is recognized by all. Nor, in reporting on past *purung,* do people tend to summarize the event, and speak in general terms of settlements, loss and gain, how much a wife is apt to cost, or whether the Butags in their *bēyaw* with the Rumyads received more or less by way of goods than the Rumyads would 'look for' in return.

> Our data, in fact, show little pattern in the cash value of prestations as related to any independent reckoning of the extent of an offense. Brides are often more expensive than bodies, and the Rumyads paid

more heavily for 'tasted goods' taken from their victim (a firearm) than for the person they killed (a brass pot). Further, even though the Rumyads were acknowledged key offenders, the Butags gave considerably more by way of gifts at a return *bēyaw* that took place in 1970 than the Rumyads had given at the first event.

Rather, most oratorical events appear to operate in piecemeal fashion, specific moves on the part of various speakers leading to anger, recompense, concession, or withdrawal, as parties try to 'curve around' the intransigence of their adversaries, urge payments, and make concessions without admitting 'defeat.'

Oratory is, then, less a matter of discovering some undetermined truth than a negotiation of relationship, a revealing – with a care that sees in 'letting out' of thoughts or words a source of anger, vulnerability, and confusion – of deep and heartfelt thoughts whose presumably 'hidden' contents are quite often things that everybody knows. When asked the point of their elaborate speech and preference for indirection, Ilongots mention everything from a hope to prolong contact and so enjoy more food and drink to feelings of 'shame' or 'fear' bound up with direct statement. Most commonly, they indicate, on the one hand, a desire to avoid disruptive outbursts, to seem contained, controlled, and ruled by 'knowledge,' and, on the other, an 'angry' hope to challenge and belittle one's opponents to the point where they abandon their demands. Unlike kinsmen who assume equality by virtue of their common blood, orators will acknowledge and manipulate the 'hiddenness' of adversary hearts; confronting one another as the representatives of opposed sides, they recognize the *liget* that each harbors in imbalance. Their discourse operates through exchange upon exchange of words and goods wherein men alternately oppose their hardened hearts and work to weld them, knowing that, if successful, they will become as equal kin, share a meal from common plates, encourage 'quick' ones to feed one another rice by hand, and even speak – as men did at the conclusion of the *bēyaw* that we saw – with warm and sincere hopes of future marriage.

'Knowledge,' 'passion,' and regulation through exchange

Good orators are knowledgeable men, men of reputed *bēya* – a designation that relates in part to their familiarity with history and their skill in witty speech,[11] but primarily to their delicate approach to human affairs. Knowledgeable speech is, of necessity, indirect, because a fellow's heart is quickly angered; it is a measured, 'slow' proceeding – the word 'slow,' or *lipalipa,* referring not to the pace of speech, which is ideally mellifluous and unbroken, but to a lack of 'sudden' (*tu'meg*) outbursts of 'intense' (*'iteg*) concern and feeling, a quality of respect that avoids calling things by name. *'Unlipalipa kisi,* 'Let's go slowly,' is something adults say to youths in Ilongot accounts of headhunting raids, just as it is a phrase that senior men use in urging hiking fellows to leave their resting place and set off on their way. When I first heard men tell me to 'move slowly,' I thought they meant for all to slow themselves in order to accommodate my awkwardness in the forest – and so proceeded to show I could make haste! Only later did I realize that *lipalipa* has more to do with caution imposed on impetuous energy and *liget* than it has to do with speed.

In oratory, one moves 'slowly' out of a desire to 'find' *('abet)* the words that can at once contain the *liget* of the youths for whom one speaks and yet be inoffensive, 'hitting' *(pukna)* aptly on the grounds for 'softened' feeling in an opponent's heart. Through indirection orators show their 'respect' *(tu'ngan)* and wisdom. They speak of 'tasted objects' rather than of weapons, of 'rice' instead of women, of 'young pups' when they have a hopeful husband in mind – much as adults are careful to avoid the names of affines, to call death an 'absence' and a burial a 'handling of dirt,' and to say that 'something kind of happened' *(kimu'kuyen* from *kuyen,* 'something,' cf. Tagalog *kwan)* instead of 'he got a little better' *(pimi'piya)* when reporting progress in a fellow who is ill. The true or 'big names' of things can be experienced as an afront and excite passions. Indirection, allusive phrases, and metaphors such as:

'Amung kamin limadeseka 'alaken,
'We are like frogs who jumped,' meaning 'We jumped into this and feel vulnerable';

qualifying words:

Bukud ma 'amung pu'una sinengtengangku dimu,
'Well, the core, in a sense, of why I called for you,' in which *'amung* means 'in a sense';

Legema sa nu 'alimbawa wade ma qimpanengtengantu dēken,
'Just in case, perhaps, there was a reason that he called me,' in which *legem* is 'just' and *'alimbawa,* from Tagalog *halimbawa,* means 'perhaps';

and a grammatical reduplication that suggests uncertainty:

Retē'retebēngku ma kuwa'an nima 'upu,
'I just guess the direction of the talk,' in which reduplication of the first syllables qualifies *reteb,* 'to guess';

Wadē'wade pay ma ramaka 'upuwenmu,
'There might be a bit that you want to say,' with reduplication qualifying *wade,* 'there is';

are all common in oratory and enforce a sense of delicacy and care.

Practically, indirection means that one is 'slow' in another sense as well. Hours went by before a man like Tayeg, insisting that as his uncle's son he could demand payment of bridewealth for his sister, let it be known that he expected a gift for not having been informed of the marriage until it was, in fact, accomplished. And we spent a good part of the night in a pea patch, shivering with cold, before Kama, present at the peace meeting, could be persuaded to accept a firearm and enter Ringen homes. Taking time like this permits opponents' hearts to 'get used to one another,' or *tagde,* and because, Ilongots say, it is impossible to know what 'flows' *(kurut)* inside the thought and breath of equal humans, a cautious pace is required if one is to become accustomed to, and trust, another's heart. With time and indirection, one can enjoy food and drink together, taking pleasure in the art of speakers. And further, taking time means that youth's passion will be subordinated to adult *bēya* because only adult men command the skills of 'crooked' speech.[12]

But there is, I think, an even deeper way in which 'slow' speech is bound up with skills that Ilongots associate with 'knowledge,' something I mislabeled in earlier work on oratory (see M. Rosaldo 1974) as an inability to persuade. What happens in an oratorical confrontation is not in any familiar sense a "trial" in which one musters facts to help decide a case and so, perhaps, negotiate its outcome. Orators confront one another's intransigent and separate hearts and must attempt, with 'curving' words, to 'hit' and so to bind them. When an opposite will not be moved, a speaker may have the wit to 'answer' *(sibēr)* each denial with new insistence, swearing to climb rocks, drink streams, or manufacture untold gifts for would-be brides and so confront, with *liget* of his own, a 'hard' opponent. But equally, the seasoned orator may, in delicacy, claim to set forth 'soft' words, words 'sweet as fruits' and 'without arrows.' Arguing kin ties with the men to whom he speaks, he may plead for 'pity' *(dē'ri)* and a reduction in demands.

Thus, when, for example, Tubeng listed all the gifts that he would see returned from his apparently futile courtship, what was in question was not at any point what happened, but rather (1) whether he should be paid for gifts now lost, or insult suffered, or for both, a question recognized as one of 'custom'; and (2) given a decision that the gifts should be repaid, whether his demands could then be tempered by a show of 'pity' *(dē'ri)* for the brother of his lost bride and her successful groom. It was unquestionably bad form when Tepdu, 'father' of Tubeng's would-be bride, indicated that only certain of the gifts received should be returned; and his quibbles in this regard met only laughter. Rather, as Tukbaw and a number of other men explained on listening to the tape after the event itself had passed, Tepdu should have proclaimed his poverty and destitution, requested 'pity' as a kinsman, and suggested that if Tubeng would not be satisfied with the few gifts that Tepdu felt he could return, the former might be happier to take his life. In fact, it was with such a strategy in mind that Rumyad men had called themselves the crippled 'fathers' of the younger orators from Butag, hoping that in sympathy for old men shivering in the night air, the Butags would – without first seeing a return for 'tasted objects' – enter and enjoy the comfort of the Rumyad homes. 'Knowledge' in contexts like this involves the establishment of a tone of discourse in which opposites can display their kin-based bonds.

But if, instead of huge demands, desiring speakers meet refusal – the insistence, in the case of marriage, that the woman's brothers simply have no 'rice' to share – the 'knowing' voice will seek to find another point of access to his opponent, and strike a chord relating less to sympathy than to the *liget* that an interlocutor has yet kept hidden in his heart. If opposites can be induced to speak, and so make known a hidden 'anger,' petitioners can then 'repay' old wrongs with small prestations, and through such payments pave the way for future interactions in which they, in turn, will have occasion to make claims. This was what happened at one of the most disturbing *purung* I attended,[13] at which Lundi, a recent widow living with her brother-in-law and sister near Kakidugen and quite far from their close kin, was sought by Wagat's cousin Bē'rak, an aging bachelor – a man who many reckoned *depyang,* an 'incompetent,' 'worthless man,' or clod. Lundi had made clear her reluctance to remarry, but concern for her children, for her lack of local connection, and for Bē'rak himself (who people thought should wed) led to the scheduling of a *purung,* in which Tukbaw would (by virtue of some very distant ties) speak Lundi's part, as her 'brother,' and Bē'rak have his suit defended by Tepeg, Wagat's brother, and a number of other men. Present when we first arrived, Lundi stayed only briefly in the house where the men were speaking – long enough to learn from Tukbaw that he hoped that she would speak her mind, but if, as a woman, she felt herself unable to broadcast the things she felt, she could trust him, as her 'brother,' to look out for her concerns. Lundi listened silently and then, protesting that the noise disturbed her tired children, left the house.

Tukbaw's message to Lundi had itself been of questionable sincerity, as in traditional marital *purung* women rarely give direct voice to their feelings, hoping brothers will 'defend' them in rejections and fearing the 'anger' of their brothers should they openly accept a lover's suit. Further, Tukbaw already knew that Lundi still felt herself in mourning for the husband who had died a year before. But what Tukbaw hoped to hear was something different: Did Lundi think Bē'rak too poor or too unmanly? Was she, perhaps, obsessed with rumors that kin of Bē'rak had killed members of her 'body' in the past? The men tried among themselves to 'find out' such a source for Lundi's 'anger,' but – reluctant to commit herself to further dealings – Lundi stayed by a granary in her sister's garden and refused to return.

Eventually, however, Lundi was persuaded to rejoin her guests and suitors, at which point Bē'rak, misunderstanding a suggestion that he give Lundi a drink, tried to embrace her. In fury, Lundi left again, then returned once more, and this time let herself admit the 'name' of what it was that had just recently made her 'angry.' But thus confronted with the cause of Lundi's *liget,* Bē'rak could insist, in 'shame,' that he be allowed to pay her in return for his offense. This accepted, Bē'rak's speakers took the opportunity to offer to enhance their gift. These actions led in turn to an agreement that Bē'rak be allowed to visit the house where Lundi was staying and help her brother-in-law in garden labor – although on last report we learned that the unhappy Lundi had fled with her children to the homes of distant kin.

Several women I knew berated the men who were involved for ignoring Lundi's stated wishes, but most agreed with Tukbaw when he argued that much of courtship assumes something of this form: A woman resists and a man hopes, through labor and repeated gifts, gradually to 'accustom' his lover's heart to interaction; and Ilongots say that if a man has *liget* necessary to persevere, he is unlikely to fail to win his suit. The 'knowing' and committed suitor tries to 'find' the things that keep a woman's feeling at a distance, and if she or her brothers 'name' their reasons for dissension, the young man's party can insist on giving gifts and so initiate further talk. Much of the talk of *purung* consists, in short, of such attempts to 'hit upon,' and make public and so accessible to resolution, what are divisive, hidden thoughts – to find (as Tukbaw did in Lundi's case) a source of 'anger' and repay it. Slow and careful speech seeks to facilitate what may be critical revelations. By 'laying out' his words and proclaiming against deception, the orator works at once to ease and stimulate the silent 'anger' in his fellows' hearts.

The careful speech of *purung* is, thus, predicated upon a particular view of people's hearts and thoughts, a view that claims that troubled feelings can be quieted if their source, once 'hidden,' is made known. One tries to find the words that will occasion revelation, just as in medicinal spells one tries to 'hit upon' words that 'find' the things that made a person ill. In magic, as in oratory, one seeks to 'name' the origins of misfortune, weaving lines such as 'even if I were contaminated by a plant,' 'licked by the sun,' 'touched' or 'cursed' or 'criticized' by a spirit, into the wording of a spell. Ilongot cures depend upon a collection of appropriately named plants, whose strength can frighten or coerce a spirit. And Ilongots assume that, whether or not familiar to them, all plants 'have names' and some – like 'gather,' 'dizzy,' 'wild boar,' 'finger,' 'thigh,' and 'toothless' – have potent names, which can be known and used. Successful spells depend upon one's luck in calling forth such 'knowledge.' Just as in oratory one seeks through subtle words to find the bases for an interlocutor's resistance, so magicians hope to 'find' the plants with names that can effect a cure. In both cases, the 'knowledge' that leads to a success is something one assumes to be already there, requiring only revelation; and so, practitioners seek to make the 'names' of troubles public because in giving voice to 'hidden' founts of *liget,* one makes them manipulable and subjects them to social action and control.

But if the knowing speaker seeks, in slow and cautious terms, to let his opposite 'make known' a hidden feeling, if speakers value openness and claim that they 'lay out' their hearts and lack disguise, good orators are also men who can 'hold on' to tortured thoughts and anger. While protesting revelation, they will use metaphors and 'crooked' speech to 'hide' their deeper meanings. Avoiding names of things in order to befuddle and exhaust their interlocutors, they hope to dazzle and to display a quality of *liget* that indicates the mettle of their side. The rounds of boasts and dueling that in the past preceded *bēyaw* – and made it something of a show of courage for men to ask for peace – are themselves testimony to the fact that orators require 'passion' as a necessary complement to knowing subtlety in their speech.

Claiming clarity, good speakers often revel in deception. Good *purung,* Ilongots say, is full of 'riddles' *(kinit)* – a particularly appropriate designation, as riddles are characteristically devices that adult men, through 'deception,' use to test the knowledge of the young. Furthermore, in riddles the 'knowledge' that is sought is cast as social knowledge, the answer being called the riddler's 'fellow bachelor,' or 'friend' *(kabuintaw).* Thus:

'I have a friend who is like a pot that can feed as many guests as happen to be present, even if the house is full,' has as its answer 'a mouth,' which 'feeds' by talking.

'I have a friend with bracelets on every arm,' bespeaks a granary with rat guards, which are like bracelets on its legs.

So, in oratory, to call a woman 'rice,' or to answer, 'You think you hear us pounding rice but really what you hear is the woodpecker's clapping,' is seen as *kinit,* 'telling riddles,' an attempt to challenge and bemuse those men whose lack of wit reveals the weakness of their side.

Successful orators hear their fellows' words and then turn them to their purpose, as did Tukbaw when he first asked Bē'rak's speakers what sort of 'rice' they hoped to find in local gardens, knowing that if they said, 'plain rice,' *mabu'u,* he could name other families who had a surplus, and if they spoke of 'glutinous rice,' *deyeket,* he could insist that in his household full of children, hungry youngsters had long ago consumed his small supply. Some brothers will 'pretend to anger' (*rayag,* 'to make a show of anger, make an unconsummated threatening gesture') at a sister's marriage, in order – others claim – to provide a cause for payments. Some see the subtlety in their *purung* as a device for 'testing' (*pabēyabēya,* 'making known') their opponents; through ruses meant to cause confusion and frustration, they hope to intimidate those speakers who, for lack of *liget,* can be summarily dismissed.

> In 1973, when men from Dekran came to announce their hopes to marry Binsing, Katan's daughter, they were intimidated by the 'angry' speeches of her kin. A history of enmity as well as rumors to the effect that men from Dekran never helped their wives, gave Binsing's father and brothers sufficient cause to feel, at best, ambivalent about the union. And so, according to reports, the 'angry' pretense in her uncles' speech – as they declared that before a Dekran suitor could move into their 'daughter's' home, he would first prove himself by climbing ladders runged with knives and sipping local rivers dry – caused the suitors such confusion that they could not decide among themselves a telling answer, and thus humiliated, withdrew. The Dekran version placed a different value on the same proceeding. They saw themselves behaving in the manner of the Christian ethic they had recently accepted, demonstrating 'knowledge' without 'passion,' and when faced with *liget,* showing themselves willing to 'give in' (see also Chapter 5).

Without *liget,* without firm words and stunning speech, one's *purung* will, then, 'fail to reach' its mark; young men lose their hoped-for brides; the brothers of new brides receive no payments; and enemies continue killing rather than redress a history of wrongs. This is, in fact, the dilemma faced in *purung* among kinsmen. Tayeg, for example, having proclaimed himself a 'child' to his uncle, said, 'If you were another sort of person, you would hear my tongue in *purung,* but I am trapped because it is my father with whom I speak.' In short, his oratory was ineffective because in recognizing kinship he was forced to forswear 'anger'; it was only an impatient aunt's outburst to the effect that she refused to see her 'daughter' marry without prestations that permitted Tayeg to give voice to the sense of insult he had 'hidden' in his heart.

Once again, there is an interesting parallel with magic. Spirits of the dead are the very opposite of living kinsmen, because the former, in their attempts at closeness, bring not succor but affliction, drawing healthy kinfolk toward themselves. Thus, 'knowledgeable' practitioners try not only to 'find out' but also to deny relation by intimidating the unwanted spirits – much as one seeks, in oratory, to convey a sense of *liget* toward opposites who are not yet acknowledged kin. Naming noxious plants as if they held them while reciting lines of magic, practitioners may claim to have such leaves as cause misfortune, and so 'deceive' the sources of disease with shows of *liget,* frighten them, and urge them to succumb. But the parallel with magic reaches even deeper. Oratory and magical spells alike achieve their goals not just by 'frightening' and 'finding out,' but rather through a negotiation of commitment – for, as Punlan once suggested, gifts offered to the spirits are similar to prestations that forge peace. In magic as in public life, dissension and disruption are dealt with through the giving of 'returns' *(ta'rat)* for troubling *liget;* and opposites who, accepting gifts, yet persevere in 'angry' violence will themselves suffer from 'vengeance' or 'contagion' *(bēret)* in a dyadic or 'reciprocal exchange' *(tubrat).* Thus, in magic, gifts to spirits, much like gifts offered at a *bēyaw,* are meant to soothe the 'anger' of the past, binding recipients to a suspension of bad feeling. And just as the participants in a *bēyaw* swear they will 'dissolve like salt water' if either violates the convenant, so spirits who are given gifts and yet continue to afflict their human victims are threatened in spells with words such as, 'Here I have the plant called "toothless"; may you be rendered toothless "in exchange" *(ta'rata).'*

Exchange, prestation, mutual offerings, and threats of mutual harm are, in fact, a good deal of the substance of a *purung* – a form of discourse that admits acknowledgment of difference and possibly unequal *liget,* so that adult men, ruled by *bēya,* can resolve their tensions through reciprocal displays of 'knowing' kindness and of equal mettle in their hearts. . Speakers in oratorical events say that they 'give' or 'hand' each other words; they may, like Kama in his *purung* with the Rumyads, pretend to 'share' *(bēret)* the 'knowledge' that they hold, or ask why soft and easy words have been reciprocated with 'thorns.' Each *purung* speech proclaims itself an 'answer' *(sibēr)* to the one that came before it, as speakers, echoing their opposites, acknowledge what they take to be the central elements of a fellow's thoughts. Thus, in response to his uncle's inquiry:

... if in fact there is some substance to that gossip, well, don't hide it from me ... and don't think I am pointing my words, don't think I am accusing you, even though I am the one who is beginning this, by asking if there is any truth, anything to believe in what I heard ...

Tayeg could proclaim:

... well, as I am the one you are looking for, and you want to hear what I have to say, I will say yes, I will be the one to talk to you; because we are father and son, I will not hide my thoughts ... Well, it is true, there is some little bit I said, something I said before. But even if I said it, I will not continue, because I know that we are father and son ...

Then the uncle, in his turn, declared, 'Thanks, then, I must give thanks, because you say, yes, you are my child . . .' Should an overly anxious speaker fail to so address his predecessor's proclamations, one of his fellows may take the floor with comments like: 'I will not go after your words right now, because I want to say I heard the words that came before.'

As the *purung* proceeds, speakers will 'give' more of their 'hidden' thoughts, articulating demands and hopes, yet trying to avoid a compromising revelation. An awkward turn of phrase may permit an opposite to say – as Tukbaw could to Bē'rak's far less talented promoters – 'You speak as though my sister were wild game, waiting for you hunters to arrive,' and so shame the careless speaker. And furthermore, if clumsy speeches are themselves seen to call forth 'anger,' and words or gestures meant to be convincing are instead construed as boasts or threats, the offender will confront demands for payment 'in return' for the distress he caused. Thus, for example, at a bridewealth transaction in Pugu we heard complaints to the effect that the groom's party was not only very large, but that some of them had brought 'even Americans' to 'beautify' their presence, and had furthermore flown with us from Kakidugen to a mission airstrip near the bride's family's home. So accused of showing off, the speakers for the groom then managed to answer the attack by setting forth a set of tokens of our voyage: brass wire, with which, they said, they 'telephoned' the airplane; red cloth with which they flagged it down. And finally, in playful flourish, they claimed the bride's family, now overwhelmed with goods, to be the real 'Americans' whereas they themselves were poor and groveling 'Japanese' – who should be given gifts 'in return' for their excessive loss!

In peace meetings, a history of enmity and deep distrust makes the 'exchange' of 'anger' and 'soft' words potentially more problematic, and negotiations may be colored by such apparently incidental facts as the number of persons gathered to support a 'side.' Thus, before the Rumyad-Butag *bēyaw* that we saw, Butag fear of Rumyad strength led to the loan of a bachelor hostage whom the Butag men had thought to hold at knifepoint, 'by the tail,' as they walked on the trail toward Ringen – and if they had so used the boy, they would have had to pay for threatening his life. Instead, the Butags chose to show their firm goodwill and fearless daring, to treat the youth as a companion, and then, 'in anger,' find the Rumyads at fault for what appeared to be excessive 'bodies' on their side. But once Rumyad had paid recompense for 'tasted' goods and killings, and the Butags, fully satisfied, had entered and set down their weapons in the ready Ringen homes, it was time for a return prestation. The Butag men were 'criticized' and forced to pay for holding loaded weapons – an unnecessary show of 'anger' in the presence of unarmed and friendly hosts. Something of the reverse occurred when, at the celebration of Burur's beheading, the hosting Kadēng, in a boastful dance, happened to call to mind a death that the visiting Da'sa caused his distant kinsman. Da'sa gave an arrow in recompense for the killing, but then saw Kadēng reciprocate with a prestation for inciting undue hostility at the celebration and, without real cause, defaming a man he had invited as his guest.

Such violations, occasioning *ta'rat,* a 'return,' 'repayment,' or 'exchange,' tend to appear casual and accidental, yet they in fact emerged in every *purung* that we heard. Unable to negotiate acknowledged differences in the 'knowing' terms appropriate to kinsmen, orators are bound in a dilemma. Demonstrating *liget* and conviction in their speech, they inevitably occasion *liget* in the men whose sympathy they seek – and such 'anger' requires a 'return.' Although speakers hedge – 'Don't think I am accusing you.' 'Don't think I put sharp prongs onto my tongue' – affronting words are rarely masked by protest. Proclaiming honorable means and goals, men nonetheless give voice to challenge and accusation. And such affronts – which have in the past been known to lead to physical assault – will themselves provide a basis for the exchanges in which differences are ultimately resolved.

Through a balancing of 'angry' claims, individual offenses and returns become aspects of a *tubrat,* a balanced, dyadic, or 'reciprocal exchange,' in which members of both sides succeed in 'finding' one anothers' hearts and so construe themselves as 'equal men,' abjuring conflict. *Purung* requires that adults align themselves on opposed sides, disguise their 'different' hearts, and display *liget* in order that complaints can be revealed, 'set down,' acknowledged, and redressed. In the course of an encounter, both parties will alternately display their strength and both may receive payment. Exchange provides the format through which imbalances are rectified, and 'angry' men, in recognizing the 'anger' in their fellows, allow that all are 'equal humans' who have no further cause for strife. A form of discourse dominated by the dual form of the verb (*Maki'upu kita,* 'We speak, one to the other, I to you'), *purung* moves from antagonism to a more fluid style of interaction. The ultimate suspension of opposing claims is symbolized by youths who hand-feed one another rice; collective participation in a concluding feast; and, if portions are sufficient, by gifts of food that individuals offer one another to indicate their mutual concern. As fellows and recipients of 'equal shares' *(bēet),* they will conclude with speech in the collective form (*Pemen'upu kisi,* 'We speak together'), suggestive of the diffuse reciprocity that should obtain in civil dealings among relatives and friends.

Reciprocal exchange within a *purung,* is, then, a device by which opposing parties move from a state of mutual ill will in which each may be contaminating and dangerous to the other to a sense of collectivity and shared concern. 'Knowing' kinlike interactions are forged through dyadically organized displays of *liget*. And *ta'rat*, or 'returns,' for 'anger' born of prior wrongs or present bluster – the sins of killers, the daring of prospective grooms, or the defensive pose of men who would at once contest and yet defend themselves against another's challenge – will themselves incline toward balanced exchange, or *tubrat*, over time. Whether in the form of an 'exchange' prestation within a *purung*, or through subsequent 'returns' of women, *bēyaw*, boasts, or even deaths, *tubrat* show that members of both sides have equal *liget* and so can 'knowingly' forge bonds as equal men.

The skillful indirection of oratorical discourse – of speech that strives at once for delicacy and respect and for the strength implied by dazzle and deception, a style of talk that seeks to call forth secrets and yet makes strategic use of hidden motives of its own – itself reflects as it facilitates such transactions. Achieving what is at best a delicate balance (and forever vulnerable to the man or woman who feels 'twisted' by a thought still unaddressed), orators enact a sort of mediation between the separate hearts of 'angry' and potentially unequal men and the far less passionate 'knowing' claims of those who share a 'body' and, as equals, can cooperate in day-to-day affairs. Their speech – like daily living – affirms the fact that Ilongots can live in civil peace only if they see themselves as 'sharing' needs as kin and equals. Yet oratory makes clear, as daily life does not, that equality itself is an achievement, always tenuous and dependent on a sense of focused purpose, of potentially destructive *liget*, which both enlivens and protects the human heart.

Exchanging liget and creating social ties

Ta'rat and *tubrat*, words that characterize exchanges in oratorical transactions, are related in their application to the word *beet* or *bēret*, 'share, revenge, contaminate,' which we have already seen as central to Ilongot interpretations of their social life. Thus, a plant that makes a spirit sick as an 'exchange' *(ta'rat)* is said to *bēret*, or 'transfer contamination'; enemies are *kabēret*, 'fellow contaminants,' and enemy 'peoples' *(bērtan)* who 'share' *(bēret)* a meal without a prior 'rubbing' and associated 'exchanges' *(ta'rat)* are apt to *bēret*, or 'contaminate' one another, making one another ill. To kill an enemy, 'to take revenge,' may be described as *bēet* as well as *tubrat;* to ask for a wife 'in exchange' *(tubrat)* for a woman given may be to ask to *kibēet*, 'have a share'; and much as *tubrat* establishes equality in *liget*, permitting friendly interaction to proceed, so *bēret*, or 'sharing,' is predicated on the assumption that such equality in fact obtains. Finally, *bērtan*, 'kind' or 'people,' a word referring to 'classes' of objects but in particular to locally based and historically associated groups of kin (see R. Rosaldo 1975), is probably related as well to the verbs denoting contamination, sharing, and exchange. Evidence for this point includes the fact that men, in explaining how many shares of game are typically distributed in a settlement, may speak of, for example, 'five *bēet*' or 'five *binartan*.' (*Binartan* comes from *bērtan*, the infix and vowel change giving the perfective sense, 'divided into kinds.') In addition, the disease caused by eating with an enemy is called *bērtan* in some dialects, *bēet* in others. Thus, the notion of discrete classes appears to be linked linguistically to ideas of exchange and conflict, as if to say that when people are of recognized separate 'kinds,' or *bērtan,* they must either be equal sharers, or enemies, *kabēret,* bent on exchanging harm.

These parallels are of interest because oratory, as the enactment of a delicate and tenuous exchange, reflects in form important aspects of the social and historical processes it is organized to address. In *purung,* Ilongots give their social lives an interpretation that is compatible not only with the particular grievances under discussion, but also with certain general ideas concerning 'knowledge,' kinship, and the 'anger' caused by recognition of imbalance and necessary to the creation of a new, cooperative equality among those who were, in 'anger,' once opposed. More particularly, people who recognize themselves as related members of one 'kind' or *bērtan* will be inclined to abjure *liget;* and those who wish or need to be cooperatively bound to fellows may, though unequal in their histories of death and insult, find that rather than redress their grievances in *purung,* they must 'resign' themselves to past inequities and slights. By contrast, an acknowledgment of *liget* requires that parties are prepared to recognize their differences and imbalances. And the resolution of their tensions – the 'discovery' of kinship and successful negotiation of a marriage or a peace – demands exchanges through which acknowledged opposites establish themselves as peers and 'equal men.' Thus, the 'sides' of *purung* are likely to consist of men who view themselves as members of opposing 'kinds,' or *bērtan* – true 'enemies' *(kabēret),* whose physical force and strength in numbers will permit them to answer 'angry' words and deeds with shows of 'anger,' and ultimately, to demand or host reciprocal *purung* 'in exchange.' This is particularly clear in Ilongot memories of past *bēyaw,* in which opposing groups are said to have begun negotiations in a flourish of reciprocal boasts and insults and a burst of dueling that lasted until shields were beaten into splintered wood.

In actual fact, however, confrontations like these are rare. Enmity is often undermined by 'knowledge' of enduring kinship; and materials on intra-Ilongot killings, at least since the turn of this century, are often difficult to sort out into discrete cases of dyadic conflict, as the identities of both killers and victims as members of discrete 'peoples,' or *bértan,* tend to vary with the point of view of those reporting the event. Men of several groups are apt to join in raids, just as individuals may have a variety of reasons for claiming kinship ties with victims. And the fact that some men have found cause to 'cut' the lives of vulnerable kin, whereas others are joined by marriage to the murderers of their 'bodies,' often means that killers are in active daily contact with individuals whose 'blood' they have shed. Redress within a group whose members are considered kinsmen may take the casual form of 'rubbings' and the exchange of minor gifts (such as those Lakay offered in Ringen) in accord with the expectation that denounces oratory among kin. And, even more telling, in cases in which members of a single 'people' or local kinship group truly massacre some other group, and deaths exceeding two or three are not 'answered' with revenge, it often turns out – as Ilongots say – that enemies 'simply marry one another,' and so forswear their differences because of kinship bonds. What happens is that weakened groups that lack the 'anger' or opportunity to enforce their claims may find themselves in the position of relations who, as kin, 'forget' their grudges – assuaging loss through an informal 'gift' of heads or women, or, more simply, through a sense of resignation in the face of what may, in fact, be necessary supportive ties.

Thus, to take just one example, the Peknar people often see themselves as member of the Rumyad *bértan* – their members 'hook together,' their genealogies are intertwined. But, in 1921, a group of Peknar men and women, having killed a lowlander and suffered ravages from soldiers in revenge, fled to Rumyad kin in Buybuyan in hopes of finding food; they came, Ilongots say, 'to share in life' (*kibiay,* from *biay,* 'life'). Welcoming them, as if they were, in fact, relations, the Rumyads yet found reason to complain about their visitors; some say that Peknar men deceived them by promising to present a bracelet they did not intend to give. A slaughter followed: Men from Rumyad, aided by relatives of the Yamu *bértan,* beheaded ten of their guests in the house where they were staying; and the Peknars, thus weakened, had no chance of revenge. Shortly afterward, however, Lakay, who was bound to both groups as a kinsman, went on a headhunting raid with Rumyad elders, and took a head under their guidance – most probably an informal 'return' for Peknar 'anger.' Then, in the 1950s, members of both groups came to live together in the Keradingan region; Radu, nephew to a victim, married the daughter of one of the beheaders; and in time, civil relations were resumed. Still, while a neighbor of the

Rumyads in Keradingan, Baket, Tukbaw's mother and a cousin of the guests who lost their heads, refused to let her daughter wed a Rumyad suitor. Subsequently, the Rumyads themselves moved southward, and more recently, Peknar people moved even further away from Rumyad kin toward Pengegyabēn and Kakidugen. Relations have continued to be peaceful, although people say that in the old days 'Ingu, son of Radu, would have heard the 'story' from his father and planned a raid in vengeance against Rumyad. And public memory of prior tensions was enlivened by the fact that, of all men in Kakidugen, Radu alone refused to join the Rumyads as kinsman in the 1969 Butag peace. Clearly, the past has hardly been forgotten. But at the same time, a sense of interlocking kinship has made it virtually impossible to acknowledge difference in order to forge a public peace.

In short: Kinsmen are unlikely to negotiate their differences in *purung* and one-sided slaughters have been frequent among peoples who were able to construe themselves as kin. It follows that opposites in a *bēyaw* are not likely to be counted as relations. When diverse groups in an 'exchange' *(tubrat)* of killings manage to take 'vengeance' *(bēret)* and so show their equal strength, they are apt to see themselves as unrelated 'peoples' *(bērtan)* in long-standing opposition, as adversaries who can only mediate their conflicts through an oratorical encounter and discover grounds for subsequent relations through a balancing of peaceful gestures over time. Thus, our data for feuds since 1900 shows a preponderance of cases of one-sided killing among people who at one time pretended to active kinship; three cases of reciprocal raids that were not resolved in formal *purung* but ended in an 'exchange' *(tubrat)* of women; and some ten feuds resolved in *bēyaws,* of which seven and possibly eight involved deaths attributed to both of the presumed unrelated 'peoples' and convenants offered up by each in turn. Formal convenant appears, in short, to require an equality of difference, strength, and 'anger.' *Bēyaws,* based on *tubrat,* require *bēyaws* in return.

So it was that, in 1970, the Butags offered Rumyad a 'return' *bēyaw* in recompense not for victims killed but for men whose prison deaths were blamed on Butags who had accused the Rumyads of a series of lowland killings and then led pursuing soldiers to their homes. And, much earlier in the century, the dynamics of reciprocal challenge and response governed the development of a much-recounted feud between the Rumyad and Dekran peoples, which ran its course through: (1) reciprocal beheadings; (2) tentative encounters, and finally, in the company of mediators from another *bērtan,* a *bēyaw* that was initiated with a dueling match in which, 'if it were not for the mediators,' people say, 'we would have bashed ourselves to death'; this was followed by (3) plans, never realized, for Dekran marriage to a Rumyad woman; and then, (4) in lieu of marriages or other active ties (and perhaps because of Dekran disappointment), a resumption of reciprocal hostilities. In subsequent years, and probably because of the earlier establishment of relation through an exchange of *bēyaw,* there were no further major *purung,* but men again established friendship, as symbolized by their joint participation in a headhunting raid against another group. Most recently, there was the unsuccessful bid to marry Binsing, a Rumyad woman, by an aspiring Dekran youth (see pp. 166, 203). The balancing of claims and revelations within particular oratorical encounters had its parallel, then, in reciprocal killings and gestures of peace between opposing *bērtan,* which led ultimately to a collective show of *liget* in a joint beheading, and the hope, as yet unrealized, for an exchange of wives. Significantly, it was the second Dekran killing of a Rumyad man that made the brother of the Rumyad maiden reluctant to accept a Dekran suitor; 'holding on' to unrequited *liget,* he indicated his resistance to relation, providing further cause for future infractions of what may always be a tenuous peace.

Not surprisingly, a similar pattern holds for marriage. Though marriages need not be formally arranged, and payments 'in return' for women may consist of little more than the game that a new husband shares in his wife's home, Ilongots recognize in marriage a natural cause for *liget* and so for oratorical transaction. Initiated through gifts of betel chews and beads, short periods of labor in the desired woman's home, and then a possible exploratory *purung* (which can in turn be met with exit, challenge, or even threats on lives), a marriage may, like a killing, be viewed as an affront and source of 'anger,' requiring payment 'in return' for affinal *liget,* and at times, a *tubrat* marriage 'in exchange' (see Chapter 5).

Close kinfolk are, of course, unlikely to give voice to 'angry' thoughts among themselves, and so require elaborate oratory for betrothals only at those times when their relationships are problematic, admitting the possibility of a breach. But when once-distant groups are joined in marriage, speakers will acknowledge prior difference, and in negotiating ties among their 'children' assert their shared commitment to a growing peace. Although covenants by themselves do not necessitate further dealings, marriages over time provide the grounds for future visits and cooperation; as such, they constitute a sort of transition from a state of difference and balanced opposition to one of mutuality and acknowledged bonds. This was, for example, the intended outcome of the unrealized Dekran–Rumyad marriage. Had Dekran been successful, the bachelor brother of the Rumyad maiden would probably have sought a Dekran wife.

Again, marriages were a crucial aspect of relations between the Tamsi and Pugu peoples, whose grievances were resolved through reciprocal peace pacts in the 1920s. At the second of these, Pugu men stole a Tamsi woman, saying, 'We will not kill her, but take her as a wife.' Though this marriage was not immediately reciprocated, a child of the union took the lead in inviting Tamsi relations – when the latter were harassed by soldiers in the late 1950s – to the safety of an upstream Pugu settlement. Their coresidence then paved the way for two subsequent *tubrat,* or exchange marriages, leading to the present sense that Tamsi and Pugu are allied.

Reciprocity in marriage makes sense for the practical reason that in-married men are like hostages in a potentially hostile and unfamiliar setting. But marital *tubrat* are not limited to the eve of formal peace. At any time when previously distant groups find themselves living close together, and, in the course of daily contact, 'discovering' forgotten ties, marital exchanges may secure their sense of kinship. It was through such exchange that Rumyad and Tamsi, finding themselves in close proximity for the first time in living memory, managed in the early 1960s to create a present sense of connection, giving substance to a memory of common origins as members of a single *bērtan* in the past. When Tamsi, fearing soldiers, moved upstream to live with Pugu kin, members of the latter group who considered themselves related to the Rumyads served as 'mediators' in arranging a reciprocal set of meetings between the estranged 'peoples' – with meals and formal *purung* offered first in Tamsi, then in Rumyad homes. The Rumyads then found cause to move within a few hours of the Tamsi settlement; and when Pawig from Rumyad began to court a Tamsi woman, Kangat of Tamsi found himself thinking that 'if they can sleep with our sisters, we should sleep with theirs in return.' But tensions lingered. Pawig took a second wife and his fickleness so angered Tamsi men that they were known to hope to kill him, and Pawig himself once went so far as to wait in ambush for the Tamsi in-laws he had chosen to reject. Happily, a subsequent set of *purung* and marital exchanges reinforced the tenuous friendship, and Pawig eventually returned to live with his abandoned Tamsi wife. In the end – as so often happens when men, by proving equal *liget,* begin to reckon themselves kin – Tamsi and Rumyad went together on a headhunting raid in which youths from both groups 'reached' their adult goal of taking heads.

Thus, although the Ilongot view of marriage as a cause of *liget* gives sense to the exchange of unions, marital ties themselves may help secure social relations and a sense of deep connection in which reciprocal 'anger' will ultimately have no place. In the case of groups as distant as Rumyad and Tamsi, marriage necessitates a *purung,* and the *liget* there acknowledged calls attention to the reciprocity of accomplished unions, the quality of balance in exchange. But not all marriages are with distant groups, and in cases in which the shifts that follow unions bring to light less easily acknowledged tensions in day-to-day affairs, associated *purung* and prestations may have more to do with an articulation of differences than with the creation of new bonds. So, in Rumyad, people say one asks for *langu,* a major bridewealth prestation, in 'return' *(ta'rat)* for a woman who is to move to her husband's home upon marriage. Such moves, violating a universal norm of uxorilocal postmarital residence, are seen as major disruptions, and although data on this point are weak, it seems likely that they have occurred at times when relations with local groups were otherwise in flux.

Certainly, the one recent Kakidugen case in which *purung* and major gifts accompanied a marriage was very much concerned with questions of the family's residential affiliations – and a conflict in preference between an aging father and his son. 'Utup's refusal to let his daughter marry a man of a *bërtan* with which he hoped to attenuate prior ties so angered the son, 'Adēlpig, that when his sister showed interest in Kakidugen's future captain, 'Adēlpig threatencd to take the lovers' lives. In order to protect his daughter, 'Utup moved his family to Kakidugen – considcrably closer to the second suitor's actual home – leaving his son to find the sister pregnant some months later. In the end, 'Adēlpig won considerable payment[14] from the captain as a 'return' for his once-flouted *liget,* and eventually movcd to Kakidugen, where we found him in 1974. Though coresidence had begun to forge a sense of kinship, relations between the brothers-in-law continued to be awkward – especially as their hopes for a more balanced resolution foundered when an exchange union between a second cousin of 'Adēlpig (his wife's brother) and the captain's 'sister' ended in the latter's accidental death.

Finally, however, the vast majority of marriages are with acknowledged kinsmen, and much as we have seen before, coresident kin are not inclined to voice their *liget,* or cast their interactions in the idioms of formal *purung.* When close kinfolk intermarry they are reluctant to view their unions as a true 'exchange' of wives. For example, when Rumyad peoples who had previously affiliated with distinct groups lived together in the Keradingan region, there was a series of intermarriages. A set of these led to the present solidarity between many of the adults in the settlements of Kakidugen and Pengegyabēn who were to host our stay. In the late 1950s, after the relevant senior kin had together built their homes and led their sons in killing, Lakay's son, Tepeg (affiliated with Kakidugen), married Midalya, his second cousin and Tukbaw's sister, and Tukbaw (affiliated with Pengegyabēn) married Wagat, Lakay's daughter. Shortly before, 'Insan, another son of Lakay, had married a daughter of Tukbaw's half brother, Kadēng, and then Maniling, son of Kadēng, made known his choice of 'Insan's cousin as his wife. A

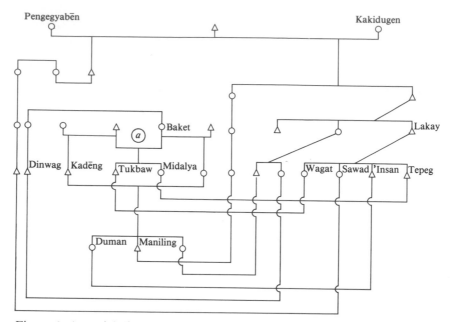

Figure 6. A partial diagram of Kakidugen–Pengegyabēn marriages, 1955–8
Note: *a*–The marriage of Baket to the father of Tukbaw and Midalya followed the deaths of her former husband and of her new husband's first wife.

genealogical diagram (see Figure 6) readily reveals these and a number of associated marriages to have the form of a reciprocal exchange or *tubrat;* yet today in Kakidugen, there is a reluctance to speak of these marriages in such terms. Adults insist that in their youths they simply 'followed' their own 'hearts' – and that what came together in their unions was not two 'sides' but a collection of individuals who shared an interest in each other and who joined in marriage out of a spirit of cooperation and a reluctance to lose healthy young bachelors to unrelated groups. In a manner parallel to that suggested for both feuds and killings, these marriages were not viewed as 'exchanges' because of an association of exchange with difference, *liget,* and the difficult words of oratory – all incompatible with the firm, enduring, and presumably unquestioned bonds of coresident kin.

Thus, although the diversity of actual marriages – as these are determined by regional differences, individual affinities, attempts by elders to forge a kinlike solidarity, and the culturally shaped inclination to *liget* and exchange – makes it difficult to characterize Ilongot unions in terms of any single pattern, the way that Ilongots interpret and discuss their marriages fits a very general cultural mold. Ilongots in different regions vary in their customary proceedings: Downstream people require *purung* and prestation for all unions, whereas Rumyads and most of the upstream and western *bērtan* have been inclined to minimize formal negotiations in the past. But for all, to marry is, potentially, to 'insult' *(bēngen)*, to affront, and so to 'anger' future affines, and such *liget* – especially when opposing, discrete groups are implicated in the union – is apt to find resolution in *purung* and reciprocal exchange. Close kin, inclined to underplay their different origins and goals, appear unlikely to see their marriages in this way, but even kin can find in marriage an opportunity to dramatize those conflicts that daily life makes difficult to address. In oratory, they can make clear the distance between affines; decide which ties they would regard as the unquestioned ones of kinship; and, challenging those men they choose to cast as their opponents, negotiate new relations through exchange.

In short, when and insofar as Ilongots see in marriages – or killings an appropriate cause for *liget,* their inclination to require gifts and then arrange for *tubrat* follows a logic that parallels that of oratory itself. Cooperating kin who 'share a body' do not display the differences in their 'hearts,' nor do they look for vengeance, require *tubrat,* or readily engage in oratorical discourse. But when the multiple and overlapping claims of differently related men come to be seen within the frame of a dyadic opposition, one can acknowledge cause for difference, and then attempt, through oratory, to demonstrate the equality in strength and knowledge that is presupposed by 'sharing' among kin. The words exchanged in oratory are at different points the 'knowing' analogues of conciliatory gifts and the sounds of a potentially disruptive 'anger' – just as speakers have, in any following, both 'knowing' adults and far more 'passionate' and energetic youths. Resolving past imbalances, they associate the 'angry' deeds that once tore them apart with youthful 'quickness'; and by asserting *liget* in their speech and presence, they show themselves to be true 'equals' who can exchange and mediate their differences in the 'knowledgeable' idioms appropriate to adults. Unconcerned with punishment, truth, or justice, successful orators manage not to right a wrong but to transform the 'anger' in their fellows' hearts into a 'knowledge' of connection – creating through opposition a sense that opposites are ultimately the 'same,' bound up in the undifferentiated nets of 'equal men.'

> It seems significant in this regard that changes in Ilongot views of themselves and their society have had an immediate consequence for the form and conduct of *purung*. Increasingly, contemporary Ilongots appear to shun the 'anger' and 'deception' of traditional oratorical discourse, and at certain times break down the dyadic form of oratory by permitting captains to rule on relevance and call out speakers' names (see M. Rosaldo 1973). But even more telling, modern mission

Ilongots do not believe that one should 'pay' for 'anger' – as such transactions tend to induce *liget* 'in return.' In the *purung* for Tubeng, the unsuccessful suitor discussed previously, people contrasted his behavior with that of Gading, his father's competitor for a woman. When Gading lost his bride to Tubeng's father, he could find relief for his 'anger' only by shedding blood – the father having pointed him in the direction of a vulnerable group of settlers. Tubeng, by contrast, was said to show his 'new' and Christian 'knowledge' by asking a return not for his 'anger' but for goods bestowed in courtship, and further, by making his demands clear and 'direct' through an insistence that he be given not used and soiled objects, but their precise equivalents in cash.

Conclusion: Liget and the knowledge of adult men

What we have said thus far suggests that Ilongots recognize a complementary relation between, on the one hand, the dyadic form of oratory, characterized by opposition and reciprocal exchange, and, on the other, the overlapping ties of family, residence, and cooperation that shape the everyday reciprocity of presumedly equal kin. Whereas the latter tend to inhibit public shows of difference, the former provides a context in which a multiplicity of conflicts may be acknowledged and redressed. Further, although cooperative local ties appear to be secured by the still-active presence of an aging senior figure – man or woman – it is for men of middle years to dominate in oratory, and the conflicts that they speak of concern, overwhelmingly, the activities of youths. What remains to be explored is the cultural rationale that shapes the subject matter of *purung*. Why do mature men have a dominant role in oratory, and why, when men acknowledge conflict, are their subjects marrying and killing, issues that primarily concern the 'anger' of the young? Answers to these questions will lean heavily on a good deal of the discussion that has preceded – showing, in particular, the intimate connections between Ilongot views of social life and their conceptions of the self.

As we have already seen, Ilongots recognize two crucial forms of differentiation in their daily social world: the first between men and women, and a second between old and young. Men, because of their experience, have 'higher hearts' than women, exceeding them in both *bēya* and *liget,* knowledge and force. But among men themselves the situation is more complex. Whereas youngsters are lacking in both knowledge and focused 'anger,' it is the unmarried youth, the bachelor, who is free to move and contemplate beheadings, who typifies the heights of *liget;* and though the very old lack 'energy,' and so are not respected for the things they 'know,' *bēya* is associated with the verbal skill and social wisdom of married adults.

In the informal contexts of daily living, these differences are reflected in the fact that men will give commands, or *tuydek,* expecting services from women – just as all adults are free in extending *tuydek* to the young. Political viability for a man depends in part on the rice he can expect his wife to feed to visitors in their household; and the cooperative ties among adult kin require them to share the labor of unmarried children and – themselves supported by such labor – to have the time and food to help in neighboring homes. Thus, it is hardly surprising that orators select, as contexts for debate, events in which the differences between women, bachelor youths, and married men are of the essence. They acknowledge grounds for conflict by associating them with the unruly 'passions' of their 'children,' with *liget* that they alone can claim the knowledge to control. Adult male orators are unique because, as married men whose children are still laborers in their households, they can enjoy the fruits of 'energy' in youths and women, while at the same time they – unlike their aging senior kin – can still assert a *liget* of their own. Arranging marriages, they allocate the labor and reproductive force – the *liget* – of their offspring; negotiating peace, they show themselves to have the 'knowledge' of kin ties and past exchanges that can diffuse or focus *liget* in the interest of collective life and common goals.

Yet it would be misleading to suggest that the dominance of adult men in oratory rests immediately on their "command" of labor – especially as, in daily life, egalitarian norms associated with the notion that all kinfolk share a common 'body' tend to minimize such claims as have their bases in admitted differences in people's 'hearts.' *Tuydek,* as we saw in Chapter 4, will often go unanswered. 'Angry' women can escape their husband's hands by fleeing to a kinsman or a granary; and youngsters can, through petulance, refuse a parent's request to stay at home because of rain or quit their play to help with cooking – because children, like their parents, cannot be moved when an intransigent *liget* rules their thoughts. Commands require that people will *teber,* 'accede,' 'proffer agreement'; and the sorts of agreements that facilitate everyday cooperation are dependent on an appreciation of the independent wills of 'equal humans,' all of whom are equally involved in labor, and none of whom enjoy privileged material rewards.

Rather than being based upon the social and economic relations that govern day-to-day affairs, oratory is an occasion for their reformulation; and in organizing diverse daily ties into the 'sides' that can engage in true exchanges, it casts a sensible but slanted light on the mundane relationships by which participants are bound. The fact that oratory concerns itself with marrying and killing is, in general, consistent with a focus in Ilongot culture on the youthful years and youthful glamour – a focus we have seen to be reflected in everything from songs, which speak primarily of romantic goals and killing, to the names that parents give their children, the majority of which describe male violence, sexual attraction, or oratorical art.

But in even more concrete terms, the orators' interests are consistent with certain of the actual sources of disruption and concern in Ilongot daily living. Because it is for youths to kill, young men (like Burur, whom we met in Chapter 2) incline to trouble. Intent on killing, youths will 'hold' the stories of the past and think to 'answer' wrongs and slights that their more 'knowing' adult kin have chosen to 'abide.' Often, it is a youth who will avenge a threatening gesture suffered by his senior kin; and our data include numerous stories of young men like Lefty, whose son 'exchanged' assaults by his mother's kin on his father's 'people' when he reached his bachelor years. Again, in marrying, the young at once promote new bonds and give shape to conflict. Often prodded to pursue a bride by taunts or more explicit statements from their elders, the young, in choosing to resist, accept, or shape envisioned marital ties not only experience themselves in conflict with their peers, but manage through their actions to give a public form to local differences and tensions, revealing hitherto hidden preferences of adults.

In short, young men who "cause" disruption when they marry, move, or kill, may in their deeds reflect unstated conflicts of their seniors; but the fact is that their actions *do* involve the forging of new obligations and new forms of alignment, and, as such, at once exhibit and give rise to 'angry' gestures and real strife. Youthful concerns are not the only sources of disruption in Ilongot social experience, but their cultural centrality has a real basis in social practice. The association of young men with what is both an admired and a fearful *liget* has a good deal to do with the real consequences of the activities in which such youths, inevitably, are involved.

By elaborating these in oratory, Ilongots not only succeed in giving cultural form to conflict, but at the same time they provide a sort of model for their dealings with their fellows, a fully "socialized" image of their world. My account throughout this text has contrasted 'angry' youths 'in search' of heads and wives with their more 'knowing' seniors; and I have spoken of their relationship as an enduring feature of social life within a local group. In daily life cooperating married men maintain a stance of 'knowing' parity with one another by recognizing all as proven peers in 'anger,' who rule – as they depend upon – the 'angry' energy of youths.

But oratorical encounters were seen as incompatible with the cooperative stance that unites all adult men within an everyday arena. Highlighting differences among mature men, youths, and women, oratory deals in opposition, confronting adult men with adult fellow, and contrasting kin and nonkin, "us" and "them." The formal idioms in which adults address and reconcile differences among themselves have no place in local dealings in which cooperation is organized by an assumption of equality, common interest, and undifferentiated 'hearts.' Thus, the men who would 'exchange' a present 'anger' for a future sense of kinlike bonds are faced with a dilemma. In order to establish grounds on which all recognize themselves as 'equal men,' they must behave as kinsmen never should, and entertain the possibility of imbalance and the threat that differences will grow. And they do this, as we have seen, by associating present tensions with the *liget* of men's youthful years – an 'anger' that is realized in a local company of young men as it was proven in the prior deeds of 'knowing' speakers, who by their ornaments and words assert a *liget* now established in their hearts.

So insisting on their 'anger' as ever-present grounds for strain, orators can acknowledge equal *liget* in their fellows. Then, as 'equals,' they are able – through exchange – to abolish cause for difference and assume the 'knowing' stance of those who reckon themselves kin. Just as, in growing up, a youth will hope to prove his 'angry' force in order to become the peer of 'knowing' seniors, so oratory provides a context in which potentially unequal male adults can demonstrate themselves as peers in 'anger' in order to accept exchange for prior delicts, to abolish tensions, and to adopt the attitudes of cooperation and concern appropriate to related men.

Thus oratory is, for Ilongots, first of all a political event, concerned with unrelated 'other men,' and directed outward. But an understanding of the form of Ilongot political discourse requires that we look as well to the relationships within a 'side.' Because of the ways that marrying and killing are significant for dealings within a local group and for the relationships of young men and seniors, they provide a grounds for politics. And again, because Ilongots consider both marrying and taking heads a proof of *liget*, it is hardly surprising that their oratory reflects in form – as it discusses, airs, and helps resolve – the strains associated with men's images of themselves as 'angry' and unequal youths who grow into more 'knowledgeable' seniors, images which, in turn, concern the nature of authority and cooperation within a local group.

In discussing headhunting (Chapter 5), we saw that a good deal of what Ilongots see as beautiful and exciting in the act of killing has to do with the dynamics of social reproduction; because adults, constrained by physical weakness, 'knowing' bonds, and nets of obligation, cannot themselves be lovely, filled with 'focused' energy, and inclined to violence, they look for their vitality to the *liget* of the young. Headhunting is the moment in which youth's *liget* finds fulfillment; invigorating to the social body, it is a token of the ways in which civil society depends for its liveliness and renewal upon the initiative of youth.

Oratory, I would claim, makes a complementary sort of statement in that it gives a 'knowing' shape to youthful *liget,* and says something about the kinds of bonds through which a healthy collectivity is composed. To have *liget,* we have seen, is to have health, force, energy, strength in numbers – yet the dynamics of emulation, by which youths prove themselves the potent 'equals' of their fellows, can be a source of strain. Orators make this clear, and by casting *liget* as a feature not of daily social life but of uneasy points of opposition, they indicate the care and conscious dealing – in short, the adult wisdom – necessary to give energy and emotional life a constructive social form. In *purung,* people see that 'exchange' as well as 'anger' is necessary if youths are to find the allies who will help them kill and celebrate their triumphs; that *bēya* as well as *liget,* measured age as well as youthful passion, may be required if children are to marry and reproduce.

Stated otherwise, oratory, in acknowledging the separateness of people's hearts – the fact that 'knowing' bonds are forged through proofs of *liget,* and that youthful 'anger' supports as it yet threatens to divide the 'knowing' kinship of adults – makes clear their necessary interdependence. A daily world in which autonomous and equal adults engage in cooperative interaction is shown, through oratory, to be as fragile as it often is – while at the same time, the very brittleness of social bonds that claim a natural source in ties of blood is made less fearful, because intelligible, in terms of the inevitable 'angry' claims of children, and the 'knowledgeable' exchanges of adults.

7. Conclusion: Self and social life

Interpretive ethnography is, to use Riceour's phrase, a matter of attributing "a meaning to a meaning" (1970:13). It is a descriptive enterprise, which promises neither to uncover "how it feels" to get inside a native's skin nor to facilitate causal generalization,[1] but rather through its organization to promote at once a taste for detail and a sense of pattern and to articulate something about the ways that cultures work by showing how they "mean." By asking what could be called "strategic questions," the anthropologist hopes to convey something of how – in general terms – distinctive cultural preoccupations inform as they are structured by the social lives of actors, and so enhance our ways of thinking about societies whose modes of discourse and relation are both similar to and different from, the complex particularities she describes. In this sense, all interpretation is, of necessity, comparative. We understand another's speech with reference to our construal of its context; and the ethnographer's constant challenge is to order – and so make sense of – foreign discourse in a way that manages to preserve the "otherness" and complexity of unfamiliar "worlds" or contexts, while rendering familiar a hitherto inaccessible form of talk.

Of course, any description that attempts to synthesize, or make sense, makes claims about the nature of connection – and mine has argued that a discourse that concerns the experiences of "the self" is patterned less by universal psychic traits than by such local "forms of life" as make for relationship and opposition in societies. Attempting throughout this text to capture the distinctive tones and patterns of Ilongot life, I have insisted that Ilongot practices and ideas that seem similar to those we know from elsewhere in the world should be interpreted first with reference to their social use and situation. This suggests that the comparative value of my account lies less in the identification of familiar traits or terms than in the ways I organized Ilongot themes to highlight crucial aspects of social process. Thus, I have not commented on the ways that *liget* in Ilongot life recalls the "gall of anger that swarms like smoke inside of a man's heart and becomes a

221

thing sweeter to him by far than the dripping of honey'' (*Iliad,* Book 18) – for fear that, noting similarities between expressions used by Ilongots and Ancient Greeks, the reader would be readily misled to assume that Ilongots, like Achilles, associate 'anger' with the "shame" that comes of slights to "honor." Aware of commonalities, one might then fail to note that whereas unrequited 'anger' urges Ilongots to kill, it operates in *The Iliad* in favor of Achilles's withdrawal from Achaean friends at war with Troy.

Similarly, I have avoided such reflections as were occasioned on the day that I returned from a long hike to learn that children, playing a tape of modern music in our house, had discovered a lovely female voice that sang – my friends reported as if they understood the words – in passionate tones, of death and love. We played the tape and found mixed in with songs by an 'old man' who turned out to be Bob Dylan, a single cut by Joan Baez, singing – in a tremolo that for Ilongots recalled the quivering tension of such songs as stir men's hearts to kill – about a soldier off to war. As history could not explain the aptness of my friends' reaction to the tape, the coincidence between Ilongot sensibilities and my own led me to think of tremolo as a "natural symbol," bound universally to love and loss. But although a sound may well evoke for many people certain themes, observations of this kind, again, seem to fall short. Baez's song protested against war and invoked mourning, whereas for Ilongots her quivering voice was like a fluttering bangle or a twisting heart. Its beauty lay precisely in its power to stir their hearts with angry thoughts – just as mourning, for Ilongots, points not to passivity and calm but to wild violence.

If I had attended simply to the song as stimulus and to its disturbed response, I would have failed, in short, to appreciate the fact that Ilongot aesthetics – intelligible as they had become – were yet quite different from my own, just as their 'passion,' though similar in many ways, was also different from the "anger" of Achilles. Fitting distinctive contexts and a distinctive form of life, affects in Ilongot terms may well resemble feelings that we know. But precisely because "meaning" is bound up with "use," affects must be understood as the constructions of a form of life, and "selfhood" as a mode of apprehension mediated by cultural forms and social logics. Or, to cast my point in somewhat different terms, it seems that if we hope to learn *how* songs, or slights, or killings, can stir human hearts we must inform interpretation with a grasp of the relationship between expressive forms and feelings, which themselves are culture-bound and which derive their significance from their place within the life experiences of particular people in particular societies.

In summary

Central to my account of 'knowledge' and 'passion' as these operate in Ilongot social life is a simple argument. I believe that folk notions of "person" and "society," "individual action" and "social form" will always be related, each illuminating the other in a way that guarantees "strategic" import to investigations of cultural constructs concerning "personhood," "human motivations," or "the self." To say this is not in any sense to claim that all individuals within a culture are the same, all "socialized" to be the ideal "persons" of their society. It is rather to insist that the reproduction of a given form of social life demands such continuities in discourse as would permit a shared and sensible frame for the interpretation of daily practice, so that the ways that individuals construe their actions show some relation to the orders that they recognize in the world. A Protestant world view, as Weber saw – though his terms were not those of modern anthropology – required Protestant motivations, a Protestant "ethic'; and a capitalist system realized through the independent and competitive pursuit of private interest has a certain coherence with notions of "abstract" and equal individuals, praised by liberal philosophers and critically analyzed in the early manuscripts of Marx. Timeless form and theatric stasis as themes in Balinese history and society are – as Clifford Geertz has shown – similarly consistent with a characteristic distaste for individuality in the well-scripted interactions of Balinese daily life (Geertz 1973b).

Equally, for Ilongots, a fluid social world whose boundaries and divisions are construed as products not of formal rule or mythic norm but of individual shows of *liget* is bound up with a certain view of how and why men act. For Ilongots, one might suggest, there is neither "individual" nor "social structure," but rather certain processes working equally in nature, social groups, and human consciousness, a set of categories that highlight similarities between the changing tenor of collective life and motivational systems of the self. Whereas people elsewhere stress the tensions among individuals or between the private person and her or his compelling public bonds, Ilongots see continuities, casting social life as a sort of "actualization" of the emotions, and viewing difference and division as the product of affective processes that are at once invigorating and stressful, ever disruptive of the ideal state of balance and equality which, at the same time, they sustain.

The continuities in Ilongot notions of human motivation and the nature of their social world permitted me, as it were, to 'follow' them, explaining first their words for feelings and then the social and practical situations to which emotional idioms were applied. My choice of two

terms – *liget* and *bēya* – as more or less focal derived from their centrality in headhunting and oratory, events that for the Ilongots themselves
appeared to merit most elaboration and concern. What is more, the
organization and contents of these events – marking, it appeared,
dramatic moments of transition in the lives of growing bachelors –
suggested the significant dimensions of social relationship that have
emerged in this account. More specifically, I found that 'knowledge' and
'passion' were notions whose use was patterned on developmental features of the Ilongot life cycle and on the social organization of marriage
and reproduction, which in turn was rooted in systems of relationship
and opposition distinguishing, on the one hand, men from women, and,
on the other, old men from young. A proper grasp of Ilongot talk of
persons required, in short, an understanding of their views of the development and change in individuals through a lifetime, and of the socially significant relationships and situations that characteristic affects
and orientations were used to order and describe.

Cultures differ, but life cycles, of course, are universal, and it is
probably in my commentary on Ilongot views of individual development that these 'people of the forest' appear most like ourselves. It
seems likely, for example, that people everywhere experience and
acknowledge increasingly differentiated and complex affectual orientations as they grow older and as their social bonds, correspondingly,
grow richer. The Ilongot child whose 'fear' gives way to 'anger,'
'shame,' and with these, an understanding of civility or 'knowledge,' is
like a child anywhere, learning to accommodate to differences in context and relational milieu. For Ilongots as for ourselves, a capacity for
deep feeling and a 'knowledge' both of skill and of relation grow together; *liget* and *bēya* are complementary in the experience of growing
children for the quite human reason that strong affect must depend in
part upon the breadth of our experience, a sense of 'focus' or 'intensity' developing in opposition to the complex and diversified orientations that characterize daily life.

But we have also seen a number of distinctive characteristics of affectual patterning in the Ilongot life cycle. The Ilongot infant is thought
to be neither the innocent babe of our maternal lore nor an evil fount of
natural desire – just as the "self," for them, is not an entity whose
"nature," either good or bad, must then be tainted, tamed, or otherwise perplexed by the demands of its society. Ilongot children do not
require "guilt" or "shame" to teach them to control innate and selfish
needs, nor will they, in their early years, be taught responsibility, individuality, and an independent "sense of self" with which to criticize
and resist the corrupting claims of sociality. Unformed, they need the

constant presence of more knowledgeable adults, not to save their souls, but for a much more this-worldly reason – to survive. 'Knowledge' and 'passion' grow together through their youthful years as increased skill requires increased effort, and differences in developmental experience as these are linked to characteristic tasks explain, for Ilongots, the distinctive orientations of women and men. In childhood years, common experiences in the home dictate that boys and girls develop in quite similar ways, attaining both a 'knowledge' of civility and the *liget* that will motivate their work. But when boys begin to follow fathers on their hunts, to travel, and in their teenage years, to forge friendships with their 'fellow bachelors,' they will develop 'higher hearts' than women who, in the Ilongot view, are limited in both *liget* and *bēya,* confronting only a familiar world whose boundaries are familiar gardens.

Continuities between the self and its experienced milieu mean furthermore that all people are potentially the same, differing primarily according to differences in their social situations. Ilongots do not speak of "personalities" forged in childhood years, or of enduring differences in moral "character." Although they recognize that people vary in their ways and moods, as 'energetic,' 'lazy,' 'knowing,' 'strong' – that some 'resign themselves' whereas others 'hold on' to 'anger' – they do not assume such consistency in the individual heart as would grant one's 'hidden' memories, prior slights, or future goals enduring and consistent consequence for individual action or psychology. Thus, 'anger' buried in a person's 'heart' need have no behavioral implications, and *liget* demonstrated in the violent actions of boasters, youths, or drunks is more likely to be attributed to contingencies of situation and immediate milieu than to innate and "inner' claims of selfish, slighted, or untutored hearts and minds.

Just as people are not reckoned good or evil in themselves, so 'anger' may be linked at once to valued and destructive ends depending on its social context. *Liget,* breeding difference and dissent as it gives voice to unacknowledged strains, can lead as well to solidarity, health, and strength – and so, when mediated by the *beya* in a 'knowing' heart, becomes a disposition sought for and desired. As killers, young men proudly realize *liget* in themselves, and in doing so 'cast off' what they had known as limits and constraints, achieving a profound emotional state that alters their experience of the world, a state that Sartre (1948) has described as one of "magicality." Women, staying close to home, do not expect or speak of such transformatory discontinuities in their lives; but boys look forward to dramatic status changes when, through violent deeds, they prove themselves the strong, autonomous 'equivalents' of adults, whose cooperation in daily living is rooted in assumptions of equality. Thus, for Ilongots, unlike ourselves, one might well claim that the individual man's most intense "sense of self" is won when, casting off a victim's head, he establishes himself forever as an 'angry' man – autonomous because constrained by none, ready to pursue and later give direction to a wife because an 'equal' in 'angry' force to his fellows.

And yet, importantly, this cultural concern for the freedom and independence of adult male hearts is complemented by a 'knowledge' of the necessity of sharing and sociality. If marriage follows taking heads, the killer frees himself and 'casts off' bonds precisely at the moment in his development when diverse and energizing claims will limit his autonomous stance, committing him to conduct ruled much less by *liget* than by a 'knowledge' that denies the relevance of unique achievements, privileges, and deeds, and subsumes differences in talk of common kinship and cooperative ties. In daily life, a potential tension in the affective orientations of men's hearts – between an 'angry' sense of independent claims and the 'knowledge' that belongs to kinsmanly cooperation – finds resolution in a sort of rough division of emotional bent between the culturally celebrated 'angry' youths and the less 'passionate' and yet more powerful adults whose *bēya* is, in fact, associated with youth's decline.

To us, what seems distinctive and most troubling here is, perhaps, the fact that Ilongots celebrate and actively pursue something that they, like us, consider disturbing and disruptive – a taste for boasting, contest, and slaughter. I found it difficult in the field to write down texts in which men dwelt in great detail not just on flashing knives, but on sinews slashed and screaming victims; and I was struck dumb during the one headhunting ceremony that I saw when friends who joined in the celebratory song appeared in face and stance to be transformed, turned strange and ugly in their boasts of violence. Perhaps because I could not fathom the psychological or moral implications of their acts; perhaps because, with headhunting on the wane, I did not have to let imagination dwell on the concrete details of killing, I found that both in fieldwork and in writing this account my interests focused less on *liget* as a psychic state realized in crazed and frightening acts than on its social and collective meaning. So doing, I "saw" less, perhaps, but "listened" more, and so discovered that in unquestionably distressing features of Ilongot life were also patterns that – though hardly unfamiliar to ourselves – took their distinctive cast from the situation of the 'angry' youth in a configuration of relationships concerning men, women, old, and young, as these are organized in Ilongot society.

Of comparison and context

One of the most striking features of a good deal of Ilongot daily life is the glamour and the restlessness of bachelors. During my first years of Ilongot research, the anxious youths who told in songs of hopes to marry and to kill recalled, at certain times, the "hoods" belonging to my high school years, or perhaps the ghetto boys who stood on Tally's Corner (Liebow 1967). And though I tried to understand their plans to sever heads as something of a very *different* sort, my hopes to come upon exotic, cosmological accounts of otherwise unconscionable proofs of manly force were quite consistently undermined. Previous interpretations of headhunting led me to seek out a set of potencies acquired through what might ultimately be construed as a pragmatic act of force – a quest for such desired things as "soul substance," friendly enemies, or healthy growth. Alternatively, these explanations advised that I should view Ilongot violent deeds in calmer, cosmic terms, and see the youthful killer as a sort of shaman in a dualistic world wherein he mediates life and death. But none of these accounts made sense to the Ilongot youths who sang about their weighty hearts and dreamed of killing. For them, the point of taking heads appeared much less concerned with godly gifts than with the joy of victory itself. For Ilongots, as we have seen, there is no "substance" gained in taking heads; the head itself is tossed away; and what one wins is not a mystic power that secures the lives of infants or of groups, but instead a puzzling "spirit" known as *'amet*, which ensures one's lively reputation. And in the end, these *'amet* are desirable precisely because they *are* the things that restless bachelors lack: a sense of pride, potency, and self-worth.

But here, in very simple terms, was my problem. Why, if they pursued such common or mundane rewards, did Ilongot headhunters care to kill and win an *'amet?* Or more generally, how could a youth's desire for self-esteem provide an adequate "motivation" for such extraordinary acts as severing and tossing human heads? The answers I developed in this text were less concerned with headhunting per se than with its placement in a particular kind of social context. Headhunting became "meaningful" in relation to a social system which, in turn, constrained the ways that Ilongots were inclined to think and talk about their times and lives. Superficially simple words, like 'knowledge' and 'passion,' were, we saw, intelligibly linked to youthful hopes to kill because of their embeddedness in Ilongot understandings of the social world around them, giving shape to the experiences that they used to explain the differences between men and women, and again, between unmarried bachelors and mature adults. It was, in short, the ways that

Ilongots of all ages understood a young man's situation in the world that made adults encourage sons in killing, as it made bachelor youths determined to prove their 'angry' potency by taking heads.

The difficulty with prior treatments of headhunting was, it seemed to me, only in part a function of such apparently peculiar facts as the Ilongot failure to preserve and save the trophy heads of victims. In other ways, Ilongot headhunting so resembles in form the violent practices of Southeast Asian neighbors as to make it seem unlikely that Ilongot killers are concerned with something very different than the "soul stuff" that neighboring Ifugao look for on their raids (Barton 1930). Headhunting throughout Asia and the Pacific is, for example, associated with such common themes as male prestige achieved, in every case, through movement that gives way to violent deeds at some great distance from the homes to which accomplished killers will return in vital triumph. Headhunting often follows deaths of leaders or close kin. And then again, reports of Southeast Asian groups suggest that killers gain, through heads returned or the performance of celebratory rites, not only a sense of vital energy and renewed collective life but also potencies that secure their future hopes to kill and that offer prophylactics against enemy revenge.[2] Finally, much as Ilongot youths who kill are then thought ready to pursue young wives, so headhunting myths quite often reward the traveling killer with a lovely and desired bride. Closest to home, the Ifugao of Luzon speak of young headhunters as the "children" of old men; in spells, they seek to make their enemies "confused," and while on the trail they rub themselves with ginger to confirm and "clarify" their fierce intentions; and even though they save their victims' severed heads, Ifugaos, like Ilongots toss these heads into the air, so that, as they put it, their trophies will be light: ". . . be (to me) like the feathery plumes of the cogon and runo grass. My feet will fly up the steeps and I shall not become fatigued" (Barton 1969:145).

No talk of "soul stuff" or cosmology will, I think, explain these commonalities in belief, nor can it help us understand Ilongot killers. Instead, it seems to me most likely that the meaning of such achievements as the severing of human heads itself depends much less on cosmic schemes than on the social meanings brought to bear on violent deeds, and these in turn depend upon the ways that personhood is understood and structured in a particular sociocultural milieu. If headhunting – as in the Ilongot case – is seen as an important part of growing up, one must then ask what makes a man adult, what privileges adults enjoy, and how an adult's understanding of his place relates to killing. Again, if headhunting grants communal joy and health, it seems important to explore relationships between the accomplishments and claims of individual men and people's views of what it is that orders and gives life to social groups.

Part of the answer to such questions in the Ilongot case probably applies as well to Ifugao and to a variety of other Austronesian groups whose heritage provides related sets of images and themes in terms of which these peoples formulate a sense of what it means to be a person. And so, Ilongot youths who prove themselves by traveling abroad – and then, through taking heads, succeed in 'concentrating' a life-giving 'anger' – may well be seen as the enactors of a quite general cultural scheme wherein young or subordinate men disperse and then return to focal "centers" where life's energy is "concentrated" and the "self" is strengthened and renewed. It is this pattern of movement from and toward a vital "center" in which energy comes to life that seems to me to underlie the common features in a wide range of Southeast Asian practices and beliefs, because it underlies as well conceptions that unite society to the living "self."

But at the same time that we note such commonalities in thought, it seems essential to insist that these conceptions are themselves adapted, in each case, to the exigencies of social context. The Ilongot "center" is, of course, a very simple home and hearth, and not the privileged station that an Ifugao killer seeks, or yet again the elevated place of kings on Southeast Asian mountains. The social facts that give Ilongot headhunting its distinctive place in the life cycles of Ilongot men would thus lead me to expect that killing, marriage, and prestige combine in very different ways in the more highly stratified Ifugao world, wherein the "energy" and "lightness" men achieve through taking heads will have quite different social meanings and political con-sequences (see, e.g., Barton 1919). Stated otherwise, my way of under-standing what headhunting means for restless bachelors in the Ilongot social world is rooted in my sense of the relationships and needs de-termining the bachelors' situation. Because, for Ilongots, a wife and *'amet* are the only things a man can ever hope to earn, the bachelor is a man without a place, defined in part by his inability to claim an adult's "knowledge." And then again, because adults do not compete among themselves for rank and status – because among Ilongot married men no one claims debts or deference from equal fellows – successful men will not attempt to dominate their peers, and their political life is not concerned with men's unequal claims, but rather with the qualities and deeds through which men can establish their equality as adults.

More specifically, my interpretation of Ilongot materials has shown that culturally acknowledged differences between women and men, realized in the social organization of production, at once legitimate the authority that brothers and husbands claim in their relationships with women and at the same time provide an idiom for men's interactions among themselves. Cultural logic dictates that women who remain, upon marriage, within the families where they were born will 'know' of family needs, be strong, and display 'anger' in their gardens. But they will not attain the 'heights' of most men's hearts, give voice to such divisive thoughts as would suggest a 'hidden' *liget* in their thoughts, or, through their interactions in a relatively unchanging local scene, become men's peers in 'knowledge.' Bachelor youths, who have no wives, are free to move and may display more 'anger' than adults, but they, like women, lack the true autonomy men enjoy when they have wives and fires of their own, and so are subject – though they may rebel – to the commands of 'knowing' seniors. But adult men, enjoying 'higher hearts' than sisters, mothers, or wives, can not only issue commands to women in their homes and speak for them in oratorical transactions, but furthermore claim equality with the adult peers with whom they will cooperate on hunts. *Liget* achieved in the headhunting exploits of a youth stands ideally as a symbol of his autonomy and freedom from constraint, his ability to engage in the cooperative enterprises of adults without fear of a humiliating domination. And at the same time, 'knowledge' won through his experience of travel and of diverse social ties not only dictates his authority as an adult male in local life, but furthermore inhibits such competitive and divisive thoughts as *liget* in itself can breed, encouraging the suppression of unequal claims of individual women and men in the interest of undifferentiated and balanced dealings among kin. Thus senior men, as adults whose marriages are secure, may claim equality in a cooperating group and prove equality in confrontations because they can not only celebrate the fame of prior 'angry' deeds but, in more concrete terms, control through 'knowledge' the 'energy' both of women and of youths.

Because, in the collective enterprises of daily life, cooperation takes the form of the assumption that all participants are 'equal' and 'the same,' displays of *liget* are abjured and inequalities between such few as everyday enjoy supportive efforts of surrounding kin and their less favored fellows receive scant recognition. Some men marry without taking heads; some wives have hearts with strength to bend their husbands' thoughts; and some headhunters live happy lives in homes of kin without managing to marry. Norms of sharing among relatives who are presumed to be 'the same' mean that in their daily lives Ilongots can sustain a flexible and egalitarian stance in which neither men nor women are constrained to work against their wills – and none can speak with certainty about the inclinations of another's heart.

Domination of older men over women and youths, and the preeminence of some, as speakers, over adult fellows, becomes clear, of course, primarily in those oratorical transactions in which all acknowledge *liget* as a source of difference and opposition, creating out of daily life two 'sides' or 'kinds' who must display their equal 'anger' in order to forswear their grudges and adopt the knowing idioms of relation and presumed equality that are associated with kin. And it is precisely in these dramas of 'reciprocal exchange,' in which adults negotiate relation, that the organization of 'equality' in Ilongot life is revealed to be a system that makes men rather than women the public guarantors of civil ties, casts bachelors as at once a source of life and of destructive tension; and requires the mediating authority of mature and married men.

What oratory makes clear is the tendency of a world in which the 'equality' of cooperating adult men depends upon their claims to wives and 'anger' to cast young men and their concern to marry and take heads as an inevitable source of conflict – much as it permits established senior men to mediate the 'anger' of their sons and to negotiate relational bonds, arranging moves and marriage. But if youth's violent bent legitimates the authority of adults, it is also the case that headhunting provides for young and old alike an image of collective 'passion' and vitality. The songs and images through which, as we have seen, Ilongots celebrate the strength of violent youths as something older men would recreate; the association of marrying and taking heads, and finally, the motivational links connecting mourning to beheading – all suggest that although killing involves such shared assumptions as promote male dominance in marriage and the relative subordination of unmarried youths, it is also in young headhunters that old men see, revitalized, their lives. If headhunting is a sort of initiation by which young men attain the 'angry' emblems of adults, its deeper resonances lead, I would suggest, much less toward magical or cosmological concerns than to the hopes of elders to assure the reproduction of their groups in the face of the inevitable facts of aging and decline.

I imagine that it is in such terms that the ideologies of headhunting groups elsewhere in Southeast Asia and the Pacific will be unraveled. In every case, the 'concentration' that a killer brings to the act of taking a head takes on significance with reference to the structures of opportunity and constraint that are provided by his social world. Thus, if myths bespeak the truth, it seems that in many cases what headhunters gain is not "soul substance"[3] but something more like *liget,* and with it, women who will reproduce. Similarly, it seems that the powers that are communicated by taking heads come not from victims but from adults who would see 'concentrated' their waning reproductive force and so transmit it, through cooperative violent deeds, to sons.[4] In yet more general terms, I would suggest that headhunting and similar violent initiations elsewhere in the world might equally be viewed in terms of the "things they say" about the relationships that bind young novices and senior men, relationships themselves constrained by the kinds of hierarchies and claims that organize particular societies. And insofar as, in the Ilongot case, the status that adults enjoy is bound up with claims to wives, it seems likely that headhunting can be interpreted along the lines developed here, as what Clifford Geertz might call a "text" concerning the adult male "self" as he is situated in relation both to women and to youths.

In short, my portrayal of Ilongot notions of the "self" in relation to the male life cycle and the social organization of marriage leads me to propose comparable investigations of other groups in which youths are 'angry' and old men 'knowledgeable' and calm – and furthermore, to suggest that headhunting deserves interpretation with reference to the related facts of marriage and of hierarchy among men. Women figure minimally in my account because of their lack of prominence in Ilongot ideology, or rather, because a view of things that they share equally with men suggests that it is primarily as horticulturalists whose labor complements men's hunts – as wives to men whose 'knowledge' binds and whose 'anger' reproduces social life – that women reckon their significance in Ilongot society. It is difficult – and often foolish – to explain the absence of what one expects to find, but it seems that the Ilongot woman's lack of a "separate" and distinctive voice is consistent, on the one hand, with norms of equality and 'sameness' that govern the local interactions men and women share, and, on the other, with the fact that inequalities among men in Ilongot society are minimal, depending more on the claims of each man to a single wife than on such imbalances as are associated with polygyny, pervasive trade, or with bridewealth payments that lay claims to women's unborn young.[5] Cultural form thus reckons women first as 'equal humans' and secondarily in their relationship to men, focusing less upon the ways that women are distinctive than on collectively valued acts that at once confirm the dominance of male adults and yet provide for all an image of vitality to which each, individually, can aspire. Furthermore, because in actual life 'knowledge' and 'passion' often make opposing claims, Ilongot notions of "the self" suggest that individuals are interdependent because always incomplete. Unlike Western men who must be "socialized" to the "controlling" expectations of a group, Ilongots are cooperatively bound by kinship unless *liget* divides them.

Final remarks

All understanding is schooled by what we know, and my interpretation of the things Ilongots did and said was shaped in part by – as it in turn informed – my understanding of quite general Southeast Asian views of concentrated "centers" that define the "self" within society. But in relating Ilongot headhunting to men's 'knowing' and 'impassioned' hearts – to terms that both describe the orientations of the "self" and serve to differentiate among the roles and claims of kinds of persons in Ilongot society – I was concerned to show that headhunting's significance in men's lives is shaped by the constraints and opportunities of a social system of a distinctive kind. My grasp of what made Ilongot bachelors very different from Ifugao killers or even Western youths who cultivate a taste for violence was thus dependent on my sense of what their world is like: of how men's lives are organized in terms provided by dynamic processes that characterize their society as a whole. The context in which Ilongot headhunting acquires sense is thus a context likely to be shared with other relatively "simple" and unstratified social groups in which inequalities between unmarried men and seniors are predicated not on debt or law, but on the proofs of potency and force that guarantee the husband's right to services from his wife, and at the same time make an adult man the equal of his fellows. Equality becomes a value in a world like this because – although their shows of force "make" men adults and energize the social group – imbalances tend inevitably to cause men to want to prove themselves, and so occasion strife.

Interpretation never really "gets inside" the native's "head," nor are ethnographers' accounts of deeper "meanings" in the things that people say exercises in speculative psychology. In learning to make sense of foreign worlds, we are, instead, involved in showing how particular modes of speaking are illuminated by the social actions and relationships such speech describes. So shifting back and forth between the sense of native terms and changing understandings of their contexts, ethnographers must draw on prior knowledge of human experience in the world and then revise it. And finally, because no human world is utterly unlike the things we know, the translation of particulars is at once a way of probing a distinctive though not wholly unfamiliar form of life and an exercise in the comparative study of human societies.

When anthropologists discuss the "meaning" of the things that people say and "mean," they are, thus, always speaking in implicitly comparative terms because interpretation is of necessity constrained by understandings – themselves comparatively informed – of the significance of certain contexts. Ilongot explanations of their world taught me how to see and hear, and at the same time they required that I "interpret" or "explain" their sense in terms of my assumptions about what mattered in Ilongot lives. The business of deciding where to look and how to hear was thus a product of both what I heard while in the field and of a particular theoretical bent that taught me to see headhunting within the life cycles of men whose ''selves'' were shaped by a distinctive set of social processes. In order, finally, to understand why killing could give rise to celebrations of collective life, I had to understand its sense within lives ultimately constrained by the relational forms of Ilongot society.

Appendix 1. Ilongot phonology

The phonological systems sketched here appears adequate to all Ilongot dialects. In some, the glides /w/ and /y/ are treated as fricatives, with consequent lowering and centering of preceeding /u/ and /i/ respectively, but local variation is associated primarily with suprasegmental features, vocabulary, and styles of speech.

Consonants

p	t	k	'
b	d	g	
m	n	ng	
	l	r	
	s		
w	y		

Vowels

i		u
	e	
	a	plus vowel length /v̄/

Certain features of the above system deserve comment:

/'/ is a glottal stop.

/ng/ is a velar nasal.

/r/ is a voiced velar fricative, with possible historical relations to (and occasional dialectical and stylistic alternation with) the consonants /g/ and /l/ and the lengthening of a vowel /e/.

/e/ is a midcentral unrounded vowel which, when lengthened (/ē/), is raised and fronted.

Vowels /i/ and /u/ have context-determined high and low allophones. High tense realizations are obligatory after voiced stops, and in the case of /i/, before nonliquid dental consonants.

Vowel length (/v̄/ in transcription) is indicated only for the vowel /e/.

Further analysis may also require the marking of length for /a/. Vowel length is distinguished from vowel doubling /$v_i v_i$/. I have indicated double vowels in all cases in which a root alternates between /v_i/ or /$v_i v_i$/ and /$v_i r v_i$/.

235

Appendix 2. Glossary

The glossary that follows represents an attempt to make accessible to the reader certain aspects of the Ilongot language and, more specifically, to provide instances of native usage that complement the discussion in the text. Sample sentences are culled from texts, lexical interviews, and notes on conversations; they are provided in an effort concerned more with cultural than formal linguistic elucidation. Thus, in all but the most obvious cases of polysemy and/or homophony, I have attempted to provide examples and glosses that show a range of semantic applications and give the reader a sense of the lively and often "literal" ways that apparent "metaphors" tend to be seen. Rather than discriminate between what might be called "basic" or "referential" and more "extended" or "metaphoric" uses, I have intentionally grouped quite diverse applications as exemplars of a relatively conjunctive "thread" of sense.

Lists of pronouns, demonstrations, and particles are included to facilitate reading of examples and for comparative interest.

(a) Pronouns

	Free Form, Actor Focus	Affix, Actor Focus	Free Form, Oblique Focus	Affix, Oblique Focus
first person, minimal	si'ak	-ak,-k	dēken	-ku,-k
second person, minimal	sika	-ka	dim(u)	-mu,-m
first, second person, minimal	sikita	kita	dēta	-ta
third person, minimal	siya	φ,-su	su	-tu
first person, nonminimal	sikami	kami	dēmi	-mi
second person, nonminimal	siki	-ki	dēki	-yu
first, second person, nonminimal	sikisi	kisi	dēsi	-si
third person, nonminimal	siyayde	'ide	'ide	-de

(b) Demonstratives

	Emphatic	Attributive	Locative
near speaker	'itut	('i)tu	ditu
near hearer	'itat	('i)ta	ditan
distant	'imat	('i)ma	diman

(c) Some common Ilongot expressives and particles

'a – and (introduces independent clause in string)
'amung, 'amunga – sort of, in a sense (hesitation, uncertainty)
'anin – oh dear!
'awan, 'away – no, none
bukud – well, as for that
di – at, in (locative preposition)
dima – plural article (focused case)
'ed, 'eg – don't, not
'iri – no
kebet – pathetically, unfortunately
kunu – it is said
kuyen – so-and-so, what-do-you-call-it
la – oh!
la'i – friend, buddy (often in supplications)
legem – just, only
ma – definite article for all but proper names (focused case)
mad – in, inside (locative preposition)
nem – counter-factual, if only
ni – definite article for proper names (nonfocused case)
nima – when, indefinite and plural article (nonfocused case)
nu – if
numpa – why?
ngade, ngaden – what?
ngu – emphatic
ngunsi – pathetic, unfortunate
ngu'dek – unfortunately
pa – still
pige – how many?
pu – now(?), continuative
say – introduces clauses, it is
sayden – and, as well as
si – having possessing; definite article for proper names (focused case)
ten – causative, precautional
tungu(y) – where?
'u – subjunctive
'uun – yes

(d) A partial glossary of terms for affects, dispositions, and kinds of speech

'abet
>   to find, catch on, be clever
>   *'inabetku ma pana* – I found the arrow
>   *'awana 'abetengku* – I can't find it; I can't figure it out (e.g., a riddle)
>   *'u'abet 'imana tu'u* – that's a clever person, someone who catches on quickly

'adiwar
>   to look for, to search, to hunt
>   *'adiwarensi ma pilak* – we'll look for the money
>   *ma 'enggēlasagēt 'amunga wade tuy ma 'adiwarentu* – the youthful one, it is as if there is something s/he is looking for
>   *'a nu mamutur legem pu nemnementu ma pen'adiwar nima kaenentu* – and if he takes a head, he will only look for food to eat
>   *rimaw 'engadiwar* – he went hunting
>   *bukud ma 'qengadenanmisu ma 'adiwar 'a ten 'awana 'entepek ma kawade'an nu side* – the reason we call (the hunt) 'seeking' is because there is no certainty about the place of game
>   *nima qimpangadiwarmi nud ma purungyu* – when we went hunting for your oratorical encounter

'adug
>   to endure, to bear, have patience
>   *'adugim 'ima lakay kebeta* – have patience with the old man for pity
>   *'adugim ta 'anak 'edmu pe'i'ibira ten sannu ngumired* – be patient with your child, don't let him/her cry because s/he might get sick
>   *ma 'u'aduge tu'u 'angen 'upuwan ma sit nima nagiat 'away ki'apirsu* – a patient person, even if someone says bad things to him/her, s/he won't get angry
>   *'adugēnsi ma bēa'eng nima bēnuwa* – we'll endure the length of the trial

'agal'agal
>   to show off
>   *'en'agal'agalentuy dima bēkirtun raki* – he shows off to his male peers
>   *'awana sinarayuna 'en'agal'agalka ten ki'abetanmuy ma pedimeta 'ipa'yakmu* – don't always show off unless you would meet up with cause for your countenance to be pitiful (i.e., unless you are looking for trouble)

'aimet, 'arimet
>   ornament, to ornament, dress up, prepare, perform a magical spell
>   *si 'aimetak nun 'uberi* – I have beautiful ornaments
>   *en'aimetak pu pa* – I'm still getting ready, dressing up
>   *'aimetengku ma ganaganak* – I'm getting my belongings together
>   *bēya'angku ma 'aimet dita dē'en* – I know the magical spells of the ancients
>   *'aimetengku ma pagi* – I do a magical spell over the rice

'akin
>   to transfer (from one container to another); to contaminate
>   *'in'akingku ma rinutu mad palanggana* – I transfer the cooked rice into the open bowl
>   *na'akinanak nima ngired* – I was contaminated with, caught, the illness

sa nu 'un'akin dēken ta pempa'nun nu rinawam – just in case I am contaminated by, 'catch,' the disturbing feelings in your heart

'aleng

to be bored, weakened, sullen, dull

me'a'alengaka 'umpedeg mad 'abung – I'm bored by staying around the house

nu me'alengka wade ma 'impabēsima 'amunga ta'en nu 'imuget puy ma rinawam – if you are sullen, there is something you took badly (something that disturbed you), as if your heart felt bad

nu si ligetka 'un'a'aleng ta rinawam – if you are angry, your heart grows weak and dull

nu man'ē'egyat ma rinawam 'unta'untabi tuy ma 'i'alengmu – if your heart jumps in confusion, it will reach the point that you grow weak

'alimet

to be distracted (cf. *'aimet, 'arimet* for a probably related root)

nu manngired kisi me'a'alimet ma rinawasi 'awan pun 'entuntun – when we are sick, our hearts are distracted and don't make sense

na'alimetak ten say dita 'emul – I'm all itchy and distracted because of these flies

nu 'away 'ed manta'en nima rinawam me'alimetka – if there is nothing that does not involve your heart (if you are thinking of too many things) you grow distracted

nu wade kesiwasiwasi, ke'alimetansi me'ugi ta rinawasi – if there is something we forget, some distracting thought, our hearts will feel bad

'amumur

equally, in kind, as well

merumakak 'amumur – I want it too, equally

sa nu tuma'eni 'egkami 'amumur 'enganyaa nu side – (we never beg for meat) lest someone think that we don't, equally, get game

'i'aa'antaka 'amumuri ma 'edmu deken 'idengē – I'll do the same to you, equally, if you don't listen to me

nakaramakkuy ma 'amumura naka'udum – I don't like that, that you, equally (i.e., my putative equal), acquired so much

la 'amumur ta rimami makaligēligetak mamun mantalabaku – (when I see how much work someone else has done, I think), well, our hands are equal (i.e., we both have hands), I too will be angry at work

'anurut

like, equivalent, the same

'away 'anurut niman – there is nothing like that

'anurut nima 'inupum – just as you said

'nan'anurut pa nguy 'ima sinikenantan – it must be that we are the same age, that our growing up was the same

nan'i'anurut – they are identical, the same (e.g., in size)
'anurutsin tu'u – our equal human being, fellow man
peki'anurutengku nud ma 'epegmu – I'll make it (the same as) your size

'apet
(a) to be envious, seek to emulate, aspire to
    nu 'edmu ramak 'awana me'apet ma rinawam – (in response to a question about the relationship of envy and desire) if you don't want something, your heart won't be envious
    'awana nanakurengku 'inalugēy man 'awanuy ma na'apetangku – I would not just happen to think something like that up if I weren't aroused by envy
    la tuy ma kasirarakik 'imapet dēkena – oh for my fellows who aspired after (?OR approached, see sense (b)) my success (e.g., on hunts)
(b) to near, come to a close
    'imapet ma getur – the knotted string is almost finished, the date is approaching
    'imapet ma masi – the night is ending, it's past midnight

'apir
(a) different
    tan 'apir tuy ma keramakangku – what I want is something different (from that)
(b) to be angry, offended
    pemen'a'apir 'ide – they are fighting with, arguing with, one another
    nu wade ki'upuwantu sa puy ma ke'apiran nima niyektun – if someone says something (i.e., in opposition) to him, that is what angers his breath
    nu me'apiranak 'amunga metunuran tuy ma rinawak – when I am angry, my heart is as if on fire

'awet
(a) to be fast, quick, able
    maka'awetka – make haste, hurry up
    'imawetak mad bēnuwa – I moved quickly on the trail
    me'awe'awet tuy ma rinawatu meli'ngesi – his/her heart moves quickly with sudden anger
    u'awet 'imana tu'u – that's a quick-moving, able person
(b) youth
    me'awet – youths, 'quick ones'
    'awana tabiyentu ma ke'u'awetmu penggipret nima betrangmu – she does not equal your youthfulness, the tightness of your body

bēngen
(a) to insult, criticize, belittle
    ngadēn pun bēngenanmun ma sit – why are you insulting someone else?
    bukud ma nginadenanmi Bēklig nud Sangpur 'amunga bēngen ten natēk-

ligēn ma kideptu – the reason we called Sangpur by the name of Bēklig had to do with insult because he was bald

(b) to be affiliated with sexually, to be recognized as a lover (used for both sexes)

'awan pu mibēngen mad bēkur – he is not yet involved with a woman

dima 'anak man'ibēbēngen 'ide pan'irarapuwa – children become sexually involved with one another to start (a marriage)

bēret, bēet

(a) to distribute, share, apportion (cf. *bērtan* for a probably related root)

bēretensi ma side mad tētengetngeg – let's distribute the game to every house

'indētu ma bēetde – he carried their portion

pēpeya'engku bēretay tu ganagansin petputengku diyu ten suma'engkay 'alaga'engku – I'll truly distribute our goods, and give to each of you, so don't think I am keeping them to myself

(b) to take revenge, contaminate, be contagious

'embēret tu ra'eka 'iman – that plant is contagious

'adurim tu 'iman 'ed kasu binaret – leave that alone, don't take revenge

'imbinatde pembē'yek – they married 'in revenge' (i.e., in exchange for a previous marriage)

'awana 'umbēet dıman ten 'inadepyang 'ide – they won't take revenge because they are worthless, incompetent

(c) in Dekran dialect, *bēet* is the name of a disease elsewhere called *bērtan*

bēriu, bēitu

news, gossip

ngadet bēritum – what is new? what is your news?

'upiyan bēita – the Gospel, "Good News"

siya'ak pu mibēita – I will be the one to be talked about

bērita'engku dimu tu kinwa'an nitu riñuwak – let me tell you the way my heart is going, let you in on my thoughts

bērtan

(a) kind, class, especially bilateral descent group

pige ma bērtan nima taiwmu – how many kinds of things do you have to sell?

pekibērtanengku ma ra'ek – I will divide the plants into categories, sets

'imat pa ta bērtantu – there is still another kind

mad bērtanmi ka'irumyadmi – among our people who are Rumyads

mad 'amung bērtanmi, ngadenmi, sikami nun 'ikeradingan – among those of what is sort of our group, our name, we who are from Keradingan

'awana metunulung ma bērtan basta ma talagan kawade'antu – (in cases of vengeance or compensation, if) the kin group membership isn't quite clear, the place where he lives is sufficient (to determine his role)

'ipeknar ma kesikenana bērtantu ten 'edde kami pu languwi – Peknar is

his/her major kin group identity as they (i.e., non-Peknar kin of father) never paid us bridewealth

ten 'upuwenyu ma nagiat ten tam bērtan puyde – now, don't speak badly, as these people are of another group

(b) share, see *bēret*

pigen bērtan ma 'ara'ensi – how many shares (of meat) should we make?

(c) name of illness caused by eating with people of a *bērtan* that has killed one's kinsfolk and not paid recompense

bētang

shame, humility, respect

nabētangan tuy ma 'anak – the child is ashamed

'embētangansi ma 'apusi 'edsi de 'engadeni – we are shameful, respectful, toward our parents-in-law and so don't name them

ma 'alig nima bētang say ma 'empa'yakensi ma dērin – an analogy for shame is looking at the ground

'away 'ara'en dēsin ma bētang nu 'edsi pan legem ma bēyasi – humility gets us nothing if we don't go ahead with what we know

betrang

body

'engkayab mad betrang – (of a song) it climbs on the body, concerns aging

'i'ai dimu nima padgēdgiw nima rinawama betrangmu – it happens that your heart would cause your body to be admired

'i'akedtu 'i'ai ma betrangtu mad bēkur – (in marriage a man) gives his body by coming to the woman

kibetrangan – people of a body, kinfolk, especially a wide net of relations, as, for example, all persons of a *bērtan*

narped ma betrang ten 'adu ma bērtantu – the body is torn, split, because s/he is associated with many kin groups

nu pasiyendet 'Ipi say mebēyaw sikami nun betrangtu – if they kill Ipi, we, of his body, will get recompense

'amung pu 'imbetrangku ma 'in'aasun 'ama – (speaking of a stepmother for whom he would demand compensation in the case of her murder) it is as if I made her my body when father took her (as his wife)

'un'adu ma betrangtu – his/her body becomes many; s/he has many children

bēya

to know, knowledge

binaya'anmi ta 'ingkana'agi'agisi – we came to know, we realized, that we are all related

'anggēn 'anakak bima'bimaya'ak nu 'ukit – even though I am a child (younger than you), I know something, a little bit (used, e.g., in oratory)

wade ma 'inaraka bērun bēya – there is a new knowledge I have acquired (used to speak of conversion to Christianity)

dima 'anak 'away suttun rinawade, bēyade, 'unsawasaway de 'eliget –

children don't have fitting hearts, fitting knowledge, and just for no purpose, get angry

*'ubēya ma raki nu say ma bēkur 'ibēgebēge'ande kisi nu wade ma 'emina
kayra'uwanmu* – men are more knowledgeable than women, they tell us
if, for instance, you say something wrong

'anggen 'ubēya ma bēkur talagan 'u'adangan ma raki – even if a woman is
knowledgeable, men are truly higher

siyay tu tuydekentu siyay ma bēya'an nima rinawatu – (in courtship) he
commands her (and if she obeys), that's how her heart becomes known

mad 'ibēyaksu 'amunga siwagi dēken ma rinawatu – (of an undesired son-
in-law) from what I can tell, it's as if his heart will separate from mine

biay, biray
(a) life, to live

nu si biayka pa 'undewep ta sambal – if you still have life, the medicine
will help

'imai dēmi de mekibiay – they came to live with us and share in life (eat our
food)

say ma bēkur ma 'entengegēn nima biay ten 'awana 'en'etan mad 'uma –
women are life's foundation because they never leave their fields (as
against men who 'travel everywhere' and make an uncertain contribution to the diet)

'iapmuy dita biminaru 'awana bēya'ande 'ibiayde bē'yekende – look at
these new-style girls, they don't know how to give life to (cook, provide
for) the ones they marry

(b) to give birth

talagasin 'embiblnhuy ngu'dek – it is our true lot to give birth, sadly

(c) to be alive, raw, undercooked

'embiray tu rinutum – the rice you cooked is still hard

dēgiw
to admire, respect, look up to

say 'idēgiwsi ma diyut – we look up to God

'aduwik kededēgiwi mad talabaku – if only I could be looked up to for my
work

'upiya ta pemasik ten 'idēgiwak dima tu'u – it's good that I killed because
people will respect me

pedgēdegiw – to show off, ask for admiration

dē'ri
to pity, be pitiable, proffer or require sympathy

say ma diyut ma 'undē'ri dēsi – God gives us pity

dima bēkur 'awana tayenande kami medēdē'ri kami – women don't leave
men (as men leave women, e.g., on travels), because we are pitiable, in
need of their care

kadēdē'ri – please, have pity

nadē'riyangku ma 'anak ten 'uira pu – I have pitied, cared for, the child because s/he was now an orphan

kadē'riyangku 'away bi'en – I should be pitied for I have no betel chew

dikrat

to be startled, made to jump, be distressed

dimikrat ma rinawak 'eta'gi, kimeyeb – my heart was startled and rose with sudden distress

nu wade tu 'ima dengerensin bērita 'a 'undikrat ma rinawasi – if there is news for us to hear, our hearts jump (fearing the worst)

nu mansinepka 'undikrat pu tuy ma rinawam 'ebēngun – if you have a dream (associated primarily with bad omens), your heart startles and wakes up

'egē

(a) to respect, be hesitant to offend

pen'egētaka ten 'ubēyaka mad kuila'an – I respect you because you are smart at school

en'egēransi bekbekay ma 'anak nima sit – we are hesitant to beat another person's child

'away 'egērantu 'upuwa – he is not ashamed to speak

(b) be dizzy (as from heights)

nu 'umgēka 'amung pun rapu ma rinawam ten 'u'adang pu 'imana keyu – if you get dizzy, it is something you will feel in your heart, because you find yourself high up a tree (e.g., when pollarding)

'enu'nu

to move, make small movements

ngadēy 'enu'nuka pa 'egka 'ensisiya – why are you squirming and refusing to be content?

'iapide pen'ē'enu'nu nima batling 'idēgiwisi nima bēkur keramaki – if they see the movements of our earrings, girls will look up to us and fall in love

dumintan 'umnu'nu ma rinawan ma napasiyan namaside – before the hearts of those in mourning start to move, they have killed

bukudkan lawi nu mepasi tu 'anaka 'itu . . . 'egka bumarubērut 'enu'nu – (line in a magical spell) as for you, feather, if this child is to die, don't move (fluttering feathers are associated with life)

'eret

(a) to knot, tie, be tied

'en'eret ma side mad bēngu – the game is tied to the backpack

'upiyan 'eretanmuy ma 'eyara – you will do the ties on the knife handle well, effectively

'awan pay bēya'antu pengrettu – he still doesn't know how to make knots (to hold a house together; therefore is too young to marry)

(b) be strong, firm, concentrated

ma 'u'eret 'uliget, ta'en nima ke'ukegkeg nima 'eret nima 'abung – a strong person is passionate, like the strength of ties on a house *maka'eretka* – make an effort, act strong

'imeret ma masi – night is strengthened, it is the dead of night

'ipget

to show conviction, make an effort

'enta'en tuy ma rinawasi 'egka pu pē' peg'ēngku 'ipgesi ma' umaka kateg-pusitu – (when we are at work), our hearts say, "wait a minute, I'll try to push the work on my garden, so it can be finished"

ma 'en'ipget 'enggi'temande 'away rekarekade – those who make an effort clench themselves and do not let up

wade ma dēdē'ena mu'lu ke'ipgetanmu – there is something that for a long time you've been decided on

'iteg

certain, emphatic, excessive

'awana 'iteg – certainly not

'iteg ngunsi tuy ma pembēge'enmu – it's really too much, inappropriate, the thing you are asking for

na'itegēn – s/he is too anxious, precipitous

'un'itegēk 'ekar – I'm dying to go

kalikal

to be restless, uncomfortable, anxious to leave or move

kalikalentu pē'kar nima ngired – he is hurrying the illness on its way

tuy ma 'engkalikal 'engrekdēd ma rinawatu, 'en'ekaruwak ngu – a person who is restless, his/her heart suddenly says, "if only I could get going"

kayub

to fear, be afraid, be timid

dima hēkur 'engkayubēnde kami ten raki kami – the women, they fear us, because we are men

nu kumayubka 'amunga 'umpedeg ma rinawam 'away 'enu'nutu – when you are frightened, it is as if your heart stops, it has no movement

nu kumayub 'engkayulēten ma rinawatu 'engkaubēbe puy ma matatu, 'amung 'engngawangawa – if someone is frightened, his/her heart is stunned, his/her eyes are lowered, as if s/he were lost

'ay 'engkayub ngut kuyen 'itut ngu 'ariyentuwak 'aruduki lilipa'i – (during a betrothal meeting, the suitor hopes the woman's side will think), ah, so-and-so is timid and is coming 'hunting' for me cautiously and slowly

'ureniyan ma rinawan ma si kayub, kala'puy ma 'uliget – the heart of a person with fear is heavy in contrast with the light heart of one who is impassioned, angry

kemnu

to be disappointed

bukud nima 'ingkapasin ma katan'agik 'a kimemnuy ma rinawak – well, when my sibling died, my heart was disappointed, saddened

'engkemnu puy ma rinawam ten 'awan pu 'irapenmu ma napasi – your

heart is saddened, despairs, because you'll never again see the dead person

'engkemnulu ta rinawak sa 'u ngu tegputengku kamuway ma 'en'ara'engku – my heart despairs, "if only I could hurry and finish what I am doing"

ki'bu

to return a selfish or deprecating gesture

siyay ma ki'buwande dēmi bēngeni – that's why they are reciprocating by insulting us

nu wade tu 'ima bēge' ensi nu 'ima sit'a'awana 'i'akedtu dēsi 'a ki' buwansi pu keligesi – well, if there is something we ask from someone and s/he doesn't give it, then we reciprocate with anger

ki'buwantaka 'amumuri ma 'edmu dēken 'idngē – I'll be equally selfish, as you won't listen to me (i.e., to my request)

kidēt

to be lazy, discouraged

'engkidētangku 'entuydek dita raki ten bēya'angkun kidētde – I've dispaired of giving men commands, because I know how lazy they are

nu kumidētak 'away 'adun 'enu'nu nitu rinawak, 'empēpedeg dēken ma rinawak 'away nemnementun bēkir – when I am lazy, discouraged, there is little movement in my heart, my heart just stays with me and thinks of nothing else

talagan kidētde –that's their true laziness, their lazy nature

kinurud

(a) to resign oneself, recognize limitation

mangkikinurudka ten 'edmu giwara – resign yourself, because you can't do it

nu manngired kisi 'a 'engkikinurud – when we are sick we have to accept it, resign ourselves

'edde pusu 'ikinurud 'ingadēni – they can't bear naming it

(b) quickly

tatan kinurud ma 'i'aaksu – it takes just a minute for me to do it

kui, kuri

energetic, industrious

'ukuiyak pu 'ungraw nima bēkur ten 'inambatlingak man – I'm quick now in going after women because I have my headhunter's earrings

'awana 'ungkurika nu 'away ngelemanmu mad dē'rem – you won't be energetic if you don't experience a pressing desire within

'enlaniklanik ma rinawak 'engkui 'engkuwa – my heart prances gaily with readiness, energy, to walk

ma kui 'anurut nima pengkuwi'kuwi nima buyeng mad kaget – industry is like the fluttering of shell baubles on a belt

'en'amumur pay ma 'urepata 'atu ta'en niman ma kuin Duman – just like a dog on the scent, that's what Duman's industry is like

kurut, kuut

to flow, course (as a river)

sima'en nuy pengkurut nu dēnum – may it be like the flowing of a river (e.g., of an illness that is directed to 'flow away' in a medicinal spell)

mad kinurut nima bēyak in the coursings of my knowledge, the place where my thought flows, the depths of my heart (especially in oratory)

kuut nu dēnum – riverbed

ladsek

to jump, startle (probably derived from *ladtuk,* 'to jump')

nu lumadsek ma rinawan dita 'anak mesigalan puy de me'ta'uri – if the hearts of children jump (in fear), they'll get skinny as a consequence

ma penladsek nu rinawa ta'en nu 'iladtuksi, 'amung 'iya'dēn, 'amung me'awa'wan – the startling of the heart is like when we jump, as if to go uphill, as if it (the heart) vanished

'amung kamin limadseku 'alaken we are like frogs that jumped, we have extended ourselves unawares (line in oratory)

liget

anger, energy, passion

'uligetak nu 'umari ma side 'enyegyeg ta rinawak – (when hunting) I am impassioned when game nears me and my heart thumps

siyay dima bēkur ma 'amunga 'uli'liget tud 'abung ten say ma pen'eg-kangde – it's the women who are, in a sense, the angry, energetic ones in the household, because they are always getting up

mad pen'anak say ma raki ma 'en'apitan nima liget ten siya put ma rapu-wan nima 'anak – in childbirth, it is the man whose passion is impli-cated, as that is the source of the child

nu manngayu kami 'awana mangewet kami sa nu merehmu'un tuy ma ligetmi – when we headhunt, we don't eat sugar cane, so that our anger will not be cooled

'edde dēmi sibēri nu 'ima 'uliget – (we speak nicely in oratory) so that they won't answer us with anger

'u'a'adang ma liget nima raki, nu me'apiran tu'megēntu tagē'a – men's anger is highest; if they are angry, they'll just go ahead and hit you

'ungreni pu ma betrangmu ma keligesim nu 'edmu 'ibu'la ma wade nud ma rinawam – your body gets heavy when you are angry if you don't let out what is in your heart

mad pinusingmu ma ligetku 'itangrarmuy man – for having broken my anger (i.e., angered me), set this down (give me this)

mega'mega

to show off, prance around

'entabēr 'enmega'mega ten madēkit pu – she is making claims and show-ing off because she is a maiden

'enmega'mega tuy ma pengkuwatu – there is bounce, pride, gaity in the way s/he walks

'en'anan 'emega'mega ma 'uputu 'ebērawbēaw – foolishly s/he is making a show of his/her speech and being loud

meted

to quiet, be quiet

metedkin 'anak 'en'upuwak – be quiet you children, I want to talk

nu 'ikapetmu ma batling mimeted pu ma rinawam – when you come to wear headhunting earrings, your heart becomes quiet

mimeted, yimamek puy ma rinawatu ten limakay pu – his heart is quieter and softer, because he is an old man

nemnem

to think, thought

'egka pa 'ennemnemak pa – wait a minute, I want to think a bit

dima raki 'away 'edtu nemnema mad kumpude 'ekwa'antu – as for men, there is nothing they don't think about in all their travels

'enngelementu nemnemay di 'amatu – he thinks desirously about his (absent) father

ma tulani penemnemtu dēsi ma penngayusi, 'ara'antu ma rinawasi pegēgē'tēra – the flute makes us think of headhunting, it makes our hearts itch

niyek, or *neyek*

breath, to breathe

'egka pa, 'enniyekak pa – wait a minute, let me catch my breath

na'ugēlet ma niyekku – my breath is awful (i.e., I am disturbed, angry, sick)

'ungrekdēd ma niyek nu wade ma dengērenmu nampiyalan gisada – your breath takes a start if there is a fine violin you are hearing (i.e., fine violin music can make your heart jump)

'away niyekmu – you have no breath, are thoughtless

say ma raki ma 'unēneyek, tuy ma 'engrasibēn nima bēkur pembēge nima raki – it is men who are truly 'of breath'; whatever women pass by, men think to mention

ngadēn or *ngaden*

(a) name (of persons, objects, kin groups), to be named, reputed, commanded

penengka'wit ma ngaden – the names hook together, they are related

sa bēt ma kasiraptu 'en'aranantud tu petutuydeki pariparisi ma ngadēngku – it is perhaps because I am a novice that he keeps commanding me and repeating my name

katyak tuy ma mengadenana simabi – I will be the one to be named, known for, reaching my goal (i.e., taking a head)

mad 'amba'an 'awana ngadenansi 'ipipiya ma ngaden nima 'en'adiwarensi – in the oratorical style, we don't name directly the name of what we are looking for

(b) what?

ngadēn nima – what is that?

ngalemkém

to tense, clutch, be angry (probably derives from *kemkem*, to clutch)

'engngalemkem ma rinawak nu meligetanak – my heart clutches with anger

mepagpag ma rinawam 'enngalemkem nu 'egka mamutur – your heart will shake loose (like leaves off a branch) and clutch (with frustration) if you don't take a head

ngasingasi

to thrive, be healthy

'angēn santu nu manngasingasiyak 'un'adang nima niyekku – even nowadays (i.e., since I am a Christian), if I am healthy, my breath rises (with ambition, pride)

'unngasingasi ma pagi nu man'udēn 'amunga 'ungruyuk ma rinawatu – rice plants thrive in the rain, as if their hearts were lengthened

ngelem

to dwell upon, be absorbed by (a thought or desire)

kimēded 'ari 'enngelem mad nemnemku pasiyengkuy 'iman – it suddenly started absorbing my thoughts that I would kill that person

'enngēngelemen nima rinawak 'en'u'ut'ut ta 'ugalitu – my heart dwells upon him as it seeks to find out his customs, intentions (e.g., of a lover)

siyuy ta 'enngelemin ta nemnemku ta bēkura 'iman – the preoccupation of my thoughts is that woman

ma 'enngelemngelem 'amunga 'ennēnemnem 'engkemkem pay ma rinawatu – someone who is desirous thinks deeply (about it) as if his/her heart were grasping

ma tulani rawentu ma rinawasi pengelemngelem – flute music causes our hearts to fall into deep musing (i.e., thoughts of killing)

pa'nun

disturbance, disruption

pa'nunmu – what's the matter?

wade ma pempa'nun nima rinawatu – there is something wrong with, something disturbing, his/her heart (often describes heart loss, insanity)

nu wade 'impa'nun nu betrangmu 'alimbawa na'egnayangka siya pu perapuwenmu ngiredmu – if something disturbed your body, like, for example, you were chilled, it is to that that you attribute the origins of your illness

pasi'ut

to force oneself, do against odds

nu mandungulukan tu rinawam 'anggen nagiat ta manukmu 'umpasi'utka 'ekar – if your heart is really fixed on something, even if your bird omens are bad, you'll insist on going anyway

'awana pasi'utengku ma kidēt – I don't force laziness, if I feel lazy I don't push myself

'awana 'ilegemta 'idupadupē tu betrangta 'ipasi'usi – let's not force things

and risk our bodies against odds (e.g., in the case of bad omens, or when the object isn't really desired)

pedeg

to stop, stay in one place

siyay ta pindegēntu – that is where s/he stayed, lived

nu mampēpedegka 'away nemnemenmun bēkir – if you remain (at home), you don't think of anything else (don't have interesting thoughts)

'inadēgem ma rinawak 'amunga pedeg – my heart was alert and expectant, as if stopped short

'away ki'apir'apirangku 'empēpedēleg ma rinawak 'awana 'ensibērak – there is nothing that angers me, my heart stays still and I don't answer back

piriw, piiw

to snatch away

dima 'anak penempiriwden ma tapinit – the children try to grab the raspberries from one another

penempiiwden mesiken mad bē'yek siyay ma penempasiyande – our elders took wives from one another, that's why they killed one another

buu pipiriwmu dēken ta pinuturkun makutay – (a successful headhunter calls, on tossing the head) hey, come and try to snatch away from me the man who I beheaded

piriwen dima me'awet ma biaymin mesiken – children snatch away the lives of us, their elders

piya, or *peya*

(a) good, to be good, better

'upē'peya tuy mana 'upu – that's a much better sort of talk

'umpiya pu ma rinawatu nu 'emana 'anurut nima pemasitu – (if a man is angry) his heart gets better when he shoots game, just like when he kills

pimi'piya – s/he got a little better

(b) true, really

pipiya pu bimaya – s/he really has achieved knowledge (e.g., can now do something on his/her own)

(c) to make

'emiya'ak nima pana – I'll make an arrow

(d) song, to sing

pipiyan piya – true songs (typically, songs of longing associated neither with work nor the celebration of beheadings)

pu'un

essence, focus, core

sat Lakay ma 'amunga pu'unmi di Kakidugen – Lakay is our focus (i.e., leading, organizing elder) in Kakidugen

say ma 'ama ma pu'un nima kayub – it is the father who is the essence of fear (i.e., our central, paradigmatic experience of fear is vis-à-vis our fathers)

say 'ara'anmi tu ra'eka 'iman mad pu'untun bēsilid – we get that herb in the center of the mountain, way up on the mountain

rekwab

to burst open, unknot

nu mampinurdut kisi 'a rekwabēnsi – if we tie our hair in a bun, then we let it loose

'ingrekwabtu pu ma rinawatu mentukep – he caused his heart that was plugged closed to burst open (in joy)

nu mepasi ma 'anaksi 'a 'utakit ma rinawasi du nu mamasi kisi 'ungrekwab ma rinawasi – if our children die, our hearts hurt, but if we kill our hearts will open up again (with joy)

rinawa

heart, to will, want, take to heart

'enganak nu rumuyuk ma rinawak – I'll eat when my heart lengthens, when I feel a little better

nu 'alila'en nima 'agimeng ma rinawam 'enggawangawaka pu – if 'Agimeng (the forest spirit) coddles your heart, you will go crazy, get lost

sima'gi mu rinawak nima dēage kē'elagku mad tengdēr – my heart rose (with fear) when I came close to falling from my pollarder's rope

nu 'away rinawa mesigalan ma tu'u – a person without a heart gets thin

tu 'emina sinanem 'amunga si rinawa ten 'embiray, nu makpit pu 'awan pu rinawatu – all cultigens seem, in a sense, to have hearts, because they are alive, but when they dry up, they have no more heart

tuy dima 'anaka 'un'ibir mē'nēlek ta rinawatu say 'enambaldēsu nimu tutu – a child who cries a lot will lose his/her heart, so they medicate him/her with the breast

nan'irinaway de – their hearts are joined, they are in love

rinawak ma 'ikitak diman – it is my heart, my wish, that I go there

ringring

(a) to relax, ease, diffuse

'engrawak 'eringring mad dēn – I'm going off to relax over there (often a euphemism for hunting)

riringringantu ma takit mad betang – s/he is trying to ease, diffuse his/her illness outside, away from the house

meringring ma rinawami nu manginum kami – our hearts relax (i.e., consciousness is marred) when we drink liquor

ma silbiyan nima dēmu say ma pengringringan nu rinawa dima 'enebteb mad keyu – the purpose of pollarding songs is to ease the hearts of those who are cutting at trees

(b) clean, clear

'uringriling ma salaming – the mirror is clean, clear, sparkling

riwa
  (a) other, different
      sit mamana 'engriwan kesipēran ma wadesu – it is another kind of happiness that s/he has (i.e., after converting to Christianity, one feels a different kind of happiness)
      nariwariwa ta rinawasin tu'u – as people, we have very different hearts, motives, intentions
      men'iriwakin ma lambung – use different (colors of) wool
  (b) to take badly, get angry, turn bad
      'enlipalipay de 'ari 'ernep ten sannu periwa'en dima pan'abung – (when coming to make a marital petition, the suitor's party) approaches slowly in entering the house, so that the house owners are not offended
      'impariwatu ma 'upuk – he took my words badly, misinterpreted me, found cause for anger in what I said
      riwa'en nima rinawak petakisi – my heart takes it badly and makes me sick
      makana'ēlebka ten riwa'enmu kapaya – think it through carefully, don't (when you speak) do badly and miss the mark

riyu, or *reyu*
      to guess, sense, figure out
      legeme perēreyuwangku dēdengera – I'm just trying to figure things out, to listen and size things up
      dima 'anak 'engriyuy 'ide 'enanakaw – the children may think they can figure out when to steal
      'engriyuki pu 'enta'en, nii 'upiya tu 'ima bērita – you guess and dare to speak out, "so the news is good"
      nu 'irapentu ma betrangmu mengreyu ma matatu dimu – (of a suitor or lover) when s/he sees your body, his/her eyes will try to get a sense of you
      riyun rinawak – the hunch of my heart, what I happen to think
      riyun 'ureni – of something that turns out to be heavy

ruyuk
      to lengthen, be long, be happy
      paru'ruyukmu tu pedeng nima belek – lengthen the tie on the pig
      'awana 'unsipēka nu 'ed mangruyuk ma rinawam – you won't be happy if your heart does not lengthen (if you don't stop being distressed)
      'ungruyuk ma sinanem ten me'udenana 'un'apē – the cultivated plants 'lengthen,' grow healthily, happily, because they are rained on and get fatter
      nima pempiyapiyam pengruyuk nima rinawam kumpude nemnemenmu rawanmu – when you are well and your heart is happy, whatever you think about you do

sawasawa
      to act wildly, distractedly, confusedly, without focus
      'ensawasawa ngu'dek ta rinawa dita bēkur – there is, unfortunately, a lack of focus, a kind of confusion, in women's hearts

'unsawasawa ma rinawam nu bēetenkan ma 'amaya – your heart will act wildly, grow distracted, if you are contaminated by the 'amaya plant

ma 'ensawasawan tu'u 'umbugkut – a person who is distracted, or crazy, is likely to run away

siya puy dima me'awet ma pesawasaway nima panginu'un 'amung pan siwasiwande ma ke'awetande – it is the youths who confuse, forget about, God, as if they were distracted by their quickness

sibēr

to answer, to answer back

dima 'away 'apirtu 'awana 'unsibēr – those who lack anger will not answer back

pemensibēr dima bekur dimu raki mad buayat – in the celebratory headhunting song, men and women answer one another, in chorus

simusimu

to be mixed up together, to act with mixed motives, to act unreliably, to rape(?)

nasimusimu kisi 'inabēbērtan – we are all mixed up with people of several kin groups

'uli'liget 'usi'simusimu ngunsi dita raki – men are angrier, and, unfortunately, more devious (e.g., inclined to seduction)

sipē

to be happy

ma 'usipē keta'entu dima 'ungkuwa 'i'awet'awet – someone who is happy is like someone walking quickly

legeme meslsipē 'amunga 'en'engit'engit – s/he just feels happy, as if laughing and laughing

say kesipēranmu 'anggen 'ed 'ekanen nu wade hi'en lalu nu 'innekmu ma bi'en – well, a cause for happiness, even if it isn't food, might be a chew of betel, especially if you have been longing for betel

tabēr

to display one's force and skill, show off

nima kalakaysi 'awana ta'en nima pedgedgiw petubēra 'ikuwasi – when we are old, it isn't like it was when (in youth) we asked for admiration and showed off as we walked

bukud nima 'empamanan tu katan'agik 'a nanta'enaki simabērmu pu pasiya – well, when my brother first shot game, I said, 'you've shown your force in killing it'

tagde

to get used to, grow accustomed to

'embētang ten 'awan pu tumagde – s/he is ashamed because still unaccustomed to things here

pementagde pu ma rinawa dima matambē'yek – the hearts of the husband and wife grow accustomed to one another, they become affectionate *takitanmi ma 'i'ekaryu ten 'impamentagde kisi* – we will be pained when you go away because we have grown used to one another

ta'rat

to exchange, do or give in exchange, pay

nansalamat pu ten 'anggēn 'awa'wan si kuyen 'itut ngu ta'rattu – (a man who has received a wife in exchange for a married sister) gives thanks, because even if so-and-so is gone, here is an exchange for her

tampay 'iturnudmi de 'ita'rat – how will we ever make demands of them in exchange?

ta'rat nima penempasi – (a missionized Ilongot declares that adultery today) is an exchange for killing, a substitute

'away 'ita'ratkusu – I have nothing to exchange, pay, for it

pangiredmu dita bēteng ta'rata – (magical spells) make the ancestor spirits sick in exchange

tebēr

to accede, comply, say yes

papdegēngku nem daput 'awana 'untebēr – I tried to convince him/her to stay, but s/he would not listen

'anggen 'ed tumbēr ma bēkur – (people of other ethnic groups force marriages) even if the woman doesn't accept (the man's suit)

tengeg

trunk, base, foundation

ma tengeg nima keyu – the trunk, base of a tree

tan tengeg – one house, one household

say ma raki ma 'entengegēn nima pen'anak ten siya puy ma 'empiyasu – men are the foundation of childbirth because they make it (the fetus)

say ma ra'ek ma tengeg nima kasambaltu ten siyay ma pepēpeyay tu'uy – herbs are fundamental to medication because it is they (and not, e.g., the words of the spell alone) that make people well

tengteng

to order, warn

'a 'imat pay ma tengtengengku dimu mad rawanmu – well, there are still some things I would order, request of you, where you are going

nu 'umkar ma tu'u 'itengtengside ma 'edde kita'en di bēnuwa – when people leave we warn them not to fall on the path

tepek

to make sense, guess, find out, come upon an idea, agree

'aam pu petpeka – come now, and explain it to me

ngaden nima petētepekengku dimu – what would you have me explain to you (i.e., isn't it obvious)?

penepeksi ma ngadēntu – we try to find out its name (e.g., of a disease), to determine what is the matter *'awana 'untepek dēken tu 'upun ma panginu'un* – the word of God (New Christian preaching) does not make sense to me

say 'innepekde ma 'abung nima katan'agide – they found out, guessed they would be welcome at, their sibling's home

nan'itepek puy ma rinawade – they agreed with one another, fell in love (?)

tukbur

to dissuade, issue a negative command

mad penukbur, 'enta'en kisi, 'edka kuyen – when we give negative commands, we say, "don't do what-do-you-call-it"

'imiteg pay ta 'edyu ketutukbura 'anak – it's excessive, the way you will not be dissuaded (do not understand what "no" means), you children

tubrat

to engage in a recirpocal exchange, to reciprocate a possibly damaging gesture

'enubratak 'embē'yek nud ma bēkurtu – I'll reciprocate and marry his sister

nan'isinubratde penempasi – they exchanged killings

di X ni Y nan'isinubratden mambē'yek – X and Y engaged in a marital exchange

tu'meg

suddenly, to act suddenly

tu'mege meligetan tu 'iman – that person will get angry very suddenly

katu'mege 'i'ekarde – their sudden exit

kasinu'mēgentu ma tolabakun ma raki, pen'unudde maman nud ma ligetde – the quick and abrupt quality of men's work follows as well from, reflects, the quality of their anger

tu'ngan

to respect, avoid offensive behavior

dima bēkur 'awana tuydekande kami pentu'ngande dēmi say 'entu'ngananmi de nu meki'ekar dēml mud rungut   women don't command us (men), they respect us; we show respect for them (and don't command them) when they come with us into the forest

tu'nganansi pay ta napasiyan 'edsi 'italabaku – we are still showing respect to the mourners, and so are not working

tuydek

to command

'awan ngu'deka metuydek dita 'anak – these children won't listen to commands

talima'engku ma 'anak nima sit ten 'away tuydekengku – I am adopting another person's child because I have no one to command, no one to help me *siya'ak ma 'entutuydekanyu nun 'anak* – am I the one that you children think you can issue commands to? (indeed!)

'uget

bad, bad feelings, bad fortune

na'ugeta tu'u – a bad person

si 'uget ma rinawak nu 'edde' ak 'en' upu' upu – my heart will be full of bad feelings if I don't speak

talagan 'ugetmu ma 'edmu man' irap nu side – it is truly your misfortune (with implication of magically induced malaise, curse) that you have not been able to see, encounter, game

wade ma 'impa' ugetkun 'ekanen – there is something I ate that I took badly, that upset me

'awana 'entalabakuwak ten 'en' uget pu tuy ma rinawak – I won't work because my heart still feels bad

'unud

to follow

pemen' unud kisi mad bēnuwa – we follow one another on the trail

'unudēn nu ngired ta 'ibunga nu bēyukan – the blossoming of the *bēyukan* is usually followed by sickness

'in' unuddēy de mad pembē' yek – they followed them in marrying (married right after them)

sa puy 'unudentu dima bēkurtu – he will follow his sisters (move to where they live)

'unudēnsi ma ma'it nud ma pagi – we plant corn after rice, as its 'follower'

'upu

word, language, speech, to talk

'awana dengērengku ta 'upuyun 'iluku – I don't understand your language, Ilocano

padudukiyengku ma 'upuk – I'll lengthen my speech, speak a bit longer

bukud ma rawentaki peki'u'upuwi – well, what I am going to say to you . . .

ma legemengku diyu 'upuwa – what I would just say to you is . . .

'upug

to collect, focus, concentrate, bring together

'u'upug ma bēnuwa – the trail is narrow

tuy ma man' iramakden bēkur nu raki 'u' upug ma rinawade – when a man and a woman desire one another, their hearts are focused, brought together

ma 'in' upugmun side – the game you collected

'entayep ma pentagem dita raki 'amunga 'en' upug ma ligetde nud 'iman – men, in dancing, hold their bodies low, compact, as if concentrating their anger in that

yated
>   to lose vitality, tension, grow stiff
>   *nu mambē'yek yimated pu tuy ma betrang* – when we marry, our bodies
>   lose their vitality
>   *'away 'edde 'empampa'a nun 'ed pu yumated ma rinawatu* – someone
>   whose heart is not yet stiff, there is nothing s/he won't think of

Notes

Preface

1 The people whom Felix Keesing characterized as "the scattered groups of the higher country now subsumed under the term Ilongot" (1962:389) in fact recognize deep commonalities in language and custom, as they all speak mutually intelligible dialects of a single language whose closest relatives are probably Ibaloi, Kallahan, and Pangasinan (Lawrence Reid, personal communication). Generally known as "Ilongot," or one of its various realizations ("Egongot," "Iyongot," or "Ixongot"), they identify themselves, according to dialect, as 'irungut or 'iyungut, 'from the forest,' or as bugkalut (a word with no recognized local meaning but appearing in an eighteenth-century cathechism [reprinted in Sheerer 1911] and in a nineteenth-century dictionary of Pangasinan [Fernandez Cosgaya 1865:86] with the sense of "any person who has not been baptized"). Occasionally, they are also designated "Ibilao," originally, according to Barrows (1905:471), a Gaddang word that contemporary Ilongots understand as a derogatory lowland term meaning "wild" or "crazy"; Abaca, the name for one local Ilongot subgroup; or Italon, a word that means 'wild' (and, specifically, 'wild carabao' in Ilongot) but that has no recognized human application today. Earliest references to the Ilongots by Augustinian chroniclers writing in 1669-76 in fact use these last two designations: "They [Igolotes, a name for certain non-Ilongot tribal groups] are opposed in all their customs to the Abacaes and Italones of the mountains of Santor in Pampanga" (Blair and Robertson 1904:244). But "Ilongot" is used universally among contemporary reporters as it is by Renato Rosaldo and myself.

2 First reports on the Ilongot appear in chronicles of the missionary efforts of Spanish Augustinian, Dominican, and Franciscan orders in Northern Luzon from the late seventeenth century. See Renato Rosaldo (1978) for an interpretation of what he calls the "rhetoric of control" as reflected in such sources as Buenaventura Campa (1891), Julian Malumbres (1919), Angel Perez (1904), and Alejandro Cacho (1904). In addition to these, a number of detailed reports by Franciscans, and the stunning summary of Jordana y Morena (1885), describe aspects of Ilongot life in the nineteenth century that are striking in their consistency with Ilongot life today. Ideas about fire trees, as detailed in the Preface and Chapter 1, were not limited to Spaniards, but appear as well in the report of an early English traveler (Savage 1904) and a contemporary would-be ethnographer of Luzon (Hill 1967). Archival work on the Ilongot past is still in progress and will be incorporated in subsequent writings by Renato Rosaldo and myself.

1 The Ilongots

1   Our census tabulations from the period 1967-9 totaled 2,090 persons. At the time we estimated a total population of 2,500. During our return visit, however, we became convinced that our estimates for Ilongots, especially in marginal areas where they live intermingled with lowland Christian populations, had been unduly conservative – leading to the present expanded estimate of a population of 3,500.

2   Wilfred Turnbull, an American administrator who investigated Jones's death, provides some of the most useful information both on Jones and on the situation of the Ilongots early in this century (see Turnbull 1909, 1929, 1937). A recent article published by the Field Museum of Natural History, which sponsored Jones's research, also gives a useful account of his death (Stoner 1971).

3   Renato Rosaldo's monograph (1980) on Ilongot social history provides a dramatic and detailed account of the movements summarized here.

4   For a full discussion of Ilongot kinship, with special reference to domestic group organization and naming, see Renato Rosaldo (1968, 1970).

5   Renato Rosaldo (975) describes Ilongot *bērtan* as "demes," showing the importance of a historical perspective to an appreciation of contemporary views of social order, and suggesting certain parallels between Ilongot social organization and that of other "bilaterally" organized groups. The historical nature of *bērtan* formation is examined in depth by R. Rosaldo (1980).

6   Ilongots in different localities vary in the rules they offer for *bērtan* reckoning. Rumyads suggest that one's 'true' *bērtan* name comes from the mother, or that the *bērtan* identity of either parent is equally valid, the father's name being dominant only if he has given extensive bridewealth gifts. But Ilongots in other regions are equally certain that *bērtan* names are inherited automatically from one's father. I am not certain as to whether such normative variation corresponds systematically to variation in bridewealth expectations, but suspect that the situation is more complex – reflecting, among other things, the immediate marital and residential histories of particular local groups.

7   For a fuller discussion of Ilongot names as they relate to kinship, affinity, and forms of friendship, see R. Rosaldo (1968, 1970).

8   Jones's diaries in fact suggest that a man named Sibley, apparently an ex-soldier and straggler from the Spanish-American War, was instrumental in encouraging Ilongot raiding at that time.

9   My notion of "interpretation" comes most directly from Clifford Geertz (1973a), who describes his interests as "hermeneutic," thereby suggesting connections with a tradition of humanistic investigation stemming from Vico and Dilthey and rooted in the assumption that *social* sciences are, by virtue of the articulate nature of their human subjects, different in kind from those sciences that explore the natural world.

10 Arthur Brittan, in *Meanings and Situations* (1973:16), cites Peter Berger(1969) to the effect that "the social is a dialectical process involving the interchange between man's externalization of his subjectivity, its objectification in symbolic form, and finally, its re-entry into consciousness by the process of internalization. In other words, man produces himself . . ." Brittan goes on to criticize social scientific explanations that use "vocabularies of motivation (that) tend to see man as a victim, or as a self-

seeking executioner," because "they seem to suspect that the human animal is best described in terms of those motives which best express the times we live in" (68-9). These remarks, highlighting as they do the *social* significance of descriptions in terms of the motivational systems used and articulated by actors, reach back, of course, to Weber, but are also useful in suggesting something of my reasons for the analysis developed in this book.

11   Suzanne Langer, whose discussion of "significant form" (1953) has deeply informed my readings of Ilongot talk and practice, recognizes this dichotomy in philosophy (though she uses the word "symbol" to describe both poles): "One conception of symbolism leads to logic and meets the new problems of the theory of knowledge; and so it inspires an evaluation of science and a quest for certainty. The other takes us in the opposite direction – to psychiatry, the study of emotions, religion, fantasy and everything but knowledge" (1942:32). And her work testifies to her special interest in the latter, "the use of symbols to attain, as well as to organize, belief" (1942:33) through forms "in which the factor of significance is not logically discriminated, but is felt as a quality rather than recognized as a function" (1953:32). My position differs from hers in insisting that "significant form" is never absent, even from logical or pragmatic discourse. In contemporary anthropology, Sperber's (1974) insistence on the criterion of irrationality as demarcating "symbolism" from "language" and meaning elaborates a distinction that is implicit in the work of theorists such as Victor Turner (for whom "symbols" have the special feature of "multivocality" [1967]) to the absurd extreme of losing touch with what precisely is most compelling about Turner's analyses: his insistence on rooting "symbolic" forms in their social, and thus meaningful, milieu.

12   As Langer (1942) makes clear, concern with "symbols" is not limited to students of the obscure or hidden but is an aspect of contemporary thought in disciplines such as linguistics and logic. Similarly, for many an American anthropologist, as Sahlins (1976) notes, the "symbol" is nothing very special at all, but refers simply to an arbitrary albeit recognized label for a (by some lights, arbitrary) cultural category of things or persons, like "mother" or "chair." This use is continuous with, for example, Schneider's (1968) discussion of the core "symbols" of American kinship, or with Geertz's definition of culture as a "system of symbols" and of "symbol" as just about anything that "serves as a vehicle for conception" (1973:91). Although I am generally sympathetic with this broader use of "symbol," I fear that the word still reminds most of us of the "other," the emotive and exotic. It is with this narrower sense that the word is used by such social anthropologists as Turner, Firth, and Douglas. And so I would suggest that persons who share my view of the ubiquity of "symbols" (and my reluctance to develop arbitrary distinctions among them) might do well to appeal to words like "culture," "discourse," and "significant objects" – lest use of the word "symbol" by itself invoke some of the conceptual problems described in the text.

13   By "two kinds" here, I am referring to the (crude) distinction between "symbolic" and "literal," which loosely parallels more motivated (though far from unproblematic) divisions between "connotative" and "denotative" in linguistics, and "affect" and "cognition" in psychology. My bias for avoiding these distinctions applies, however, to another, which relates at one remove to the above. Word "meanings" – which, however, con-

notatively laden, are thought to operate by virtue of their capacity for reference (see Waldron 1967) – have been opposed to the "meanings" associated with objects, events, and so on, that need not themselves "refer." My hunch is that this distinction is more problematic than has been acknowledged by most semanticists; but whatever its virtues for the lexicographer, my claim here is that a strict view of referential meaning gets in the way of the use of native terms and sentences in cultural analysis.

14   The relationship of "universal" premises and empirical "generalizations" to the adamantly culture-specific analysis developed here is a complex one (see, e.g., Giddens 1976), and is addressed in part in my conclusion. What I am alluding to at this point is the simple fact that generalization always requires abstraction from context,and that a separation of the "symbolic" from the literal, cognitive, or everyday appears to promote unselfconscious abstractions of this kind – as evidenced, for example, by the tendency of many a social anthropological account to appeal to universal pragmatic, and/or physically grounded motivational schemes. Anthropologists will, I imagine, never free themselves from some more or less sophisticated version of the battle of etics and emics, but for the translator, this fact itself must be a source of unending concern. To represent *liget* as "anger" – or, more material still, as "adrenalin" – is part of a process of translation, but it can easily keep us from discovering much about what *liget* "means." The issue is not one of rampant relativism, for, as Wittgenstein suggests, one would not translate *liget* with a word like "anger" if it were not in important ways similar to it – just as one cannot "imagine a case in which people ascribed pain *only* to inanimate things; pitied *only* dolls" (1953, para. 282). Rather it is one of giving local contexts their due account.

15   To say that the symbolic pervades the everyday is, in general, to develop a habit of "construing social expressions on their surface enigmatical" (Geertz 1973:5). Paul Ricoeur, who begins by isolating a special "symbolic" mode of "double meaning" (1970:7), or "plurivocal expression" (1970:11), makes the useful observation that the notions of "symbol" and "interpretation" should, in effect, delimit one another, the "symbol" being precisely such an expression as is felt to require an interpretive account. He then winds up with the most compatible conclusion that, in spite of the apparent univocity of certain utterances, "multiplicity cuts across the whole of discourse," for "If man interprets reality by saying something of something, it is because real meanings are indirect; I attain something only by attributing a meaning to a meaning" (1970:32). In these remarks he seems to suggest that we must address anything we consider significant – and so any human action – as symbolic and thus demanding an interpretation if it is to be "attained," apprehended, understood.

16   My stress on sentences and "modes of speaking" as opposed to "words" or "semantic systems" derives, of course, from Wittgenstein's insistence that to understand an expression is always to understand its use, a view that puts my stance closer to the "ethnography of communication" proposed by Hymes (e.g., Gumperz and Hymes 1972) and others (e.g., Bauman and Sherzer 1974) than to traditional investigations of "language and culture" or to their present heir, American ethnoscience. Most work in the "ethnography of communciation," however, has been more con-

cerned with specifying "rules" for "appropriate" performance and with detailing "kinds" of speaking than with raising questions about the relationship between the form of expressions and their culturally acknowledged functions – questions that my somewhat different concern for "interpretation," or perhaps "translation," would seem to require.

17   Victor Turner's physiological or "sensory" (1967) pole of symbolic reference is of course designed to address this question of "effectiveness." Lévi-Strauss, whose work can be read as an argument for the ultimately "logical" or "linguistic" organization of affect (see, in particular, Lévi-Strass, 1963b), raises the question of the "effectiveness of symbols" in what for him is an uncharacteristic paper (1963a) of that title. Harriet Whitehead (in press), building on Lévi-Strauss's suggestions, has recently argued that it is not "symbols" per se that are "effective" in, for example, religion and therapy, but certain interactional dynamics and associated psychological processes that may, in turn, account for the genesis of the "symbolic" form of rites. For a treatment of ritual that avoids the question of "effectiveness," see Sherry Ortner (1978).

18   I use the word "self" interchangeably with "person" to suggest all concerns that bear on folk understandings of human action, and not the narrower set of implications associated with notions of individualism, self-concept, self-esteem, and the like that have a technical use in Western philosophy and psychology and are not particularly applicable to Ilongot understandings of themselves. I am aware that my use of "self" in this way may be confusing, but find equally problematic the word "person" which, in anthropology, has been associated with normative, legalistic, and/or cosmological specifications of the individuals' "position" within a social structure (see, for example, the collection of African views of the person edited by M. Dieterlen [1973]). See Amelie Rorty (1976) for a discussion of the historical background of these and related terms.

19   Maurice Bloch (1977) has recently criticized Geertz in an argument that is virtually the opposite of my own, insisting that Geertz's treatment of Bali errs precisely in confusing the "ritual" or "symbolic" with the everyday. Bloch is correct in raising the question of whether Geertz's analysis has any bearing on such "real" political events as the violent 1965 massacres. But his answer – that the "real" political and economic practices of the Balinese undermine Geertz's discussion – seems misplaced. I would argue, against him, that Geertz's treatment requires a specification of its contextual application, and such qualification as would be necessary to interpret contexts in which the behavioral patterns he identifies are not likely to obtain. Geertz specifically denies the implication that the "system" he identifies operates with the same sort of coherence and integrity in all contexts, suggesting rather that what he has described is a flexible but nonetheless widely ramifying pattern whose contextual ramifications are various and open to change. What we need is not to factor out the "ritual" (or "cultural") from the "real" ("empirical") but to develop our grasp of the dialectal relationship of action and reflection, so making "cultural analyses" sensitive to contextual variation and historical change.

20   Takeo Doi's analysis (1973) of the Japanese concept of "dependence" or *amae* as one absent from Western psychoanalytic discourse, and yet necessary to the understanding of a number of characteristic behavioral patterns and psychological problems among the Japanese, takes just this step. It shows the significance of "folk" psychological categories for pro-

fessional psychotherapy and suggests as well the possible contribution of Japanese discourse on the subject of "dependence" to psychological theory in general.

21 My dissertation, *Context and Metaphor: Ilongot Oral Tradition* (1972a), is essentially an exploration of the speech acts and genre associated with Ilongot notions of 'knowledge' or *bēya*. See also M. Rosaldo (1972b, 1973, 1975) and Rosaldo and Atkinson (1975).

2 Knowledge, passion, and the heart

1 It is probably fair to link this tradition to Durkheim and the British social anthropology that followed from him. Although Durkheim's *Elementary Forms of the Religious Life* (1915) is definitely concerned with "sentiments" his stress on the social use of such emotional responses as "collective effervescence" tended to support a style of inquiry that assumed a universal social psychology and did not explore the cultural specificity of affective form.

2 I am indebted to Harold Conklin for these comparative materials.

3 This sentence was offered as an explanation for a familiar line of magical spells concerned with health: *Sima'en nuy pentenggal nu 'utlek nu nagi,* 'May he/she be like the springing up of the leaves of the *nagi* (?a rattan).' *Tenggal* can also be used to describe the physical movements of a sick person who has begun to arise: *Simē'tenggal* means 'She/he sat up a bit.' I would cite this example as one that captures particularly well my difficulty in making systematic distinctions among "metaphoric" and "literal" uses of terms to describe the (very real, as far as Ilongots are concerned) motions of the heart. Hearts are, in the magical line, compared to *nagi,* but it is not clear (to me at least) that *tenggal* has a "literal" use in the second case that contrasts with the first. Rather, it seems to bespeak a world in which (as was suggested earlier in the text) there is a good deal of similarity in the ways that people think and talk about the lives of human hearts and plants. In some cases, of course, heart attributions are clearly metaphoric; this is the case with *bekag,* 'unfold,' discussed in the text. But other instances are more complex. *Limadsek ma rinawak,* 'My heart jumped, was startled' – *Ladsek,* 'to jump, startle,' seems almost metaphoric in especially when one notes its probable derivation from *ladtuk,* 'to jump, as from a height.' But the fact is that *ladsek* itself is used only rarely for nonemotional sorts of movement and so "belongs," in a sense, to the heart.' *Agēr* (or *'agēw*), in *Bukud nima 'ingkatagiwku na'a'agēwak,* 'Well, when I am hungry, I feel drowsy,' appears to mean something like 'drowsy, weakened'; but it is difficult to decide if the root is polysemic, or, alternatively, the literal base or, yet again, a metaphoric extension of a use of the following sort: *Bukud nima 'intengdērkun ma keyu 'a 'inagērtuwak,* 'Well, when I pollarded the tree, it nearly knocked me over.' Decisions as to the status of terms – as "mere" idioms, coincidental homonyms, literal descriptors, or metaphors indicative of chance imaginative flights – are not irrelevant to my discussion, but they can, I think, lead the translator to much narrower readings than are merited by materials at hand. For my purposes (and whether or not particular usages are intended as metaphors) what matters most is first of all the fact that Ilongots are quite literal in construing emotional life as a matter of motion and as a matter involving *both* "physical" and "psychological" dimensions; and second, that their habitual discourse – like any other – makes

sense because of connections they actively recognize between diverse areas of experience (e.g., between plants and people, or again, between the movement of violin strings and the way violin music 'feels' in the heart). I take it that the unraveling of such connections is the very core of cultural analysis.

4 To the set of terms mentioned here – *'alimet,* 'preoccupied,' *'alimudeng,* 'dizzy,' and *'alinsukun,* 'turn back upon, be distracted' – could be added a number of others, e.g., *'aliga'ga,* 'to be startled,' *'alibat,* 'stagger, sway from side to side (as when drunk),' *'aligenggeng,* 'to look around in confusion,' *'alika'yeng,* 'grumbling sound of churning stomach,' and *'alibudbud,* 'whirl, as of wind,' all of which begin with the prefix *'ali* and have a sense that includes a notion of casting about, turning around and around, and so forth. My hunch is that the meaning of the prefix itself derives from the root *'uri,* 'return,' which is, of course, used regularly in Ilongot glosses of many of these words (e.g., *'alinsukun,* discussed in the text, was glossed as *'en'uri nud 'iman,* 'it turns back on the same things'). More important to me, however, is the way that a sort of onomatopoeia, associated with many Ilongot descriptive terms, lends a peculiar concreteness to Ilongot descriptions, blurring (at least for the outsider) not only distinctions between metaphors and literal meanings (see note 3), but also between words and things. It is a far leap, but I feel that this latter observation is, in the overall, consistent with the "powers" that Ilongots recognize in certain kinds of utterances (e.g., in the case of magical spells, oratory, naming) and sounds.

5 In an interesting essay, Siegel (1966) discusses two Atjehnese terms that are in many ways similar to *liget* and *bēya.* One is *hawa nafsu,* which suggests spontaneous and violent "nature," and the other is *akal,* "reason," which gives human actions form. For the Atjehnese, however, the two are related as "nature" to "culture," and Siegel interprets events that give rise to the former as escapes, providing individuals with an opportunity to confront one another directly, without the constraints of culture, as "natural" men. The Ilongots, by contrast, see both *liget* and *bēya* as products of social experience, developing together (as we shall see in Chapter 3) in the course of the individual's life.

6 A number of readers of drafts of this book have been puzzled by the fact that *liget* appears to bear no relation to notions of sexual "passion" or physical "desire." By way of explanation for such a striking "silence," I would remind the reader that *liget* – like all Ilongot emotions – is not associated with any form of spontaneous, physical, or "natural" impulse, be it sexuality, hunger, or thirst; rather, passions are generated through and coordinate with patterns of action, processes of conflict, emulation, and competition in social life. I would add that attempts by Renato Rosaldo and myself to explore Ilongot conceptions of sexuality routinely met with disappointment. Ilongots of both sexes insisted that they enjoyed sexual intercourse, but tended to associate their pleasure more with feelings of affection and 'familiarity' *(tagde)* toward their partners than with physical sensations associated with desire and release.

7 A probably related fact is that most, though not all, reduplicated roots in Ilongot suggest repeated and often senseless action: *Sawasawa* and *ngawangawa* both mean to act pointlessly, to be crazy; *ngelemngelem* is the constant twisting and longing of the heart; *kuwikuwi* means to swing back and forth, to flutter; *ngasingasi* is to be vibrant, upright, lively.

Further, these reduplications contrast neatly with those that repeat only a first syllable punctuated by a glottal stop, suggesting incomplete, truncated, or partial actions and states of affairs: *Pimi'piya*, from *piya*, 'to be good,' plus the imperfect infix -*im*-, means 'he got a little better'; *Bima'bēya*, from *bēya*, suggests 'He learned a little, sort of knows.'

3 Knowledge, identity, and order in an egalitarian world

1 My account of Ilongot views of childhood development focuses on aspects of that development that were explored through interviews on such "emotion words" as *liget* and *bēya*, as well as through my general observations and discussions concerning the life cycle. Not being interested in personal development from a traditional psychological point of view, I was less concerned with such classic issues as weaning, crawling vs. walking, toilet training, sibling rivalry, and so forth, than with Ilongot construals of personhood as these were illuminated by their actions toward, and way of talking about, young children. In addition, Renato Rosaldo's life history of an Ilongot (1976) provided useful direction and detail.

2 In fact, a celebration followed soon afterward. This was the event discussed in Chapter 2.

3 Children under about four years of age always sleep with adults. Beyond that age there is considerable flexibility, but there is a pervasive sense among Ilongots that no one likes to sleep alone.

4 My analysis throughout this chapter owes a great deal to C. Geertz's "Person, Time and Conduct in Bali" (1973), which makes the point that characteristic affects and styles of action are likely to be related to names, identities, and ways of denoting "persons," as well as to H. Geertz's "The Vocabulary of Emotion: A Study of Javanese Socialization Process" (1959). The latter article demonstrates a similar development for Javanese children, for whom 'fear' and 'shame' are related, but the overall direction of affect is different, 'shame' leading, among the Javanese, to a much more submissive and accepting attitude than Ilongots would find desirable.

5 In Ilongot thought, house 'centers' parallel the 'centers' of rice field and forest (see Chapter 4) in a number of suggestive respects: (1) both are the loci of intense activity; (2) certain rituals, now abandoned, involve bringing a mortar and pestle into the center of the house to call spirits, much as spirits are called to the 'centers' of garden and forest; (3) in headhunting celebrations, a crosslike ornament, called *tagdēy*, is planted in the center of the room where men tie leaves to it and boast, suggesting that the 'centers' of houses – like 'centers' of gardens – can be foci of *liget* as well. This relation of 'replication' (see Vogt 1965) between house and productive spaces is also reflected in that fact that *tugutug* spells that smoke away spirits from the 'edges' of forest and garden have their parallels in *tugutug*, 'to smoke away illness,' performed either on platforms near windows or in the yard of a house.

6 Double and most adjacent vowels in Ilongot indicate roots that are occasionally realized with an intervocalic /-r-/, the alternation sometimes, but not always, being associated with the difference in grammatical function. Thus, *bēet* and *bēret* are recognizable, respectively, as nominal and verbal intransitive, as against verbal transitive, variants of a single root.

7 *'Adal* is a borrowing from the Tagalog *aral,* "to learn," and alternates with perfective forms of the verb *bēya,* 'to know,' as in *Bimaya,* 'He learned, came to know.' The importance Ilongots attach to collective action is perhaps reflected in the availability of prefixes that distinguish things done by a single (or a united group of) actor(s), from dual or collective activities. Thus, *'En'upu,* 'He/she speaks,' can be contrasted with *(Ma)ki'upu,* 'They speak dyadically, reciprocally, to one another,' and again, with *Pemen'upu,* 'They speak together, as several voices.'

8 In noncentral dialects, *lulu* alternates with *dungi* for male infants, and female infants may be *'umig, lupi,* or *tempi.*

9 See Renato Rosaldo (1970) and (1971) for a discussion relating affinal status and reciprocal names.

4 Horticulture, hunting, and the 'height' of men's hearts

1 In two and a half years of living in Ilongot houses, I only once saw a man raise his hand to a mature woman (his daughter); most couples report no more than one beating in their mutual history, and that, in the first years of marriage.

2 The pattern I am describing here is most pronounced in the central and upstream regions; downstream settlements – for reasons not yet clear to me, but possibly related to their more dense forms of settlement and more elaborate marital exchanges – encourage relatively more collective labor throughout the agricultural year.

3 Today, Ilongots use small harvesting knives, but still feel uncomfortable with large blades for reaping. This seems consistent with the fact that the traditional taboos prohibited use of metal in cutting both rice and the umbilical cord of a new baby – an association that probably derives from a desire to differentiate female concerns from the 'cutting' of forests and persons associated with men.

4 Like the pollarder's tightropes, these tall racks appear to be unique to Ilongot cultivators – at least on Luzon. Their ten-tier height is determined by the fact that yields are measured in units of ten bundles, called *penge.*

5 The above statement holds true particularly for sardinelike small river fish *(bēyek)* and catfish *(dalag);* a larger and fleshier whitefish *(rudung)* is, in areas where it is prevalent, a casual addition to the diet. It is also the object of large-scale fishing trips when Ilongots – often from several settlements – gather together to dam and poison *(pa'duweg)* a stretch of one of the larger rivers, collect the stunned fish, and dry and distribute the quantities they are unable to consume. Such trips are also the stuff of warm recollections because they involve the excitement of collected numbers, extended voyage, and drama on the part of men who spear the fish. No such interest attaches to fish netted by women, or gathered by women from the dams. For a more detailed account of fishing, see R. Rosaldo (1970).

6 This sort of hunt is more common in the more densely settled downstream region, where the product of a single day's hunting is unlikely to make a significant contribution to the ten to twenty cooperating households of which a settlement may be composed.

7 If, however, the game was bagged in distant reaches of the forest, the men will have butchered it on the spot of the kill.

8 *'Apu* in Ilongot is a kin term for grandparents and grandchildren, parents-

and children-in-law, but here Ilongots seem to be following Ilocano usage, in which "apo" can be "senior" or "patron/boss."

9   In 1974 a kilo of dried meat brought $2.50 to $3.50 (U.S.) in lowland markets; before Martial Law, it could be exchanged with traders for bullets and is now sold for cloth, kerosene, salt, or cash.

10   See M. Rosaldo (1974) for a general discussion of the implications of a contrast between women's "domestic" and men's "public" orientations from a cross-cultural point of view.

11   All magical spells, or *nawnaw,* belong to a larger category of speech acts that Ilongots call *'eyap,* or 'invocations.' They range from an informal 'Go, go away cold,' which elders mumble to themselves on taking aspirin, to prolonged and rhythmic chants invoking spirits and involving the manipulation of sets of from one to ten or twenty potent and metaphorically significant plants. Spells for health, or *sambal,* contrast with *'aimet,* 'preparations,' uttered to excite the 'hands' of harvesters and hunters, to 'anger' *(liget)* dogs and 'quicken' *('awet)* bow strings, to bring 'rice hearts' *(rinawa nu pagi)* to a ripened garden, or to alert a newly filled granary to a coming year of use. *Kuiri,* spells that promise safety to headhunters on a raid, are occasionally classed as *'aimet,* but these are generally distinguished from the more various and elaborate performances, which – combining language, herbs, and gesture – at once call forth desired produce and 'prepare' the gardener and hunter for their respective tasks.

12   This paragraph and the two that follow are derived from a discussion by Rosaldo and Atkinson (1975); for further details on Ilongot magic and the use of magical plants, see M. Rosaldo (1972a and b, 1975). M. Rosaldo (1973) discusses spells and invocations in the context of an indigenous classification of speech acts.

13   The fact that 'news' *(beita)* of good harvests 'circles' like the reputations of killers underlines the ways in which women gain self-esteem from their work. But not surprisingly, the reputation of gardeners depends upon guests who visit their households, and does not, like the glory of killers, gain circulation from songs, boasts, and ornaments worn in travels to distant locales. Women *do* achieve respect for their efforts, but their fame travels less widely than that of men.

14   Our data indicate that in 1974 we were eating between one-half to two-thirds the amount of game enjoyed in 1967-9.

5 Headhunting: a tale of 'fathers,' 'brothers,' and 'sons'

1   All Ilongot songs are "composed" by their singers insofar as the words used vary from one performance to another, even though stock phrases, tunes, and themes appear in all. New tunes and themes are recognized as the creation of specific singers, but this point is not relevant for discussion here. Furthermore, very few songs are arranged in verses, lines, or scansion patterns – a fact reflected in the loose prose translations offered in the text.

2   Ilongot songs *(piya, depyug)* are classified in terms of functional associations: lullabies *(meara),* farewells *(mina'naw),* celebratory songs *(buayat, tarapandet),* magical invocations *('amamet, dinawig, 'anitu),* songs for pollarding *(dēmu),* and finally 'true songs' *(pipiyan piya)* for amusement, which 'climb' *(kayab)* either on a story (as is the case with ballads) or on

desires to marry, kill, grow older, or recover a lost youth. Songs of this last variety typically involve a sort of objectification, in which the singer speaks of himself or herself sometimes in the first, sometimes in the second, person ('oh, poor bachelor . . .') and adopts a tone associated with 'exclamations of pity' *(dimet)* – such as 'oh dear' *(qanin, ngu'dek)* – which appears again to dissociate the song and singer from the self addressed in song.

3   Ilongots use Tagalog- and Spanish-based loan words to talk of external forms of political and moral authority: *batat,* Tagalog *batas,* 'law'; *'uldin,* Spanish *orden,* 'order'; *gubildnu,* Spanish *govierno,* 'government'; *diyut,* Spanish *dios,* 'god.' And, probably because both government and mission are seen by them as opposed to their traditional forms of magic, contest, and killing, they use these to characterize, equally, the authority of the Philippine National Government and of the fundamentalist Christian God.

4   Ilongots distinguish proper 'raiding' *(ngayu),* which includes both 'raids from ambush' *(ta'nēb)* and 'storming' *(bēgbēg)* of households, from killing 'by stealth' *(ka'abung)* in a supposedly friendly home. In the latter case, a typical strategy is called *'agē* – a decoy visits and invites a lack of caution among chosen victims, while his fellow raiders wait to attack the unsuspecting house.

5   After raids, men can boast of their achievement of 'beheading' *(putur),* 'capturing' *(dēkep),* or 'stabbing' *('etbung)* the victim, or of tossing the head for a second *(ta'wad)* or third *(taubutub)* time.

6   Tukbaw approached us to explain that disaffection among the senior men might keep a celebration from occurring, and so suggested that we buy a pig for sacrifice – so shortcutting some of the problems concerned with responsibility for Burur's achievement, and permitting us to see a traditional 'sacrifice for beheadings' *(dēwak).* I imagine that had we not complied, Burur's celebration would have waited for, and been joined to, the sacrifices that followed raiding in 1972.

7   The symbolic uses of teeth could be further explored if I knew more about the traditional Ilongot practice of filing flat the front six teeth, top and bottom, of both male and female adolescents, for reasons Ilongots characterize as aesthetic: Blackened filed teeth provide, they say, a stunning contrast to betel-stained red lips. I should add that if tooth loss is read, in a classic Freudian manner, as an "equivalent" to beheading or death, which in turn "equals" castration – an issue which, according to psychoanalytic theory, must be confronted by young boys in the process of growing up – our tale of "fathers and sons" might be seen to have an essentially Oedipal shape. Certainly, headhunting as a ritual involving young men and 'fathers' and serving ideally as a prerequisite to marriage can be seen as a local "resolution" to Oedipal dilemmas. But although such an interpretation might be useful in an exploration of the psychological dilemmas of individual Ilongots, I lack the projective materials necessary to support this kind of account.

8   In fact, of several hundred names recorded, over half had no agreed upon significance, and of the others, the vast majority – names for boys and girls alike – touched either on the question of beheading, or the related facts of marriage and of skill in formal talk. See Chapter 4.

9   I have no data indicating what novice raiders who did not manage to take a head do at the time of headhunting celebrations, but I would guess that

they do not participate with their fellows in the boasts and chorus singing; they probably keep themselves "on the sidelines," as did Kugkug at Burur's celebration, when he felt he could not join in joyous singing because his heart was 'heavy' with the thought of his son Sideng who, at the time, had not yet taken a head.

10   Actually, our data are inconsistent on the place of zithers in these schema. Some informants say that the zither accompanies 'true songs' – flutes and violins – before a raid. The reason for the inconsistency would appear to have to do with some ambiguity as to the relevant boundary between after-raid celebration and before-raid desire, which for some informants depends on performing a major sacrifice, and for others on an end to a sort of "*buayat* spirit" as people come to think of their immediate tasks and future raids.

11   Downs (1955) has developed an analysis of the frequent association of headhunting, mourning, and fertility in Indonesian materials, but his account, based on an assumption of dual organization, does not capture what Ilongots share with the Indonesian groups. A more promising comparative tactic, and one that might complement the analysis developed here, would take its cue from Freud's *Mourning and Melancholia* (1916); certainly, the characteristic behavior of Ilongot novices bears striking resemblance to Freud's description of melancholics. But there would be two difficulties. First, in the Freudian account, melancholia is derivative of mourning, whereas the Ilongot materials suggest that the association of headhunting and mourning is derivative of the psychological and cultural significance of headhunting for unaccomplished youths. Second, one would have to ask why Freud's melancholics turn violence "inward," whereas violence in the Ilongot case is directed outside the self.

12   A reluctance to name the dead made genealogical reckoning of relationships quite difficult for us as analysts; Ilongots had often forgotten the names of relevant linking kin. Our genealogical interviewing was furthermore made problematic by a real discomfort about naming the departed; once, after a long day of such interviews, my 'sister' Wagat complained that the deceased had probably heard us and would come to haunt her in her dreams.

13   The myth of the *masina* tree is strikingly similar to the South American Bororo myth of men who go out to fetch Arara birds, used as a "key" point in Lévi-Strauss's analysis in *The Raw and The Cooked* (1970). In that study, a brother of the bride is abandoned by his new brother-in-law in a treetop; he is saved by a jaguar, a "wild cat" related to the civet; and on "returning to the ground," he enters a new series of social relationships which, presumably, look forward to his marriage (see also T. Turner, n.d.). My hunch is that these similarities may be understood in part with relation to similarities in social organization: Both myths come from societies that practice uxorilocal residence, in which a primary differentiation exists between married and unmarried men. That the Ilongot youths are 'fellow bachelors' whereas the Bororo boys are affines may have to do with a tendency in Ilongot society to minimize the differentiation associated with affinity; bachelors who compete for a single girl are, in the analysis developed here, quite similar to brothers-in-law who also have competing interests in the fate of a single maiden.

14   In fact, reciprocal naming appears to be most common among male affines

– men who are bound to share their adult lives and labor, but find themselves, perhaps, reluctant to be defined by the asymmetrical prohibition that forbids a husband to name the siblings or parents of his spouse.

15   Probably some five to ten percent of Ilongot men reach their forties without every marrying – the usual explanation being a physical deformity that makes them undesirable and 'ashamed.' Spinsterhood is virtually unknown among women who reach their middle age – the imbalance having less to do with polygyny, of which we saw only two cases in the entire contemporary Ilongot population, than with a tendency for men and not women to remarry upon the death of a spouse.

16   Wild carabao (*'itarun*) are reported in Jones's diaries, and Ilongots in the downstream region recall hunting them earlier in this century. They are unknown today.

17   The taunt that houses are too weak to hold the weight of game or killers is probably related to the Ilongot idea that a final accomplishment of a youth before marriage is his ability to 'tie knots' that fasten housewalls and posts. 'Tying' (*'eret*), as was shown in Chapter 2, is related to notions of 'strength' and force.

18   A second common cause of feuding was, informants say, the theft of food from gardens; because such thefts usually followed destitution, it seems likely that Ilongots killed thieves less because of challenges to property than because of the vulnerability of the weak. At the same time, however, theft of food from gardens would have carried the additional implication of 'theft' of, or laying claims to, local women, and so would have been a source of insult and *liget* in a manner consistent with the analysis in the text.

19   'Red' and 'angry,' these earrings can themselves strike down the man who dares to wear them – especially while eating – if he does not have an *'amet* of his own.

20   Another set of leaves called *'amaya* binds rice hearts and plenty within a granary; and the sun can *'amaya,* or 'call away,' the hearts of humans, causing illness unless the hearts are magically recovered by leafy charms, also called *'amaya.*

6 Negotiating anger: oratory and the knowledge of adults

1   *Sinapang* ('to speak obscenely') is a word used to describe vulgar utterances in a context where they are inappropriate – especially, in the company of affines of the opposite sex or senior generation, or of cross-sex 'siblings.' Sexual gestures and intimate physical contact – including, for example, presence at a birth – between people of these categories are seen as 'shameful,' and often have supernatural sanctions. At the same time, vulgarity between 'fathers' and 'daughters,' or 'mothers' and 'sons,' though restricted by a general respect toward senior kinfolk, is not systematically forbidden. The interpretation suggested here is that senior kin (and it is particularly old men, like Lakay, who engage in sexual repartee), insofar as they lack *liget,* can neither affront nor feel themselves threatened by sexual innuendo; rather, their linguistic license is a token of the general atmosphere of affectionate ease ideally bound up with their presence.

2   There is no single term in Ilongot that is equivalent to the English "kin-

ship.'' When speaking of kinfolk of unspecified relation, one can say *Katan'agimide*, 'They are our siblings; *'Kibetrangak nud X*, 'I share a body with X'; or *Kabetrangangkut X*, 'My fellow in body is X.' The word *matrem*, 'blood,' can be used alternately with *betrang*, 'body,' but in general is more limited in extension, referring primarily to collateral and immediate lineal relations, as in *Ma kametreman say dima katan'agilisi biyang nima katan'agisi mad betang nasawasawa dima*, 'The fellow in blood is our true sibling, not our siblings on the outside, they (their blood? their connection to us?) are lost, diffused.'

3   Even now my grasp of Ilongot terms for various marital *purung* and prestations is weak, in part because of considerable local group variation. *Kabe'ruwan* is virtually universal and appears to refer either to the oratory that arranges a marriage or the labor that a man does in his desired affinal household. *Pu'rut* means, for some, a premarital prestation, and in particular, the gift giving by parents who plan a marriage during their child's youth; for others, it is no different from a major bridewealth prestation, or *langu*. *Pi'yat* also varies in its application, some seeing it as a premarital exploratory talk, others as a sort of *langu*, and still others as equivalent to a *singgepan* (from *tegep*, 'to go up into'), a major *purung* and meal that marks the man's entrance into his wife's household and that in some local groups was traditionally required before the new husband could bring his bow into the house. Finally, *langu* describes a major bridewealth prestation; one can *pi'yat* as many times as new affines request to 'taste the hand' of the new husband, but *langu* – in retrospect at least – are the ultimate prestation and can only happen once. *Langu* are routine in the downstream region, where one of their functions appears to be a delimitation of the kindred of the groom – who will then be able to request prestations for the groom's daughters. But in Rumyad, people insist that *langu* are possible only when marriages cross *bērtan* lines, and that they require movement of the woman to her husband's home. Traditionally, prestations appear to have involved primarily a collection of dried meat and sugarcane wine for feasting, with the possible addition of one or two 'metal' ('*uteng*, meaning 'metal,' is also used to describe all bridewealth gifts) objects – knives, brass wire, pots – acquired through trade. Recently, however, there has been something of an explosion of marital prestations of all kinds (quite probably related to changes in local social relationships and the corresponding "meaning" of *purung*, as suggested on p. 215-16) and people seem uncertain as to whether these are *langu*, *pi'yat*, or something else.

4   For a full analysis of *bērtan* as locally based bilateral descent groups see Renato Rosaldo (1975). What is important for our purposes is: (1) that although *bērtan* labels are multiple and overlapping, often being merged with names of localities, (2) Ilongots speak as though their social universe were divided into unambiguous and discrete descent-based classes, a not unreasonable "illusion" because (3) it is in fact as members of well-bounded *bērtan* that they confront one another in *purung*, especially in *bēyaw*, public negotiations of peace.

5   Peace requires three ritual steps: (1) *tangrar*, 'laying down' of gifts as a 'return' for victims slaughtered; (2) *redred*, 'rubbing,' a ritual act in which participants from both sides hold onto 'hard' and strengthening brass and renounce their differences, so removing the danger of ulcerous sores (called *bērtan*, the name for 'kinds of people'; see discussion on pp. 207-8)

should enemies 'eat from the same leaf'; interestingly, *redred* between men and women– the killers spitting on and rubbing a brass bracelet that is worn by or handed to the women – is a necessary aftermath of killings, lest sharing meals with killers cause a more 'soft' and fragile women harm; and further, after medicinal spells to cure someone of *bertan* affliction, practitioners take a knife or other metal object (metal being considered a strength-giving substance) and touch all those within the household who have not killed, a gesture not called 'rubbing' but said to protect inhabitants from new afflic-tion by 'contagion' *(beret)* (see Endicott 1970 for an account of a related symbolism of metal objects among the Malay); (3) *dewak*, the sacrifice of a pig that constitutes the 'covenant' *(beyaw)*, during which representatives of both sides hold salt and dip their hands in sacrifical blood as they pro-claim that violators of the covenant will dissolve like salt in water, scatter like beads from a broken necklace, and fail to reproduce.

6   Kiga, father to Lakay, had joined with other kin in a peaceful oath 'by salt' with the Butags, but Luku, present at their encounter yet harboring the memory of a prior threat on his father's life by Butag killers, did not swear with his fellows, instead taking the opportunity to familiarize himself with Butag territory. Shortly afterward, he went on a raid. Informed of Luku's murders and fearful that he and his children would suffer ravages of 'salt,' Kiga then hastened to renew his friendship with the Butags. But on his way, a gun was accidentally triggered by friendly hunters as they unloaded a catch of wild boar; Kiga, standing beside it, received the wound that took his life. All agree today that Kiga died of the curse of 'salt' brought on by Luku's violation. But interestingly, 'anger' for the death was not directed toward Luku, but toward the Butags who had in Kiga their 'exchange' for Luku's killings – and toward Mengsiw, an in-married man and owner of the gun in question, who himself died before Lakay's children found an opportunity to kill him 'in exchange.'

7   Tayeg's *purung* is described at length in M. Rosaldo (1973), in which cer-tain crucial actors are, however, given different names. Interested readers are referred to that article with the warning that my translations and in-terpretations were based only on our first field stay with the Ilongots, and research in 1974 has led me to revise them. In particular, the article under-plays the importance of deception and exchange in oratory – probably because the centrality of *liget* in Ilongot culture became clear to me only after our second stay in the field.

8   For Ilongots, only two diseases– *bertan* (see discussion on p. 208) caused by eating with an enemy, and 'salt' or *sigem*, which afflicts those who violate a peace – are directly referable to infractions of appropriate social behavior. A person can be diagnosed as afflicted by either disease on the basis of symptoms alone (any severe and prolonged illness, but especially stomach pains and sores in the case of *bertan*, chills and fever in the case of 'salt') or a recognized violation of social rules, but identification of a specific infraction is never itself necessary to an effective cure. The as-sociation of *bertan* with bodily sores is interestingly consistent with the sort of symbolic logic identified by Mary Douglas (1966), who would not be surprised to discover that a transgression of social boundaries has as its symptoms a skin disease that violates the ''boundaries'' of the self.

9   The Tagalog word *batas – batat* in Ilongot – is consistently invoked in oratory as a model of orderly proceedings; much to my horror, pistol-wielding captains were said to be able to enforce *batat* and forestall vio-

lence on occasions when traditional Ilongot orators could not! Importantly, *batat,* though in some ways antagonistic to traditional Ilongot *purung,* is consistent with its stress on slow and careful speech, on delicacy and 'knowledge'; speakers claim to 'know *batat'* when they mean to deny *liget* in their dealings, and knowledge of *batat* is associated with the 'new knowledge' *(berun bēya)* of Ilongot Christians, which, like lowland law, is said to forbid crooked speech and indirection, and to require (because all Churches have leaders) the coordinating efforts of a single person in a position of authority.

10   I could glean little of the importance of the spleen *(bērsit* or *bēsit)* in Ilongot folk anatomy, but did note that it is used in a number of contexts as an equivalent of the otherwise interchangeable words for 'knowledge,' 'breath,' and 'heart,' e.g., *'Ingrawtu mad bērsittu* or *Mad rinawatu,* 'He took it to his spleen, heart; he took it seriously'; *'Away niyektu* or *'Away bērsittu* or *'Away bēyatu,* 'He has no breath, spleen, knowledge; he is shameless, lacking knowledge.'

11   The Ilongot word *'amba'ān* describes the style of *purung* speech that combines 'slowness,' wit, and deception with verbal ornaments and phonological 'flourishes' *(bēira)* said to 'beautify' *(beri)* one's talk. *'Amb'an* style is clearly in decline and although I managed to hear bits of what all recognized as good oratory and gleaned a further sense of its quality from related flourishes in song, Ilongots spoke nostalgically of truly spectacular speakers whom I, unfortunately, had not 'reached.' Even today, however, Ilongots in both oratory and play display a grasp and appreciation of the fully elaborated witty style, using it for boasts on tapes, for short flourishes in actual *purung,* and, in daily talk, as a semihumorous vehicle for the expression of sudden anger, a way of taunting one another, and in particular, a strategy for testing the depth of my understanding of 'deep' speech.

12   Significantly, modern *batat*-dominated oratory is also dominated by men younger than those who are likely to speak in traditional *purung.* Bachelors and young married men who have been to school, who are familiar with lowland languages and legal terms, and who know how to write down speakers' names are the people most vocal in criticizing traditional oratorical indirection – though increasingly, they are the people whom all Ilongots are willing to hear.

13   Lundi's case was exceptional for reasons that became quite clear after the event. Many women are 'persuaded' to accept an initially unattractive spouse, but most can manage to avoid an undesirable alliance either by convincing their male "protectors" of their preferences, or by fleeing and establishing themselves as the 'daughters' or 'sisters' of some other group of kin. The latter was, of course, what Lundi did. That she had to flee a considerable distance and at great emotional cost had to do with two factors: First, having children, it was assumed that she needed men (and preferably, a husband) to 'care for' them; second, because of the extent of non-Ilongot settlement in her natal region and her own earlier marriage to a lowlander, Lundi had very few Ilongot connections to mobilize as an alternative set of relations. A woman's ability to control her marital experience depends – in a way that a man's does not – on such connections and on their willingness to assume the supportive role of kin.

14   There was some question, in Kakidugen, as to whether the captain's rather extensive gifts to 'Adēlpig (including a previously unheard-of prestation of

a carabao along with a radio) did not constitute a *langu* – and 'Utup, fearing such an interpretation, insisted that he had not 'sold' his daughter and would not have her leave his home. But I imagine that the interpretation of the captain's gifts – as a *langu*, or a simple payment for 'Adēlpig's 'anger' – will be revised depending on future residential choices. For a short period, the captain and his wife did in fact leave 'Utup's home, moving in the direction of the former's kinfolk; were such a residential arrangement to be revived (perhaps on 'Utup's death), people might well argue that the captain gave a *langu* for his wife.

7 Conclusion: Self and social life

1 For a fuller discussion of these and related issues in the interpretive understanding of ethnographers, see Geertz (1976).

2 Robert McKinley (1976), in a paper with a very different analytical slant, cites a number of these myths, and I am indebted to him for such references as: Perham (1896), who reports the Iban story of Klieng's War Raid to the Sky, in which Klieng must conquer the cruel Tedai who has captured the parents of Kumang, whom he hopes to wed; Geddes (1957), whose report of the Land Dayak myth of Kichapi again requires the hero to behead the killer of the parents of his desired bride; and Downs (1955), who recounts a number of Toradja myths, including the story of Tambuja, a hero who beheads in vengeance for his parents' death, thereby acquiring an enemy daughter as his wife. The Marind-anim pig totem myths (Van Baal 1966) suggest that headhunting was taught, as a custom, by a supernatural wife to her pig/human husband; and though Ifugao headhunting stories (Barton 1955) do not associate wives and killing, their ceremonies – like many in Indonesia (Downs 1955) – link headhunting to the fertility of women and of crops. It would seem possible to perform a comparative analysis, relating these variations in headhunting, ritual, and mythology to differences in the social organization of marriage and in the social meanings associated with taking heads.

3 Needham (1976; see also M. Rosaldo 1977) summarizes and critiques evidence that has supported interpretations of headhunting as a quest for "soul substance" in such works as Hutton (1938) on the South Asian Naga; Kruyt (1906), who writes on Indonesia; and Furness (1902) and Elshout (1926), who provide accounts of Bornean groups. McKinley (1976) provides an innovative interpretation of headhunting rites as an occasion for the acquisition not of "soul substance," but of friendly enemy names and/or skulls. Downs (1955, 1956) rejects the "soul substance" theory and proposes instead an interpretation in terms of social and cosmic dualism – a dualism which, in the Ilongot case at least, appears more as a *product* of specific and divisive shows of *liget* than as its *occasion*.

4 My thoughts on this matter were stimulated by an unpublished paper by Gayle Rubin (1976), which discusses gender conceptions among such lowland New Guinea groups as the Etoro (see also Kelley 1976), who engage not only in headhunting but in a ritualized form of male homosexuality, through which elders literally "inseminate" and so transfer strength and reproductive force to unmarried youths.

5 For an elaboration of this argument with reference to comparative materials, see Collier and Rosaldo (1975, 1978).

Bibliography

Barrows, David P. 1905. "Population," in *Census of the Philippine Islands: 1903* 1.

Barth, Frederick. 1965. *Political Leadership Among the Swat Pathans.* London: Athlone Press.

Barton, R. F. 1919. *Ifugao Law.* Berkeley: University of California Publications in American Archaeology and Ethnology.

1930. "Hunting Soul Stuff," *Asia* 30.

1955. *The Mythology of the Ifugaos.* Philadelphia: Memoirs of the American Folklore Society 46.

1969. "The Religion of the Ifugaos." New York: Kraus Reprint Co. (originally published by the American Anthropological Association, 1946).

Bauman, R. and J. Sherzer. 1974. *Explorations in the Ethnography of Speaking.* Cambridge: Cambridge University Press.

Benedict, Ruth. 1946. *The Chrysanthemum and the Sword.* New York: Houghton Mifflin.

Berger, Peter. 1969. *The Social Reality of Religion.* London: Faber.

Blair, E. H. and J. A. Robertson. 1904. *The Philippine Islands, 1493–1898.* Vol. 14. Cleveland: Clark.

Bloch, Maurice. 1977. "The Past and the Present in the Present," *Man* 12.

Brittan, Arthur. 1973. *Meanings and Situations.* London: Routledge & Kegan Paul.

Cacho, Alejandro. 1904. "Manifiesto Compendioso del Principio y Progresos de la Mision de Italones que los Religiosos de N.P. San Agustin de la Provincia del Santisimo Nombre de Jesus de Filipinas Mantienen en los Montes de la Pampanga, Hacia el Oriente de Dicha Privincia," in *Relaciones Agustinianas de las Razas del Norte de Luzon,* ed. Angel Perez. Manila: Bureau of Public Printing.

Campa, Buenaventura. 1891. "Una Visita a las Rancherias de Ilongotes," *El Correo Sino-Anamita* 25.

Collier, J. and M. Rosaldo. 1975. "Marriage, Motherhood and Direct Exchange." Paper presented at the Meetings of the American Anthropological Association.

1978. "Politics and Gender in Simple Societies." Unpublished paper.

Conklin, Harold. 1957. *Hanunóo Agriculture.* Rome: Food and Agricultural Organization of the UN.

Dieterlen, M. 1973. *La Notion de Personne en Afrique Noire.* Paris: Edition de la Centre National de la Recherche Scientifique.

Doi, Takeo. 1973. *The Anatomy of Dependence.* Tokyo: Kodansha Int.

Douglas, Mary. 1966. *Purity and Danger*. New York: Praeger.
Downs, R. E. 1955. "Headhunting in Indonesia," *Bijdragen tot de Taal-Land-en Volkenkunde* 3.
   1956. *The Religion of the Bare'e-speaking Toradja of Central Celebes*. The Hague: Uitgeverij Excelsior.
Durkheim, Emile. 1915. *Elementary Forms of the Religious Life*. New York: Macmillan.
Elshout, R. 1926. *De Kenja-Dajaks uit het Apo-Kajangebied:bijdragen tot de Kennis van Centraal-Borneo*. The Hague: Martinus Nijhoff.
Endicott, Kirk. 1970. *An Analysis of Malay Magic*. Oxford: Clarendon Press.
Evans-Pritchard, E. E. 1937. *Witchcraft, Oracles and Magic Among the Azande*. London: Oxford University Press.
Fernandez Cosgaya, Fray Lorenzo. 1865. *Diccionarío Pangasinan-Español*. Manila.
Firth, Raymond. 1973. *Symbols: Public and Private*. Ithaca, N.Y.: Cornell University Press.
Freud, Sigmund. 1916. "Mourning and Melancholia," in *Collected Papers,* Vol. 4 (1925). London: Hogarth Press.
Furness, W. H. 1902. *The Home Life of Borneo Headhunters: Its Festivals and Folk-Lore*. Philadelphia: Lippincott.
Geddes, W. R. 1957. *Nine Dayak Nights*. Melbourne: Oxford University Press.
Geertz, Clifford. 1973a. *The Interpretation of Cultures*. New York: Basic Books.
   1973b. "Person, Time and Conduct in Bali," in *The Interpretation of Cultures*. New York: Basic Books.
   1976. " 'From the Native's Point of View': On the Nature of Anthropological Understanding," in *Meaning in Anthropology,* ed. K. Basso and H. Selby. Albuquerque, N.M.: University of New Mexico Press.
Geertz, Hildred. 1959. "The Vocabulary of Emotion: A Study of Javanese Socialization Process," *Psychiatry: Journal for the Study of Interpersonal Process* 22.
Giddens, A. 1976. *New Rules of Sociological Method*. New York: Basic Books.
Gumperz, J. and D. Hymes. 1972. *Directions in Sociolinguistics: The Ethnography of Communication*. New York: Holt, Rinehart and Winston.
Hallowell, A. I. 1954. "The Self and Its Behavioral Environment," *Explorations* II.
   1967. *Culture and Experience*. New York: Schocken Books.
Hill, R. 1967. "Ilongots, Boundary of Nueva Ecija and Nueva Vizcaya," *Unitas* 40.
Hutton, J. H. 1938. *A Primitive Philosophy of Life*. Oxford: Clarendon Press.
Jones, William. 1907-9. *The Diary of William Jones*. Typewritten copy. Chicago National History Museum.
   1908. Letter of 25 August 1908 to Franz Boas. Typescript. Chicago Natural History Museum.
Jordana Y Morena, Ramon. 1885. *Bosquejo Georgráfico e Histórico-Natural del Archipiélago Filipino*. Madrid: Imprenta de Moreno y Rojas.
Keesing, Felix. 1962. *The Ethnohistory of Northern Luzon*. Stanford, Ca.: Stanford University Press.
Kelley, R. 1976. "Witchcraft and Sexual Relations: An Exploration in the Social and Semantic Implications of the Structure of Belief," in *Man and*

Woman in the New Guinea Highlands, ed. P. Brown and G. Buchbinder. Washington: American Anthropological Association.

Kruyt, A. C. 1906. *Het Animismein de Indischen Archipel.* The Hague: Mortinus Nijhoff.

Langer, Suzanne. 1942. *Philosophy in a New Key.* Cambridge, Mass.: Harvard University Press.

——— 1953. *Feeling and Form.* New York: Scribner.

Lattimore, Richard, trans. 1951. *The Iliad of Homer.* Chicago, Ill.: University of Chicago Press.

Leach, Edmund R. 1954. *Political Systems of Highland Burma.* Cambridge, Mass.: Harvard University Press.

Lee, Dorothy. 1959. *Freedom and Culture.* Englewood Cliffs, N.J.: Prentice-Hall.

Lévi-Strauss, Claude. 1963a. "The Effectiveness of Symbols," in *Structural Anthropology.* New York: Basic Books.

——— 1963b. *Totemism.* Boston: Beacon Press.

——— 1970. *The Raw and the Cooked.* New York: Harper & Row.

——— 1970. *Tristes Tropiques.* New York: Atheneum.

Liebow, R. 1967. *Tally's Corner.* Boston: Little, Brown.

Lienhardt, Godfrey. 1961. *Divinity and Experience.* London: Oxford University Press.

Malumbres, Julien O. P. 1919. *Historia de Nueva Vizcaya y Provincia Montañosa.* Manila: Imprenta del Colegio de Santo Tomás.

Mauss, Marcel. 1938. "Une Categorie de l'Esprit Humain: La Notion de Personne Celle de 'Moi'," *Journal of the Royal Anthropological Institute* 68.

McKinley, Robert. 1976. "Human and Proud of It! A Structural Treatment of Headhunting Rites and the Social Definition of Enemies," in *Studies in Borneo Societies: Social Process and Anthropological Explanation.* ed. G. N. Appell. DeKalb, Ill.: Center S. East Asian Studies, N. Illinois University.

Needham, Rodney. 1972. *Belief, Language and Experience.* Chicago, Ill.: University of Chicago Press.

——— 1976. "Skulls and Causality," *Man* 11.

Ortner, Sherry. 1978. *Sherpas Through Their Rituals.* Cambridge: Cambridge University Press.

Perez, Angel. 1904. *Relaciones Agustinianas de las Razas del Norte de Luzon.* Manila: Bureau of Public Printing.

Perham, Arch. J. 1896. "Klieng's War Raid to the Sky," in *The Natives of Sarawak and British North Borneo,* Vol. 1, ed. Henry L. Roth. London: Truslove and Hanson.

Reid, Lawrence. 1974. Personal communication.

Riceour, Paul. 1970. *Freud and Philosophy.* New Haven, Conn.: Yale University Press.

Rideout, Henry Milner. 1912. *William Jones: Indian, Cowboy, American Scholar, and Anthropologist in the Field.* New York: Lippincott.

Rorty, Amelie. 1976. "A Literary Postscript: Characters Persons, Selves, Individuals," in *The Identities of Persons,* ed. A. Rorty. Berkeley: University of California Press.

Rosaldo, Michelle Z. 1972a. *Context and Metaphor in Illongot Oral Tradition.* Unpublished Ph.D. dissertation, Harvard University.

——— 1972b. "Metaphor and Folk Classification," *Southwestern Journal of Anthropology* 28(1).

1973. "I Have Nothing to Hide: The Language of Ilongot Oratory," *Language in Society* 2.

1974. "Woman, Culture and Society: A Theoretical Overview," in *Woman, Culture and Society,* ed. M. Rosaldo and L. Lamphere. Stanford, Ca.: Stanford University Press.

1975. "It's All Uphill: The Creative Metaphors of Ilongot Magical Spells," in *Sociocultural Dimensions of Language Use,* ed. M. Sanches and B. Blount, New York: Seminar Press.

1977. "Skulls and Causality," *Man* 12(1).

Rosaldo, Michelle Z. and J. Atkinson. 1975. "Man The Hunter and Woman," in *The Interpretation of Symbolism,* ed. R. Willis. London: Dent.

Rosaldo, Renato. 1968. "Ilongot Kin Terms: A Bilateral System of Northern Luzon," in *Proceedings of the VIIIth International Congress of Anthropological and Ethnological Sciences, 1968, Tokyo and Kyoto* II. Tokyo: Science Council of Japan.

1970. *Ilongot Society: The Social Organization of a Non-Christian Group in Northern Luzon, Philippines.* Unpublished Ph.D. dissertation. Harvard University.

1971. "Fellow-Bulldozer." Paper presented at the Meetings of the American Anthropological Society.

1975. "Where Precision Lies: The Hill People Once Lived on a Hill," in *The Analysis of Symbolism,* ed. R. Willis. London: Dent.

1976. "The Story of Tukbaw," in *The Biographical Process: Studies in the History and Psychology of Religion,* ed. F. Reynolds and D. Capps. The Hague: Mouton.

1978. "The Rhetoric of Control: Ilongots Viewed as Natural Bandits and Wild Indians," in *Forms of Symbolic Inversion,* ed. B. Babcock. Ithaca. N.Y.: Cornell University Press.

1980. *Ilongot Headhunting, 1883–1974: A Study in History and Society.* Stanford, Ca.: Stanford University Press.

Rubin, Gayle. 1976. "Coconuts." Unpublished paper.

Sahlins, Marshall. 1976. *Culture and Practical Reason.* Chicago, Ill.: University of Chicago Press.

Sartre, Jean-Paul. 1948. *The Emotions: Outline of a Theory.* New York: The Philosophical Library.

Savage Landor, A. Henry. 1904. *The Gems of the East: Sixteen Thousand Miles of Research Travel Among Wild and Tame Tribes of Enchanting Islands.* London: Macmillan.

Scheerer, Otto. 1911. "On a quinary notation among the Ilongots of Northern Luzon," *Philippine Journal of Science* 6.

Schneider, David. 1968. *American Kinship: A Cultural Account.* Englewood Cliffs, N.J.: Prentice-Hall.

Siegel, James. 1966. "Prayer and Play in Atjeh: A Comment on Two Photographs," *Indonesia* 1.

Siskind, Janet. 1973. *To Hunt in the Morning.* New York: Oxford University Press.

Sperber, Dan. 1974. *Rethinking Symbolism.* Cambridge: Cambridge University Press.

Stoner, Barbara. 1971. "Why Was William Jones Killed?," *Field Museum of Natural History Bulletin* 42.

Turnbull, Wilfrid. 1909. *Report of an Inspection Trip Through the Ilongot*

Rancherías and Country On and Near the Cagayan River. Typescript. Chicago, Ill.: Philippine Studies Center, University of Chicago.

1929. "Among the Ilongots Twenty Years Ago," *Philippine Magazine* 26.

1937. "Return to Old Haunts," *Philippine Magazine* 34.

Turner, Terrence. n.d. "The Fire of the Jaguar." Typescript.

Turner, Victor, 1967. *The Forest of Symbols*. Ithaca, N.Y.: Cornell University Press.

Van Baal, J. 1966. *Dema: Description and Analysis of Marind-Anim Culture*. The Hague: Martinus Nijhoff.

Vogt, E. Z. 1965. "Structural and Conceptual Replication in Zinacantan Culture," *American Anthropologist* 68.

Waldron, R. A. 1967. *Sense and Sense Development*. New York: Oxford University Press.

Weber, M. 1958. "The Social Psychology of the World Religions," in *From Max Weber,* ed. H. H. Gerth and C. W. Mills. New York: Oxford University Press.

Whitehead, Harriet. In press. *Scientology*. Cambridge: Cambridge University Press.

Wittgenstein, L. 1953. *Philosophical Investigations.* London: Macmillan.

Index